Logistics

D0478109

WITHDRAWN

WITHDRAWN

5/2007

Ingram 11/03

Logistics
An Introduction to Supply Chain Management

Donald Waters

palgrave
macmillan

© Donald Waters 2003

All rights reserved. No reproduction, copy or transmission of this publication may be made without written permission.

No paragraph of this publication may be reproduced, copied or transmitted save with written permission or in accordance with the provisions of the Copyright, Designs and Patents Act 1988, or under the terms of any licence permitting limited copying issued by the Copyright Licensing Agency, 90 Tottenham Court Road, London W1T 4LP.

Any person who does any unauthorised act in relation to this publication may be liable to criminal prosecution and civil claims for damages.

The author has asserted his right to be identified as the author of this work in accordance with the Copyright, Designs and Patents Act 1988.

First published 2003 by
PALGRAVE MACMILLAN
Houndmills, Basingstoke, Hampshire RG21 6XS and
175 Fifth Avenue, New York, N.Y. 10010
Companies and representatives throughout the world

PALGRAVE MACMILLAN is the global academic imprint of the Palgrave Macmillan division of St. Martin's Press, LLC and of Palgrave Macmillan Ltd. Macmillan® is a registered trademark in the United States, United Kingdom and other countries. Palgrave is a registered trademark in the European Union and other countries.

ISBN 0–333–96369–5 paperback

This book is printed on paper suitable for recycling and made from fully managed and sustained forest sources.

A catalogue record for this book is available from the British Library.

Library of Congress Cataloging-in-Publication Data

Waters, C. D. J. (C. Donald J.), 1949–
    Logistics : an introduction to supply chain management / Donald Waters.
        p. cm.
    Includes bibliographical references and index.
    ISBN 0–333–96369–5 (paper)
    1. Business logistics. 2. Industrial management. I. Title.

HD38.5 .W384 2002
658.5—dc21
                                        2002073544

Editing and origination by Aardvark Editorial, Mendham, Suffolk

10 9 8 7 6 5 4 3 2 1
12 11 10 09 08 07 06 05 04 03

Printed in Great Britain by
Ashford Colour Press Ltd, Gosport

To Dan and Sue

Contents

List of Figures

Preface

SUBJECT

This is a textbook about logistics. It describes the way that materials move into an organisation from suppliers, through the operations within an organisation, and then out to customers. As you can see, we take a broad view of logistics, looking at every kind of 'organisation', moving every kind of 'material'. We talk about manufacturers moving tangible goods – and service providers moving materials for their intangible services.

Every organisation needs a reliable flow of materials. Logistics is an essential function, and managers have to make the movement of materials as efficient and effective as possible. This is best done by an integrated function that is responsible for all aspects of material movement. The results are important, as they directly affect customer service, costs – and just about every other measure of performance.

Logistics is not contained within an organisation, but has a unique position in linking external suppliers and customers. Organisations increasingly recognise that they do not work in isolation, but form part of a supply chain whose aim is to satisfy customers. To emphasise this broader role, some people prefer to talk about 'supply chain management'.

This is a particularly fast-moving field. Developments in operations – such as just-in-time, lean operations, efficient customer response, enterprise resource planning, e-commerce, globalisation, and increasing customer service – are rapidly changing the demands on logistics. This book gives an up-to-date view of logistics, emphasising current trends and developments. It covers important issues, such as:

- increasing strategic importance of logistics
- global operations and increasing international competition
- integration of organisations and activities in the supply chain
- changing requirements from logistics to deal with new types of operations
- better communications allowing closer co-ordination of movements
- new requirements from aspects of e-commerce
- increasing emphasis on quality and customer-based service
- environmental concerns.

APPROACH OF THE BOOK

The book gives an introduction to logistics. It can be used by anyone who is meeting the subject for the first time. You might be a student taking a course in business studies, or another subject that needs some knowledge of logistics – or you might read the book to learn more about a central area of management. The book gives a broad description of logistics, covering all the main concepts. It discusses the topics in enough depth to provide material for a complete course, but it does not get bogged down in too much detail. By concentrating on key issues, we have kept the text to a reasonable length.

The book has a number of features. It:

● is an introductory text and assumes no previous knowledge of logistics or experience of management
● can be used by many types of student, or people studying by themselves
● takes a broad view, covering all types of organisation
● sets logistics within its strategic context
● describes a lot of material, concentrating on topics that you will meet in practice
● develops the contents in a logical order
● is practical, presenting ideas in a straightforward way, avoiding abstract discussions
● illustrates principles by examples drawn from international organisations
● includes a range of features, including chapter aims, examples of logistics in practice, case studies, projects, worked examples, chapter reviews, problems, discussion questions and useful readings
● is written clearly, presenting ideas in an informative and easy style.

CONTENTS

The book follows a logical path through the decisions of logistics. An obvious problem is that the topics are all related, and decisions are made simultaneously rather than consecutively. In the book we effectively have to make a linear journey through a complex web of material. To make this easier, we have divided the book into three parts. The first part gives an overall introduction to logistics. It defines key terms, discusses the role of logistics, its aims, importance, trends and the general context of supply chain management. It shows how logistics has developed into a single, integrated function.

The second part looks at the planning for a supply chain. This starts with the design of a logistics strategy, and then shows how this strategy can be implemented. Important decisions include the structure of the supply chain and the location, number and size of facilities. These decisions lead to lower level plans to organise activities and resources. The supply chain keeps changing, so we look at ways of measuring and improving the performance of logistics.

The third part of the book focuses on some specific functions of logistics, including procurement, inventory management, warehousing, transport of materials and international logistics.

Together these chapters cover some of the most important decisions made in any organisation.

CONTACTS

If you have any comments, queries, requests or suggestions for the book or associated material, the author and publisher would be very pleased to hear them. You can contact the author at donaldwaters@lineone.net.

PART I

Introduction

This book is divided into three parts. Part I contains two chapters and gives an overall introduction to logistics, as well as setting the scene for the rest of the book. It introduces some important issues which are developed in later chapters.

Chapter 1 defines the key terms, discusses the role of logistics, its aims, importance and the general context of supply chain management. Chapter 2 describes current trends, and shows how logistics has developed into a single, integrated function.

Parts II and III look at planning in the supply chain, and focus on different activities of logistics.

CHAPTER 1

The Context of Logistics

CONTENTS

AIMS OF THE CHAPTER

After reading this chapter you should be able to:

- DEFINE 'logistics' and associated terms

- UNDERSTAND the role and structure of supply chains

- LIST different activities of logistics and understand the relationships between them

- DISCUSS the aims of logistics

- SHOW how logistics contributes to customer satisfaction

- RECOGNISE the importance of logistics to every organisation

INTRODUCTION

All organisations move materials. Manufacturers build factories that collect raw materials from suppliers and deliver finished goods to customers; retail shops have regular deliveries from wholesalers; a television news service collects reports from around the world and delivers them to viewers; most of us live in towns and cities and eat food brought in from the country; when you order a book or DVD from a website, a courier delivers it to your door. Every time you buy, rent, lease, hire or borrow anything at all, someone has to make sure that all the parts are brought together and delivered to your door. **Logistics** is the function that is responsible for this movement. It is responsible for the transport and storage of materials on their journey between suppliers and customers.

On a national scale, logistics involves a huge amount of effort. The USA has a gross domestic product (GDP) of US$10 trillion,[1] so its population of 280 million produces and consumes an average of US$36,000 of goods and services. The world's seven largest economies (USA, Japan, Germany, UK, France, Italy and Canada) have a combined GDP of US$20 trillion. All of this – whether it is oil produced in Canada, consumer electronics in Japan, cars in the UK or dairy products in France – relies on logistics to collect materials from suppliers and deliver it to customers. Millions of people are involved in this effort, and it costs billions of dollars a year to keep everything moving.

Ordinarily we only notice a small part of logistics. We might see lorries driving down a motorway, visit a shopping mall, drive through a trading estate, or have a parcel delivered to our homes. These are the visible signs of a huge industry. In this book, we take a more detailed look at this complex function. We discuss the issues and developments, and see how managers can get the best results from their logistics.

DEFINITIONS

Supporting operations

Every organisation delivers **products** to its customers. Traditionally we have described these products as either goods or services. Then manufacturers like Sony and Guinness make tangible goods, while AOL and Vodafone provide intangible services. In reality, this view is rather misleading, and every product is really a complex package that contains both goods and services. Ford, for example, manufacture cars, but they also give services through warranties, after-sales service, repairs and finance packages. McDonald's provide a combination of goods (burgers, cutlery, packaging, and so on) and services (when they sell food and look after the restaurant). It is more accurate to describe products as lying on the spectrum shown in Figure 1.1. At one end of this spectrum are products that are predominantly goods, such as cars and domestic appliances; at the other end are products that are predominantly services, such as insurance and education. In the middle are products with a more even balance, such as restaurant meals and hospitals.

At the heart of an organisation are the **operations** that create and deliver the products. These operations take a variety of inputs and convert them into desired outputs, as shown in Figure 1.2. The inputs include raw materials, components, people, equipment, information, money and other resources. Operations include manufacturing, serving, transporting, selling, training, and so on. The main outputs are goods and services. The Golden Lion restaurant, for example, takes inputs of food, chefs, kitchen, waiters, and dining area; its operations include food preparation, cooking and serving; the main outputs are meals, service, customer satisfaction, and so on.

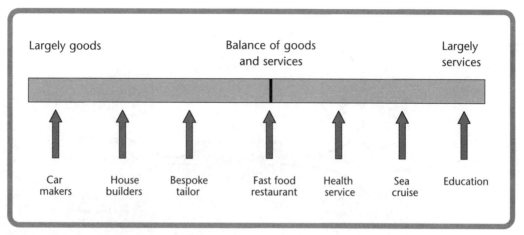

Figure 1.1 Spectrum of products

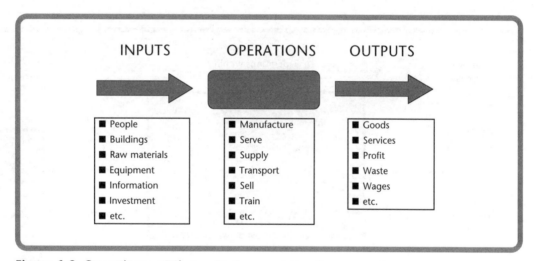

Figure 1.2 Operations creating outputs

The products created by an organisation are passed to its customers, giving the cycle shown in Figure 1.3. This shows customers generating demands, with operations using resources to make products that satisfy them. Logistics moves materials around this cycle.

The operations are usually divided into a number of related parts, in the way that a hospital has an emergency room, surgical ward, purchasing department, heart unit, operating theatre and so on. So logistics also moves materials through the different parts of an organisation, collecting from internal suppliers and delivering to internal customers (as shown in Figure 1.4). This leads to our basic definition.

LOGISTICS is the function responsible for the flow of materials from suppliers into an organisation, through operations within the organisation, and then out to customers.

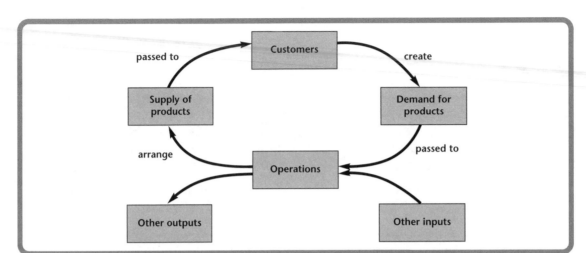

Figure 1.3 Cycle of supply and demand

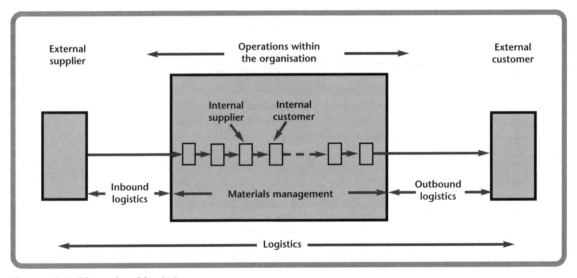

Figure 1.4 The role of logistics

Moving materials into the organisation from suppliers is called **inbound** or **inward logistics**; moving materials out to customers is **outbound** or **outward logistics**; moving materials within the organisation is **materials management**.

Materials

In these definitions we have talked about the movement of materials – but what exactly do we mean by **materials**? Sometimes this is obvious when, for example, a power station brings coal from a mine, a farmer moves potatoes to a wholesaler, or a computer manufacturer delivers PCs to a warehouse. At other times it is less clear when, for example, a television company delivers entertainment to its viewers, a telephone company provides a communications service, or a research company creates new knowledge. Tangible goods clearly have to be moved, and you can easily see the role of logistics. Even organisations providing the most intangible services move some goods around – perhaps paperwork or consumables – so they still need logistics. However, we can take a broader view and say that logistics also moves less tangible things, such as information and messages. Then a television company uses logistics to move around its production facilities, and also to transmit programmes to customers. In different circumstances, logistics is responsible for moving raw materials, components, finished products, people, information, paperwork, messages, knowledge, consumables, energy, money and anything else needed by operations. To simplify things, we describe all of these as **materials**.

MATERIALS are all the things that an organisation moves to create its products. These materials can be both tangible (such as raw materials) and intangible (such as information).

THE SUPPLY CHAIN

Definition

So far, we have focused on the movement of materials through a single organisation. In reality, organisations do not work in isolation, but each one acts as a customer when it buys materials from its own suppliers, and then it acts as a supplier when it delivers materials to its own customers. A wholesaler, for example, acts as a customer when buying goods from manufacturers, and then as a supplier when selling goods to retail shops. A component maker buys raw materials from its suppliers, assembles these into components, and passes the results to other manufacturers. Most products move through a series of organisations as they travel between original suppliers and final customers. Milk moves through a farm, tanker collection, dairy, bottling plant, distributor, and supermarket before we buy it. A toothbrush starts its journey with a company extracting crude oil, and then it passes through pipelines, refineries, chemical works, plastics companies, manufacturers, importers, wholesalers and retailers before finishing in your bathroom. A sheet of paper moves through several organisations before it reaches our desk (illustrated in Figure 1.5).

People use different names for these chains of activities and organisations. When they emphasise the operations, they refer to the **process**; when they emphasise marketing, they call it a **logistics channel**; when they look at the value added, they call it a **value chain**,[2] when they see how customer demands are satisfied, they call it a **demand chain**. Here we are emphasising the movement of materials and will use the most general term of **supply chain**.

A **SUPPLY CHAIN** consists of the series of activities and organisations that materials move through on their journey from initial suppliers to final customers.

Every product has its own unique supply chain, and these can be both long and complicated. The supply chain for Cadbury starts with cocoa beans growing on farms and ends with the delivery of bars of chocolate to hungry customers. The supply chain for Levi jeans starts with cotton growing in a field and ends when you buy the jeans in a shop. The supply chain describes the total journey of materials as they move 'from dirt to dirt'.[3] Along this journey,

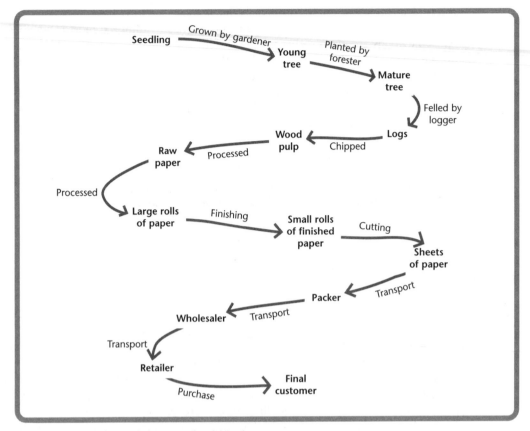

Figure 1.5 Outline of the supply chain for paper

materials may move through raw materials suppliers, manufacturers, finishing operations, logistics centres, warehouses, third party operators, transport companies, wholesalers, retailers, and a whole range of other operations. Sometimes, the supply chain goes beyond the final customer to add recycling and re-use of materials.

Structure of the supply chain

The simplest view of a supply chain has a single product moving through a series of organisations, each of which somehow adds value to the product. Taking one organisation's point of view, activities in front of it – moving materials inwards – are called **upstream**; those after the organisation – moving materials outwards – are called **downstream**.

The upstream activities are divided into **tiers** of suppliers. A supplier that sends materials directly to the operations is a first tier supplier; one that send materials to a first tier supplier is a second tier supplier; one that sends materials to a second tier supplier is a third tier supplier, and so on back to the original sources. Customers are also divided into tiers. One that gets a product directly from the operations is a first tier customer; one that gets a product from a first tier customer is a second tier customer; one that get a product from a second tier customer is a third tier customer, and so on to final customers (see Figure 1.6).

In practice, most organisations get materials from many different suppliers, and sell products to many different customers. Then the supply chain converges as raw materials move in

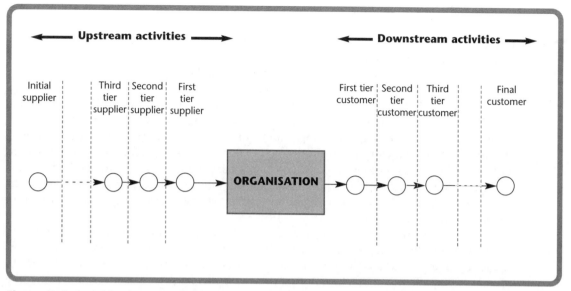

Figure 1.6 Activities in a supply chain

through the tiers of suppliers, and diverges as products move out through tiers of customers. A manufacturer might see sub-assembly providers as first tier suppliers, component makers as second tier suppliers, materials suppliers as third tier suppliers, and so on. It might see wholesalers as first tier customers, retailers as second tier customers, and end users as third tier customers (as illustrated in Figure 1.7).

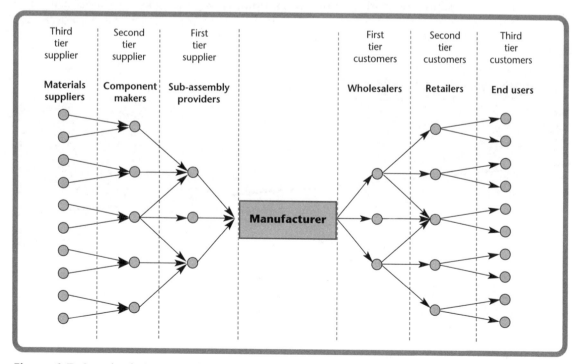

Figure 1.7 Supply chain around a manufacturer

It is fairly easy to imagine the shape of a manufacturer's supply chain, but most other organisations use the same general approach. Airlines, for example, move passengers from pick-up points, through local feeder services to major 'hub' airports, on to another hub, and then back out through local services to their destinations; banks collect all cheques in central clearing houses before sending them back to branches and customers; blood transfusion services have regional centres that act as wholesalers for plasma.

Each product has its own supply chain, and there is a huge number of different configurations. Some are very short and simple – such as a cook buying potatoes directly from a farmer. Others are surprisingly long and complicated. An everyday product like a shirt has a long journey from the farm growing cotton through to the final customer. It also has several chains merging as buttons, polyester, dyes and other materials join the main process. In the same way, when you buy a computer, many strands of the supply chain merge as Intel provide the processor, Matshita the DVD drive, Agfa the scanner, Hewlett-Packard the printer, Microsoft the operating system, and so on.

Supply chains diverge to meet demand from different types of customer. Manufacturers of car components, for example, sell some products to car assembly plants, some to wholesalers for garages doing repairs, some to retail shops for individual customers, and some directly to customers through websites. Then the supply chain divides into separate strands with the same product following alternative routes.

As you can see, our picture of supply chains is getting more complicated, with various mergers and divisions along their length. The reality is even more complex, as each organisation works with many – often thousands – of different products, each of which has its own supply chain. The French company Carrefour is Europe's largest retailer, and this comes at the end of tens of thousands of supply chains; Corus makes steel that is used in countless final products, DEL makes computers that are used for huge amounts of information transfer.

Some people argue that the term 'supply chain' gives too simple a view, and they prefer to talk about a **supply network** or **supply web**. However, we will stick to the usual name, and recognise that it refers to a complex pattern of movements. You can get some idea of the size and complexity of these from the Logistics in Practice example of Wal-Mart.

LOGISTICS IN PRACTICE

Wal-Mart

In 1962 Sam Walton opened a discount store in Rogers, Arizona. He attracted customers with a combination of low prices, a wide range of goods and friendly service. Sam called his store Wal-Mart, and was so successful that he quickly opened more branches. In 1983 he opened a SAM'S Club warehouse for members, and in 1988 the first 'Supercenter' selling groceries. By 1991 Wal-Mart had become the leading retailer in the USA, and started its international expansion. It moved into Mexico, Puerto Rico and Canada, and then into South America, Asia and Europe. Most of its later expansion came through buying local companies, such as ASDA in the UK.

Wal-Mart always kept the same emphasis on low prices, a wide range of products and friendly service. The scene is set at the front door of each store, where a staff

member greets customers and tells them about special offers and promotions. By 2000 Wal-Mart was the world's largest retailer with 4000 stores, serving 100 million customers a week, employing 1.2 million staff – or 'associates' – an annual turnover of US$175 billion and profit of US$6 billion a year.

You can imagine the size of the logistics in Wal-Mart. On mainland USA they have 85,000 suppliers sending $1.5 billion dollars' worth of materials a week to 62 main distribution centres, and on to 1800 Walmart stores, 800 Supercenters, 460 SAM's clubs and 13 Neighbourhood Markets. A large part of Wal-Mart's operating expenses depend on the efficiency of their logistics. When margins are tight, a small change in logistics performance and costs has a considerable effect on profit. This is why Wal-Mart use the 'industry's most efficient and sophisticated distribution system'. Their success can be judged by continuing expansion, with annual sales up 20 per cent in the first quarter of 2000, and like-for-like sales up 5 per cent.

Sources: Wal-Mart reports and website at www.walmartstores.com

Benefits of supply chains

Supply chains are so complicated that you might wonder if there is some way of avoiding them. Sometimes this is possible, when we move products directly from initial producers to final customers – when, for example, farm shops sell vegetables directly to consumers, or authors publish their works on the Internet. In general, though, there are very good reasons for having a longer supply chain. Suppose the population of a town decides to buy vegetables from a farm shop. This would have a minimal supply chain, but the whole population would travel separately to the farm. It would make more sense to have a transport company collect the vegetables and deliver them to a central location in the town – like a supermarket. If the transport company delivers to one town, it can easily deliver to other nearby towns, perhaps stopping at a depot to organise local deliveries. As there is a depot, vegetables can be put into storage while the supply is plentiful, and removed when there are shortages. If the vegetables need cleaning or preparation, the transport company can divert to a processing plant. Continuing in this way, you can see why a long supply chain develops, and what benefits it brings.

Supply chains exist to overcome the gaps created when suppliers are some distance away from customers. They allow for operations that are best done – or can only be done – at locations that are distant from customers or sources of materials. For example, coffee beans grow in South America, but the main customers are in Europe and North America. The best locations for power stations are away from both their main customers in cities and their fuel supplies.

As well as moving materials between geographically separate operations, supply chains allow for mismatches between supply and demand. The demand for sugar is more or less constant throughout the year, but the supply varies with the harvesting of sugar cane and beet. When there is excess supply, stocks are built-up in the supply chain, and these are used after the harvests finish. Supply chains can also make movements a lot simpler. Imagine four

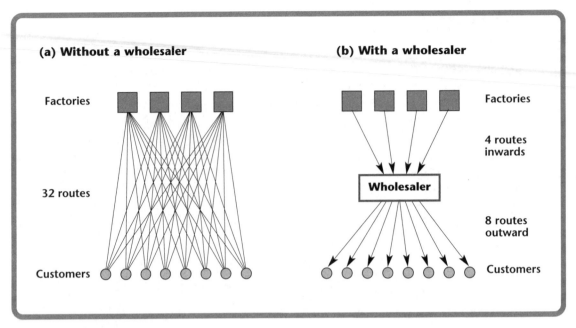

Figure 1.8 Using intermediaries to simplify the supply chain

factories directly supplying products to eight customers (as shown in Figure 1.8). Logistics has to organise 32 different delivery routes but, if the factories use a central wholesaler, the number of routes is cut to 12.

The following list suggests some other benefits of well-designed supply chains (where we use the terms 'wholesaler' and 'retailer' as a convenient label for intermediaries):

● Producers locate operations in the best locations, regardless of the locations of their customers.
● By concentrating operations in large facilities, producers can get economies of scale.
● Producers do not keep large stocks of finished goods, as these are held further down the supply chain nearer to customers.
● Wholesalers place large orders, and producers pass on lower unit costs in price discounts.
● Wholesalers keep stocks from many suppliers, giving retailers a choice of goods.
● Wholesalers are near to retailers and have short lead times.
● Retailers carry less stock as wholesalers provide reliable deliveries.
● Retailers can have small operations, giving a responsive service near to customers.
● Transport is simpler, with fewer, larger deliveries reducing costs.
● Organisations can develop expertise in specific types of operation.

ACTIVITIES OF LOGISTICS

Separate activities

Logistics is responsible for the movement and storage of materials as they move through the supply chain. But what activities does this include? If you follow some materials moving through an organisation, you can see that the following activities are normally included in logistics.

Procurement or purchasing. The flow of materials through an organisation is usually initiated when **procurement** sends a purchase order to a supplier. This means that procurement finds suitable suppliers, negotiates terms and conditions, organises delivery, arranges insurance and payment, and does everything needed to get materials into the organisation. In the past, this has been seen as a largely clerical job centred on order processing. Now it is recognised as an important link with upstream activities, and is being given more attention. We describe procurement in more detail in Chapter 8.

Inward transport or traffic actually moves materials from suppliers to the organisation's receiving area. This has to choose the type of transport (road, rail, air, and so on), find the best transport operator, design a route, make sure that all safety and legal requirements are met, get deliveries on time and at reasonable cost, and so on. We describe transport in more detail in Chapter 11.

Receiving makes sure that materials delivered correspond to the order, acknowledges receipt, unloads delivery vehicles, inspects materials for damage, and sorts them.

Warehousing or stores moves materials into storage, and takes care of them until they are needed. Many materials need special care, such as frozen food, drugs, alcohol in bond, chemicals that emit fumes, animals, and dangerous goods. As well as making sure that materials can be available quickly when needed, warehousing also makes sure that they have the right conditions, treatment and packaging to keep them in good condition. We describe warehousing in more detail in Chapter 10.

Stock control sets the policies for inventory. It considers the materials to store, overall investment, customer service, stock levels, order sizes, order timing and so on. We describe stock management in more detail in Chapter 9.

Order picking finds and removes materials from stores. Typically materials for a customer order are located, identified, checked, removed from racks, consolidated into a single load, wrapped and moved to a departure area for loading onto delivery vehicles.

Materials handling moves materials through the operations within an organisation. It moves materials from one operation to the next, and also moves materials picked from stores to the point where they are needed. The aim of materials handling is to give efficient movements, with short journeys, using appropriate equipment, with little damage, and using special packaging and handling where needed. We describe materials handling in more detail in Chapter 10.

Outward transport takes materials from the departure area and delivers them to customers (with concerns that are similar to inward transport).

Physical distribution management is a general term for the activities that deliver finished goods to customers, including outward transport. It is often aligned with marketing and forms an important link with downstream activities.

Recycling, returns and waste disposal. Even when products have been delivered to customers, the work of logistics may not be finished. There might, for example, be problems with delivered materials – perhaps they were faulty, or too many were delivered, or they were the wrong type – and they have to be collected and brought back. Sometimes there are associated materials such as pallets, delivery boxes, cable reels and containers (the standard 20 foot long metal boxes that are used to move goods) which are returned to suppliers for reuse. Some materials are not reused, but are brought back for recycling, such as metals, glass, paper, plastics and oils. Finally there are materials that cannot be used again, but are brought back for safe disposal, such as dangerous chemicals. Activities that return materials back to an organisation are called **reverse logistics** or **reverse distribution**.

⬤ *Location.* Some of the logistics activities can be done in different locations. Stocks of finished goods, for example, can be held at the end of production, moved to nearby ware-houses, put into stores nearer to customers, passed on to be managed by other organisa-tions, or a range of alternatives. Logistics has to find the best locations for these activities – or at least play a significant role in the decisions. It also considers related questions about the size and number of facilities. These are important decisions that affect the overall design of the supply chain. We discuss location decisions in more detail in Chapter 5.

⬤ *Communication.* Alongside the physical flow of materials is the associated flow of informa-tion. This links all parts of the supply chain, passing information about products, customer demand, materials to be moved, timing, stock levels, availability, problems, costs, service levels, and so on. Co-ordinating the flow of information can be very diffi-cult, and logistics managers often describe themselves as processing information rather than moving goods. Christopher supports this view by saying that, 'Supply chain compet-itiveness is based upon the value-added exchange of information'.[4] The Council of Logis-tics Management also highlights the combination of materials and information flow in their definition:

> Logistics is the process of planning, implementing and controlling the efficient, cost-effective flow and storage of raw materials, in-process inventory, finished goods and related information from point of origin to point of consumption for the purpose of conforming to customer requirements.[5]

Depending on the circumstances, many other activities can be included in logistics. Some-times an organisation might include sales forecasting, production scheduling, customer service management, overseas liaison, third party operations, and so on. The important point is not to draw arbitrary boundaries between functions, but to recognise that they must all work together to get an efficient flow of materials. In the example of Augulla, logistics may not be organised particularly well; you might consider the problems that this brings and how you might start improving things.

LOGISTICS
IN PRACTICE

Augulla Limited

In its Bombay factory, Augulla Limited makes a range of basic clothes such as plain T-shirts and underwear. The process is fairly straightforward, but the company's chair-man, Pradhir Augulla, is disappointed at the time it takes a product to reach the final cus-

continued

tomer. He is considering buying other companies in the supply chain to see if he can improve overall performance. To help with this decision he has collected information about the average times taken by different activities, starting with the purchase of fibres on the open commodity market and ending with delivery to the final customer.

Start of supply chain with fibre available on the open commodity market:

- Store fibre in commodity warehouses (140 days)
- Buy fibre and move to spinners (11 days)
- At spinners:
  - store raw fibre (21 days)
  - spin to form yarn (13 days)
  - store yarn as finished goods (11 days)
- Buy yarn and move to knitters (8 days)
- At knitters:
  - store yarn (6 days)
  - knit to form fabric (9 days)
  - store work in progress as grey stock (12 days)
  - dye standard colour and finish fabric (7 days)
  - store fabrics as finished goods (8 days)
- Buy fabric and move to Augulla Limited (7 days)
- At Augulla Limited:
  - store fabric (12 days)
  - cut to form components (5 days)
  - store buffer of components (6 days)
  - sew components to form garments (14 days)
  - store garments as finished goods (18 days)
- Deliver to regional distribution centre and store (21 days)
- Deliver to local wholesaler and store (17 days)
- Deliver to retail shop and store (19 days)

End of supply chain when customer buys garment from shop.

You can see that it takes an average of 365 days for materials to move through the supply chain. The main operations of spinning, knitting, dyeing, cutting and sewing only take 48 days, and various aspects of logistics fill the rest.

Sources: Pradhir Augulla and company records

Organising logistics

It is probably easiest to imagine the activities that make up logistics in a manufacturer, with forklift trucks unloading pallets from lorries and moving them around warehouses. But the

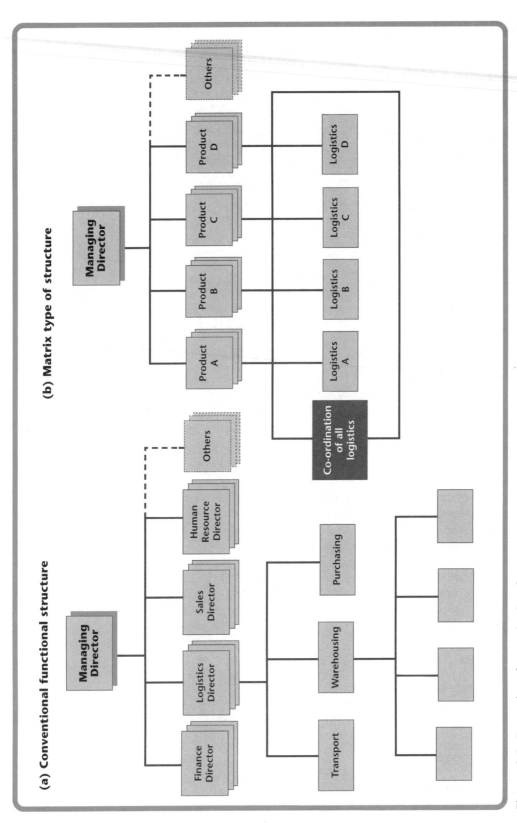

Figure 1.9 Examples of organisational structure

same principles apply in any other organisation. When a rock band goes on tour they carry huge amounts of equipment. Procurement buys everything that is needed on the tour, transport packs it and moves it to the next destination, receiving makes sure that everything arrives safely, warehousing keeps things safe until they are needed, materials handling moves things between trucks and the stage, location decides where to perform. The same types of decision are made with even the most intangible service. Insurance companies, for example, decide what kind of branch network to have, where to locate offices, who to buy telephone and other services from, how to deliver information to customers, and so on.

You can see logistics in every organisation, and it obviously comes in a huge number of different forms. The activities can be arranged in many ways within an organisation, and there is certainly no single 'best' arrangement. A small organisation might have one person looking after everything. A medium sized organisation might have one department with different sections for purchasing, transport, stock control, distribution, and so on. A large organisation might have a logistics division employing thousands of people and running huge transport fleets. Sometimes all the activities are organised in a single department reporting to a logistics director; sometimes they are part of a larger department such as marketing or production; sometimes they are spread out in small pockets throughout the organisation; sometimes they are contracted out to third-party suppliers.

The current trend is towards an organisation where logistics is a single integrated function, with a logistics director – or equivalent – at its head. This follows a traditional functional structure, with the logistics director working with directors in production, finance, sales, human resources, and so on (as shown in Figure 1.9a). There are many variations on this, with a common one found in companies organised around products or projects. Then some logistics might exist in each division, with a matrix structure allowing co-ordination of the overall function (shown in Figure 1.9b).

AIMS OF LOGISTICS

Logistics is responsible for the flow of materials through a supply chain. This function is also called **supply chain management**. Some people argue that logistics is somewhat narrower and concentrates on the movement within a single organisation, while supply chain management takes a broader view of movement through related organisations. This is, however, largely an argument over semantics rather than real differences in practice. Here we will stick to the convention that the two terms refer to exactly the same function. This view is supported by the Institute of Logistics and Transport – the main professional body within the UK – who give the following definitions.[6]

LOGISTICS is the time-related positioning of resources, or the strategic management of the total supply-chain

---

The **SUPPLY-CHAIN** is a sequence of events intended to satisfy a customer.

Some people also talk about logistics management, business logistics, distribution management, materials management, merchandising, or a series of other terms. Sometimes you have to be careful as these terms can refer to specific parts of the supply chain or slightly different activities. When someone talks about, say, 'distribution management' you should be clear about whether they mean transport, physical distribution, the whole of logistics, or some other function.

With our broad view, logistics managers have two main aims. The first is to move materials into, through, and out of their own organisation as efficiently as possible. The second aim is to contribute to an efficient flow through the whole supply chain. Traditionally, managers concentrate on the first of these, focusing on those parts of the supply chain that they directly control. Hopefully, if each organisation looks after its own logistics properly, materials will move efficiently through the whole chain, thus achieving the second aim. To some extent this is true. It is not, however, inevitable and organisations really need a more positive approach to co-operation. We will discuss this in the next chapter. Here, though, we look at the more immediate aims of logistics within an individual organisation.

We have said that managers aim for an efficient movement of materials – but what exactly do we mean by 'efficient'? There are several answers to this, including fast deliveries, low costs, little wastage, quick response, high productivity, low stocks, no damage, few mistakes, high staff morale, and so on. Although these are all worthy goals, they are really indicators rather than real aims. To find the real aim of logistics, we must relate it to the wider objectives of the organisation.

Ultimately, the success of every organisation depends on customer satisfaction. If it does not satisfy customers, it is unlikely to survive in the long term, let alone make a profit, have high return on assets, add shareholder value, or achieve any other measure of success. So organisations must deliver products that satisfy customers. Unfortunately, customers judge products by a whole series of factors. When you buy a DVD, for example, you judge its contents, appearance, how easy it is to buy, how long you wait, how expensive it is, whether the right DVD was delivered, whether it was damaged, how courteously you were treated by sales staff, and so on. Some of these factors clearly depend on logistics – the availability of the DVD depends on stocks; the delivery time depends on transport; damage is prevented by good material handling; the price is affected by logistics costs. So we can phrase the overriding aim of logistics in terms of customer service. It has to organise the movement of materials in the best way to achieve high customer satisfaction.

Any organisation can give outstanding customer service if it is prepared to allocate enough resources. The problem, of course, is that more resources come with higher costs. There is a limit to the amount that customers will pay for a product and, therefore, on the service that can be given. Then a realistic aim for logistics balances the service given to customers with the cost of achieving it.

The overall **AIM OF LOGISTICS** is to achieve high customer satisfaction. It must provide a high quality service with low – or acceptable – costs.

We can phrase this balance in terms of perceived customer value. Logistics adds value by making products available in the right place and at the right time. If a product is available at the place it is needed, logistics is said to have added **place utility**; if it is delivered at the right time, logistics has added **time utility**. Then we can phrase the aim of logistics in terms of getting the highest customer utility or perceived value. In essence, we are trying to maximise the difference between perceived value and actual costs.

People often summarise the aims of logistics as getting, 'the right materials, to the right place, at the right time, from the right source, with the right quality, at the right price'. This is broadly correct, but it depends on how we define 'right'. In different circumstances, logistics is judged by completely different measures of performance. When you post letters, you sometimes want them delivered quickly, sometimes as cheaply as possible, sometimes with high security, sometimes at a specified time, and so on. Managers have to design logistics that are flexible enough to satisfy a variety of needs. There are two aspects to this. The first is concerned with planning, when managers take a strategic view and design the best possible supply chain for their circumstances. We look at these strategic decisions in Chapters 3 and 4. The second concern is about execution, when materials move through this chain as efficiently as possible. Harrington summarises this double role by saying that, 'logistics is both the glue that holds the materials/product pipeline together and the grease that speeds product flow along it'.[7]

IMPORTANCE OF LOGISTICS

Essential and expensive

Logistics is essential for every organisation. Christopher[8] says that, 'Logistics has always been a central and essential feature of all economic activity'. Shapiro and Heskett[9] agree, saying that, 'There are few aspects of human activity that do not ultimately depend on the flow of goods from point of origin to point of consumption'. Without logistics, no materials move, no operations can be done, no products are delivered, and no customers are served.

Not only is logistics essential, but it is also expensive. Organisations may reduce their overheads as much as possible, but they are often left with surprisingly high logistics costs. Unfortunately, it is difficult to put a figure to these, and there is a good deal of uncertainty in the area. Normal accounting conventions do not separate expenditure on logistics from other operating costs, and there is some disagreement about the activities to include. As a result, very few organisations can put a precise figure on their logistics expenditure, and many have almost no idea of the costs.

The cost of logistics varies widely between different industries. Building materials, such as sand and gravel, have very high logistics costs compared with, say, jewellery, pharmaceuticals and cosmetics. However, one rule of thumb suggests that logistics costs are 15–20 per cent of turnover. The USA has a GDP of $10 trillion, so it might spend $1–2 trillion dollars a year on logistics, with half of this spent on transport.[10] You have to interpret such figures carefully as other studies give different views. The UK government, for example, says that 12 per cent of the GDP comes from wholesale and retail trades and 6 per cent comes from transport and storage.[11] These figures suggest that overall logistics costs are considerably higher – perhaps supporting an earlier estimate by Childerley that logistics accounted for 32.5 per cent of the UK GDP.[12]

LOGISTICS IN PRACTICE

Konigshaven Suppliers

Konigshaven Suppliers is a food wholesaler, delivering to supermarkets in southern Denmark. Its standard accounting systems do not identify separate logistics costs, and this makes it difficult to identify areas with particularly high costs, or those that need improving. To get a clearer picture, the company ran a survey in one main warehouse. It used some estimates and simplifications, but feels that the following figures give a reasonable view. These figures show the costs incurred for each €100,000 of net sales.

a. *Cost of sales: €58,000*
    The cost of purchasing products sold on to customers, including administration of the purchasing office

b. *Transport inwards: €3000*
    Cost of bringing goods from suppliers and delivering to the warehouse

c. *Other costs of delivery to warehouse: €4000*
    A general category covering any other costs of relations with suppliers

d. *Warehousing and handling: €7000*
    Costs of receiving materials, checking, sorting, moving to the warehouse and storing

e. *Stock financing: €1000*
    The cost of financing stock, including debt charges

f. *Sales force: €12,000*
    Salaries and costs of the sales office

g. *Special promotions: €3000*
    Including presentations, visits and samples

h. *Delivery to customers: €5000*
    Costs of taking goods out of the warehouse and delivering to customers

i. *Debt financing: €2500*
    Costs of financing plant and equipment

j. *Information processing: €2000*
    Including all aspects of order processing

k. *Returns and recycling: €500*
    Cost of recovering pallets and any other materials returned to the warehouse

These figures are open to some interpretation, but they show that transport accounts for 12 per cent of sales and warehousing for 8 per cent. Several other costs might be included in logistics, including some purchasing, sales, information processing and recycling.

Sources: company reports and publicity

Despite the differences in these figures, everyone agrees that logistics can be very expensive. Whether it is getting more expensive is open to debate. Some people say that fuel, land, safety, environmental protection and employee costs are all rising and making logistics more expensive. They argue that this is a long-term trend that will inevitably continue. An opposing view says that improvements in logistics are more than compensating for price rises, and the overall cost is falling. By improving methods and replacing outdated practices, logistics costs continue to fall as a proportion of product value. The true picture depends on circumstances within each organisation.

Effects on financial performance

As an expensive function, logistics has an impact on an organisation's overall financial performance. We can give many illustrations of this, but will start with the effects on the return on assets (ROA).

The return on assets is defined as the pre-tax profit earned by an organisation divided by the value of the assets employed.

$$\text{Return on assets} = \frac{\text{profits earned}}{\text{assets employed}}$$

This gives a measure of how well available resources are used and, in general, the higher the value, the better the organisation's performance. Assets are usually described as current (cash, accounts receivable, stocks, and so on) or fixed (property, plant, equipment, and so on). Improving the flow of materials reduces the amount of stock. This clearly lowers current assets, but we can argue that it also reduces fixed assets and increases profit. This argument is summarised in Figure 1.10.

● *Current assets.* More efficient logistics reduces the current assets through lower stock levels. Reducing the investment in stock can also free up cash for other more productive purposes and reduce the need for borrowing.

● *Fixed assets.* Fixed assets include property, plant and equipment. Logistics is a heavy user of these resources, and the warehouses, transport fleets, materials handling equipment and other facilities needed to move materials through the supply chain form a major part of fixed assets.

● *Sales.* By making a more attractive product, or making it more readily available, logistics can increase sales and give higher market share.

● *Profit margin.* More efficient logistics gives lower operating costs, and this in turn leads to higher profit margins.

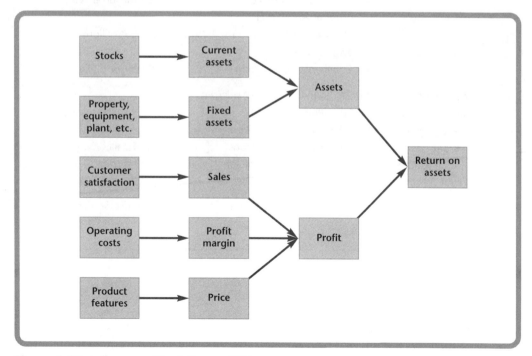

Figure 1.10 Influence of logistics on ROA

● *Price.* Logistics can improve the perceived value of products – perhaps making them more easily available, giving faster delivery or shortening lead times. More attractive products can get premium prices.

As you can see, the first two points give lower assets, while the last three increase profits. All of these effects raise ROA, and consequently affect other measures of performance, such as share price, return on investment, borrowing, and so on.

WORKED EXAMPLE

J. Mitchell currently has sales of £10 million a year, with a stock level of 25% of sales. Annual holding cost for the stock is 20% of value. Operating costs (excluding the cost of stocks) are £7.5 million a year and other assets are valued at £20 million. What is the current return on assets? How does this change if stock levels are reduced to 20% of sales?

Solution

Taking costs over a year, the current position is:

Cost of stock	=	amount of stock × holding cost	
	=	10 million × 0.25 × 0.2	= £0.5 million a year
Total costs	=	operating cost + cost of stock	
	=	7.5 million + 0.5 million	= £8 million a year
Profit	=	sales – total costs	
	=	10 million – 8 million	= £2 million a year
Total assets	=	other assets + stock	
	=	20 million + (10 million × 0.25)	= £22.5 million
Return on assets	=	profit / total assets	
	=	2 million / 22.5 million	= 0.089 or 8.9%

The new position with stock reduced to 20% of sales has:

Cost of stocks	=	10 million × 0.2 × 0.2	= £0.4 million year
Total costs	=	7.5 million + 0.4 million	= £7.9 million a year
Profit	=	10 million – 7.9 million	= £2.1 million a year
Total assets	=	£20 million + (£10 million × 0.20)	= £22 million
Return on assets	=	2.1 million / 22 million	= 0.095 or 9.5%

Reducing stocks gives lower operating costs, higher profit and a significant increase in ROA.

Summarising the importance

Logistics has the awkward combination of being both essential and expensive. It affects customer satisfaction, the perceived value of products, operating costs, profit and just about every other measure of performance. Novich says that, 'Poor logistics are the cause of roughly

50 per cent of all customer complaints'.[13] No organisation can expect to prosper if it ignores logistics and organising logistics properly can give a huge competitive advantage. We can, then, summarise the importance of logistics by saying that it:

- is essential, as all organisations, even those offering intangible services, rely on the movement of materials
- is expensive, with costs often forming a surprisingly high proportion of turnover
- directly affects profits and other measures of organisational performance
- has strategic importance with decisions affecting performance over the long term
- forms links with suppliers, developing mutually beneficial, long-term trading relationships
- forms links with customers, contributing to customer satisfaction and added value
- has a major affect on lead time, reliability and other measures of customer service
- determines the best size and location of facilities
- gives public exposure with visible locations, advertising on trucks, 'corporate citizenship', and so on
- can be risky, because of safety, health and environmental concerns
- prohibits some operations, such as moving excessive loads or dangerous goods
- can encourage growth of other organisations – such as suppliers and intermediaries offering specialised services.

CHAPTER REVIEW

- ❑ Every organisation creates products to satisfy customer demand. The operations that create these products need an effective and efficient flow of materials. In this sense, 'materials' are all the goods and services needed to create products.

- ❑ Logistics is the function that is responsible for the flow of materials into, through and out of an organisation.

- ❑ Materials move through a series of related activities and organisations between initial suppliers and final customers. These form a supply chain. Each product has its own supply chain.

- ❑ There are many possible structures for supply chains, but the simplest view has materials converging on an organisation through tiers of suppliers, and products diverging through tiers of customers.

- ❑ Although it is a single function, logistics consists of a series of related activities. These range from procurement at the beginning of operations, through to physical distribution at the end.

- ❑ An overall aim for logistics is to achieve high customer satisfaction or perceived product value. This must be achieved with acceptable costs.

- ❑ Every organisation depends on the movement of materials, and the way this is done affects costs, profits, relations with suppliers and customers, customer service, and virtually every other measure of performance.

In 1996 a survey by Deloitte & Touche in Canada[14] found that 98 per cent of respondents described logistics as either 'critical' or 'very important' to their company. The same survey emphasised the rate of change in the area, with over 90 per cent of organisations either currently improving their supply chain or planning improvements within the next two years.

C A S E   S T U D Y   *Ace Dairies*

Ace Dairies gives a home delivery service for milk, dairy products and a range of related goods. Roger Smitheram has run the dairy for the past twelve years. His product is a combination of goods (the items he delivers) and services (the delivery and associated jobs he does for customers).

At the heart of operations is an information system which contains full details of all Roger's 500 customers, including their regular orders, special orders, where to deliver, how they pay, and so on. Every day the system calculates the likely sales of all products in two days time. Roger adds some margin of safety, allows for likely variations and passes his order to Unigate Dairy in Totnes in Devon (about 150 km away). This Unigate depot acts as a wholesaler for milkmen in Wales and the southwest of England. The following evening it delivers to a holding depot in Camborne, and then takes Roger's goods 10 km to a cold store in Hayle. At 5.30 the following morning Roger collects the order from his cold store and starts delivering to customers. This normally takes until 1.30 in the afternoon, but on Fridays he spends more time collecting money and often finishes after 5.00 pm.

There are several specific problems facing Ace Dairies. There is, for example, some variation in daily demand, so Roger has to carry spare stock. He cannot carry too much, as dairy products have a short life and anything not delivered quickly is thrown away. Roger aims at keeping this waste down to 2 per cent of sales. There are also problems maintaining a service during holidays, or when Unigate has difficulties with their deliveries.

Perhaps Roger's main concern is maintaining his sales over the long term. Demand for doorstep deliveries is declining, as people buy more milk at supermarkets. The number of milkmen in Hayle has declined from ten in 1987 to three in 2002. Most of Roger's customers have been with him for many years, but he generates new custom by canvassing, delivering leaflets, special offers, carrying a range of other products, and so on.

Source: Roger Smitheram and internal reports

CASE STUDY
Questions

- Describe the supply chain for milk.
- Where does Ace Dairies fit into this? What specific activities form the logistics in Ace Dairies?
- What are the main problems that Ace Dairies has with logistics?

PROJECT
Websites

You can find a huge amount of information about logistics on different websites. Many of these advertise services, but others are aimed at giving information and offering advice. Search the Web and collect a list of useful sites. The following list gives a useful starting point.

www.iolt.org.uk	– Institute of Logistics and Transport in the UK
www.lmi.org	– Logistics Management Institute
www.clm.org	– Council for Logistics Management in the USA
www.supply-chain.org	– Supply Chain Council
www.cips.org	– Chartered Institute of Purchasing and Supply
www.infochain.org	– Canadian Association of Logistics Management

DISCUSSION QUESTIONS

1. Is it true that every organisation has to move materials to support its operations? What do service companies like Internet service providers move? Give some examples from different types of organisation to support your views.
2. How important is logistics to the national economy? What proportion of employment and gross domestic product is due to logistics? How has this proportion changed over time?
3. The supply chain is a convenient notion, but organisations are only really interested in making products that they can sell to customers. Provided they have reliable supplies of materials, and reasonable transport for finished products, logistics is irrelevant. Do you think this is true?
4. Very few organisations deal with the final customer for a product. Most operations work upstream and form one step of the supply chain, often passing materials to internal customers within the same organisation. How does the type of customer affect the organisation of logistics and the measures of customer satisfaction?
5. The cost of logistics varies widely from organisation to organisation. What factors affect these costs? Are the costs fixed or can they be controlled?
6. How could you find the best balance between service level and costs?

REFERENCES

1. United Nations (2001) *Industrial Statistics Yearbook*, UN, New York.
2. Porter M.E. (1985) *Competitive Advantage*, Free Press, New York.
3. Cooper M.C., Lambert D.M. and Pagh J.D. (1997) Supply chain management, *International Journal of Logistics Management*, **8**(1), 2.
4. Christopher M. (1996) Emerging Issues in Supply Chain Management, Proceedings of the Logistics Academic Network Inaugural Workshop, Warwick.
5. Council of Logistics Management, promotional material and website at www.clm.org.
6. Institute of Logistics, (1998 to 2001) *Members' Directory*, Institute of Logistics and Transport, Corby.
7. Harrington L. (1996) Untapped savings abound, *Industry Week*, **245**(14), 53–8.
8. Christopher M. (1986) *The Strategy of Distribution Management*, Heinemann, Oxford.
9. Shapiro R.D. and Heskett J.L. (1985) *Logistics Strategy*, West Publishing, St Paul, MN.
10. US Statistical Abstract (2001) *Survey of Current Business*, Department of Commerce, Washington DC.
11. Office of National Statistics, (2001) *Annual Abstract of Statistics*, HMSO, London.
12. Childerley A. (1980) The importance of logistics in the UK economy, *International Journal of Physical Distribution and Materials Management*, **10**(8).
13. Novich N.S. (1990) Leading-edge distribution strategies, *The Journal of Business Strategy*, November/December, 48–53.
14. Factor R. (1996) Logistics trends, *Materials Management and Distribution*, June, 17–21.

Further reading

There are many books on logistics, and the following list gives a useful starting point.

Arnold J.R.T. (1996) *Introduction to Materials Management* (2nd edn) Prentice Hall, Englewood Cliffs, NJ.

Brewer A.M., Button K.J. and Hensher D.A., (2001) *Handbook of Logistics and Supply Chain Management*, Pergamon, London.

Christopher M. (1998) *Logistics and Supply Chain Management*, FT Prentice Hall, London.

Coyle J.J., Bardi E.J. and Langley C.J. (1996) *The Management of Business Logistics* (6th Edition), West Publishing, St Paul, MN.

Dix C. and Baird C. (1998) *Front Office Operations*, Addison Wesley, Reading, Massachusetts.

Gattorna J.L. and Walters D.W. (1996) *Managing the Supply Chain*, Palgrave – now Palgrave Macmillan.

Handfield R.B. and Nichols E.L. (1998) *Introduction to Supply Chain Management*, Prentice Hall.

Hill E.R. and Fredendall L. (1999) *Basic Supply Chain Management*, St. Lucie Press.

Simchi-Levi D., Kaminsky P. and Simchi-Levi E. (1999) *Designing and Managing the Supply Chain*, Irwin/McGraw Hill, New York.

Waters D. (1999) *Global Logistics and Distribution Planning*, Kogan Page, London.

CHAPTER 2

Integrating the Supply Chain

CONTENTS

- Aims of the chapter
- Progress in logistics
- Current trends in logistics
- Integrating logistics within an organisation
- Integration along the supply chain
- Achieving integration
- Chapter review
- Case study – Friedland Timbers asa.
- Project – Supply partnerships
- Discussion questions
- References

AIMS OF THE CHAPTER

After reading this chapter you should be able to:

- OUTLINE the way that logistics has developed over time

- SEE how logistics is responding to pressures for change

- DISCUSS the benefits of creating a single, integrated logistics function

- DESCRIBE ways of achieving internal integration

- APPRECIATE the benefits of further integration along the supply chain

- DESCRIBE different approaches to this integration

PROGRESS IN LOGISTICS

Early views

Despite its obvious importance, logistics has not always received its fair share of attention. Historically, organisations put all their effort into making products and gave little thought to the associated movement of materials. Managers recognised that transport and storage were needed, but they were viewed as technical issues that were not worth much attention – they were simply the unavoidable costs of doing business. Some early work in the 1920s began to look more carefully at the transport of finished goods.[1-3] In 1962, though, Drucker could still describe logistics as, 'the economy's dark continent'[4] and say that this formed 'the most sadly neglected, most promising area of ... business'. Since then there have been considerable changes.

Perhaps the main reason for change was the recognition that logistics was expensive. By the 1970s[5,6] and 80s[7-10] surveys were suggesting that the movement and storage of materials typically accounted for 15–20 per cent of revenue. In the last chapter we said that it is difficult to get accurate figures for this, and in 1994 Hill could still say that, 'many distributors are unaware of the costs of the distribution service they provide'.[11] However, logistics had been identified as a high cost function, and one where organisations can make significant savings.

WORKED EXAMPLE

JL Francisco & Partners run a wholesale fruit business around Rio del Plata. In normal circumstances the company makes a gross profit of 5% of sales. A consultant's report has recently suggested that 22% of their operating costs are due to logistics, and that improved efficiency might reduce this by 10%. How much extra profit would this generate? If they do not improve logistics, how much would sales have to rise to get the same increase in profit?

Solution

Gross profit is 5% of sales, so if we take sales of $100, operating costs amount to $95. At present, 22% of this, or $95 \times 0.22 = \$20.90$, is due to logistics.

If the company reduces the cost of logistics by 10%, it would save $20.90 \times 0.1 = \$2.09$. Assuming that there are no changes to the selling price or other costs, this is a direct contribution to profit. A 10% reduction in logistics costs raises profit from $5 to $7.09, or an increase of 42%.

Without the reduction in logistics costs, the company would have to increase sales by 42% to get the same increase in profit.

Pressures to improve logistics

As well as potential savings, many other factors are encouraging organisations to improve the management of their supply chains. The following list suggests some of these pressures:

● Customers are more knowledgeable, and demand higher quality, lower costs and better service.

● Competition is getting fiercer, and organisations must look at every opportunity to remain competitive.

● There is changing power in the supply chain. Very large retail chains, such as Wal-Mart, Tesco, Toys-R-Us and McDonald's, demand customised logistics from their suppliers.

● Other changes in retail markets include the growth of 24-hour opening, home deliveries, out-of-town malls, retail parks, telephone and on-line shopping.

● International trade continues to grow. This is encouraged by free trade areas such as the European Union and North American Free Trade Area.

● Organisations are introducing new types of operation, such as just-in-time, lean operations, time compression, flexible manufacturing, mass customisation, virtual operations, and so on.

● Some organisations are turning from a product focus (where they concentrate on the end products) to a process focus (where they concentrate on the way products are made). This encourages improvement to operations, including logistics.

● There have been considerable improvements in communication. These allow electronic data interchange (EDI), item coding, electronic fund transfer (EFT), e-commerce, shared knowledge systems, and other new practices.

● Organisations are outsourcing peripheral activities and concentrating on their core operations. Logistics is a useful area for third-party operators, with specialised companies offering a range of services.

● Organisations are increasing co-operation through alliances, partnerships, and other arrangements. This integration is important for logistics, which is usually the main link between organisations in a supply chain.

● Managers are recognising the strategic importance of the supply chain.

● Attitudes towards transport are changing, because of increased congestion on roads, concerns about air quality and pollution, broader environmental issues, government policies for the real cost of road transport, privatisation of rail services, deregulation of transport, and a host of other changes.

This is, of course, only a partial list and there are many other pressures for change, including uncertain market conditions, political change, deregulation of business, rising costs, shortage of skilled staff, fluctuating exchange rates, and so on. In the next section, we will see how logistics is responding to these pressures.

CURRENT TRENDS IN LOGISTICS

Improving communications

Logistics continually meets new challenges, and is changing faster now than at any time in the past. Perhaps the most obvious change is the increasing use of technology. Some of this appears directly in the movement of goods – such as electronic identification of packages, satellite tracking of lorries and automatic guidance systems – but the greatest impact has come with communications.

When a company wants to buy something, it typically has to generate a description of the goods, request for price, purchase order, order confirmation, contract terms, shipping papers, financial arrangements, delivery details, special conditions, invoices, and so on. In the past, all of these – and mountains of other paperwork – had to be printed and posted between organisations. This could make even a simple transaction seem complicated and time consuming. Telephones did not help much, as Sam Goldwyn pointed out, 'a verbal contract isn't worth the paper it's written on'.

In the past few years technology has revolutionised these communications. Initial progress came with fax machines that could send electronic copies of documents between distant locations in seconds rather than days. The drawback with fax machines is that documents produced by one computer still have to be printed, fed into a fax machine, transmitted over telephone lines to someone else who reads the text and enters the information to their own computer.

By the 1990s the obvious next step had arrived with **electronic data interchange** (EDI). This allowed remote computers to exchange data without going through any intermediaries. Early users were supermarkets, who linked their stock control systems directly to suppliers' order processing systems. The supermarket checkouts recorded sales of each item, and when stocks got low the system automatically sent a message asking for another delivery. This use of **EPOS** – electronic point-of-sales data – gave less paperwork, lower transaction costs, faster communications, fewer errors, more integrated systems, and closer business relations.

By 1997 about 2000 companies in the UK used EDI for trade with suppliers.[12] Over the next few years electronic trading became more sophisticated and widespread. The mushrooming of e-mail was followed by all kinds of e-business, e-commerce – and soon 'e-anything'. The efficient transfer of information has been particularly useful for purchasing, which has developed into **e-purchasing** or **e-procurement**. This comes in many forms, all based on the direct exchange of data between a supplier's computer and a customer's. Two main versions are **B2B** (business-to-business, where one business buys materials from another business) and **B2C** (business-to-customer, where a final customer buys from a business). By 2002 around 83 per cent of UK suppliers used B2B,[13] and the worldwide value of B2B trade was over US$2 trillion.[14]

Two associated technologies have developed to support EDI. The first is **item coding**, which gives every package of material moved an identifying tag. The tag is usually a bar code or magnetic stripe that can be read automatically as the package moves through its journey. Then the logistics system knows where every package is at any time, and automatic materials handling can move, sort, consolidate, pack and deliver materials.

The second technology is **electronic fund transfer** (EFT). When the delivery of materials is acknowledged, EFT automatically debits the customer's bank account and credits the supplier's. This completes the loop, with EDI to place orders, item coding to track the movement, and EFT to arrange payment.

Improving customer service

It is normally in everyone's interests to make logistics costs as low as possible. Logistics managers want low costs so that they remain competitive, and their users want to pay as little as possible. Many organisations have reduced their logistics costs to levels that affect their whole operations. Lower transport costs, for example, make it feasible to sell products over a wider geographic area. The cost of transport for, say, Japanese manufacturers is so low that they can offer goods at prices that are comparable to those offered by domestic companies. Similarly, efficient transport can move products quickly over long distances, so there is no need to build traditional warehouses close to customers.

While striving for lower costs, organisations obviously have to maintain their service levels. Improved logistics means giving the service that customers want at the lowest possible cost. A problem, of course, is finding the features that customers really want and the level of service they are willing to pay for. These vary widely in different circumstances, but a key factor is the **lead time**. This is the total time between ordering materials and having them delivered and available for use. Again, it is normally in everyone's interest to make this delay as short as possible. When customers decide to buy something, they want it delivered as soon as possible; suppliers want to keep customers happy with fast service, and with no products hanging around and clogging the supply chain. Ideally, the lead time should be as close to zero as possible, and one approach to this uses **synchronised material movement**. This makes information available to all parts of the supply chain at the same time, so that organisations can co-ordinate material movements, rather than wait for messages to move up and down the chain.

Another key factor for customer satisfaction is personalised products. Instead of buying a standard textbook, for example, you describe the contents you want and a publisher supplies a volume with exactly these specifications. This is **mass customisation**, which combines the benefits of mass production with the flexibility of customised products. It uses B2C to give direct communications between a final customer and a manufacturer, and it needs supply chains that are flexible, that move materials very quickly, and respond to varying conditions.

Dell Computers was one of the first companies to use mass customisation. They do not build standard computers, but wait until a customer places an order on their website. Then they build a computer for the specific order. Logistics makes sure that the necessary materials are always available for manufacturing, and it delivers the finished machine quickly to the customer.

Dell work so closely with their suppliers that they have developed 'virtual integration', where they all seem to be part of the same company. This works well with Dell, who have 50 main components, but would it work with a car manufacturer and their three thousand components? Flexible manufacturing here would put severe pressures on the supply chain, but the '3DayCar Programme' suggests that 80 per cent of cars in the UK could be built to order by 2010.[15,16]

Other significant trends

Apart from increasing technology and emphasis on customer satisfaction, there are several other important trends in logistics. The following list includes some of the most significant.

- *Globalisation:* Improved communications and better transport mean that physical distances are becoming less significant. Organisations can become global in outlook, buying, storing, manufacturing, moving and distributing materials in a single, worldwide market. As a result, international trade and competition are continuing to rise. Organisations used to look for competitors in the same town, but now they are just as likely to come from another continent.

Efficient logistics makes a global market feasible, and other factors that encourage international trade include less restricted financial systems, consumer demand for imported products, removal of import quotas and trade barriers and the growth of free trade areas. You can see the effects in manufacturing, where producers look for economies of scale in large facilities located in areas with low production costs. The unit production cost is low, and efficient logistics keeps the delivered price down. This is the reason why German companies open large plants in Poland, American companies work in Mexico and Japanese companies work in China.

⬤ *Reduced number of suppliers:* In the past, organisations have used a large number of suppliers. This encouraged competition, ensured that they got the best deal and maintained secure deliveries if one supplier ran into difficulties. The current trend, however, is to reduce the number of suppliers and develop long-term relationships with the best. As we shall see later, working closely with a small number of organisations can bring considerable benefits.

⬤ *Concentration of ownership:* Large companies can get economies of scale, and they have come to dominate many supply chains. There are, for example, many shops and transport companies – but the biggest ones continue to grow at the expense of small ones. The result is a continuing concentration of ownership, which you can see in many logistics sectors ranging from food wholesalers to cruise lines.

⬤ *Outsourcing*: More organisations realise that they can benefit from using specialised companies to take over part, or all, of their logistics. Using a third party for materials movement leaves an organisation free to concentrate on its core activities. McKinnon says that, 'Outsourcing has been one of the dominant business trends of the 1980s and 1990s'[17] and surveys suggest that around 30 per cent of logistics expenditure is outsourced in the EU.[18]

⬤ *Postponement*: Traditionally, manufacturers move finished goods out of production and store them in the distribution system until they are needed. When there are many variations on a basic product, this can give high stocks of similar products. Postponement moves almost-finished products into the distribution system, and delays final modifications or customisation until the last possible moment. You can imagine this with 'package-to-order', where a company keeps a product in stock, but only puts it in a box written in the appropriate language when it is about to ship an order.

Manufacturers of electrical equipment, such as Phillips and Hewlett-Packard, used to build into their products the transformers and plugs needed for different markets. Then they had to keep separate stocks of products destined for each country. Now they make the transformer and cables as separate, external units. They only keep stocks of the basic, standard products, and customise them for different markets by adding the proper transformers and plugs at the last minute. The result, of course, is much lower stocks. In the same way, Benetton used to dye yarn different colours, knit sweaters and keep stocks of each colour to meet varying demand. Now they knit sweaters with undyed yarn, keep much smaller stocks of these, and dye the finished sweaters to meet actual orders.

● *Cross-docking:* Traditional warehouses move materials into storage, keep them until needed, and then move them out to meet demand. Cross-docking co-ordinates the supply and delivery, so that goods arrive at the receiving area and are transferred straight away to a loading area, where they are put onto delivery vehicles. This dramatically reduces stock levels and associated administration.

There are two basic forms of cross-docking. In the first, packages are moved directly from arriving vehicles and onto departing ones. This does not really need a warehouse and a simple transfer point is enough. In the second form there is some additional work as materials arrive in larger packages which are opened, broken into smaller quantities, sorted, consolidated into deliveries for different customers and transferred to vehicles.

Cross-docking can develop to the point where nothing actually moves through a warehouse. Any stock is kept within vehicles, giving **stock on wheels**. A related arrangement uses **drop-shipping**, where wholesalers do not keep stock themselves, but co-ordinate the movement of materials directly from upstream suppliers to downstream customers. As warehousing is expensive and time-consuming, these methods can give much more efficient flows, and allow methods such as **quick response** and **efficient customer response** (which we discuss in Chapter 7).

● *Direct delivery:* More customers are buying through the Web, or finding other ways of trading earlier in the supply chain, such as mail order or buying directly from manufacturers. This has the benefits of reducing lead times, reducing costs to customers, having manufacturers talking directly to their final customers, allowing customers access to a wider range of products, and so on. It also means that logistics has to move small deliveries quickly to final customers. This has encouraged the growth of couriers and express parcel delivery services such as FedEx, UPS and DHL.

● *Other stock reduction methods:* Keeping stock is expensive, so organisations continually look for ways of reducing the amount stored in the supply chain. There are many ways of doing this. One approach uses just-in-time operations to co-ordinate activities and minimise stock levels. Another approach has **vendor managed inventory**, where suppliers manage both their own stocks and those held further down the supply chain. Improved co-ordination reduces overall costs and can give economies of scale.

● *Increasing environmental concerns:* There is growing concern about air pollution, water pollution, energy consumption, urban development and waste disposal. Logistics does not have a good reputation for environmental protection – demonstrated by the emissions from heavy lorries, use of green field sites for warehouses, calls for new road building, use of extensive packaging, ships illegally flushing their fuel tanks, oil spillages from tanker accidents, and so on.

On the positive side, logistics is moving towards 'greener' practices. Operators use more energy efficient vehicles, control exhaust emissions, reuse packaging, switch to environmentally friendly modes of transport, increase recycling through reverse logistics, add safety features to ships, develop brown-field sites, and so on. They increasingly recognise that careful management can bring both environmental protection and lower costs. A fair assessment might be that logistics is making progress on environmental issues, but it has some way to go.

● *More collaboration along the supply chain:* Organisations in a supply chain increasingly recognise that they have the same objectives – which are satisfied final customers. They should not, therefore, compete with each other, but should co-operate to get final customer satisfaction. This is an important point. It means that competitors are not other organisations within the same supply chain, but are organisations in other supply chains. Christopher[19] summarises this by saying that 'supply chains compete, not companies'.

In summary

We could continue this list, describing all types of changes in logistics. Our aim, though, is not to be exhaustive, but to illustrate some of the main trends. These are not independent, but are all related. Increasing technology, for example, can give less stock, lower costs, shorter lead times, higher customer satisfaction, and so on. If we take an overview of the trends, we can suggest three main themes. The first looks for a more efficient flow of materials through the supply chain. It might, for example, give faster deliveries, reduce stock levels, reduce handling, or give lower costs. This approach is characterised by **lean logistics**,[20,21] which grew from the ideas of lean operations, and tries to remove all waste from the supply chain. Its characteristic approach is to analyse operations, and then systematically remove all the wasted effort, movement, materials, time, and other resources. This seems a simple idea, but it can give dramatic improvements in performance.

The second theme has logistics becoming more flexible and responsive. It might, for example, give a customised service or respond quickly to changing demands. This approach is characterised by **agile logistics**,[22] which focuses on customer satisfaction.

The third theme looks at increasing **integration** of the supply chain. Organisations cannot work in isolation, but must co-operate with other organisations in the supply chain to achieve their wider objectives.

Unfortunately, people often assume that there is some conflict between these three themes. They assume, for example, that leanness needs standard operations which reduce flexibility, or that integration needs more complicated systems that increase costs, or that agility needs extra resources that lower average utilisation. To some extent this is true, but the three themes are not mutually exclusive and we can design logistics that are lean, agile and integrated.[23,24]

Three important themes for logistics consider **LEANNESS**, **AGILITY** and **INTEGRATION**. Ideally, logistics should aim for all three of these.

INTEGRATING LOGISTICS WITHIN AN ORGANISATION

Problems with fragmented logistics

Figure 2.1 summarises our view of logistics within an organisation, where a series of related activities add value to the final product. These activities have traditionally been managed separately, so that an organisation might have a distinct purchasing department, transport department, warehouse, distribution fleet, and so on. Unfortunately, dividing up logistics in this way creates a number of problems.

Purchasing might look for the most reliable suppliers, inventory control for low unit costs, warehousing for fast stock turnover, materials management for easy handling, transport for full vehicle loads, and so on. These aims all seem worthy, so it might be sensible for each activity to judge its own performance in the most appropriate way. Unfortunately, we soon hit

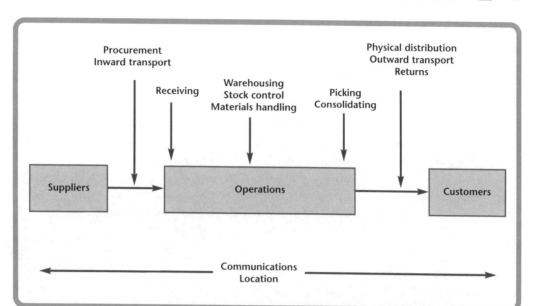

Figure 2.1 Summary of logistics activities

problems when the aims come into conflict. For example, warehousing might save money by reducing the stock of raw materials – but this leads to more frequent shortages and raises the costs of expediting for purchasing and emergency deliveries for transport. Similarly, purchasing can reduce its administrative costs by sending fewer, larger orders to suppliers – but this increases stock levels and raises the amount of money tied up in the warehouse. Using sea transport rather than airfreight reduces transport costs – but increases the amount of stock held in the supply chain. In reality, the different activities of logistics are very closely related, and policies in one part inevitably affect operations in another.

LOGISTICS IN PRACTICE

RP Turner Corp.

RP Turner Corp. makes pipeline valves for the oil industry in western Canada. It buys materials from Japan, the USA and eastern Canada, manufactures valves in Edmonton, Alberta and ships the finished products to oil fields in the North.

The company grew by emphasising the high quality of its products, which work reliably in the harsh weather conditions of the Arctic. Transport to remote customers is expensive, and in 2000 the company looked for ways of reducing the cost of logistics. It soon found that separate functions worked more or less independently. This was sometimes all too obvious when the three main departments – Marketing, Production and Finance – were in different locations. Production was in Edmonton, as the nearest major city to the oil fields; Marketing was in Calgary near to oil company headquarters; Finance (including procurement) was in Vancouver near the port and financial

LOGISTICS
IN PRACTICE

continued

centre. To appreciate the potential problems, you have to remember that Canada is a big country, so Production was a thousand kilometres away from Finance, 500 kilometres away from Marketing and over two thousand kilometres from delivery points.

The company was rewarding different departments for different types of performance. Not surprisingly, when the departments were asked for their priorities, they had different views.

Marketing wanted:

- high stocks of finished goods to satisfy customer demands quickly
- a wide range of finished goods always held in stock
- locations near to customers to allow delivery with short lead times
- production to vary output in response to customer orders
- emphasis on an efficient distribution system
- an optimistic sales forecast to ensure production was geared up for actual demand.

Production wanted:

- high stocks of raw materials and work in progress to safeguard operations

- a narrow range of finished goods to give long production runs
- locations near to suppliers so that they could get raw materials quickly
- stable production to give efficient operations
- emphasis on the efficient movement of materials through operations
- realistic sales forecasts that allowed efficient planning.

Finance wanted:

- low stocks everywhere
- few locations to give economies of scale and minimise overall costs
- large batch sizes to reduce unit costs
- make-to-order operations
- pessimistic sales forecasts that discouraged underused facilities.

Despite good communications, the company felt that it was too widely spread out. It decided to centralise operations at its main plant in Edmonton. This brought the logistics functions geographically closer together, and major reorganisation over the next two years brought a unified view of the supply chain.

Sources: Ray Turner and internal company reports

The problems at RP Turner are almost inevitable if logistics is divided into separate functions. Each part will move in a different direction, and there is duplicated effort and wasted resources. Imagine a wholesaler who has one fleet of vehicles run by materials management to bring materials in from suppliers, and a separate fleet run by distribution to deliver the same goods out to customers. This might work, but you can picture the duplicated effort and waste in managing two separate vehicle fleets. Another organisation might have three stocks – raw materials, work in progress and finished goods – each run by different departments and using different standards and systems.

A fragmented supply chain also makes it difficult to co-ordinate the flow of information through different systems. Suppose a production department knows that it is running short of a material and needs a new delivery. This information should pass seamlessly to purchasing. If, however, it has to pass from one system to another there is a greater chance of error, uncertainty, delay and inefficiency – resulting in late delivery, emergency orders, expediting and shortages.

To put it briefly, fragmenting logistics into different parts has the disadvantages of:

- giving different, often conflicting, objectives within an organisation
- duplicating effort and reducing productivity
- giving worse communications and information flows between the parts
- reducing co-ordination between the parts – leading to lower efficiency, higher costs and worse customer service
- increasing uncertainty and delays along the supply chain
- making planning more difficult
- introducing unnecessary buffers between the parts, such as stocks of work in progress, additional transport and administrative procedures
- obscuring important information, such as the total cost of logistics
- giving logistics a low status within an organisation.

Bringing activities together

The obvious way of avoiding these problems is to consider logistics not as a series of distinct activities, but as a single integrated function. Then all the parts work together to get the best overall result for the organisation. This is why Sheehy, former Chairman of BAT, could say, 'I believe that a well designed, integrated logistics system is a vital prerequisite for commercial success'.[25]

> ■ **INTEGRATING LOGISTICS** within an organisation has all the related activities working together as a single function.
> ■ This is responsible for all storage and movement of materials throughout the organisation.
> ■ It tackles problems from the viewpoint of the whole organisation, and looks for the greatest overall benefit.

In practice, it is difficult to integrate all the logistics within an organisation. The supply chain consists of many different activities, with different types of operation, using different systems and geographically dispersed. The usual approach has the integration developing over time. One department might slowly take over all aspects of ordering and receiving raw materials. Another department might slowly take over all aspects of delivering finished products to customers. Some organisations are tempted to stop when they reach this stage, and they work with two functions:

- *materials management*, aligned with production and looking after the inwards flow of raw materials and their movement through operations; and

- *physical distribution*, aligned with marketing and looking at the outward flow of finished goods.

However, this still leaves an artificial break in what is essentially a continuous function. The obvious step is to combine the two into a single function responsible for all material movement into, through and out of the organisation. This completes the **internal integration** of an organisation's logistics.

Despite the obvious benefits of integrated logistics, there can still be practical difficulties. Perhaps the obvious one is finding someone with the knowledge, enthusiasm, ability and authority to carry through necessary changes. This needs a senior manager who has the necessary power to start the changes – with effects then percolating through all levels of the organisation. New practices and relationships come from individuals working together, developing a culture that is based on teamwork and co-operation rather than self-interest and conflict.

Another factor that encourages internal integration is the analysis of **total logistics cost**. We can define this as:

Total logistics cost = transport cost + warehouse cost + stock holding cost + packaging cost
+ information processing cost + other logistics overheads

The traditional view considered each of these separate costs as independent, so reducing, say, the transport cost automatically lowered the total cost. In the 1960s organisations began to take a 'systems' view of logistics, and analyse the interactions between activities. It became clear that reducing the cost of one activity increased the cost of another – and the total logistics cost might be reduced by increasing the amount spent on certain activities. Lewis et al.[26] gave an early example of this. They found that airfreight was much more expensive than alternative road transport, but faster delivery eliminated the need for local stocks and warehouses, and gave considerable overall savings

One other important factor for integration is the availability of integrated information and control systems. Managers need a system to collect, store, analyse, distribute and present information ranging from the strategic aims of the organisation down to details of each transaction. Most organisations use local networks or intranets for this, but the Internet is increasingly seen as an efficient route for logistics information. The information can be used by a control system that assesses current circumstances, makes decisions and implements the results. An information system might show that stocks are running low, and a control system uses this information to place an order with suppliers.

LOGISTICS
IN PRACTICE

International Business Systems

International Business Systems (IBS) is the largest international vendor of software for supply chain management. It is listed on the Stockholm Stock Exchange, but works internationally with more than 5000 customers in 40 countries. It was formed in 1969, and now has 2400 employees working in 90 offices.

IBS offer many software products including a range of fully integrated modules that improve performance of the supply chain. In other words, they provide the information and management controls for looking

after 'the flow of goods and information in such a way that you give better customer service and achieve shorter lead times, with less capital tied up, thereby releasing resources for more profitable activities'.

The IBS system has modules based around core activities such as purchasing, distribution, sales, finance, production, and so on. These modules contain many different components for order processing, forecasting, sales analysis, Internet trading, bar coding, warehouse management, bar codes, inventory management, vendor managed

continued

inventory, spare part handling, customer relations management, after sales support, project management, and so on.

The aim of IBS is to give a sophisticated system that is comprehensive, but easy to run and use. Concise, well-presented and rapid information about all aspects of the supply chain helps organisations to manage their integrated logistics and 'puts them in control of the supply chain'.

Sources: IBS promotional material and website at www.ibsuk.com

Stages in integration

We have now described how logistics has moved from being a low priority, fragmented function, to a strategic, integrated one. This is a major change, which typically goes through the following stages:

Stage 1   Separate logistics activities are not given much attention or considered important.

Stage 2   Recognising that the separate activities of logistics are important for the success of the organisation.

Stage 3   Making improvements in the separate functions, making sure that each is as efficient as possible.

Stage 4   Internal integration – recognising the benefits of internal co-operation and combining the separate functions into one.

Stage 5   Developing a logistics strategy, to set the long-term direction of logistics.

Stage 6   Benchmarking – comparing logistics' performance with other organisations, learning from their experiences, identifying areas that need improvement and finding ways of achieving this.

Stage 7   Continuous improvement – accepting that further changes are inevitable and always searching for better ways of organising logistics.

By Stage 4 an organisation has integrated logistics, and the last three stages show how the function can be improved. Stage 5 emphasises the need for a strategic view, Stage 6 looks at other organisations for comparisons and lessons, and Stage 7 recognises that logistics must continually evolve. However, this is not the end of the story. Once an organisation has efficient, integrated and strategic logistics, it can start looking at integration along more of the supply chain.

INTEGRATION ALONG THE SUPPLY CHAIN

Problems with fragmented supply chains

We have described the benefits of integrating logistics within an organisation. Now we can extend this argument, and suggest the same benefits for integrating logistics along more of the

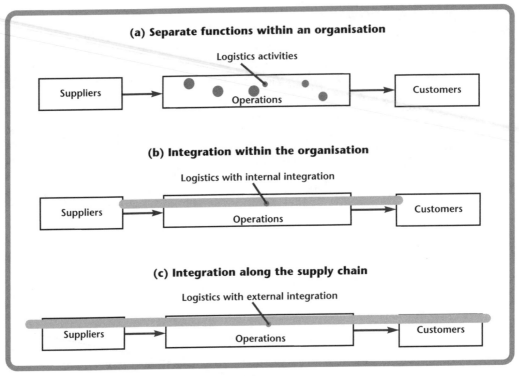

Figure 2.2 Three levels of logistics integration

	A	B	C	D	E	F	G	H
1	Week		1	2	3	4	5	6
2								
3	Customer							
4		Demand	100	105	100	100	100	100
5								
6	Retailer							
7		Demand	100	105	100	100	100	100
8		Opening stock	100	100	105	100	100	100
9		Closing stock	100	105	100	100	100	100
10		Buys	100	110	95	100	100	100
11								
12	Local wholesaler							
13		Demand	100	110	95	100	100	100
14		Opening stock	100	100	110	95	100	100
15		Closing stock	100	110	95	100	100	100
16		Buys	100	120	80	105	100	100
17								
18	Regional wholesaler							
19		Demand	100	120	80	105	100	100
20		Opening stock	100	100	120	80	105	100
21		Closing stock	100	120	80	105	100	100
22		Buys	100	140	40	130	95	100
23								
24	Manufacturer							
25		Demand	100	140	40	130	95	100
26		Opening stock	100	100	140	100	130	95
27		Closing stock	100	140	100	130	95	100
28		Makes	100	180	0	160	60	105

Figure 2.3 Varying demand

supply chain. If each organisation only looks at its own operations, there are unnecessary boundaries between them, disrupting the flow of materials and increasing costs. **External integration** removes these boundaries to improve the whole chain. Christopher advises this move, saying that 'Most opportunities for cost reduction and/or value enhancement lie at the interface between supply chain partners'.[22]

This effectively gives three levels of integration. The first has logistics as separate activities within an organisation; the second has internal integration to bring them together into a single function; the third has external integration, where organisations look beyond their own operations and integrate more of the supply chain (as illustrated in Figure 2.2).

- ■ Organisations within the same supply chain should **CO-OPERATE** to get final customer satisfaction.
- ■ They should not compete with each other, but with organisations in other supply chains.

Forrester[27] described one interesting effect of a fragmented supply chain. Imagine a retailer who notices that demand for a product rises by 5 units in a week. When it is time to place the next order, the retailer assumes that demand is rising, and orders ten extra units to make sure it has enough. The local wholesaler sees demand rise by ten units, so it orders an extra 15 units to meet the growth. The regional wholesaler sees demand rise by 15 units, so it orders another 20 units. As this movement travels through the supply chain, a relatively small change in final demand is amplified into a major variation for early suppliers.

W O R K E D
E X A M P L E

In a simple supply chain, each organisation holds one week's demand in stock. In other words, each buys enough materials from its suppliers to make its closing stock at the end of the week equal to the demand during the week. Demand for a product has been steady at 100 units a week. One week, demand from final customers is five units higher than usual. Assuming that deliveries are very fast, how does this affect movements in the supply chain?

Solution

The spreadsheet in Figure 2.3 shows this for the first week when demand of 100 units moves through the supply chain. For each tier, you can see:

- ■ demand – which equals the amount bought by the next tier of customers

- ■ opening stock at the beginning of the week – which equals its closing stock in the previous week

- ■ closing stock at the end of the week – which must equal demand in the week

- ■ number of units bought – which equals demand plus any change in stock:

  buys = demand met + (closing stock – opening stock)

WORKED EXAMPLE
continued

In week 1 everything is going smoothly, with the usual 100 units flowing down the supply chain. Then in week 2 customer demand goes up to 105 units. The retailer must buy 105 units to meet this demand, plus an additional 5 units to raise its closing stock to 105. So it buys 110 units from the local wholesaler. The local wholesaler has to supply this 110 units, plus an additional 10 units to raise its closing stock to 110 units. So it buys 120 units from the regional wholesaler. The regional wholesaler has to supply this 120 units, plus another 20 units to raise its closing stock to 120 units. So it buys 140 units from the manufacturer.

In week 3 we get the reverse effect as customer demand returns to 100 units. The retailer now reduces closing stock to 100 units, so it only has to buy 95 units from the local wholesaler. The local wholesaler reduces its closing stock by 15, so it only has to buy 80 from the regional wholesaler. The regional wholesaler reduces its closing stock by 40, so it only buys 40 from the manufacturer. The manufacturer would like to reduce its closing stock by 100 units, but its demand is only 40 units so it stops production and meets all demand from stock.

A variation in customer demand of five units in one week, has made manufacturing vary by 180 units a week, with an effect continuing for several more weeks.

Benefits of integration

Confederated Bottlers used to deliver bottles from their main plant in Elizabethville to a brewery in Johnston, 115 miles away. The brewery filled the bottles and took them to a distribution centre 20 miles outside Elizabethville. Both companies used their own trucks to deliver products, returning empty. Eventually, they formed a joint transport company that used the same trucks for both deliveries. Not surprisingly, the transport costs almost halved. This example shows one obvious benefit of integration, but there are many others.

Any uncertainty in the supply chain – such as the amplified variation of demand seen in the last example – encourages organisations to hold higher stocks to give themselves a margin of safety. These stocks increase costs and make the chain slow to react to changing conditions (when customers demand new products, all the stocks of old products in the supply chain have to be sold-on before the new ones appear). If you continue thinking along these lines, you find the following benefits from external integration:

- ⬤ genuine co-operation between all parts of the supply chain, with shared information and resources
- ⬤ lower costs – due to balanced operations, lower stocks, less expediting, economies of scale, elimination of activities that waste time or do not add value, and so on
- ⬤ improved performance – due to more accurate forecasts, better planning, higher productivity of resources, rational priorities, and so on
- ⬤ improved material flow, with co-ordination giving faster and more reliable movements

- better customer service, with shorter lead times, faster deliveries and more customisation
- more flexibility, with organisations reacting faster to changing conditions
- standardised procedures, becoming routine and well-practiced with less duplication of effort, information, planning, and so on
- reliable quality and fewer inspections, with integrated quality management programmes.

Many organisations have moved towards external integration[28] and a survey by P-E Consulting in 1997[29] found that 57 per cent of companies had some form of integration of their supply chains. More than 90 per cent of companies expected further integration, with a quarter looking for 'fully integrated' systems (although there were clearly different opinions about what this meant).

The benefits of external integration may be clear, but there are many practical difficulties of achieving them. Many organisations simply do not trust other members of the supply chain, and they are reluctant to share information. Even with sufficient trust, there can be problems with different priorities, competition, data exchange, appropriate systems, skills, security, the complexity of systems, and so on. This raises the obvious question of how to achieve integration?

ACHIEVING INTEGRATION

Co-operation and conflict

Normally, a supply chain consists of distinct organisations, each working for their own benefit. So why should they co-operate? Why should one company work to benefit another? The answer is that external integration brings benefits that can be shared among all members of the supply chain, as you can see in the Perman Frère example.

LOGISTICS
IN PRACTICE

Perman Frère

Perman Frère is a small manufacturer based in Brussels. It exports most of its products and has a finished goods warehouse near the port of Ostende. Van Rijn is one of its customers, also based in Brussels. It imports most of its materials and has a raw materials warehouse near the port of Rotterdam.

The two companies have traded for many years and in 2001 they started looking for ways of increasing co-operation. It was soon obvious that they could make a number of small adjustments to improve logis-

tics. As an example, some parts were made by Perman Frère in Brussels, sent to their warehouse in Ostende, delivered to van Rijn's warehouse in Rotterdam, and then brought back to Brussels. It was fairly easy to organise deliveries directly between the companies. This gave a much shorter journey across Brussels, reduced transport and handling costs, removed excess stocks, simplified administration, and reduced the lead time from five days to three hours. They also co-ordinated deliveries to towns in northern

France, so that one vehicle could deliver products from both companies.

Both companies benefited from these changes. When they were introduced people in both companies said that they had been aware of the problems for a long time, but could not find any mechanism for overcoming them.

_____

Sources: Georges Perman and internal company reports

The first problem with external integration is overcoming the traditional view of organisations as adversaries. When an organisation pays money to its suppliers, people assume that one can only benefit at the expense of the other. If the organisation gets a good deal, it automatically means that the supplier is losing out: if the supplier makes a good profit, it means that the organisation pays too much. This adversarial attitude has major drawbacks. Suppliers set rigid conditions and, as they have no guarantee of repeat business, they see no point in co-operation and try to make as much profit from each sale as possible. At the same time, organisations have no loyalty, and they shop around to get the best deal and remind suppliers of the competition. Each is concerned only with their own objectives and will – when convenient to themselves – change specifications and conditions at short notice. The result is uncertainty about the number and size of orders, constantly changing suppliers and customers, changing products and conditions, different times between orders, no guarantee of repeat orders and changing costs.

To avoid these problems, organisations have to recognise that it is in their own long-term interest to replace conflict by agreement. This often needs a major change of culture. The following table suggests some specific adjustments.

Factor	Conflict view	Co-operation view
Profit	One organisation profits at the expense of the other	Both share profits
Relationship	One is dominant	Equal partners
Trust	Little	Considerable
Communication	Limited and formal	Widespread and open
Information	Secretive	Open and shared
Control	Intensive policing	Delegation and empowerment
Quality	Blame for faults	Solving shared problems
Contract	Rigid	Flexible
Focus on	Own operations	Customers

Different types of co-operation

There are several ways that organisations can co-operate. They can, of course, simply do business together. If an organisation has a good experience with a supplier, it will continue to use them and over some period will develop a valuable working relationship. Sometimes the co-operation is more positive, such as small companies making joint purchases to get the same quantity discounts as larger companies; EDI links to share information; combining loads to reduce transport costs; agreed package sizes to ease material handling, lists of preferred suppliers, and so on. The key point with these informal arrangements is that there is no commitment. This is probably how you shop, as you have favourite shops but are not obliged to use them. Japanese companies take this approach further forming *Keiretsu* – which are groups of organisations that work together without actually forming partnerships.

An informal arrangement has the advantage of being flexible and non-binding. On the other hand, it has the disadvantage that either party can end the co-operation without warning, and at any time that suits them. This is why many organisations prefer a more formal arrangement, with a written contract setting out the obligations of each party. These are common when organisations see themselves as working together for some time. An electricity company, for example, might agree to supply power at a fixed price for the next three years, provided a customer buys some minimum quantity. More formal agreements have the advantage of showing the details of the commitment, so that each side knows exactly what it has to do. On the other hand, they have the disadvantage of losing flexibility and imposing rigid conditions. In 2001, for example, there were power cuts in California when electricity suppliers found that their long-term contracts with customers specified prices that were too low to cover the rising costs of generation.

Strategic alliances

When an organisation and a supplier are working well together, they may both feel that they are getting the best possible results and neither could benefit from trading with other partners. Then they might look for a long-term relationship that will guarantee that their mutual benefits continue. This is the basis of a **strategic alliance** or **partnership** (shown in Figure 2.4).

The supplier knows that it has repeat business for a long time, and can invest in improvements to products and operations; the organisation knows that it has guaranteed – and continually improving – supplies. These arrangements are now common, and you often hear statements like 'Abbey National treats its suppliers as partners'.[30] Ellram and Krause prefer the term **supplier partnering** and give the following definition.[31]

SUPPLIER PARTNERING is 'an ongoing relationship between firms, which involves a commitment over an extended time period, and a mutual sharing of information and the risks and rewards of the relationship.'

The following list gives the main features of alliances:

- organisations working closely together at all levels
- senior managers and everyone in the organisations supporting the alliance
- shared business culture, goals and objectives
- openness and mutual trust
- long-term commitment
- shared information, expertise, planning and systems
- flexibility and willingness to solve shared problems
- continuous improvements in all aspects of operations
- joint development of products and processes
- guaranteed reliable and high quality goods and services
- agreement on costs and profits to give fair and competitive pricing
- increasing business between partners.

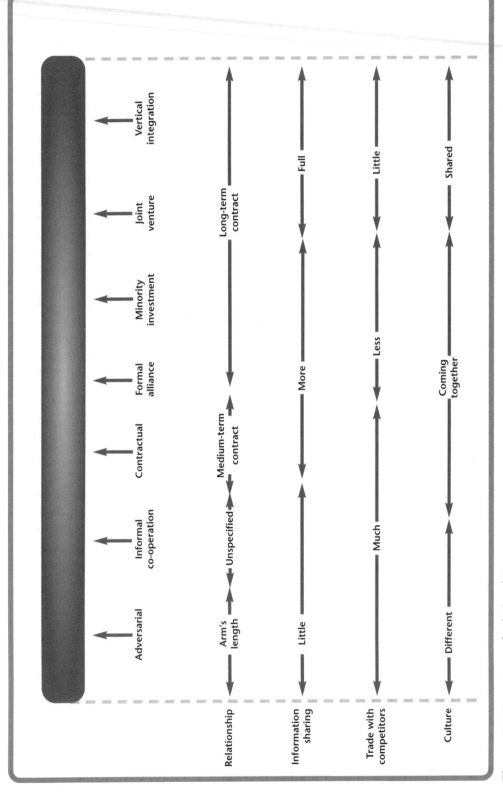

Figure 2.4 Spectrum of relationships

Partnerships can lead to changes in operations. For example, the stability of a partnership might encourage suppliers to specialise in one type of product. They give such a commitment to the alliance that they reduce their product range, make these as efficiently as possible, and concentrate on giving a small number of customers a very high quality service. They share information with customers without the threat that this will be used to get some form of trading advantage. At the same time, customers reduce their number of suppliers, as they no longer need to look around to get the best deals. Japanese companies were among the first to develop strategic alliances, and at the time when Toyota had formed partnerships with its 250 suppliers, General Motors was still working separately with 4000 suppliers.

It can be difficult to form a successful partnership. A useful starting point is to analyse current operations and future plans to see if alliances would be useful. A company cannot really expect any benefits from an alliance if it only buys a few materials, or is changing its manufacturing base, or is sensitive about confidentiality, or cannot find reliable suppliers. Most organisations, however, can see potential benefits, and they should start looking at possible arrangements. Typically they form a project team to identify potential partners, define objectives, set timetables, list resource implications, negotiate terms, and so on. When this project team makes its initial report, potential partners can be approached and negotiations begin. The following example shows how one company set about this.

LOGISTICS IN PRACTICE

Petro-Canada

Petro-Canada (PC) is the largest oil company in Canada, with 4500 employees and over $6 billion in sales. It owns 750 million barrels of proved reserves, but its main income comes from 1700 retail petrol stations. The Canadian government originally founded PC to compete with major international companies, and it still owns 18% of the shares.

In the 1990s PC started to form strategic alliances with its major suppliers. It was looking for ways of reducing costs, and supplier partnerships were a clear option for a company that spent over $2 billion a year on materials other than oil.

To find the best way of forming strategic alliances, PC benchmarked other companies who reported a history of successful partnerships, including Motorola and Dow Chemicals. In practice, growing pressure to improve performance meant that PC had to get results quickly, and they developed their own approach. This had targets of reducing costs by 15% in a first phase, and eventually by 25%.

PC quickly realised that without guaranteed product quality it could make no further progress, so it consolidated its use of total quality management. This included Deming's[32] '14 principles' which advise organisations not to buy products on the basis of cost alone, but to include a range of factors such as quality, reliability, timing, features, trust, and so on.

Now it had done the preparation, PC could start talking to prospective partners. It chose these from companies that it currently did most business with, and those whose products were critical. There were already long-standing, informal relationships with many of these, and PC extended them to create more formal alliances. Important considerations were that the suppliers were

continued

committed to high quality, emphasised customer satisfaction, and had the potential to become 'the best of the best'.

This gave PC its likely partners, and the next stage was to form joint development teams, including representatives from the purchasing and user departments. Because of the time pressure, this team looked for quick improvements. Their aim was to get the initiative moving, get some quick returns, generate enthusiasm for the ideas, and then move the partnership forward over the longer term.

We can summarise PC's approach to developing partnerships in the following stages:

1. prepare the organisation for alliances with research, training, systems and practices
2. assess the risk and benefits of partnerships, setting aims and targets
3. benchmark other partnership arrangements
4. select qualified suppliers
5. form joint teams to manage the initiative and move it forward
6. confirm the partnership's principles, commitments, relationships and obligations
7. formalise the terms and conditions
8. continue training and improving.

Sources: internal company reports and website at www.petro-canada.com

Of course, forming a partnership is only the first step, and it still needs a lot of effort to make it a success. Some factors that contribute to a successful partnership include a high level of achieved service, real cost savings, a growing amount of business, compatibility of cultures, and so on. Rowley[33] gave a more general list of key factors as management commitment, a contract specifying costs and responsibilities, agreed performance indicators, agreed objectives, shared culture and joint information systems. Lambert et al.[34] summarised these as:

- *drivers*, which are the compelling reasons for forming partnerships, such as cost reduction, better customer service, or security

- *facilitators*, which are the supportive corporate factors that encourage partnerships, such as compatibility of operations, similar management styles, common aims, and so on

- *components*, which are the joint activities and operations used to build and sustain the relationship, such as communication channels, joint planning, shared risk and rewards, investment, and so on.

Alliances are certainly not the best answer in every circumstance. Some purchases are so small, or materials are so cheap, that the effort needed for an alliance is not worthwhile; sometimes managers do not want to lose control or share information; sometimes an organisation may not be able to find a partner willing to make the necessary commitment; organisational structures or cultures may be too different; it may be impossible to reach the necessary level of trust; there may be nobody with the necessary skills and enthusiasm, and so on. Several years after starting its supplier partnership initiative, Petro-Canada still bought 20–40% of materials through traditional supplier–customer relationships.

However, it is clear that alliances are becoming increasingly popular. As Ewer[35] says, we have 'the powerful combination of improved technology which can enable better partnering, a growing consensus that partnering enabled by e-B2B is essential, and a growing public profile for partnering issues in general'.

Vertical integration

If an organisation wants to go beyond partnerships, it has to own more of the supply chain. One common arrangement has an organisation taking a minority share in another company. This gives it some say in their operations, but it does not necessarily control them. A manufacturer, for example, might take a minority share in a wholesaler, to get some influence in the way that its products are distributed.

Another option is for two organisations to start a **joint venture**, where they both put up funds to start a third company with shared ownership. A manufacturer and supplier might together form a transport company for moving materials between the two.

The most common arrangement has one organisation simply buying other organisations in the supply chain. This increases its level of **vertical integration**.

> **VERTICAL INTEGRATION** describes the amount of a supply chain that is owned by one organisation.

If an organisation buys materials from outside suppliers and sells products to external customers, it does not own much of the supply chain and has little vertical integration (as shown in Figure 2.5). If the organisation owns initial suppliers, does most of the value adding

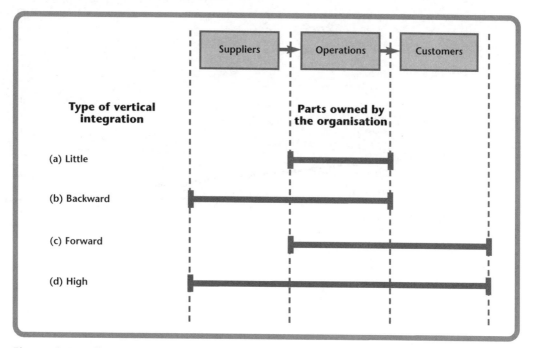

Figure 2.5 Different levels of vertical integration

operations, and distributes products through to final customers, it owns a lot of the supply chain and is highly vertically integrated. If the organisation owns a lot of the supply side it has **backward** or **upstream integration**; if it owns a lot of the distribution network it has **down-stream** or **forward integration**.

In some circumstances vertical integration is the best way of getting different parts of the supply chain to work together. Ford of America, for example, has at different times owned everything from steel mills through to distributor networks and repair shops. More often, widespread vertical integration would be very expensive, leading to huge organisations that spread their resources too thinly, needing specialised skills and experience that one organisation does not have, reducing flexibility to respond to changing conditions, and so on. So vertical integration is not necessarily desirable, and it is usually impossible for even the biggest organisation to own much of their supply chains. Heinz, for example, cannot buy all the farmers, processors, steel mills, canners, wholesalers, retailers and other organisations in the supply chain for their baked beans.

LOGISTICS
IN PRACTICE

GZ Rexam

In 1996 Rexam Pharmaceutical Packaging and Grafica Zannini formed a joint venture called GZ Rexam. Its primary aim is to supply packaging to the pharmaceutical industry in Europe. This is an important area, as over 50% of pharmaceutical companies' product recalls are caused by faults in printed material, and each recall costs several million pounds.

GZ Rexam looks for the benefits of partnerships with its customers. John Stevenson, the Sales and Marketing Director, says, 'The days of the conventional supply chain where everyone existed as an independent entity … are no longer'. He quotes three reasons for partnerships:

■ Lower costs – due to better co-ordination, elimination of duplicated effort, less bureaucracy, quantity discounts, and economies of scale. GZ Rexam estimates that it can save up to 60% of packaging costs through partnerships.

■ Shorter lead-times – from improved co-ordination, procedures and administration. With Eli Lilly they reduced lead times from six to two weeks, with just-in-time deliveries for specific orders.

■ Higher quality – with uniform standards, collaboration in quality initiatives, less reliance on inspections and a commitment to long-term improvements.

Once the objectives of a partnership have been agreed, the two key factors for success at GZ Rexam are commitment to the long-term success of the partnership and good communication between everyone concerned.

Source: Stevenson J. (1999) Partnering – Improving the Supply Chain, *Logistics Focus*, **7**(2) 9–11

CHAPTER REVIEW

❑ In the past, logistics did not receive much attention. More organisations now recognise its importance. By organising logistics properly, cost can be reduced, customer service improved, and other organisational objectives achieved.

❑ There are many pressures on logistics. It is responding to these by introducing new practices and methods. Perhaps the most obvious changes are related to new technology for improving communications.

❑ There are three important trends towards lean, agile and integrated logistics. These are not mutually exclusive, and an organisation can make progress on all three.

❑ Traditionally, logistics has been organised as a series of distinct activities within an organisation. This inevitably leads to conflicts and inefficiencies. A better approach develops a single integrated function that is responsible for all logistics.

❑ Integration can be difficult and involve major changes. There are, however, many benefits, and most companies have moved in the direction of internal integration.

❑ There are also the benefits of extending integration to more organisations in the supply chain. There are several ways of organising this external integration, ranging from informal agreements to vertical integration. The most popular has some form of strategic alliance or partnership.

C A S E   S T U D Y — *Friedland Timbers asa*

Johann Klassen is the Managing Director of Friedland Timbers asa. which makes specialised wood products for the construction industry. He has recently been worried by late deliveries to some important customers. The industry is very competitive, and Johann knows that customers will go to other suppliers if he cannot guarantee deliveries. The marketing manager is particularly upset because he has worked with these customers for a long time, and promised deliveries that were not made.

Johann asked the production manager for an explanation. She told him that 'Our own suppliers were late in delivering certain types of wood. This shortage of a key raw material disrupted our production plans. We cannot be blamed for this. If anyone in the company is to blame, it is the warehouse manager who does not keep enough stocks of raw materials to cover for late deliveries.'

Johann then went to the warehouse manager to see what was happening. 'There can't be anything wrong here', he was told. 'Stocks have been climbing for the past year, and last month they were at an all time high. In part, this is a deliberate decision, as I want to improve service levels to production. In part, though, stocks seem to have just drifted upwards. Now we have high stocks of most items, but there are still occasional shortages. These high stocks are causing me problems with space, and are stretching my budget. I think that the blame lies in purchasing, who do not order the amounts that we request.'

Johann saw that some stocks were drifting upwards because purchasing were buying large quantities of some materials. At the same time, they were delaying some purchases, and this produced the shortages. The purchasing manager explained to Johann, 'Let me remind you that eight months ago you instructed me to reduce materials costs. I am doing this by taking advantage of the discounts given by suppliers for larger orders. Often I order more than requested under the assumption that we will need the material at some stage, so I get a discount and the material is already in stock when we need it. Sometimes keeping things in stock would take too much space or be too expensive, so then I might delay an order until I can combine it with others to get bigger discounts.'

Johann thought that he was near the source of his problems, and might ask for the purchasing policies to be reviewed. Then he talked to the transport manager who was not so sure. 'It is much more efficient for me to bring larger quantities into the company', he said. 'If you reduce the average order size, the transport costs will rise. Our budget is already being squeezed, as we have to pay for expensive express deliveries of materials that production classify as urgent. If you lower the order size, there will be more shortages, more express deliveries and even higher costs.'

Johann talked to some major suppliers to see if they could somehow improve the flow of materials into the company. Unhappily, while he was talking to one company, they raised the question of late payments. This was contrary to Friedland's stated policy of immediate payment of invoices, so he asked the accounting section for an explanation. He was given the unwelcome news that 'The company's inventory and transport costs are so high that we are short of cash. We are delaying payments to improve our cash flow. As it is, we had to use a bank overdraft to pay suppliers for last month.'

C A S E   S T U D Y   *continued*

Later that day Johann found that the late customer deliveries which had started his investigation, were actually caused by poor sales forecasts by the marketing department. They had seriously underestimated demand, and planned production was too low. All the employees at FT were doing their best, but things seemed to be going wrong.

C A S E   S T U D Y
Questions

- ⬤ Why do all the logistics costs seem to be rising at the same time?
- ⬤ What do you think are the basic problems in Friedland?
- ⬤ What would you recommend Johann do?

P R O J E C T
Supply Partnerships

Find a particular product whose supply chain is easy to study, such as petrol, a telephone service, cars, a restaurant chain, or a computer game. Discuss the amount of integration in the supply chain. What alternatives are there for integration? See if different organisations making similar products have the same approach, and explain any differences. Say why the existing patterns of logistics have developed, and discuss the benefits of this level of integration.

DISCUSSION QUESTIONS

1. What do you think are the main factors that encourage logistics to change? How is it responding to these pressures? What changes do you think there will be in the next decade?
2. When logistics is divided into separate functions, each is likely to have its own objectives. Is this necessarily a bad thing, or can there be positive benefits?
3. An integrated supply chain is a convenient notion, but it does not reflect real operations. An organisation is only really concerned with its own customers and suppliers, and does not have time to consider other organisations further along the chain. Do you think that this is true?

4. When Christopher[19] says that 'supply chains compete, not companies' what exactly does he mean?
5. Decker and van Goor[36] say that integration in the supply chain can be at the level of:
    ● Physical movement
    ● Shared information
    ● Integrated control
    ● Integrated infrastructure
    What do they mean by this?

REFERENCES

1. Shaw A.W. (1916) *An Approach to Business Problems*, Harvard University Press, Cambridge, MA.
2. Clark F.E. (1922) *Principles of Marketing*, Macmillan, New York.
3. Borsodi R. (1927) *The Distribution Age*, D. Appleton, New York.
4. Drucker P. (1962) The economy's dark continent, *Fortune*, April, 4, p. 103.
5. Ray D. (1976) Distribution costing, *International Journal of Physical Distribution and Materials Management*, **6**(2), 73–107.
6. Little W.I. (1977) The cellular flow logistics costing system, *International Journal of Physical Distribution and Materials Management*, **7**(6), 305–29.
7. Firth D., Denham F.R., Griffin K.R. and Heffernan J. et al. (1980) (eds) *Distribution Management Handbook*, McGraw-Hill, London.
8. Ray D., Gattorna J. and Allen M. (1980) Handbook of distribution costing and control, *International Journal of Physical Distribution and Materials Management*, **10**(5), 211–429.
9. McKibbin B.N. (1982) Centre for Physical Distribution Management national survey of distribution costs, *FOCUS on Physical Distribution*, **1**(1), 16–18.
10. Delaney R.V. (1986) Managerial and financial challenges facing transport leaders, *Transportation Quarterly*, **40**(1), 35.
11. Hill G.V. (1994) Assessing the cost of customer service, in Cooper J. (ed.) *Logistics and Distribution Planning* (2nd edn), Kogan Page, London.
12. Stafford-Jones A. (1997) Electronic commerce: the future with EDI, *Logistics Focus*, **5**(9), 9–10.
13. MRO Software (2001) *Supplying the Goods*, MRO Software, London.
14. The Gartner Group (2001) Website at www.gartner.com.
15 Holweg M., Judge B. and Williams G. (2001) The 3DayCar challenge: cars to customer orders, *Logistics and Transport Focus*, **3**(9), 36–44.
16. 3DayCar Programme (2001) Website at www.cf.ac.uk/3DayCar.
17. McKinnon A.C. (1999) The outsourcing of logistical activities, Ch. 14 in Waters D. (ed.) *Global Logistics and Distribution Planning*, Kogan Page, London.
18. Marketline International (1997) *EU Logistics*, Marketline International, London.
19. Christopher M. (1996) Emerging Issues in Supply Chain Management, Proceedings of the Logistics Academic Network Inaugural Workshop, Warwick.
20. Jones D., Hines P. and Rich N. (1997) Lean logistics, *International Journal of Physical Distribution and Logistics Management*, **27**(3/4), 153–73.
21. Womack J. and Jones D. (1996) *Lean Thinking*, Simon & Schuster, New York.
22. Christopher M. (1999) Global logistics: the role of agility, *Logistics and Transport Focus*, **1**(1).
23. Rowley J. (2001) Lean and agile, *Logistics and Transport Focus*, **3**(6), 52–7.

24. Evans B. and Powell M. (2000) A pragmatic view of lean and agile, *Logistics and Transport Focus*, **2**(10), 26–32.

25. Sheehy P. (1988) Quality – the springboard to success, *Focus on Physical Distribution and Logistics Management*, **7**(8), 3–9.

26. Lewis H.T., Culliton J.W. and Steel J.D. (1956) *The Role of Air Freight in Physical Distribution*, Harvard Business School, Boston, MA.

27. Forrester J. (1961) *Industrial Dynamics*, MIT Press, Boston, MA.

28. Guinipero L.C. and Brand R.R. (1996) Purchasing's role in supply chain management, *International Journal of Logistics Management*, **7**(1), 29–37.

29. P-E Consulting (1997) *Efficient Customer Response – Supply Chain Management for the New Millennium?* P-E Consulting, Surrey.

30. Abbey National (2002) Website at www.abbeynational.plc.uk.

31. Ellram L.M. and Krause D.R. (1994) Supplier partnerships in manufacturing versus non-manufacturing firms, *International Journal of Logistics Management*, **5**(1), 43–53.

32. Deming W.E. (1986) *Out of the Crisis*, MIT Press, Cambridge, MA.

33. Rowley J. (2001) Outsourcing across borders in Europe, *Logistics and Transport Focus*, **3**(1), 54–6.

34. Lambert D.M., Emmelhainz M.A. and Gardner J.T. (1996) Developing and implementing supply chain partnerships, *International Journal of Logistics Management*, **7**(2), 1–17.

35. Ewer G.A. (2001) View point, *Logistics and Transport Focus*, **3**(2), 2.

36. Decker H. and van Goor A. (1998) Applying Activity-based Costing to Supply Chain Management, Proceedings of the 1998 Logistics Research Network Conference, Cranfield University.

PART II

Planning the Supply Chain

This book is divided into three parts. The first part gave a general introduction to the subject of supply chain management. This is the second part, which discusses the planning needed for a supply chain.

There are six chapters in this part. Chapter 3 discusses the strategic significance of logistics, alternative strategies, and the choice of most appropriate. Chapter 4 discusses the implementation of this strategy and approaches to change. Chapter 5 shows how the shape of the supply chain is set by the location of facilities. Chapters 6 and 7 describe some approaches to planning resources. Chapter 8 shows how to measure and improve performance.

This part of the book looks at different types of planning. It starts with the logistics strategy which sets the scene for all other decisions in logistics. Then it describes different aspects of planning, making sure that the supply chain can work efficiently. The last part of the book focuses on different activities of logistics.

CHAPTER 3

Logistics Strategy

CONTENTS

AIMS OF THE CHAPTER

After reading this chapter you should be able to:

- SEE how a logistics strategy fits into an organisation's broader decisions

- OUTLINE the strategic importance of logistics

- DEFINE a logistics strategy and DISCUSS its focus

- DISCUSS alternative logistics strategies

- APPROACH the design of a logistics strategy

STRATEGIC DECISIONS

Types of decision

Some decisions are very important to an organisation, with consequences felt over many years. Other decisions are less important, with consequences felt over days or even hours. We can use their importance to classify decisions as:

- *Strategic decisions* are most important and set the overall direction of the organisation; they have effects over the long term, involve many resources and are the most risky
- *Tactical decisions* are concerned with implementing the strategies over the medium term; they look at more detail, involve fewer resources and some risk
- *Operational decisions* are the most detailed and concern activities over the short term; they involve few resources and little risk

A traditional view has senior managers making the strategic decisions that set their organisation on its course. These strategic decisions give the objectives, constraints and context for the tactical decisions made by middle managers. These, in turn, give the objectives, constraints and context for operational decisions made by junior managers. This is still the usual approach to decisions, but new styles of management and improved technology have encouraged changes. Now you rarely see such a strict hierarchy, even among conventionally rigid organisations like the armed forces. Most decisions are discussed, negotiated and agreed rather than simply passed down. There is also a growing recognition that the best person to make a decision is the person most closely involved – and this is often a junior manager who is on the spot rather than a remote, senior manager. You can see this effect with empowerment (which devolves decisions to the lowest possible level) 'delayering' (to remove unnecessary layers of management) and lean organisations (which remove all unnecessary activities).

There are several types of strategic decision (as shown in Figure 3.1). People use different names for these, but the most common are:

- *mission* – a statement to give the overall aims of the organisation;
- *corporate strategy* – which shows how a diversified corporation will achieve its mission;
- *business strategy* – which shows how each business within a diversified corporation will contribute to the corporate strategy;
- *functional strategies* – which describe the strategic direction of each function, including logistics.

Essentially the higher strategies set the goals and general direction of the organisation, and the functional strategies show how to achieve these. So the business strategy shows what has to be done, and the logistics strategy shows how the supply chain will help achieve this. If an organisation has a business strategy of being the lowest cost provider of some product, the logistics strategy shows how it will reduce logistics costs to a minimum; if the organisation is working to get fast deliveries to customers, the logistics strategy defines policies for achieving this. This assumes, of course, that logistics really has a strategic role. Perhaps we should review the evidence to support this.

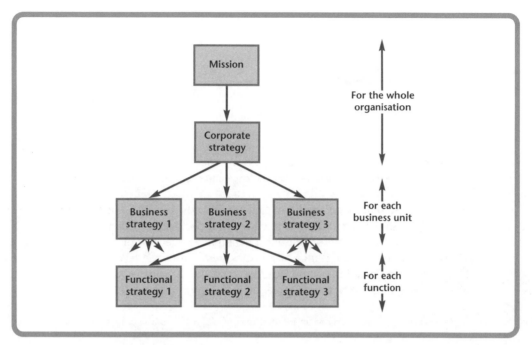

Figure 3.1 Types of strategic decision

Strategic role of logistics

The last two chapters showed that logistics is essential for every organisation, even those supplying intangible services. We said that it is concerned with major decisions that have a clear strategic impact, such as the design of the supply chain, size and location of facilities, relations with other organisations, partnerships and alliances. We showed that logistics is a major user of resources, including transport and storage; it has an impact on organisational performance, including profit and financial measures such as the return on assets; it affects lead time, perceived product value, reliability and other measures of customer service; it gives public exposure, raises safety and environmental, issues, encourages some operations and prohibits others.

You can see more evidence of the strategic role of logistics in mission statements, which often have some explicit reference to the supply chain. It is, of course, not surprising that companies offering specialised logistics services refer to the supply chain in their missions. The mission of Roadway Express, an American transport company, says:

> We will contribute to customer success and satisfaction by providing reliable, responsive, and efficient service. Our principal product will be less-than-load transportation on 2-day and longer lanes within North America, and on international lanes to and from North America.[1]

Similarly, Mercia Software is the largest Europe-based provider of software for supply chain management, and they say that:

> Mercia's mission is to provide customers with optimum value business solutions in demand and supply chain planning.[2]

Retailers often form the links to final customers, and their long-term survival depends on their ability to manage supply chains and move materials efficiently. Boots the Chemist says:

> Our vision is to be the world's leading retailer of products and services that help make our customers look good and feel good.[3]

Sainsbury's objectives include:

> To provide unrivalled value to our customers in the quality of the goods we sell, in the competitiveness of our prices and in the range of choice we offer.
> To achieve efficiency of operation, convenience and customer service in our stores … .[4]

Neither of these statements mentions logistics directly, but they both emphasise the supply of products to customers, and their implicit reliance on logistics. The point, of course, is that the long-term survival of every organisation depends on the flow of materials through its supply chains. The strategic importance of logistics stems from the basic fact that without logistics there can be no operations – and no organisation. You can see this message clearly in many mission statements. GKN, for example, include a commitment:

> To treat our suppliers fairly as an integral part of our total capability to serve our customers.[5]

We could continue discussing the evidence for a strategic role for logistics, but the facts are so clear that there is little point. This is, however, a relatively new opinion. For many organisations the recognition that logistics has a strategic impact is one of the most important developments of recent years. It changes the way that they manage the supply chain, and links it more closely with other strategic decisions. Logistics has a new, prominent role and gets the same attention as other core functions. Senior managers make the decisions, based on more relevant information and a broader view of the organisation's objectives. The recognition that logistics has a long-term effect on overall performance has moved it from the periphery to the centre of decision making.

LOGISTICS STRATEGY

Definition

All the long-term decisions about logistics form a logistics strategy.

> The **LOGISTICS STRATEGY** of an organisation consists of all the strategic decisions, policies, plans and culture relating to the management of its supply chains.

The logistics strategy forms a link between the more abstract, higher strategies and the detailed operations of the supply chain. While the corporate and business strategies describe general aims, the logistics strategy concerns the actual movement of materials needed to support these aims. The business strategy of UPS calls for 'outstanding service' to its customers, and this translates into a logistics strategy of organising a very fast parcel delivery service to almost any point in the world.

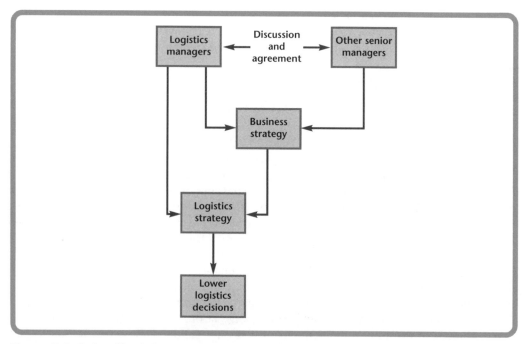

Figure 3.2 Role of logistics managers in strategic decisions

The higher strategies set the context for the logistics strategy. However, logistics managers do not simply respond to this context, they actively contribute to its formulation. Their views on what levels of performance are actually achievable by logistics form one of the inputs for the design of higher strategies (as shown in Figure 3.2). For UPS the recognition that it really can achieve efficient logistics allows it to have a business strategy of aiming at outstanding service.

There are, of course, many factors other than logistics to consider in designing a business strategy. But the amount that logistics contributes to the formulation of higher strategies can have a significant effect on operations. At one end of a spectrum (shown in Figure 3.3) are organisations where logistics contributes hardly anything to the higher strategies. Logistics managers simply accept the higher strategies designed by others, and design operations to

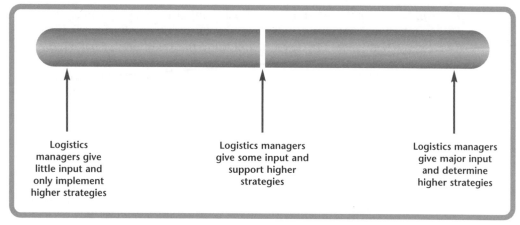

Figure 3.3 Different amounts of input from logistics managers

make sure these can be achieved. At the other end of the spectrum are organisations whose logistics really dictate the higher strategies. The Channel Tunnel, for example, offers a unique logistics service, and all its higher strategies are based on its logistics operations.

Focus of the logistics strategy

Organisations can only survive by supplying products that customers view as somehow better than those from competitors. Logistics affects the lead time, availability, cost, customer support, damage, and so on – and hence the customers' view of a product. In this sense, logistics actually contributes to the design, quality, perceived value and success of a product. But which factors are most important for this contribution and should be emphasised in a logistics strategy? We can start to answer this by taking a traditional view from marketing which says that organisations compete by concentrating on the 'four Ps' – product, place, promotion and price. Here logistics has a role in the 'product' (through its contribution to the overall product package), 'place' (through its delivery of materials) and 'price' (through its effect on operating costs). A logistics strategy could usefully emphasise these features.

A broader view says that customers are concerned with cost, quality, service level, reliability, availability, flexibility, delivery speed, location, sourcing, supplier relations, environmental impact, recycling, and a whole range of other things. These all depend on different aspects of logistics. In different circumstances, therefore, almost any facet of logistics can be important for customer satisfaction, and could be emphasised by the logistics strategy. In practice, a logistics strategy is most likely to emphasise the following:

⬤ *Cost:* Most organisations want low costs, but some adopt a positive strategy of minimising their logistics costs. This leads to higher profits for the organisation and lower prices for customers.

⬤ *Customer service:* Logistics controls stock levels, delivery times, speed of response, and other measures of customer service. By concentrating the logistics strategy on customer service, organisations can get a long-term competitive advantage.

⬤ *Timing:* Customers generally want products as soon as possible, so a common logistics strategy guarantees fast deliveries. Timing can also mean rapid supply of new products, or delivering at the time specified by a customer.

⬤ *Quality:* Customers demand higher quality in all products. A common logistics strategy guarantees high quality service, even though it can be difficult to say exactly what we mean by 'high quality logistics' (we return to this question in Chapter 12).

⬤ *Product flexibility:* This is the ability of an organisation to customise products to individual specifications. One logistics strategy is based on a specialised or customised service, such as Pickfords' removals.

⬤ *Volume flexibility:* Changing levels of business can cause severe problems for logistics, as you can see during the morning rush hour in any major city. Volume flexibility allows an organisation to respond quickly to changing levels of demand.

⬤ *Technology:* Logistics uses a wide range of technologies for communications, tracking loads, sorting parcels, identifying products, recording stock movements, and so on. Some organisations have a strategy of developing and using the latest technologies.

● *Location:* Customers generally want products to be delivered as close to them as possible. This might mean that a book club delivers directly to your door, a shop has a convenient location in a town centre, or a wholesaler has a regional logistics centre near to major cities. One logistics strategy is to provide a service in the best possible location, such as bus stations in town centres.

In principle, organisations should do everything well, giving low cost, good customer service, fast delivery, flexibility, using high technology, and so on. In practice, this is unrealistic. Organisations have to compromise, perhaps balancing the level of service with the cost of providing it. Effectively they choose a specific **focus** for their logistics strategy, showing which factor they consider to be most important. Some organisations, such as Ryanair, focus on cost, giving a cheap service; others, such as FedEx, focus on delivery speed; others focus on reliability; or a customised service, and so on. One of the key decisions for logistics managers is choosing the strategic focus.

LOGISTICS IN PRACTICE

The Schenker Group

The Schenker Group was founded in Germany more than 125 years ago, and has been working internationally ever since. They employ 28,000 people, serving customers in 1000 locations. Schenker now provide a range of logistics services, including international air and ocean freight, logistics management and land transport. They provide seamless movement of customer products and information across global supply chains, using the latest technology and developing sophisticated systems for e-commerce. However, their strategic focus is on customer service.

Schenker opened in the USA in 1947 and now have 46 offices in major cities. All of these are ISO 9002 certified, which is in line with their strategy of complete customer satisfaction. This strategy is clear from their statement that, 'Our customers are our future. Without them – there is no future.' To support this view, the company gives a number of guarantees, starting with:

Our customers will always be the centre of our complete attention.

We will earn our customers' trust everyday, and we will never take their business for granted.

Our customers are our partners in business. Their needs will be our needs.

Schenker also describe the ways that they will achieve customer satisfaction, such as:

We will service our customers in an innovative, pro-active manner. We will always be aware of how our service impacts their business.

This overriding strategy of customer satisfaction sets the scene for all other logistics activities. When they work with Copeland Corporation in Alabama, their primary goal remains customer satisfaction, but to achieve this they have to attain the secondary goals of shorter stock cycles, faster delivery, lower stocks and lower costs.

Source: promotional material and websites at www.schenker.com and www.schenkerusa.com

STRATEGY OPTIONS

Each organisation designs its own logistics strategy, but they often move along similar lines. The logistics strategies of Ford and Volkswagen, for example, are broadly similar, as are the strategies of Lufthansa and Air France. This allows us to describe a few generic strategies. Michael Porter[6] suggested that there are two basic strategies:

- *cost leadership*, makes the same, or comparable, products more cheaply;
- *product differentiation*, makes products that customers cannot get from other suppliers.

Lyons Bakeries compete by cost leadership, selling standard cakes at low prices; La Patisserie Française competes by product differentiation, selling cakes that are not available anywhere else. Similarly, easyJet compete by cost leadership, offering the cheapest fares; Execujet compete by offering a uniquely luxurious service.

In logistics, these two approaches are usually phrased in terms of **lean** and **agile** strategies. As we saw in Chapter 2, organisations with a focus on lean logistics are aiming at low costs; those with a focus on agile logistics are aiming at high customer satisfaction.

Lean strategies

No organisation can completely avoid the cost of logistics, so the next best option is to make it as cheap as possible. Then a reasonable objective is to minimise the total cost of logistics, while ensuring acceptable levels of customer service. This approach is generalised into **lean logistics**.

The aims of a **LEAN STRATEGY** are to do every operation using less of each resource – people, space, stock, equipment, time, and so on. It organises the efficient flow of materials to eliminate waste, give the shortest lead time, minimum stocks and minimum total cost.

Early work on lean operations was done in the motor industry, led by Toyota.[7,8] This work concentrated on 'lean production' but the methods got such good results that they spread into other areas, eventually developing a 'lean enterprise'. The approach is summarised in five main principles:[9]

- *value* – designing a product that has value from a customer's perspective
- *value stream* – designing the best process to make the product
- *value flow* – managing the flow of materials through the supply chain
- *pull* – only making products when there is customer demand
- *aim of perfection* – looking for continuous improvements to get closer to the aim of perfect operations.

The first of these principles, 'value', sets the target for the organisation, seeing how to add value for the final customer of the product. The second principle, 'value stream', designs a means of making this product, and effectively sets the requirements of the supply chain. The last three principles refer directly to the supply chain. The third, 'value flow', gets an efficient flow of materials, eliminating waste, interruptions, waiting and detours. The fourth principle, 'pull', shows how to control the flow of materials by pulling them through (we return to this theme in Chapter 7). The fifth principle, 'aim of perfection', describes a continuing search for improvement. This is a common theme for management initiatives which often say that areas of waste should be continually identified and eliminated.

Robert Townsend says that, 'All organisations are at least 50% waste – waste people, waste effort, waste space and waste time'.[10] During their development work, Toyota identified the following areas of the supply chain where this waste is most likely to occur:[11]

- *Quality* – that is too poor to satisfy customers (either external or internal).
- *Wrong production level or capacity* – making products, or having capacity, that is not currently needed.
- *Poor process* – having unnecessary, too complicated or time-consuming operations.
- *Waiting* – for operations to start or finish, for materials to arrive, for equipment to be repaired, and so on.
- *Movement* – with products making unnecessary, long, or inconvenient movements during operations.
- *Stock* – holding too much stock, increasing complexity and raising costs.

A lean strategy looks for ways of eliminating this waste. The typical approach does a detailed analysis of current operations, and then removes operations that add no value, eliminates delays, simplifies movements, reduces complexity, uses higher technology to increase efficiency, looks for economies of scale, locates near to customers to save travel, and removes unnecessary links from the supply chain.

One warning is that low costs do not automatically mean lean operations. Lean operations maintain customer service while using fewer resources – they do not just minimise costs. A greengrocer could minimise its inventory costs by having no stock, but it would not generate much customer satisfaction. Some people also suggest that lean operations might work in the mass production car industry, but lessons do not necessarily transfer to other supply chains. In particular, lean operations might not work when there are variable and uncertain conditions. An alternative is a more flexible strategy based on **agility**.

Agile strategy

An agile strategy concentrates on the other side of the 'efficient versus responsive' – or lean versus agile – debate. Its supporters say that lean operations put too much emphasis on costs, and cannot deal with changing conditions, increasing competition, or more sophisticated and demanding customers. If demand for a product is steady at 100 units a week, lean logistics will remove all the waste and have enough capacity to deliver these 100 units. Unfortunately, if demand suddenly rises to 110 units, lean operations cannot cope. As markets are demanding more variety and customisation, logistics should be more flexible.

> The aim of an **AGILE STRATEGY** is to give a high customer service by responding quickly to different or changing circumstances.

There are two aspects of agility. First, there is the speed of reaction; agile organisations keep a close check on customer demands and react quickly to changes. Second, is the ability to tailor logistics to demands from individual customers. These are, of course, different aspects of customer service, and the implication is that end-customer satisfaction is a prime concern, even if this comes at somewhat higher price.

Organisations that put a lot of emphasis on customer satisfaction are said to have a **customer focus**. The justification for this strategy comes from the obvious importance of customers. Without customers an organisation has no sales, no income, no profit, no business – and soon no organisation. As Michael Perry of Unilever says,[12] 'To sustain competitive advantage requires a total commitment to your customer'. Organisations with a customer focus will typically:

● aim for complete customer satisfaction
● allow customers easy access to the organisation
● find exactly what they want
● design logistics to meet, or exceed, these demands
● be flexible and respond quickly to changing customer demands
● get a reputation for outstanding quality and value
● do after-sales checks to make sure the customers remain satisfied
● look outwards so that they are always in touch with customers, potential customers, competitors, and so on.

Organisations with satisfied customers have the obvious benefit of bringing them back with repeat business – remembering the rule of thumb that it costs five times as much to attract a new customer as it does to retain an existing one. Satisfied customers also attract new business, as they recommend a good service to four or five other people – compared with dissatisfied customers who warn a dozen potential customers about a bad experience.

Lean versus agile

At first sight the aims of lean and agile operations seem contradictory. One looks to minimise costs, and sees customer service as a constraint; the other looks to maximise customer service, and sees costs as a constraint. This seems to lead to important differences.

Factor	Lean logistics	Agile logistics
Objective	Efficient operations	Flexibility to meet demands
Method	Remove all waste	Customer satisfaction
Constraint	Customer service	Cost
Rate of change	Long-term stability	Fast reaction to changing circumstances
Measures of performance	Productivity, utilisation	Lead time, service level
Work	Uniform, standardised	Variable, more local control
Control	Formal planning cycles	Less structured by empowered staff

In practice, of course, there is not such a clear divide between the two strategies. If a supplier improves EDI links with its customers, it can both reduce costs and increase customer service – becoming both leaner and more agile. Similarly, a manufacturer selling materials through a website and a wholesaler introducing cross-docking become both leaner and more agile. Both strategies accept that customer satisfaction and low costs are dominant themes, but they use different descriptions of the process to achieve them. Organisations need not choose one strategy at the expense of the other. Evans and Powell[13] discuss the use of both strategies and conclude that 'lean and agile are not mutually exclusive, they both have their merits, but also limitations, especially if an individual aspect is taken, in isolation, to the extreme'.

Strategic alliances

A third strategy develops the ideas of integration that we discussed in Chapter 2. An organisation can put so much emphasis on close co-operation with other parts of the supply chain that it has a strategy of forming alliances with suppliers and customers. The purpose of this strategy is to get efficient supply chains, with all members working together and sharing the benefits of long-term co-operation.

Usual reasons for a strategy of forming partnerships include better customer service, increased flexibility, reduced costs, avoidance of investment in facilities, and lack of expertise within the organisation. In Europe over a quarter of all logistics expenditure uses specialised contract suppliers, usually in some form of long-term partnership. The most common area for partnerships is transport, where around three quarters of companies use contract providers. Other areas for collaboration include warehousing, import/export services, materials storage and information processing.

LOGISTICS IN PRACTICE

Ellis and Everard

Ellis and Everard is a major distributor of chemicals. It has a turnover of £600 million working from 70 locations in the USA and Europe, and employing 2000 people.

The company has been developing long-term partnerships for many years, and is considered a leader in the field. It has partnerships forward with customers (such as Merck, 3M and Sterling organics) and backward with suppliers (such as ICI, Solvay Interox and Junbunzlauer). Around 95% of its supplies, and 6% of customer demand are met through partnerships. Chris Whincup, Director of Sales, says that, 'Partnerships make our lives simpler, and as such more productive and effective'.

Among the benefits Ellis and Everard get from partnerships are:

- faster decision making
- higher sales and easier introduction of new products
- stability, making long-term planning easier and more reliable
- removal of unproductive administration
- on-time payments from customers
- easier introduction of new initiatives, such as EDI for stock levels and automatic delivery scheduling.

Sources: company annual reports, Partnership Sourcing Limited's websites at www.pslcbi.com

Other strategies

We have described three general strategies based on leanness, agility and alliances. There are several other general strategies, where organisations emphasise other aspects of performance. Here we will mention a few of the more common.

● *Time-based strategies*

In the simplest view, time-based strategies aim for a guaranteed faster delivery of products. Benefits from these strategies include lower costs (by having less stock in the supply chain, less expediting, and so on), improved cash flow (by not having to wait so long for payment), less risk (by reducing changes to orders, obsolete stock, and so on) and simpler operations (by eliminating delays and unnecessary stores). The main assumption, though, is that faster delivery gives better customer service. This is not necessarily true, and you can find many examples of faster logistics reducing the quality. A delivery company might speed-up order processing, but increase the number of mistakes; an airline might rush passengers and make them feel uncomfortable; a shipping line might reduce delays by stopping in fewer ports.

One important strategy based on time is **time compression**. This is similar to the lean strategy, but concentrates on wasted time in the supply chain. Its aim is to eliminate all the non-value-adding time. Beesley[14,15] says that 'In typical UK manufacturing supply chains at least 95% of the process time is accounted as non-value adding'.

There is clearly scope for reducing the time materials spend in the supply chain and getting the associated benefits. Carter et al.[16] discuss seven ways of doing this:

1. *simplification* – making operations simpler
2. *integration* – improving information and material flows
3. *standardisation* – using standard procedures and materials
4. *concurrent operations* – moving away from serial operations and towards parallel working
5. *variance control* – ensuring high quality and avoiding waste
6. *automation* – to improve effectiveness and efficiency
7. *resource planning* – to remove bottlenecks and ensure a smooth flow of materials.

As you can see, most of these are general suggestions for improvement rather than specific features of time compression. You would, of course, expect this. A strategy that focuses on one aspect of performance cannot ignore all the others; it still has to achieve performance that is acceptable when judged by a range of different criteria.

● *Environmental protection strategies*

A small, but increasing, number of organisations are developing strategies based around environmental protection. The Body Shop, for example, designs products with natural ingredients and based on sustainable development. It uses the same principles in its logistics, with reusable containers and recycling of materials. There are good reasons for other organisations to adopt similar policies of environmental protection.

In 1993 a survey of UK companies suggested that most were aware of environmental pressures – mainly from EU and government regulations – but they only changed their practices when there were significant cost benefits.[17] The major environmental concerns were waste and packaging disposal (25% of respondents), noise and emission (23%), public perception of HGVs (15%), fuel use (12%) and road congestion (11%). Only 19% of companies reported a logistics environmental policy. Despite huge amounts of discussion in the area, there have been relatively few changes since this survey.

Most organisations assume that 'going green' raises costs. There may be some benefits from customer approval, but in a competitive environment it is difficult to justify the higher overheads. The reality, though, is that many programmes for environmental protection actually reduce costs. Better insulation of warehouses, for example, gives lower heating bills. In the same way, regular maintenance of road vehicles reduces both fuel consumption and emissions, as does minimising the distance travelled, avoiding congestion, travelling outside peak hours and avoiding built-up areas. Packaging is another area with large potential savings. You may be surprised when a pack of chocolate biscuits has three layers of wrapping – but this is only the consumer wrapping, and you do not see the three layers of industrial packaging that protects goods during transport. Careful design and reusable containers can save much of this packaging and considerably reduce costs.

⬤ *Increased productivity strategies*

These strategies use available resources as fully as possible. Facilities, such as warehouses, have high fixed costs and using them at full capacity spreads these costs over more units. It follows that increasing the utilisation of resources reduces the delivered cost of products.

This is really a variation of a lean strategy, but there are important differences. Imagine a facility that is working at 60% of capacity. Obviously, there is spare capacity that is raising unit costs. The lean approach would look for ways of removing the 40% spare capacity – and then continue looking for further reductions over time. A high productivity strategy is more likely to accept the present capacity, and start looking for alternative uses for the excess. An office or warehouse might rent out space, while a vehicle fleet might carry materials for other organisations.

⬤ *Value-added strategies*

The supply chain consists of a series of activities, each of which adds value to the final product. Then a reasonable strategy has an organisation adding as much value as possible. This value is, of course, taken from the customer's perspective. Organisations can also add value by adding time and place utility, or doing more work on the product. Imagine a company that delivers washing machines to customers' houses. It adds value by delivering to the place and and at the time preferred by customers, or by doing more work such as installing the machines, testing them, giving instructions on their use, removing old machines, offering service contracts, and so on.

⬤ *Diversification or specialisation strategies*

These strategies look at the range of services offered by logistics. Some organisations have strategies of diversification, offering the widest range of services and satisfying as many customers as possible. This is the approach of a department store which sells every product you can imagine. Other organisations have a strategy of specialising in a very narrow range of services, but being the best provider in their chosen area. They target a few customers and provide a service that cannot be found anywhere else – like a bespoke tailor. Some transport companies, for example, have a strategy of diversification and move every kind of load from letters through to oversize loads. Others have a strategy of specialisation in, say, small packages, high security or tanker deliveries.

● *Growth strategies*

Many aspects of logistics get economies of scale, and larger operations can give both lower costs and better service. One common strategy, then, is based on growth. There are several ways of achieving growth, perhaps taking over competitors, expanding the geographical area covered, diversifying into more logistics activities, moving different types of materials, or simply increasing market share.

LOGISTICS IN PRACTICE

Tesco plc

Tesco is the largest supermarket chain in the UK, with 700 stores taking 16% of the food retail market. It also has stores in Asia and central Europe, giving total sales of £25 billion a year in 1000 stores, with 250,000 employees. Their strategy is based on low cost, but also includes growth, high customer service and increasing product range.

The core purpose of Tesco is, 'Creating value for customers, to earn their lifetime loyalty'. This leads to a business strategy based around four elements – strong UK core business of food retailing, non-food sales, retail services such as personal finance and international operations. The logistics strategy supports this business strategy, with a huge logistics network. This has evolved over time to meet changing customer demands, 'Following the customer – as customers' shopping habits change, we change and respond by providing new products and services'.

You can see this effect in their stores. In the 1970s most of Tesco's sales were in fairly small supermarkets in town centres. Over the next 20 years it closed many of these smaller stores and focused on larger ones – up to 100,000 square feet – in out-of-town developments. More recently, Tesco has adopted a flexible approach, building a range of shops to suit various needs. In 2001 it had 18 million square feet of sales area in:

■ 23 Extras at around 100,000 square feet
■ 274 Superstores at around 40,000 square feet
■ 96 Compact superstores at around 20,000 square feet
■ 38 Metro stores at around 2000 square feet
■ 45 Express stores at around 2000 square feet
■ 216 other stores.

The range of products offered by these stores has also changed, with the Extras and larger superstores offering a full range of non-food products, and growing sales of services from personal financial service to pharmacies. There are plans to open 100 more Express stores on Esso petrol station forecourts, and extending opening hours so that 300 stores are open 24 hours a day.

For the longer term, a significant change for Tesco's logistics is the growth of e-commerce. This business grew from 13,500 customers in 1999, to 370,000 in 2000, and a million in 2001. With £300 million of annual sales and 70,000 deliveries a week, Tesco has become the largest on-line grocer in the world.

Sources: company annual reports and website www.tesco.co.uk

DESIGNING A LOGISTICS STRATEGY

Setting the scene

The important point about a logistics strategy is that it does not happen by chance, but needs careful decisions. So we can ask, 'How do organisations make these decisions?' Why should a company base its logistics strategy on flexibility rather than cost? Why does one company choose to specialise, while a similar one chooses to diversify?

The starting point for designing a logistics strategy examines the higher strategies and sees how logistics can contribute to these. Then we can summarise the results in a **logistics mission**. This gives a simple statement of the aims for supply chain management, like the following example.

> Our mission in logistics is to contribute to corporate aims by moving the materials needed by production into the company, moving work in progress through the company, and moving finished products out to customers. We aim to give a flexible, reliable and cost effective service that completely satisfies our customers, both internal and external.[18]

Logistics missions are useful for setting the scene, and showing the overall direction and priorities. They are much less common than mission statements for the whole organisation, but they can suffer from the same weaknesses. Organisations tend to be ambitious and include aims of being 'acknowledged leaders', 'the best', 'world class', and so on. Smith[19] says that such flowery statements fail in three ways. First, they are over-ambitious, setting targets that the organisations cannot realistically achieve. Second, they are so vague that no one can tell whether the mission is actually being achieved or not. Third, they miss the opportunity of using a powerful tool that can really help manage the logistics.

It is useful to start designing a strategy with a logistics mission, but the next steps are less clear. There is certainly no single best strategy for any particular circumstance, and there is no standard procedure for designing a good strategy. Gooderham[20] says:

> No one 'right' way to develop and implement strategy exists. The key to successful planning is to get the best fit between the chosen tools and techniques, the organisation's current culture capabilities and business environment and the desired outcome.

This leads to the usual advice of finding the best balance between the organisation's internal strengths and the external constraints – matching what the organisation is good at to what customers want. So now we have three factors that managers must consider when designing a logistics strategy – the higher strategies, the business environment and the organisation's distinctive competence (shown in Figure 3.4).

1. *Higher strategies* set the organisation's goals and the context for all logistics decisions. The mission sets the overall aims, and the corporate and business strategies show how these aims will be achieved. The logistics strategy must support these higher strategies. If, for example, the business strategy calls for high customer service, the logistics strategy must show how logistics will achieve this.

2. The *business environment* consists of the factors that affect logistics, but over which it has no control. These include:

   ⬤ *customers* – their expectations, attitudes, demographics

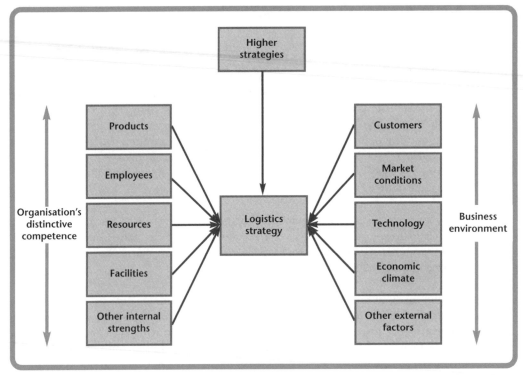

Figure 3.4 Factors in the design of a logistics strategy

- *market conditions* – size, location, stability
- *technology* – current availability, likely developments, rate of innovation
- *economic climate* – gross domestic product, rate of growth, inflation
- *legal restraints* – trade restrictions, liability and employment laws
- *competitors* – number, ease of entry to the market, strengths
- *shareholders* – their target return on investments, objectives, profit needed
- *interest groups* – their objectives, strengths, amount of support
- *social conditions* – customers' lifestyles, changing demands, significant trends
- *political conditions* – stability, amount of governmental control, external relations.

3. All competing organisations work in a similar business environment. Each can only succeed if it has a *distinctive competence* that sets it apart from competitors. This is defined by the factors that are under the organisation's control, and which it uses to distinguish itself. A distinctive competence stems from an organisation's assets, which include:

- *customers* – their demands, loyalty, relationships
- *employees* – skills, expertise, loyalty
- *finances* – capital, debt, cash flow
- *organisation* – structure, relationships, flexibility
- *products* – quality, reputation, innovations
- *facilities* – capacity, age, reliability
- *technology* – currently used, plans, special types
- *processes* – structures, technology used, flexibility

● *marketing* – experience, reputation
● *suppliers* – service, flexibility, partnerships
● *other assets* – knowledge, innovation, patents.

In essence, the business environment and distinctive competence show where an organisation is now, and the higher strategies show where it wants to be in the future. The logistics strategy shows how to move from one to the other.

Logistics audit

We can get a clear idea of current operations by doing a **logistics audit**. This describes the details of all current logistics activities.

> The purpose of a **LOGISTICS AUDIT** is to collect relevant information about existing practices and performance of logistics. It gives a systematic review of current operations, describing the procedures, costs, resources, utilisation, performance, products, and all other relevant details.

There are two main parts to a logistics audit, essentially getting information about the business environment and distinctive competence. First, an external audit looks at the environment in which logistics work. This reviews the nature of customers, types of demand, accepted service levels, locations, competitors and their operations, benchmarks and comparisons, services available, trends in the industry, economic conditions, geographical and political constraints, and any other relevant external information. Second, an internal audit looks at the way things are done within the organisation and identifies areas for improvement. It reviews the structure of the supply chain, warehouse locations and size, stock holdings, methods of materials handling, achieved service levels, lead times, transport arrangements, order processing, damage, productivity, and any other relevant internal information.

You can see that this approach is similar in principle to a **SWOT analysis**, which lists an organisation's:

● *Strengths* – what the organisation does well, features it should build on
● *Weaknesses* – problems the organisation has, areas it should improve
● *Opportunities* – openings that can help the organisation
● *Threats* – hazards that can damage it.

Strengths and weaknesses concern the organisation's internal operations and show its distinctive competence. Opportunities and threats relate to external features, concentrating on the business environment. A SWOT analysis by Synergistic Logistical Services listed their strengths as expertise, innovation and local contacts; weaknesses as small size, local operations and gaps in experience; opportunities from the increasing use of information technology, growing interest in logistics, and service-based local economy; threats from larger competitors, high overheads and a possible take-over.

By this stage we have the aims of logistics set out in a logistics mission. We also have details of current performance from the audit. We know where we want to go, and where we are at the moment. The next stage is to identify gaps between these two and show how to bridge the gaps.

Developing the strategy

Usually, the single most important factor for a logistics strategy is the type of demand. A lean strategy, for example, works best when demand is stable – or at least predictable. It is most successful when there are few changes to customers, products, or logistics, and when price is an important factor for competition. This is typical of commodities or staple food items, where the lowest cost is the main determinant of success. On the other hand, an agile strategy works best for organisations offering a wider range of products, where demand varies and is less predictable. It is most successful for organisations that do not really know demand until customers place orders, with make-to-order operations or mass-customisation, such as the fashion industry.

It would be useful to have some formal procedure that considers factors such as the type of demand, and then suggests the best logistics strategy. Unfortunately, we have already said that there is no single 'best' strategy, and no method that always gives a good solution. The best that we can do is use some guidelines. Novich,[21] for example, recommends four steps for designing a strategy – understand and measure customer needs, find the weaknesses of current logistics, benchmark, and simplify the whole logistic system. A more systematic approach builds on the analyses we have already mentioned, and has the following eight steps:

1. Do a logistics audit. The external audit gives an analysis of the business environment in which logistics work. It shows the factors that lead to success in this environment, and the importance of each one.

2. The internal audit analyses higher strategies from a logistics viewpoint, giving the context and overall aims for logistics, its strategic focus and perhaps includes a logistics mission.

3. Design the general features of supply chains that can best deliver the desired services. This includes the design of the network, location of facilities, capacity, technology used, and so on.

4. Set specific goals to show what each logistics activity must achieve. The internal audit shows how well the current logistics achieve these goals, and identifies areas that need improving.

5. Design the best organisational structure, controls and systems to support the logistics network.

6. Benchmark logistics, looking at the performance of leading organisations, defining measures to compare actual performance with planned, optimal and competitors' performances.

7. Implement the strategy, setting the conditions for lower levels of logistics decisions.

8. Monitor actual performance, continually look for improvements, keep the strategies up to date, and give feedback.

These steps give a guideline for designing and implementing a logistics strategy. The first two points focus on current circumstances, and are based on a logistics audit. Steps 3 to 5 design the logistics strategy, describing the general features of the supply chain, goals and supporting structures. Remember that the strategy only deals with broad principles over the long term, and does not get involved with the tactical and operational detail. Step 6 looks at operations in the best competitors and sees if there are any lessons to learn. The last two steps are concerned with implementation, and adjustments to keep the strategy up to date.

We discuss some issues of implementation in the next chapter. Before we go there, however, we should mention the presentation of the logistics strategy. This might seem a minor concern, but the way the strategy is presented can be an important factor in its ultimate success.

A logistics strategy consists of a set of aims, procedures, structures, facilities, beliefs, systems, and so on. These are typically presented in a **logistics plan**. This plan might contain many parts,[22] with the following list including the most common.

⬤ a broad summary, giving an overview of the logistics strategy and how this relates to other parts of the organisation

⬤ the aims of logistics within the organisation, what performance levels are needed and how these can be measured

⬤ a description of the way that logistics as a whole will achieve these aims, what changes are involved and how these will be managed

⬤ a description of how the separate functions of logistics (procurement, transport, inventory control, materials handling, and so on) will contribute to the plan, the changes involved and how operations can be integrated

⬤ projections to show the resources needed by the strategy

⬤ projections of the costs and financial performance

⬤ a description of the way that this strategy affects the rest of the business, particularly in terms of performance achieved and contribution to customer value and satisfaction.

LOGISTICS IN PRACTICE

Bjorg's Pharmaceuticals

Bjorg's Pharmaceutical (BP) is a biotechnology company that develops and markets specialised drugs for Alzheimer's disease. It is one of the smaller companies competing against giant internationals, and its success comes from concentrating on a niche market.

Last year, BP was concerned that a major competitor was introducing a treatment that was similar to one of its own best-selling products. BP felt that the best way to compete was to improve its customer service by opening regional warehouses in its major markets of Northern Europe. These warehouses would guarantee same day delivery. To make sure that this was a sensible move, the company did a survey of 60 major customers. This survey confirmed that delivery time was by far the most important factor to them. The following table summarises the results when customers were asked to rate the importance of factors on a scale of 1 (not important) to 5 (very important).

Factor	Average response
Same day delivery	3.1
Next day delivery	4.9
Delivered when promised	2.7
Products delivered from stock	3.4
Cost of products	1.3
No errors in delivered products	2.8
No errors in paperwork	1.5
Ease of order entry	1.7
Ease of payment	1.4
Ease of access to customer relations	2.1
Knowledge of customer relations	2.5

LOGISTICS
IN PRACTICE
continued

Although same day delivery was fairly important, it seemed that most customers would be happy with next day delivery. From the survey, BP also found that its competitors only guaranteed next day delivery for 60% of orders. Another interesting finding, was the perception that BP did not share information with customers, and did not publish details of product lead times, products that might have shortages, likely delays, and so on.

Based on this information, BP adopted new policies to meet the competition. First, it cancelled the planned regional warehouses, saving over a million dollars a year. Second, it adopted a policy of next day delivery for 95% of orders, giving it the best logistics performance in the industry. Third, it improved its communications, publishing more material on its websites and encouraging customers to contact them.

Source: internal company reports

CHAPTER REVIEW

❑ Strategic decisions affect an organisation over the long term. There are several types of strategic decision. Higher strategies set the general goals and direction for the organisation, while functional strategies show how these will be achieved.

❑ The strategic importance of logistics is clear from its role as an essential function, its inclusion in mission statements, its involvement in important decisions, its effect on long-term performance, and so on.

❑ A logistics strategy describes the long-term decisions, plans, policies and culture for logistics. It is a functional strategy that shows how logistics will contribute to an organisation's success.

❑ Many aspects of logistics can have a strategic importance; the focus of the strategy shows which is considered most important. We can use the focus to describe some generic logistics strategies. Common ones focus on lean or agile logistics, developing partnerships, time based strategies, and so on.

❑ A logistics strategy has to be designed, bearing in mind the aims described in higher strategies, strengths of the organisation and the business environment. There is no 'best' strategy for any particular circumstance.

❑ Although we can give guidelines, there is no standard method of designing a logistics strategy. Managers have to do appropriate analyses and balance a number of factors before making their decisions.

CASE STUDY — Hessingen Herb Farm

Conrad and Elizabeth Kole moved into Hessingen Farm in 1983. Over the past few years their income from milk and traditional crops has dropped because of lower market prices. They have supplemented this income from other sources, including the conversion of old barns into holiday homes.

Eight years ago Elizabeth took over a small field and started growing herbs. She sold a small range of herbs to local people who wanted fresh, organic produce for cooking. Passing tourists would also buy an unusual souvenir, and the herb business began to grow. Five years ago Elizabeth started growing more unusual herbs, expanded her growing area into a second field and opened a visitors' centre. People now came to look at the growing and preparation of herbs, and taste samples in various foods. Three years ago Elizabeth introduced a new range of herb products. This was a major expansion, converting some of the farm buildings into a 'herb kitchen' and making products for cooking (sauces, dressings and marinades), perfumes (posies, pot-pourri and sachets of dried herbs) and what she called 'healthy stuff' (herb mixtures traditionally said to have beneficial effects). The farm is now widely advertised as a tourist attraction. The website is particularly useful, as Elizabeth uses it to collect orders. She currently delivers 100 parcels a week to regular locals (up to about 50 km away) and posts 200 parcels to more distant customers.

Herbs started as a small business to generate additional income for the farm, but have now become its main activity. Elizabeth is considering another expansion. She could expand the product range even further and move all the processing to an industrial estate 15 km away. Supporting this would need sales around ten times the current postal sales. Elizabeth plans to generate these by introducing a mail-order catalogue and increasing use of the website.

CASE STUDY
Questions

- How does Elizabeth currently organise her logistics? What do you think are her aims and priorities?
- What would be the effect of the expansion on logistics? What problems would Elizabeth face, and what options does she have to overcome them?

P R O J E C T

Mission and Strategy

Many organisations refer, either explicitly or implicitly, to logistics in their mission. Sometimes you can find statements about the role of logistics in corporate strategies, objectives, aims, publicity and related documents. Search through the documents published by different types of organisation, and see how they mention the strategic role of logistics. You might, for example, look for references made by certain types of manufacturer, airlines or banks. What differences are there between different industries, and companies in the same industry?

DISCUSSION QUESTIONS

1. To what extent is logistics a strategic function? Does it really have a long-term effect on an organisation? Is it possible to be 'essential' but not 'strategic'?
2. When customers judge products, they include factors like availability, lead time and after-sales service – and these are part of logistics. Is it reasonable to say, therefore, that logistics plays a role in the design of a product?
3. What are the main options for a logistics strategy?
4. What factors affect the choice of logistics strategy? Take an organisation that you are familiar with, and say exactly how you would set about designing a logistics strategy.
5. There is only one 'best' logistics strategy in any circumstances, and managers should look for this. Do you think this is true?
6. In 1996 a survey of Canadian logistics companies[23,24] listed the main benefits expected from outsourcing logistics as follows.

Factor	% of companies
Reduce total cost	79
Focus on core competency	67
Improve financial performance	66
Improve customer service	53
Improve flexibility	53
Access to new technology or systems	41
Enhance competitiveness	41
Increase capacity	37
Provide alternative logistics channels	29
Increase market share	21
Broader market coverage	20

Are these benefits likely to be different in other countries, or to have changed over the past few years?

REFERENCES

1. Roadway Express Company Annual Reports and website at www.roadway.com.
2. Mercia promotional material and website at www.mercia.com.

3. Boots Company Annual Reports and website at www.boots-plc.com.
4. J. Sainsbury Company Annual Reports and website at www.j-sainsbury.co.uk.
5. GKN Company Annual Reports and website at www.gknplc.com.
6. Porter M.E. (1985) *Competitive Advantage*, Free Press, New York.
7. Ohno T. (1988) *Toyota Production System*, Productivity Press, New York.
8. Womack J., Jones D. and Roos D. (1990) *The Machine that Changed the World*, Rawson, New York.
9. Womack J. and Jones D. (1996) *Lean Thinking*, Simon & Schuster, New York.
10. Townsend R. (1970) *Up the Organisation*, Coronet Books, London.
11. Monden Y. (1983) *Toyota Production System*, Industrial Engineering and Management Press, Atlanta, GA.
12. Perry M. (1996) Talk at the Marketing Council, London.
13. Evans B. and Powell M. (2000) Synergistic thinking: a pragmatic view of 'lean' and 'agile', *Logistics and Transport Focus*, **2**(10), 26–32.
14. Beesley A. (1995) Time compression – new source of competitiveness in the supply chain, *Logistics Focus*, **3**(5), 24–5.
15. Beesley A. (1999) Time compression in the supply chain, Ch. 11 in Waters D. (ed.) *Global Logistics and Distribution Planning*, Kogan Page, London.
16. Carter R., Melnyk P.L. and Handfield S.A. (1994) *Identifying Sources of Cycle Time Reduction*, Quorum Books, Texas.
17. Szymankiewicz J. (1993) Going green – the logistics dilemma, *Focus on Logistics and Distribution Management*, **12**(5), 36–41.
18. Waters D. (2001) Strategic Logistics, Eastern Logistics Forum, New York.
19. Smith R.J. (2000) The logistics mission, *Members' Directory*, pp. 22–7, The Institute for Logistics and Transport, Corby.
20. Gooderham G. (1998) Debunking the myths of strategic planning, CMA magazine, May.
21. Novich N.S. (1990) Leading-edge distribution strategies, *The Journal of Business Strategy*, November/December, 48–53.
22. Murray R.E. (1980) Strategic distribution planning, Proceedings of the Eighteenth Annual Conference of the National Council of Physical Distribution Management.
23. Deloitte & Touche Consulting Group (1996) *Canadian Trends in Supply Chain Management and Logistics Service Outsourcing*, Deloitte & Touche, Toronto.
24. Factor R. (1996) Logistics trends, *Material Management and Distribution*, June, 17–21.

CHAPTER 4

Implementing the Strategy

AIMS OF THE CHAPTER

After reading this chapter you should be able to:

- DESCRIBE the steps involved in implementing a logistics strategy

- APPRECIATE the problems of implementation

- CONSIDER the decisions needed for implementing the logistics strategy

- RECOGNISE the importance of continual change in the supply chain

- DISCUSS the management of change, particularly the rate of change

RELATING STRATEGY TO LOWER DECISIONS

Links with lower decisions

In the last chapter we looked at the design of a logistics strategy. This contains all an organisation's long-term decisions, policies, plans and culture relating to logistics. Senior managers design the logistics strategy, and then the remaining managers have to see how the strategy affects their work. They have to answer questions such as:

- How does the strategy affect the logistics network?
- Should we change our warehouse and transport operations?
- Will our approach to planning and scheduling change?
- Do we have, or can we get, the necessary resources?
- Do we have, or can we train, people with the necessary skills?
- How will the strategy affect present and potential customers?
- What are the impacts on staff, facilities, organisation, technology, and so on?

As you can see, these are not strategic questions, but they are concerned with more detailed tactical and operational decisions. So the logistics strategy leads to more detailed, lower level decisions. A strategic decision to sell products through a website leads to medium-term tactical decisions about warehousing, investment in stock, transport, materials handling, recruiting and training, customer service, and so on. These tactical decisions, in turn, lead to short-term operational decisions about resource scheduling, inventory control, expediting, vehicle routes, and so on.

The distinctions between strategic, tactical and operational decisions are not really this clear. Inventory, for example, is a strategic issue for decisions about building a warehouse for finished goods or shipping directly to customers, a tactical issue when deciding how much to invest in stock, and an operational issue when deciding how much to order this week. Customer service is a strategic issue when designing the supply chain, a tactical issue when organising transport for delivery, and an operational issue when scheduling the next delivery. The important point is to recognise that the strategy leads to a whole series of related decisions at different levels. What you call these levels and where you draw the boundaries is a matter of convenience.

When we talk about 'implementing a logistics strategy' we mean making the lower decisions, and translating the general aims of the strategy into positive actions. We actually **do** what is necessary to achieve the aims of the strategy. So implementation takes us from the fairly vague aspirations of the strategy to the nuts-and-bolts of how to move materials.

Strategies only become effective when they are **IMPLEMENTED**. This means that the long-term aims are translated into lower decisions, and the work is carried out to achieve them.

Tesco plc

In the last chapter we showed how the overriding strategy of Tesco is based on its core purpose of 'Creating value for customers, to earn their lifetime loyalty'. This leads to policies of low cost, growth, high customer service and increasing product range.

The logistics strategy supports these aims through the design and working of its supply network. Implementing the logistics strategy means translating the aims into positive actions. These include:

■ a concerted effort to give even better customer service

■ improving buying – with, for example, new non-food sourcing hubs in Hong Kong, India, Thailand and Central Europe that ensure competitive prices by buying products on a global scale

■ improving distribution – including a new state-of-the-art freezer centre in Daventry and a grocery centre in Thurrock

■ improving stock replenishment – moving from batch to continuous re-ordering with tills sending hourly reports of goods sold; this has increased availability by 1.5%, reduced stocks by 10% and significantly increased productivity

■ direct delivery of fast-moving items, such as carbonated drinks, in packs that go straight on display with no unpacking or shelf-filling

■ improving store design – giving stores that are easier for both staff and customers to use, and are cheaper to build

■ paperless communications giving faster and more reliable deliveries

■ a new knowledge-management system in all businesses around the world, making it easier to improve communications and share knowledge.

Sources: company annual reports and website www.tesco.co.uk

Difficulties with implementation

It can be difficult to translate a logistics strategy into lower decisions. This is obviously true when the strategy is poorly designed, and lower managers have to translate vague concepts like 'global leadership' into actual operations. It can also be true when there is a good strategy that has been properly designed. A strategy based on good customer service, for example, seems sensible and might be translated into a target of delivering all orders within two working days. Now managers have to design the detailed logistics procedures to achieve this, and this is where the difficulties appear. It might simply be impossible to achieve this target, or it might be achievable, but only at very high cost or with too much strain on the supply chain.

There are two options at this point. First, managers can say that the strategy has been carefully designed, and everyone must work harder or find new, innovative ways of achieving the targets. This might seem too rigid, but managers may believe that goals should be demanding enough to stretch the organisation. Second, managers can say that the practical difficulties are too great, and that there was a mistake in setting unrealistic targets. This is more worrying, as it means that the logistics strategy was badly designed and all the work has been wasted. It also suggests that the strategy designers do not have a clear enough view of operations.

An obvious point when designing a logistics strategy, is to make sure that it can be implemented, and that the long-term plans lead to realistic tactical and operational decisions. Ideally the strategy should set goals that are demanding (forcing the organisation to perform as well as it can) but achievable (so that it can actually be implemented). Unfortunately, there is a common problem here, especially with organisations that are rigid hierarchies. Then one group of senior managers designs the strategies, while a different group of more junior managers implements them. The two groups have different objectives, goals, information, experience and skills. Even with good communications, senior managers become remote from operations – they see the financial ratios, but have little idea how the logistics are really implemented. On the other hand, people working with the details of day-to-day operations, have little time for corporate ideals. Lofty aims such as 'being acknowledged leaders' have no relevance for someone who is rushing to make an overdue delivery.

The following list gives some common problems with implementing logistics strategies:

- people who design the strategies are not responsible for their implementation
- strategies are badly designed, perhaps with the wrong aims or focus
- it is impossible, or very difficult, to implement them properly
- they do not take enough account of actual operations, perhaps because there were not broad enough discussions
- they are over-ambitious, or somehow not realistic
- they ignore key factors, or emphasise the wrong features
- people only pay lip-service to supporting the strategies
- enthusiasm for the strategies declines over time.

One surprisingly common mistake is to design a logistics strategy and then think about implementing it. The obvious way to avoid this is to think about implementation all the way through the design, and always consider the practical effects of any policies. This needs widespread participation in the design process, particularly from those most closely involved with implementation. Some other factors that help devise a strategy that can be used are:

- an organisational structure that is flexible and allows innovation
- formal procedures for translating the strategy into reasonable decisions at lower levels
- effective systems to distribute information and support management decisions
- open communications which encourage the free exchange of ideas
- acceptance that strategies are not fixed, but continue to evolve over time
- control systems to monitor progress
- convincing everyone that the strategy is beneficial, so they conscientiously play their part in implementation
- developing an organisational culture that supports the strategy.

AREAS FOR DECISIONS IN IMPLEMENTATION

Types of decision

When looking at implementation, it is convenient to describe two types of strategic decision. The first type sets out the principles we work with, and the second type shows how the organisation will achieve these principles. So 'rapid delivery of customer orders' is a principle that

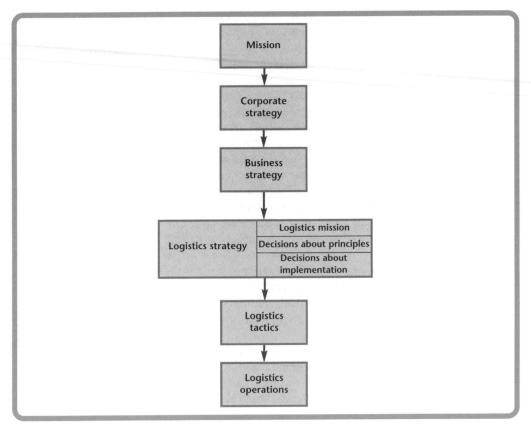

Figure 4.1 Levels of decision in logistics

the organisation is adopting, while 'building warehouses close to customers' is a practical way of achieving this: 'easy customer access' is a principle, while 'using websites to collect orders' is one means of doing this. All these decisions are strategic, as they clearly have long-term consequences. However, the first type is more concerned with aims and designs, and the second type is more concerned with practicalities and implementation. In the last chapter we looked more at the aims and designs; here we will look at the practicalities of implementing these (as illustrated in Figure 4.1).

A traditional view is summarised by Ballou[1] who says that when moving to the implementation of a strategy, we need to concentrate on four areas; customer service, facility location, inventory policy and transport. This is a fairly restricted view, and only considers a few of the functions of logistics. A more inclusive view is given by Helming and Zonnenberg,[2] who suggest decisions in five areas: supply chain configuration, enabling practices, strategic relationships, organisation and application of information technology. They also emphasise the importance of implementation by saying, 'Companies hurl staggering sums of money and human resources at their supply chain infrastructure, only to fail at implementing their supply chain strategy'.

An even broader view of implementation says that we should consider decisions in every function of logistics from procurement through to final delivery. We will look at these decisions in the next few chapters. Here, though, we will consider some general features that set the overall structure of the supply chain. In particular, we will look at the location of facilities, ownership and outsourcing, enabling practices and capacity.

Structure of the supply chain

From an organisation's point of view, the supply chain for a product consists of tiers of suppliers feeding materials from original sources into its operations, and then tiers of customers moving materials out to the final customers (as shown in Figure 4.2).

In practice, there are many variations on this basic model. Some supply chains have few tiers of customers and suppliers, while others have many; some chains have very simple flows of materials, while others have complex and convoluted networks. Different types of products clearly need different structures in their supply chain, and building sand needs a far different chain to DVD players. Important factors are the product's value, bulk, perishability, availability, profitability, and so on. Sand has low value, is bulky and is readily available, so it is best to have a short supply chain with the suppliers as close as possible to the final customer. DVD players are small, have high value, and are made in specialised factories, so they have a longer chain.

Different strategies also lead to different types of supply chain, so a company focusing on fast delivery will build a different chain to one focusing on low costs. Other factors that affect the structure of the supply chain are the type of customer demand, economic climate, availability of logistics services, culture, rate of innovation, competition, market and financial arrangements.

Organisations should consider all such factors, and then design an appropriate structure for their supply chains. In other words, they decide the types of intermediary (who form the suppliers and customers in the chain), numbers of these intermediaries, warehousing arrangements, work done in logistics centres, customers served from each centre, modes of transport, delivery speed, and so on. Perhaps the key questions here concern the supply chain's length and breadth (illustrated in Figure 4.3).

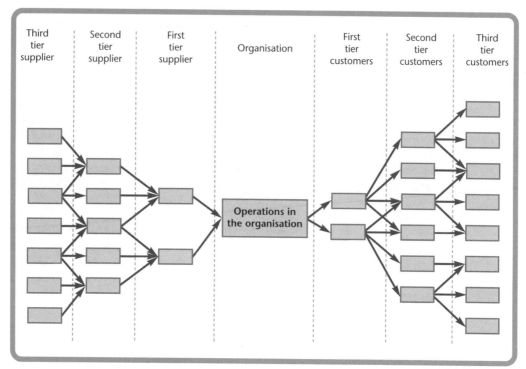

Figure 4.2 Structure of a supply chain

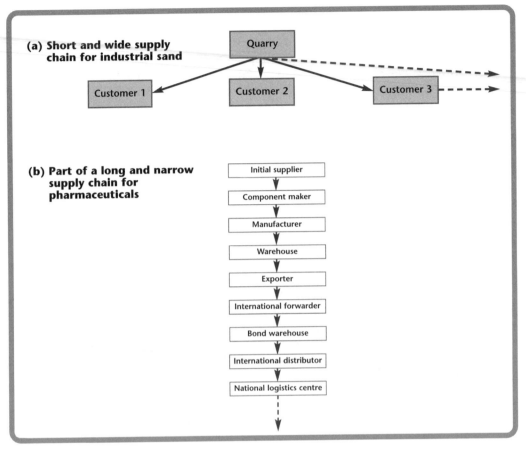

Figure 4.3 Different shapes of supply chain

● *Supply chain length* is the number of tiers, or intermediaries, that materials flow through between source and destination. We might think of a supply chain in terms of suppliers, wholesalers and retailers. In reality, some supply chains are shorter than this when, for example, producers sell directly to final customers. On the other hand, supply chains are often longer with many intermediaries, perhaps including several stages of manufacturing each of which is connected through intermediaries. Similarly, exporters might use a series of logistics centres, transport operators, agents, freight forwarders, brokers and agents to move materials through different parts of their journey.

● *Supply chain breadth* is the number of parallel routes that materials can flow through. You can imagine this in terms of the number of routes out to final customers. Cadbury's has a broad supply chain, which means that you can buy their chocolate in a huge number of retailers; Thornton's has a narrower chain, and most of their chocolate sells through their own shops; Pigalle et Fils has a very narrow chain and they only sell their chocolate in two shops in Belgium.

The best choice of length and breadth depends on many factors, with three of the most important being the amount of control that an organisation wants over its logistics, the quality of the service and the cost. A manufacturer delivering directly to customers has a short, narrow supply chain. This gives a lot of control over logistics, but it may be difficult to achieve either high customer service or low costs. Broadening the chain gives higher customer service, but it increases costs and reduces the manufacturer's control. Making the supply chain long and narrow can use intermediaries to reduce costs, but the manufacturer loses some control and the customer service does not improve. Making the supply chain both long and broad removes most control from the manufacturer, but customers get good service.

We can illustrate some of the options for a supply chain with a basic product, such as shoes. Figure 4.4 gives a simplified view of some options, assuming that final customer demand is met by either direct sales (mail order, websites or factory shops) or retailers (specialised shoe shops, clothes shops, supermarkets, large multiple retailers, small multiple retailers or mixed retailers). Then we can add other types of retailer, such as shopping clubs, discount stores, retail warehouses, and door-to-door sales. We can also add different types of intermediaries, such as manufacturers' wholesalers, retailers' wholesalers, buying groups, agents, brokers, co-operatives, and so on. Then there are specialised services such as transport, warehousing, finance, freight forwarders, and so on. The whole picture soon becomes very complicated.

A series of analyses can help managers with their design of a supply chain. The obvious ones estimate the total cost of delivery to final customers, and the time needed to satisfy an order. They might include less tangible factors, such as the efficiency of the supply chains, or customer satisfaction. Unfortunately, there is never a single 'best' solution and ultimately they have to choose the compromise that comes closest to achieving the aims of the logistics strategy. One clear trend, though, is towards shorter supply chains. Organisations of every type are realising that they can reduce costs and increase customer service by moving materials quickly through a short supply chain. This usually means removing layers of intermediaries, and concentrating logistics in fewer facilities. Manufacturers increasingly deal directly with their final customers, removing many of the traditional tiers of intermediaries. Within the

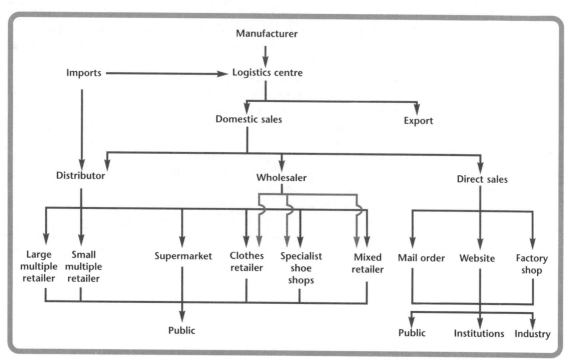

Figure 4.4 Simplified supply chain for distributing shoes

European Union the free movement of materials means that companies can replace national warehouses by a single European logistics centre. Similarly, efficient transport within the United States allows companies to work from one major centre.

Location of facilities

The structure of the supply chain sets the number of participants, including wholesalers, warehouses, logistics centres, and so on. The next question concerns the best location for each of these.

The best location for facilities depends on many factors. A warehouse, for example, might be near to factories, customers, transport or areas with development grants. The location clearly has an effect on logistics performance. If an organisation wants fast delivery, it will use local warehouses that are physically close to final customers; if it wants low costs, it will concentrate stocks in large, centralised warehouses that are inevitably some distance away from customers; if it imports and exports a lot of materials it might use warehouses near to ports or rail terminals; if it manufactures goods, it will have a stock of finished products near the factory.

Questions of location should be tackled very carefully, as they have a considerable impact over the long term. Once a facility is open it is difficult to close it down or move it. An important point, though, is that location is not an isolated decision. It leads to a series of related decisions about the work done in each location, size of each facility, level of technology used, layout of resources, customers to serve from each location, and so on. We look at location in more detail in Chapter 5.

Ownership and outsourcing

In Chapter 2 we showed that one organisation does not have to own a supply chain to get the benefits of integration. Suppliers and customers can get mutual benefits by working together, typically in a strategic alliance. We have concentrated on supplier–customer partnerships, as these are easiest to imagine and they have most effect on the supply chain. However, a similar arrangement can cover a whole range of services, such as electricity supply, banking service, and office cleaning. A common form of partnership for logistics has a specialised company looking after all of an organisation's transport. This arrangement has the advantages of an efficient and experienced specialist to look after the transport, while the organisation can concentrate on its core operations. But why stop at transport? An organisation can form partnerships with other companies to look after warehousing, purchase of materials, materials handling, and many of the other functions of logistics. When one company uses other companies to run its logistics, it is called **third party** or **contract logistics**.

Later in the book we will look at these arrangements for warehousing (Chapter 8) and transport (Chapter 11). In essence, though, the use of third party logistics is a special type of 'make-or-buy' decision. Sometimes it is better to keep logistics within the organisation, and at other times it is better to use a specialist. Rowley summarises the benefits by saying that 'The results of successful outsourcing are service improvement, cost reduction and quality enhancement'.[3] A fuller list of potential benefits includes:

- lower fixed costs, with customers only paying for services they use
- specialist suppliers who have expertise and use the best systems and practices
- suppliers can combine work from several customers to get economies of scale
- guaranteed high, and agreed, levels of customer service

- flexible capacity, dealing effectively with peaks and troughs in demand
- lower exposure to risk from, say, varying demand
- increased geographical coverage and local knowledge
- a convenient way of entering new markets.

Of course, there are disadvantages to be set against this, such as reduced control, inability to respond to unusual circumstances, more complicated communications, conflicting objectives, less control over costs, and so on. Nonetheless, the advantages of third party are becoming clearer, with more organisations moving in this direction. Surveys[4] put the value of the European logistics market at over $150 billion, with contract logistics accounting for $40 billion and rising by 8% a year.

LOGISTICS IN PRACTICE

European contract logistics

Contract logistics is a huge business in Europe. Datamonitor estimate the total cost of logistics was $150 billion in 1999, with 26% of this involving third party suppliers. By 2003 the proportion of contracted business will be 30% higher – increasing the market from $38 billion to $57 billion.

Germany is the biggest European market for logistics services (28% of the total) followed by France (20%) and the UK (17%). Because each of the economies has developed differently, and because of the different logistics requirements, the use of third parties varies quite widely. In the UK almost 40% of logistics is contracted, while in Greece it is nearer 12%. If you multiply the size of the logistics market by the proportion that is outsourced, you see that Germany, France and the UK each spend about $10 billion a year on third party logistics. These are continuing to grow at about 8% a year, but growth will be faster in Italy and Spain which currently have large logistics markets, but relatively low levels of outsourcing.

The two main issues facing contract logistics are consolidation of logistics into fewer, large companies, and geographical expansion of these companies. The European Union has encouraged trade throughout an integrated market, and larger logistics companies are emerging to service the whole market. Few of these companies are expanding by organic growth, but are looking for mergers, acquisitions and strategic alliances with other logistics companies.

Sources: Anon. (1999), European contract logistics, *Logistics and Transport Focus*, 1(3), European logistics 2000 and other reports from www.datamonitor.com

Enabling practices

Enabling practices are the activities associated with the supply chain that allow it to work efficiently. We might, for example, say that reliable information processing is an enabling practice that allows logistics to function properly.

After an organisation has designed the structure of its supply chain, and found the best locations for facilities, there are many ways of managing the flow of materials through the chain. It could, for example, use just-in-time methods to reduce stocks, EDI to link with partners, or procurement via websites. These activities are not necessarily part of the supply chain itself, or they may not be considered core activities. They do, however, ensure a smooth flow of materials to help the supply chain work as planned. In a bus company, the maintenance of vehicles does not contribute directly to the movement of people, but it is an enabling practice that helps the company work properly.

The idea of the enabling practices as supporters of logistics can be important. If you look at a series of organisations in the same business, it is likely that they will have evolved in similar ways, and have similar structures for their supply chains. Most whisky distillers or detergent manufacturers have supply chains with the same general shape. They cannot, therefore, compete by having a better supply chain structure, but they can use enabling practices to get a competitive advantage. These allow different methods and procedures to improve performance.

Capacity

The capacity of a supply chain is the largest amount of materials that can flow through it in a given time. A lorry might have a capacity of 25 tonnes that it can carry on a journey, while an airline has a capacity of 450 passengers on a flight, a warehouse can unload 210 lorries a week, or a retail shop can serve 120 customers an hour. Not all parts of a chain have the same capacity, so the overall capacity is set by the part with the smallest individual capacity. This forms the **bottleneck**. If wholesaling forms the bottleneck with a capacity of 200 units of a product an hour, this sets the capacity of the whole supply chain – even if other parts have a much higher capacity (as shown in Figure 4.5). The only way of increasing the capacity of the supply chain is to increase the capacity of the bottleneck; adding more resources elsewhere has no effect, it only increases the amount of spare facilities and reduces the utilisation. This seems an obvious point, but you can often see companies spending money on the wrong areas – for example an airline buying more planes, when its passenger numbers are limited by its landing slots at an airport.

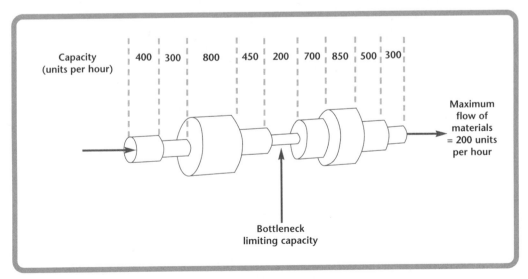

Figure 4.5 Capacity of a supply chain set by the bottleneck

To get a smooth flow of materials through the supply chain, we have to make sure that each part has an appropriate capacity. This means that the overall capacity matches total demand, and the capacity of each part is matched, so that there are no restrictive bottlenecks. We consider these problems of capacity planning in Chapter 6.

LOGISTICS IN PRACTICE

Ralston Energy Systems

Ralston Energy Systems s.r.o. (RES) works in the Czech Republic as an affiliate of Eveready Battery Company (EBC). EBC has manufacturing plants in America, Europe and Asia, and has distribution branches in almost every country of the world. Its main products are its leading brand range of batteries and torches.

Until 1998 RES ran two warehouses within the Czech Republic (illustrated in Figure 4.6). The first was a bonded warehouse used to store imported materials. Some of these materials were transferred to the RES main site in Prague, while others were re-exported to other countries. This warehouse was 50 km from Prague and was run under contract by a specialised international logistics company. The second warehouse was a 'sales warehouse' run by RES on its main site. This organised the distribution of products made in Prague, which were either destined for the domestic Czech market, or exported. Local transport from the sales warehouse was organised by a domestic company that gave a good and flexible service. Two other trucking companies were

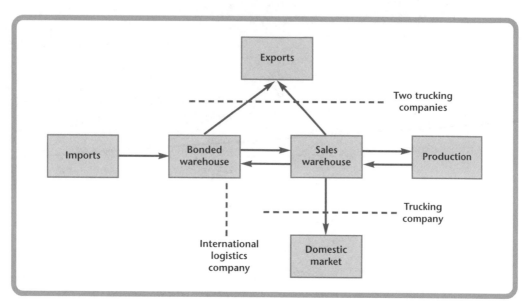

Figure 4.6 Summary of logistics at Ralston Energy Systems s.r.o.

LOGISTICS
IN PRACTICE
continued

involved in export and import operations. The sales warehouse was about three times the size of the bonded warehouse.

This structure had a number of weaknesses:

■ The sales warehouse was leased from a company which two years previously had become a competitor of RES. The company did not feel that it was appropriate to store finished goods in a competitor's facilities

■ The sales warehouse had become too small, and RES was having to store finished goods in the manufacturing plant

■ The sales warehouse had poor arrangements for loading and unloading trucks, which significantly increased the times needed

■ All goods imported into the Czech republic were sent to the bonded warehouse, and were then moved by weekly transport to the manufacturing plant

■ Local distributors charged high rates for each truck load delivered.

RES looked for a solution that would improve logistics and solve their problems. Their solution was to outsource logistics to a third party. They negotiated an agreement to run the bonded warehouse with a new operator, who also took over distribution from the sales warehouse. RES effectively closed its sales warehouse, and moved these activities to the new operator. There were various problems and disruptions for about eight months, and then everything settled down and gave a much-improved service. The new service brought the following benefits:

■ Flexible warehousing space; RES expanded into the Ukraine, and the new operator could deal with their increased requirements

■ Variable warehousing costs – based on the volumes actually stored and processed, without the substantial fixed costs

■ Variable distribution costs – again based on the amounts actually moved

■ Increased service quality – with new methods and procedures

■ Associated services from the operator – such as labelling, display rack assembly, preparation of promotional bundles, and so on

■ Saving overhead costs of management in the warehouse

■ Extending opening times from 0700 to 1900

■ Removing the conflict of interest with a competitor-owned warehouse

■ Managing remote stock in Slovenia from the same facilities.

The move took place without any disruptions to service. One week two-thirds of the stock was transferred to the new warehouse while staff continued working from the remaining stock. The following week staff moved across and started working from the new warehouse, where they were followed by the remaining one-third of stock. Overall, the move took about two years to plan and implement.

Source: internal reports

MANAGING CHANGE

Change is inevitable

The design of a logistics strategy is based on a range of internal and external factors. Unfortunately, these are constantly changing. Within the organisation there are changes to employees, goals, products, plans, processes, costs, suppliers, customers, and so on. Externally the organisation has to deal with changing customers, markets, economic conditions, competitors, technology, and so on A consequence of these continuous changes, is that the logistics strategy also has to evolve over time. Managers cannot design a strategy and then just work on its implementation – they also have to keep adjusting strategy.

As the strategy evolves, the operations of the whole logistics function must adjust and move forward. New practices affect everyone. Unfortunately, this presents a problem, as most of us do not really like changes. We might claim to welcome change, as it stops us from stagnating and getting bored. The truth, however, is that changes need a lot of effort, forcing us to abandon old and familiar practices, to learn new skills, new ways of doing things, new procedures, and to form new relationships. Change moves us away from a reasonably predictable future to one with uncertainty and risk.

Many organisations prefer to stick to their old practices. Unfortunately, this allows more flexible competitors to gain an advantage, and their performance inevitably declines. Some signs that an organisation is not changing to meet new circumstances include:

- low sales and falling market share, as old products are overtaken by competitors
- many customer complaints, particularly about quality and delivery dates
- reliance on a few customers, especially with long-term, fixed-price contracts
- old-fashioned attitudes and operations
- poor industrial relations, with low employee morale and high staff turnover
- poor communications within the organisation and with trading partners
- too much inflexible top management with no new appointments
- inward-looking managers who are out of touch with operations or customers.

Change is a normal part of business and if we do not respond we will fall behind competitors. To be more positive, we should welcome change as it creates opportunities, improves work conditions, gives better practices and performance, and more interesting, better-paid and more secure jobs. This new attitude does not happen by chance, but it needs careful management. One suggestion is that organisations need a **champion**, or **change manager**, who leads them away from their present position. This manager has the vision to see how an organisation can improve, and the ability to move it in the right direction. Unfortunately, this can be a traumatic journey, and organisations typically move through a series of stages:[5,6]

1. *Denial* – where employees deny that there is a need for change
2. *Defence* – defending the current way of doing things and criticising new proposals
3. *Discarding* – beginning to move away from the old ways and towards the new ones
4. *Adoption* – using the new ways and accepting that they are beneficial
5. *Integration* – assuming the new ways are normal and using them naturally.

The key point is that change must be managed. People have to do things differently, and they must be convinced that changes are both essential and beneficial. Getting this message across is the difficult part of change management.

Concerns about the supply chain

In 2001 Warwick Business School's Operations Management Group ran a survey to identify concerns about the supply chain. The most common management worries were:

Costs	100%
Integration of the supply chain	86%
Globalisation	71%
Procurement	57%

Integration of the supply chain is clearly a concern of most organisations. We would imagine that they are aware of the benefits of closer integration and are moving in this direction, probably through alliances and partnerships. Certainly 70% of respondents said that more integration was needed to reduce costs.

However, the survey found that there was a considerable gap between the stated desire for more integration and its actual achievement. Few organisations had made any real progress at all, and almost none had achieved widespread integration. The main problem stated by 88% of organisations was the difficulty of merging systems and consolidating EDI.

Similarly, 57% of organisations were concerned about procurement. Many people regard e-business as the major challenge – and opportunity – facing business. For the respondents to this survey, between 50 and 70% of their costs were attributed to purchases. Yet less than 40% felt that e-procurement was a strategic issue, and only 36% had a written strategy for e-procurement.

Sources: Anon. (2001) *Logistics and Transport Focus* 3(1), 48–9 and www.lefevre.co.uk

Rate of change

One important feature of change is the rate at which it occurs. Some organisations change very quickly, such as Intel which works at the frontiers of technology and is continually developing new products. Others change very slowly, and even make a virtue out of stability, such as Morgan sports cars whose basic design originated in the 1930s.

Major changes can be very disruptive, so organisations generally prefer a series of small adjustments. This iterative approach gives **continuous improvement** which is known by the Japanese name of *kaizen*. A stream of relatively minor changes can be absorbed by the organisation without major interruptions. There is also little risk, as any of the 'improvements' that do not work can easily be reversed. Over time, this incremental approach builds a momentum for improvement, and makes sure that the logistics system is always getting better.

Suggestions for iterative improvements come from many sources, such as customers, competitors or suggestion boxes. Sometimes there is a more formal arrangement, such as the **plan–do–check–act cycle**, or **Deming wheel** (shown in Figure 4.7).

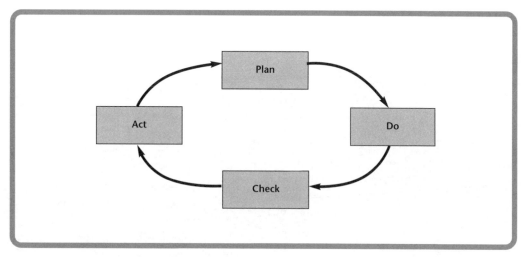

Figure 4.7 Deming wheel

This uses a team of people who positively look for improvements to logistics using the cycle:

● *plan* – looking at the existing logistics, collecting information, discussing alternatives, and suggesting a plan for improvement
● *do* – where the plan is implemented, and data is collected on subsequent performance
● *check* – which analyses the performance data to see if the expected improvements actually appeared
● *act* – if there are real improvements the new arrangements are made permanent, but if there are no improvements, lessons are learnt and the new arrangements are not adopted.

The team is continuously looking for improvements, so at this point they return to the beginning of the cycle, and consider more changes.

LOGISTICS
IN PRACTICE

Hotpoint

Hotpoint is a major supplier of domestic appliances in the UK, owned by GE. In 1988 it worked as an independent company, but was not responding quickly enough to changing conditions. It distributed its own finished products, but the operations were inefficient and costs were rising rapidly. The company decided to overhaul its distribution, with the aims of:

■ reducing costs
■ increasing customer service which had fallen to unsatisfactory levels
■ strengthening the management team
■ renegotiating pay and conditions for staff
■ introducing systems to measure and monitor performance

LOGISTICS
IN PRACTICE
continued

■ reducing the amount of damage to products in transit

■ designing a distribution strategy for the next five years.

As a starting point the company designed a mission for distribution, which was: 'To deliver Hotpoint goods to the customer; when expected and agreed; in the manner expected; in good condition; at an acceptable cost to the company.' This laid the foundation for a new culture, based on customer satisfaction and competitive performance. It took a huge effort of communication, negotiation, training, changing long-standing practices, and introducing new systems. The logistics slowly improved, and progress was monitored by benchmarking other companies, such as TNT, Exel and TDG.

An important factor for Hotpoint was control over the supply chain. It put a lot of emphasis on its home delivery service, where retailers take orders and Hotpoint deliver appliances directly to customers. This allowed drivers to make sure the appliances were in good condition, installed properly and working. Hotpoint aimed for a high quality service, with guaranteed delivery in a specified time slot, removal of packaging, collection of old appliances for recycling, and so on.

To achieve this service, Hotpoint designed a wide and short distribution network, with satellite depots around the country giving daily deliveries to all main towns and regular visits to rural areas. These depots are largely stockless, being fed each day with their requirements. They are also used for the distribution of parts sent from the national distribution centre at Peterborough.

The new arrangements set the scene for logistics over the next decade. During this period the supply chain grew in importance, and became more responsive. Lead times were reduced, more frequent deliveries were made, stocks were lowered by 50%, operating costs were significantly reduced, customer service was increased, and staff morale improved. The company won a Motor Transport Award for 'Excellence'. Changes made throughout the 1990s moved the distribution system from 'a sleeping dinosaur to a cost effective and customer-driven entity'.

Sources: Grange C. (1999) The long and winding road, *Logistics and Transport Focus* 1(4), 36–41, Grange C. (1999) The long and winding road, presentation to the Institute of Logistics and Transport Annual Conference, and www.hotpoint.co.uk

Business Process Re-engineering

Some people say that small continuous improvements to operations are not the best approach. They suggest that small adjustments only tinker with details and make no real difference. If you have a poor logistics system, the way of improving it is not to tinker with the details, but to take a broad stroke and look for dramatic improvements. The best-known approach of this kind is **business process re-engineering** (BPR). Hammer and Champy[7] define this as follows:

BUSINESS PROCESS RE-ENGINEERING is the fundamental rethinking and radical redesign of business processes to achieve dramatic improvements in critical, contemporary measures of performance, such as cost, quality, service and speed.

The idea behind re-engineering is that you do not look for improvements in your current operations, but you start with a blank sheet of paper and design a new process from scratch. This is rather like running an old car. You can tinker with it and keep it going a bit longer, but the re-engineering solution is to buy a new car. If you have a poor logistics system, you should not waste time tinkering to find small improvements, but should throw away the whole system and design a new one from scratch. Ford of America gave one classic example of this approach.

LOGISTICS IN PRACTICE

Accounts payable at Ford

In 1988 the accounts payable department of Ford of America had 500 people working with a standard accounting system. In this:

1. The purchasing department sent a purchase order to the supplier and a copy to the accounts payable department

2. The supplier shipped the goods ordered and sent an invoice to accounts payable

3. When the goods arrived at Ford, they were checked and sent to stores. A description of the goods arriving was sent to accounts payable

4. Accounts payable now had three descriptions of the goods – from the purchasing department, supplier and arrivals. If these matched they paid the invoice

5. Sometimes the paperwork did not match, and problems had to be sorted out. This took a lot of effort, often lasting several weeks.

Ford could have improved this system, and estimated that they might save 25% of staffing costs. Instead they chose a more radical solution and re-engineered the whole system. At the centre of this was their purchasing database, so the new system had:

1. The purchasing department sent a purchase order to a supplier and updated the database

2. The supplier shipped the goods

3. When the goods arrived at Ford they were checked against outstanding orders on the database

4. If the details matched, the goods were accepted, the database was updated to show that they had arrived, and the supplier was paid

5. If the details did not match, the goods were not accepted and were sent back to the supplier.

Suppliers soon learnt that the new system would not allow any mistakes in deliveries, and they were quickly eliminated. The streamlined system reduced Ford's accounts payable department to 125 people, giving a 400% increase in productivity.

Source: Hammer M. and Champy J. (1993) *Re-engineering the corporation*, HarperCollins, New York

BPR does not give new methods, but it consolidates several related ideas. Some of its main principles for the supply chain are:

- a supply chain should be designed across functions and allow work to flow naturally, concentrating on the whole supply chain rather than the separate parts
- managers should strive for dramatic improvements in performance by radically rethinking and redesigning the supply chain
- improved information technology is fundamental to re-engineering as it allows radical new solutions
- all activities that do not add value should be eliminated
- activities should be carried out where they make most sense – information processing, for example, becomes a part of logistics rather than a separate function
- decisions should be made where the work is done, and by those doing the work
- you do not have to be an expert to help redesign a supply chain, and being an outsider without preconceived ideas often helps
- always see things from the customer's point of view.

One important point is that BPR does not replace continuous improvement. It is possible to have a series of radical improvements, and still introduce smaller continuous improvements (as shown in Figure 4.8).

BPR is a general approach to change rather than a formal procedure, so we cannot say, 'this is how to re-engineer a process'. Perhaps because of this, organisations have mixed experiences with its use. Some have reported outstanding results – like the early work in the IBM Credit Corporation which increased output by a factor of 100. But around three-quarters of organisations fail to get the improvements they hoped for.[8]

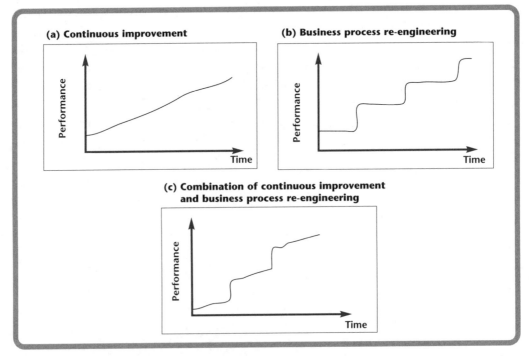

Figure 4.8 Rate of performance improvement

CHAPTER REVIEW

❑ The logistics strategy sets the overall direction for logistics. Implementing the strategy translates this into a series of lower decisions and actions.

❑ Unless the strategy is designed properly, implementation can be difficult or impossible. To avoid these problems, managers should consider implementation during the design of the strategy, they should involve those involved in implementation, and so on.

❑ Some strategic decisions are concerned with principles, while others are more concerned with achieving the principles. The first of these are considered more in the design of a strategy, while the second are considered more in the implementation.

❑ Important decisions for implementing the logistics strategy include the structure of the supply chain (length, breadth, number of tiers, type of intermediaries, and so on), location of facilities, outsourcing, enabling practices and capacity.

❑ The supply chain must continually evolve to keep up with changing conditions. These changes can be difficult, and need careful management.

❑ An important question concerns the rate of change. Continuous improvement uses a series of small adjustments to build up a momentum for change-over time. Business process re-engineering looks for more radical changes.

CASE STUDY — *Passenger Interchange*

In most major cities the amount of congestion on the roads is increasing. Some of this is due to commercial vehicles, but by far the majority is due to private cars. There are several ways of controlling the number of vehicles using certain areas. These include prohibition of cars in pedestrian areas, restricted entry, limits on parking, traffic calming schemes, and so on. A relatively new approach has road-user charging, where cars pay a fee to use a particular length of road, with the fee possibly changing with prevailing traffic conditions.

Generally, the most effective approach to reducing traffic congestion is to improve public transport. These services must be attractive to people who judge them by a range of factors, such as the comfort of seating, amount of crowding, handling of luggage, availability of food, toilets, safety, facilities in waiting areas, availability of escalators and lifts, and so on. However, the dominant considerations are cost, time and reliability.

CASE STUDY *continued*

Buses are often the most flexible form of public transport, with the time for a journey consisting of four parts:

■ *joining time, which is the time needed to get to a bus stop*
■ *waiting time, until the bus arrives*
■ *journey time, to actually do the travelling*
■ *leaving time, to get from the bus to the final destination.*

Transport policies can reduce these times by a combination of frequent services, well-planned routes, and bus priority schemes. Then convenient journeys and subsidised travel make buses an attractive alternative.

One problem, however, is that people have to change buses, or transfer between buses and other types of transport, including cars, planes, trains, ferries and trams. Then there are additional times for moving between one type of transport and the next, and waiting for the next part of the service. These can be minimised by an integrated transport system with frequent, connecting services at 'passenger interchanges'.

Passenger interchanges seem a good idea, but they are not universally popular. Most people prefer a straight-through journey between two points, even if this is less frequent than an integrated service with interchanges. The reason is probably because there are more opportunities for things to go wrong, and experience suggests that even starting a journey does not guarantee that it will successfully finish.

In practice, most major cities such as London and Paris have successful interchanges, and they are spreading into smaller towns, such as Montpellier in France. For the ten years up to 2001 the population of Montpellier grew by more than 8.4 per cent, and it moved from being the 22nd largest town in France to the eighth largest. It has good transport links with the port of Sète, an airport, inland waterways, main road networks and a fast rail link to Paris. In 2001 public transport was enhanced with a 15 kilometre tramline connecting major sites in the town centre with other transport links. At the same time, buses were rerouted to connect to the tram, cycling was encouraged for short distances, park-and-ride services were improved, and journeys were generally made easier. As a result, there has been an increase in use of public transport, a reduction in the number of cars in the town centre, and improved air quality. When the tram opened in 2000, a third of the population tried it in the first weekend, and it carried a million people within seven weeks of opening. In 2005, a second tramline will add 19 kilometres to the routes.

Sources: Hellewell D.S. (2000) Improving passenger interchange, *Logistics and Transport Focus*, **2**(6), 32–6; Gemmell C. (2001) An integrated public transport system, *Logistics and Transport Focus*, **3**(3), 36–42; DTI (1998) A new deal for transport (White Paper, Cmnd 3950), HMSO

CASE STUDY
Questions

- Are the problems of moving people significantly different from the problems of moving goods or services?
- What are the benefits of public transport over private transport? Should public transport be encouraged and, if so, how?
- What are the benefits of integrated public transport systems?

PROJECT
Structure of a Supply Chain

Have a look at the supply chain for a familiar product, such as a brand of lager or a CD. Describe the structure of this chain, emphasising its length and breadth. Why does it have this particular structure? Discuss the alternative structures and point out their benefits and disadvantages.

DISCUSSION QUESTIONS

1. What exactly is meant by 'implementing the logistics strategy'?
2. We suggested a difference between strategic decisions that set the principles for logistics, and those concerned with the practicalities of implementation. Do you think that this is a real difference? What kind of decisions fit into each category?
3. It is often more difficult to implement a logistics strategy than to design one. This is why most logistics plans fail in the practice rather than the theory. Do you think that this is necessarily true? What can organisations do to improve the implementation?
4. What are the main areas for strategic decisions in logistics?
5. Supply chains are not usually designed from scratch, but evolve over time. What problems does this create? Can you suggest a better approach?
6. Can you find any examples of good logistics strategies that have given poor results because of poor implementation? What could have been done better?

REFERENCES

1. Ballou R.H. (1981) Reformulating a logistics strategy, *International Journal of Physical Distribution and Materials Management*, **11**(8), 71–83.
2. Helming W. and Zonnenberg J.P. (2000) The five fulcrum points of a supply chain strategy, *Supply Chain and Logistics Journal*, Winter.
3. Rowley J. (2001) Outsourcing across borders in Europe, *Logistics and Transport Focus*, **3**(1), 54–6.
4. Datamonitor (2000) *European Logistics 2000*, Datamonitor, London.
5. Cubitt B. (2000) Change: the final frontier? *Logistics and Transport Focus*, **2**(3), 39–42.
6. Carnall C. (1991) *Managing Change*, Routledge, London.
7. Hammer M. and Champy J. (1993) *Reengineering the Corporation*, HarperCollins, New York.
8. Hammer M. (1996) *Beyond Reengineering*, HarperCollins, New York.

CHAPTER 5

Locating Facilities

AIMS OF THE CHAPTER

After reading this chapter you should be able to:

- UNDERSTAND the importance of location decisions

- DISCUSS factors that affect the choice of location

- DESCRIBE a hierarchical approach to locating facilities

- USE an infinite set approach, such as the centre of gravity

- COMPARE locations using costing and scoring models

- USE models for locating facilities on networks

- COMBINE location decisions into a broader approach to planning

IMPORTANCE OF LOCATION

Location decisions

In the last chapter we looked at the design of a supply chain. This sets the number and type of facilities involved in logistics. Now we are going to see where these facilities should be located.

FACILITIES LOCATION finds the best geographic locations for the different elements in a supply chain.

Location decisions are needed whenever an organisation opens new facilities. When Toyota build a new assembly line, or Carrefour open a new store, or Burger King open a new restaurant, or Pfizer extend into new markets, they have to make decisions about the best locations. These are important decisions that affect the organisation's performance for many years.

If an organisation makes a mistake and opens facilities in a poor location – perhaps after an investment of millions of euros – it cannot simply close down and move to a better place. Working in the wrong location can give very poor performance, but moving can be equally difficult. The only solution, of course, is to choose the right location in the first place. When Nissan opened a factory in Sunderland in the north-east of England, they put a lot of effort into choosing the best site, and now have Europe's most productive car plant. But if they had chosen a poor location, they could have low productivity, unreliable suppliers, poor materials, low-quality products and high costs.

The right location does not guarantee success, but the wrong location will certainly guarantee failure. This is why you do not find nightclubs in residential areas where most people are retired, big petrol stations on country lanes where they cannot attract passing customers, factories in city centres where their costs are too high, or oil refineries far away from ports where inward transport would be too expensive. Nonetheless, you can find examples of organisations working in the wrong place – and going out of business. Sometimes, people do not recognise that a location is poor, and some sites around town centres have a string of cafes or clothes shops closing down shortly after they have opened. Some organisations forget that location decisions are for the long term and are tempted by short-term benefits, such as development grants, temporary rent reductions, or tax breaks. Such sweeteners can be attractive, but they rarely form the basis of good decisions. You can also see cases where organisations make the right decisions, but circumstances change – such as garages that were in good locations before a new bypass opened.

Location decisions are invariably difficult, and organisations have to consider many factors. Some of these can be measured – or at least estimated – such as operating costs, wage rates, taxes, currency exchange rates, number of competitors, distance from current locations, development grants, population, reliability of supplies. Many other factors are non-quantifiable, such as the quality of infrastructure, political stability, social attitudes, industrial relations, legal system, future developments of the economy, and so on. When organisations look at all the circumstances, they often come to similar conclusions. This is why certain areas or trading estates become popular, as many organisations identify them as the best place to locate. This leads to certain trends in location. For example, thousands of plants have opened in the Maquiladoras on Mexico's northern border. These aim for the low operating costs in Mexico, while being close to the major market of the USA. Other rapidly growing areas are in China, central Europe and the Pacific Rim. Within these broad regions, specific areas are popular, such as Shanghai, Warsaw and Singapore.

There are other trends in location, such as a growing number of out-of-town malls, super-markets and retail estates. The major trend towards shorter supply chains means that layers of intermediaries are disappearing, and logistics is concentrated in fewer facilities. Free trade and good transport within the European Union, for example, encourages companies to replace national warehouses by a single European logistics centre.

Call centres give an interesting example of the concentration of operations in fewer loca-tions. Good communications – with low business telephone costs – mean that organisations do not need small call centres within each country or region, but they can open a huge, effi-cient centre in one convenient location. IBM, for example, employ 800 people in their centre in Greenock near Glasgow, answering questions from customers in 90 countries. Delhi has 40 major call centres, and is expanding this business to employ a quarter of a million people. When you call the customer service department of any major company, you do not really know the continent you are calling, let alone the country.

Alternatives to locating new facilities

Choosing a good location is one of the most common problems that organisations face. There are several reasons why they need to consider location, including:

- the end of a lease on existing premises
- expansion into new geographic areas
- changes in the location of customers or suppliers
- changes to operations – such as an electricity company moving from coal generators to gas
- upgrading facilities – perhaps to introduce new technology
- changes to transport – such as a switch from rail transport to road
- changes in the transport network – such as the opening of the Channel Tunnel or road bridge between Sweden and Denmark
- mergers or acquisitions giving duplicate operations that must be rationalised.

You might think that one way of avoiding the problem of locating new facilities is simply to alter existing ones. This is, however, still a location decision, as it assumes the current site is the best available. In practice, when an organisation wants to change its facilities – either expand, move or contract – it has three alternatives:

- expand or change existing facilities at an existing site
- open additional facilities at another site while keeping all existing facilities
- close down existing operations and move.

As a rule of thumb, around 45% of companies expand on the same site, a similar number open additional facilities, and 10% close down existing operations and move. The most radical option of completely relocating often has very high costs and is disruptive. The most conservative option of expanding existing facilities involves little risk and can give economies of scale.

Even when new facilities are clearly needed, there are different ways of managing them. Imagine a manufacturer that is expanding, and wants to work in a new market. This seems like a standard problem of finding the best location for new facilities, but there are several alterna-tives that are not so expensive. The following list gives five options in order of increasing investment:

1. *Licensing or franchising:* local organisations make and supply the company's products in return for a share of the profit.
2. *Exporting:* the company makes the product in its existing facilities and sells it to a distributor working in the new market.
3. *Local distribution and sales:* the company makes the product in its existing facilities, but sets up its own distribution and sales force in the new market.
4. *Local assembly and finishing:* the company makes most of the product in existing facilities, but opens limited facilities in the new market to finish or assemble the final product.
5. *Full local production:* the company opens complete facilities in the new market.

If it opens new local facilities, an organisation has the benefits of more control over products and the supply chain, higher profits, avoidance of import tariffs and quotas, and closer links with local customers. On the other hand it has more investment, risk and complex and uncertain operations. The best choice depends on many factors, such as the capital available, organisation's attitude towards risk, target return on investment, existing operations, timescale, local knowledge, transport costs, tariffs, trade restrictions and available workforce.

WORKED EXAMPLE

Warwick Supplies is planning to expand into Europe. It is considering a number of options, each of which has a fixed annual payment (for rent, electricity, and other overheads) and a variable cost that depends on throughput (handling, depreciation, staff, and so on). The following table shows a simplified view of these costs.

Alternative	Fixed cost	Variable cost
A exporting from existing facilities	€800,000	€900
B using a local distributor	€2,400,000	€700
C open a facility for local finishing	€9,000,000	€520
D open limited production facilities	€8,000,000	€360
E open larger production facilities	€12,000,000	€440

Alternatively, Warwick can avoid entering the market by licensing a local manufacturer to make the product in return for a royalty of about 2% of sales. How might it approach this decision, if it is planning on selling about 10,000 units a year with a contribution to profit of 10%?

Solution

We have a limited amount of financial information, and can use this for a break-even analysis. You can see from Figure 5.1 that alternatives C and E are never cheapest. This leaves a choice between alternatives A, B and D.

■ Alternative A is the cheapest for throughput, X, from 0 until:

$$800,000 + 900X = 2,400,000 + 700X \quad \text{or} \quad X = 8,000$$

W O R K E D
E X A M P L E
continued

- After this alternative B is cheapest until:

$$2,400,000 + 700X = 8,000,000 + 360X \quad \text{or} \quad X = 16,471$$

- After this point D remains the cheapest.

With production of 10,000 units a year, alternative B, using a local distributor, is cheapest with costs of (2,400,000 + 10,000 × 700 =) €9.4 million. Alternative A, exporting directly with existing facilities is not much more expensive at (800,000 + 10,000 × 900 =) €9.8 million, and is probably easier to organise.

Option B has an average cost of €940, and adding a contribution to profit of 10% gives a selling price of 940 × 1.1 = €1034, and total profit of €940,000. If Warwick negotiated a royalty of 2% of sales, they would get a profit of only 1034 × 0.02 × 10,000 = €206,800.

Of course, these figures only give the starting point for a decision. Now Warwick have to look at the more detailed costs, their aims, longer term plans, amount of control they want, and a whole series of other factors.

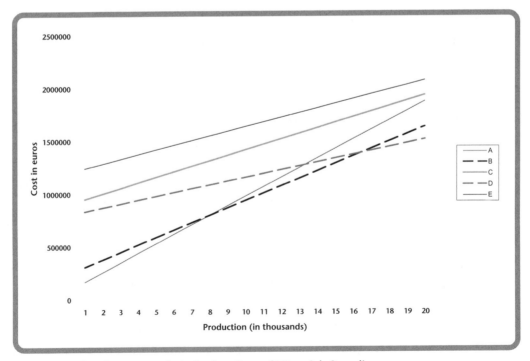

Figure 5.1 Break-even analysis for location of Warwick Supplies

CHOOSING THE GEOGRAPHIC REGION

Overall approach

Facility location involves a hierarchy of decisions. At the top of this are the broad decisions about which geographic regions to work in. Then come more local views that consider alternative countries or areas within this region. Then we look more closely at alternative towns and cities within this area. Finally we consider different sites within a preferred town (as shown in Figure 5.2). In the 1990s, for example, Marks & Spencer looked at ways to expand its retail network in central Europe. It worked with a franchisee, and considered various countries, including the option of opening branches in Poland. It looked at cities within Poland and decided to open a branch in Warsaw. After looking at available sites it opened a store next to the Cultural Palace in the city centre.

The broad decisions about geographical regions and countries come from the business strategy. An organisation with a strategy of global operations or expansion must continually look for new locations. In the 1990s it was Marks & Spencer's business strategy to expand and get close to new customers that led to its shop in Poland. By 2001, however, the company's strategy had changed and it closed many of its European operations to concentrate on the UK market (as a franchise, the Warsaw branch is not affected).

Obvious choices for location are to get close to customers, or close to suppliers. Toyota opened plants in the USA to get near to the major car market, and Exxon operate in the

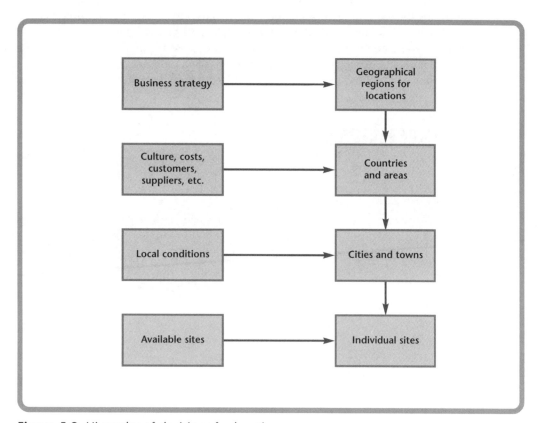

Figure 5.2 Hierarchy of decisions for locations

Middle East to get near to sources of oil. Another option is to open facilities in areas that give lower operating costs. Manufacturers move to areas with low production costs, even when these are some way from both their customers and suppliers. This puts more pressure on logistics. The supply chains become more complicated, but logistics has to be so efficient that lower production costs are not swamped by higher logistics costs.

A problem with moving to areas with low cost operations is that they might give higher total costs than expected. Many people assume that low wage rates automatically mean low total cost. This is not necessarily true, as low wages can be accompanied by very low productivity: there is no point in halving wage rates if productivity is cut by three quarters. At the same time, many operations, particularly in manufacturing, are automated so that wages form a very small part of overall costs. It makes little sense for a high technology company to move away from its main markets and work in a low wage economy when wages only form 2% of costs.

Another problem is that transport costs change quickly, and rises can make them more important than operating costs. Large, efficient steel mills in Japan, Taiwan and South Korea, for example, have low operating costs – but importing coal and iron ore, and transporting finished steel is so expensive that their delivered price is high. South Africa breweries make very good beer, but little of it is exported to Europe because of the high transportation costs.

One example of these effects came in 1980 when Tandy Corporation decided to move production of its latest computer to South Korea. Then rising shipping costs, long lead times for the sea voyage to the USA, the changing value of the dollar, and more automation in the process, encouraged them to reconsider their location. In 1987 they moved back to Fort Worth, Texas and reduced costs by 7.5%.

Perhaps the overriding consideration is that costs may not be a dominant factor in location. A logistics strategy might focus on quality, flexibility, speed of response, reliability, customer service and so forth, rather than lowest cost. As we shall see in the next section, this means that organisations prefer to locate in areas that are near markets, have reliable suppliers, good infrastructure, high productivity, guaranteed quality and skilled workforce.

LOGISTICS
IN PRACTICE

Millicra Electronic Components

Millicra Electronic Components grew as a supplier of parts to the car industry. Until 1997 their operations were based in Pittsburgh and Detroit, and their main customers were assembly plants around Detroit. Although they had a largely automated process, their costs were still high by world standards, and they worked in an intensively competitive market.

In 1998 the main US car manufacturers – General Motors, Ford and Chrysler – were all planning assembly plants in the Philippines. These would meet the rapidly growing domestic market, which was currently dominated by Japanese manufacturers (Toyota 22%, Mitsubishi 21%, Honda 12% and Nissan 11%) and they would give a low-cost production base for export to other countries in the region.

Millicra made a decision to join the carmakers in the Philippines. They were a relatively small company, and rather than

spreading operations over three sites, they decided to close their plants in America. There were several advantages to this:

- production costs in the Philippines would be much lower than in America

- they could get economies of scale from a single location

- they could introduce the latest methods and technology

- they would be near a growing market, with easy transport back to their existing customers

- the Philippine government gave a six year income tax holiday and other tax breaks

- there was a pool of cheap labour ready for training.

The company allowed six months to move equipment and other materials from America and another six months to iron out production problems. Only one or two of their experienced managers moved to the Philippines, and the rest took early retirement or moved to other employers. All of the hourly paid workers in the American plants were laid off. Millicra found it fairly easy to recruit staff in Manila, but language and cultural problems became more obvious when they started training. The company found it difficult to implement their new procedures, and there were a series of problems with supervision, training and operations, which gave much lower productivity than expected.

There were also problems with transport. Shipping costs rose, increasing the cost of importing components and delivering finished products to the US. The long sea journeys inevitably increased uncertainty, tied up stock in the supply chain and slowed responses to both customers and suppliers.

By 2001 Millicra's old customers in the US had formed alliances with a new local supplier, and demand in the Philippines was lower than forecast. The world economy was slowing, particularly in Japan and the USA, and many local economies moved into recession. Millicra could see no end to their problems, and ceased trading in August 2001.

Sources: Marozzi J. (1998) Chrysler and GM follow Ford's path to Philippines, *Financial Times*, 17 April and internal company records

Considerations in choosing regions

Organisations have to consider many factors when choosing the general regions to work in. The following list includes some of the most important:

- *Location of customers:* Service providers must generally be close to their customers – which is why you find shops, buses, libraries, restaurants, solicitors, banks and so on in town centres. The same arguments hold for manufactured products which have a high cost of delivery to final customers – which is why there are many local bakers, brewers, dairies and double glazing factories. Sometimes being close to customers is particularly important, as with just-in-time operations (which we describe in Chapter 7).

● *Location of suppliers and materials:* Manufacturers are more likely to locate near to supplies of raw materials, particularly if these are heavy or bulky. This is why coal-burning power stations are close to coalmines and pulp mills are near to timber forests. Some operations have to be close to perishable materials – encouraging fruit and vegetable processors to move close to farms, and frozen seafood companies near to fishing ports.

● *Culture:* It is easier to expand into an area that has a similar language, culture, laws and costs, than to expand into a completely foreign area. A company currently operating in Belgium would find it easier to expand in France than in, say, Korea. The decision to build Disneyland Europe near Paris gives one example where moving a successful American operation to a European culture met with less initial success than expected.

● *Government attitudes:* National and local government policies can seriously affect an area's attractiveness. Investment in Hong Kong, for example, has fallen since its return to rule by China. Many governments offer incentives for companies to move into an area – but others are less welcoming, perhaps trying to control foreign influences on the economy. Some areas encourage particular types of industry (particularly high technology or finance companies), but are less keen on, say, nuclear, chemical or polluting industries.

● *Direct costs:* These are the costs of operations, including wages, materials, overheads and utilities. They can vary widely. The most attractive locations offer a combination of low direct costs and high performance. Often there is a balance, with higher productivity coming at higher cost. Many organisations prefer to locate in high cost areas to get the other benefits they bring.

● *Indirect costs:* There can be many indirect costs of doing business, including local taxes and charges on the payroll such as social insurance, pension and social costs. There may also be controls on company ownership (often including a controlling local partner), currency exchange and repatriation of profits.

● *Exchange rates:* These can appear as indirect costs, but they are much less predictable. What seems like a good location one year can become much less attractive after a re-alignment of currency values.

● *Social attitudes:* Some countries put more emphasis on social welfare than others, and there may be higher union membership or emphasis on individual rather than corporate benefits. Other areas do not necessarily admire 'high productivity' methods and there might be higher absenteeism and staff turnover.

● *Organisation:* An organisation can keep a close check on new operations by controlling these from existing headquarters and giving local operations very little autonomy. This is, however, inflexible, and it does not allow local organisations to adapt to their own conditions or develop skills. An alternative is to devolve decisions. Then a company might become international (maintaining its headquarters in the home country and running worldwide activities from there), multinational (opening subsidiary headquarters around the world so that each area is largely independent) or global (treating the whole world as a single, integrated market).

● *Operations:* If you go into a McDonald's hamburger restaurant anywhere in the world you will see virtually identical operations. It is easier to control operations in this way, but it loses the benefit of local knowledge and practices. Other organisations blend into the local environment and adapt their operations so they are more familiar to their host countries.

LOGISTICS IN PRACTICE

McDonald's in Moscow

In 1990 the world's largest McDonald's hamburger restaurant with 700 seats opened just off Pushkin Square in Moscow. This is operated jointly by McDonald's of Canada and local Russian companies. McDonald's has opened branches throughout the world, but this was one of the most difficult, with negotiations starting twenty years previously with the Soviet Union.

The inside of the restaurant is exactly as you would expect, with the standard menu, colour scheme and decor, staff training, levels of cleanliness and cooking. Everything follows the standard McDonald's pattern, but this was only achieved after considerable effort. As well as the initial political difficulties, there were major practical problems. Beef in Moscow was not readily available and the quality was variable. McDonald's had to import breeding cattle and start a beef farm to supply the restaurant. Potatoes were plentiful, but they were the wrong type to make McDonald's fries. Seed potatoes were imported and grown. Russian cheese was not suitable for cheeseburgers, so a dairy plant was opened to make processed cheese.

When the restaurant opened it was a huge success, with 27,000 people applying for a single job, 50,000 people served a day and queues half a mile long outside the restaurant. Now there are 58 outlets in Russia and a workforce of 450. But the path is still not easy. Russia suffered an economic collapse in 1998, and this has affected wages, sales and profits. The initial set up cost was so high that the restaurant does not expect to make a profit in the foreseeable future.

Sources: company reports and Cockburn P., Big Mac, big trouble, *Independent*, 14/11/2000

INFINITE SET APPROACHES

After making a decision about the geographical region and country, an organisation has to look in more detail at the areas, towns, cities and individual sites. There are several ways they can approach these decisions, and the best depends on specific circumstances. One approach that is **not** recommended is personal preference. There are many examples of poor locations where managers simply chose a site they liked – perhaps in the town they lived or grew up in, or the area they spent their holidays. Of course, such decisions can be successful, but their main weakness is unreliability. It is always safer to do some analyses than to rely on intuition and guesswork.

Two distinct approaches to location decisions are:

1. *Infinite set approach* – which uses geometric arguments to find the best location, assuming that there are no restrictions on site availability.
2. *Feasible set approach* – where there are only a small number of feasible sites, and an organisation has to choose the best.

An infinite set approach finds the best location in principle and then looks for a site nearby; a feasible set approach compares sites that are currently available and chooses the best. These approaches are often used together, with an infinite set approach finding the best location in principle, and then a feasible set approach comparing available sites near to this. We will start by describing an infinite set approach, and then move on to look at methods for comparing sites.

Simple models

Hoover[1] was the first person to specify the three basic alternatives for location. First, a facility can be located near to customers; this gives good customer service and low costs for transport out to customers, but high cost for transport in from suppliers. Second, it can be located near to suppliers; this moves products quickly into the supply chain, gives low costs for inward transport, but high costs for outward transport. Third, it can be located at some point between suppliers and customers, giving a compromise with reasonable service and lower costs (as illustrated in Figures 5.3 and 5.4).

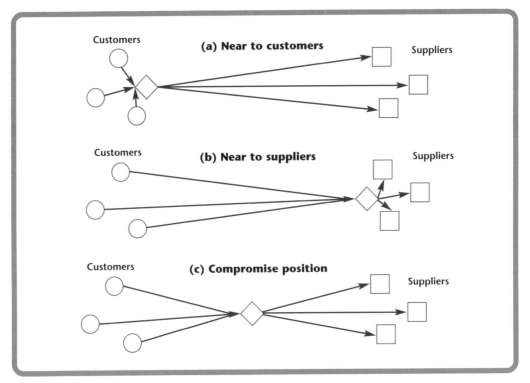

Figure 5.3 Alternative choices of location

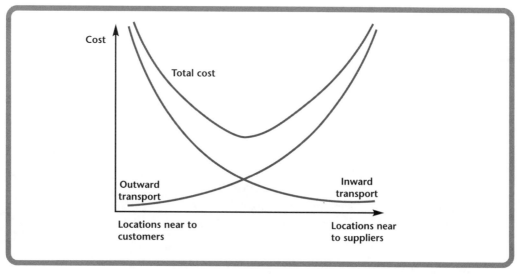

Figure 5.4 Variation in transport cost with location

A simple way of finding the best compromise location calculates the **centre of gravity** of supply and demand.[2] The co-ordinates of the centre of gravity are:

$$X_0 = \frac{\sum X_i\, W_i}{\sum W_i} \qquad Y_0 = \frac{\sum Y_i\, W_i}{\sum W_i}$$

Where:

$(X_0,\, Y_0)$ are the co-ordinates of the centre of gravity which gives the facility location

$(X_i,\, Y_i)$ are co-ordinates of each customer and supplier, i

W_i is expected demand at customer i, or expected supply from supplier i

WORKED EXAMPLE

Van Hendrick Industries is building a central logistics centre that will collect components from three suppliers, and send finished goods to six regional warehouses. The locations of these and the amounts supplied or demanded are shown in the following table. Where should they start looking for a site?

Location	X,Y co-ordinates	Supply or demand
Supplier 1	91,8	40
Supplier 2	93,35	60
Supplier 3	3,86	80
Warehouse 1	83,26	24
Warehouse 2	89,54	16

EXAMPLE
continued

Location	X,Y co-ordinates	Supply or demand
Warehouse 3	63,87	22
Warehouse 4	11,85	38
Warehouse 5	9,16	52
Warehouse 6	44,48	28

Solution

Figure 5.5 shows a spreadsheet for these calculations.

As you can see, the centre of gravity is $X_0 = 45.5$ and $Y_0 = 50.3$, which you can check by calculating:

$$X_0 = \frac{\sum X_i W_i}{\sum W_i} = \frac{16,380}{360} = 45.5$$

$$Y_0 = \frac{\sum Y_i W_i}{\sum W_i} = \frac{18,108}{360} = 50.3$$

A good place to start looking for locations is around (45.5, 50.3). As this is very close to warehouse 6 it might be better to expand on this site rather than look for an entirely new location (as shown in Figure 5.6).

	A	B	C	D	E	F
1	Centre of gravity					
2						
3						
4		X	Y	Weight	X*Weight	Y*Weight
5	Supplier					
6		1 91	8	40	3640	320
7		2 93	35	60	5580	2100
8		3 3	86	80	240	6880
9						
10	Warehouse					
11		1 83	26	24	1992	624
12		2 89	54	16	1424	864
13		3 63	87	22	1386	1914
14		4 11	85	38	418	3230
15		5 9	16	52	468	832
16		6 44	48	28	1232	1344
17						
18	Totals			360	16380	18108
19						
20	Centre of			X =	45.5	
21	Gravity			Y =	50.3	

Figure 5.5 Calculation of centre of gravity

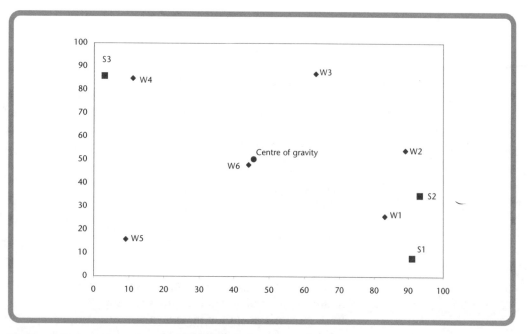

Figure 5.6 Locations for van Hendrick Industries

The centre of gravity can give a reasonable location, but we can easily show one of its weaknesses. Suppose you work in Alberta, Canada and want to deliver 20 tonnes of materials a day to Edmonton and 40 tonnes a day to Calgary. These two cities are connected by a straight road 300 km long (see Figure 5.7). If the costs of getting deliveries from suppliers are the same regardless of location, where would you build a warehouse?

The centre of gravity is $((40 \times 300 + 20 \times 0)/60 =)$ 200 km from Edmonton. A warehouse here would have to deliver 200×20 tonne/kilometres to Edmonton and 100×40 tonne/kilometres to Calgary, giving a total of 8000 tonne/kilometres. But if you built the warehouse in Calgary, you would only have to move $20 \times 300 = 6000$ tonne/kilometres to Edmonton. This gives one rule of thumb, which says that a good location is in the centre of highest demand.

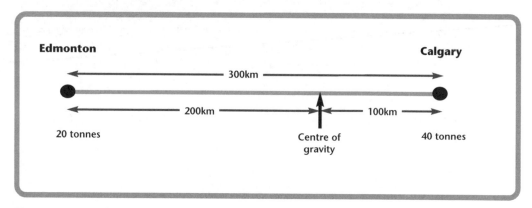

Figure 5.7 Weakness of the centre of gravity method

Adjusting the model

We can improve the basic centre of gravity model in many ways. We can, for example, use actual road distances rather than the straight-line distances of our calculation. Often the speed of delivery is more important than the distance, so we can replace distance by travel time, or we can use some more direct measure of cost. We can also adjust the basic calculation, perhaps replacing the straightforward tonne/kilometre measure by a weighted value or some function of cost. Another approach is to use an iterative calculation which keeps searching for a better location. One method of this kind takes an initial location, and then iteratively improves it using the equations.[3]

$$x^{n+1} = \frac{\sum c_j w_j x_j / d_j}{\sum c_j w_j / d_j}$$

$$y^{n+1} = \frac{\sum c_j w_j y_j / d_j}{\sum c_j w_j / d_j}$$

where: x^{n+1} and y^{n+1} are the next iterated values for the facility co-ordinates
x_j and y_j are the co-ordinates of customers and suppliers
c_j = cost of moving one unit of material a unit distance
w_j = weight moved to or from location j
d_j = distance from the last iterated position of the facility to location j

Infinite set approaches only need a limited amount of data, typically the locations of customers and suppliers and some measure of distance or cost. But even this data has to be approximated, as few organisations know exactly who their customers will be until they start local operations. Another problem is that the location suggested might not be practical. There may be no suitable site available anywhere near the solution, or available sites may be too expensive, or further development may be prohibited, or there may be no roads or workforce, or the solution might be at the top of a mountain or in the sea. To get around such problems, we can use the alternative approach of identifying available sites and choosing the best.

LOGISTICS IN PRACTICE

Warehouse locations in the USA

For many products we can use the population of an area as a surrogate for the demand. The population of Stockholm is three times the population of Oslo, so we can assume that the demand for a wide range of products is also three times as large. Then we can look at the population distribution, and use the centre of gravity of population to approximate the centre of gravity of demand.

In the UK the centre of gravity of population is near to Birmingham, and this might be a useful place to start looking for a facility. In the USA the centre of gravity of population is in Terre Haute, Indiana.

We can go further with this approach and find the best locations for two or more facilities. With continental USA as an example we get the following results.

Number of facilities	Best locations	Average distance to a customer
1	Terre Haute, IN	859 miles
2	Chillicothe, OH; Fresno, CA	490 miles
3	Allentown, PA; Paducah, KY; Fresno, CA	378 miles
4	Caldwell, NJ; Cincinnati, OH; Stockton, CA; Dallas, TX	322 miles
5	Summit, NJ; Macon, GA; Dallas, TX; Stockton, CA; Gary, IN	268 miles

With ten facilities, the average distance to a customer is 174 miles. These figures are based on raw population data, but we could refine the approach to look at different parts of the population or target markets. A lot of software combines geographic and demographic data, and does this kind of analyses to find the best locations for serving different types of market.

Sources: Anon. (1998) Are you putting goods in the right location? *Purchasing* **124**(6), 115 and report by Chicago Consulting

FEASIBLE SET APPROACHES

Costing models

Feasible set approaches identify available sites, compare them, and find the best. An obvious analysis calculates the total cost of working from each location and finds the cheapest. In practice, many of the costs of running a facility are fixed regardless of its location. Then instead of looking at the total cost, we can concentrate on those costs that vary, particularly the transport and operating costs.

Total variable cost = Operating cost + Inward transport cost + Outward transport cost of a facility

Locations near to customers have higher costs of inward transport, and those near to suppliers have higher costs of outward transport, so the best location is likely to be somewhere in between. An obvious problem, though, is that we do not know the real costs before we actually open a facility. How, for example, can we know the cost of outward transport when we do not know in advance who our customers will be or how much they will demand? Even if we have good forecasts of demand, the costs will change over time and the analysis becomes outdated. As a result, these cost calculations are useful for comparisons, but they are not necessarily the costs that will actually be incurred.

If we can only use the costs for comparisons, we might as well make the calculations as easy as possible. For example, the operating costs in nearby locations might be virtually the same, so we can remove these from the equation and concentrate of transport costs. It is difficult to find the exact cost of delivering to any particular customer, so we can assume that the transport cost is proportional to the distance moved. In practice, of course, the cost depends on more than distance, and is also affected by the type of vehicles, frequency of journeys, routes taken, ways of combining customer orders, organisation of drivers, order patterns, and so on. Nonetheless, we are only using these figures for comparison, so can use any reasonable approximations. Another shortcut uses map references or co-ordinates to find the rectilinear distance between points.

$$\text{Rectilinear Distance} = \frac{\text{Difference in}}{\text{X co-ordinates}} + \frac{\text{Difference in}}{\text{Y co-ordinates}}$$

Then we can use this simple measure to identify the location with the lowest total value of load × rectilinear distance moved.

WORKED EXAMPLE

Bannerman Industries want to build a depot to serve seven major customers located at co-ordinates (100, 110), (120,130), (220, 150), (180, 210), (140, 170), (130, 180) and (170, 80). Average weekly demands, in vehicle loads, are 20, 5, 9, 12, 24, 11 and 8 respectively. Three alternative locations are available at (120, 90), (160, 170) and (180,130). Which is the best site if operating costs and inward transport costs are the same for each location?

Solution

Figure 5.8 shows a map for this problem.

As operating and transport inward costs are the same for all three locations, we only need a way of comparing the costs of local deliveries from each. For simplicity we will use the rectilinear distance to customers. Then the distance from A to customer 1 is:

difference in   + difference in   = (120–100) + (130–110) = 40
X co-ordinates   Y co-ordinates

The calculations for this problem are given in Figure 5.9, which shows that site B is clearly best.

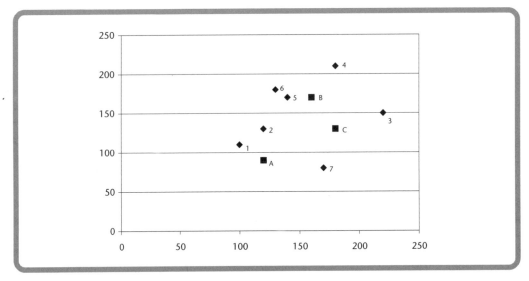

Figure 5.8 Map for Bannerman Industries

	A	B	C	D	E	F	G	H
1	Customer		Site A		Site B		Site C	
2		Load	Distance	Distance * Load	Distance	Distance * Load	Distance	Distance * Load
3	1	20	40	800	120	2400	100	2000
4	2	5	40	200	80	400	60	300
5	3	9	160	1440	80	720	60	540
6	4	12	180	2160	60	720	80	960
7	5	24	100	2400	20	480	80	1920
8	6	11	100	1100	40	440	100	1100
9	7	8	60	480	100	800	60	480
10								
11	Totals			8580		5960		7300

Figure 5.9 Comparison of sites

We can use a version of this costing model to find the best number of facilities. The argument runs as follows.

● If an organisation concentrates activities in a few key locations – such as main logistics centres – inward transport consists of large deliveries made to a few facilities and the cost is low. However, the few facilities are, on average, further away from customers and the outward transport cost is high.

● If there are a large number of spread-out facilities – such as retail shops – inward transport consists of small deliveries to more destinations and the cost is high. The facilities are, on average, nearer to customers, so they have the benefits of higher customer service and lower outward transport cost.

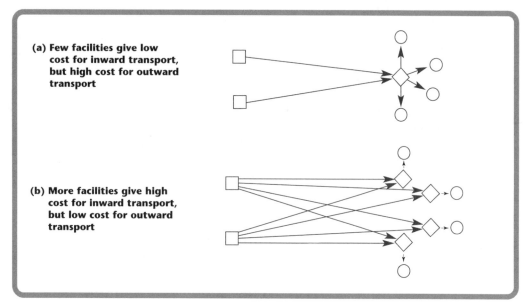

Figure 5.10 Variation in transport cost with number of facilities

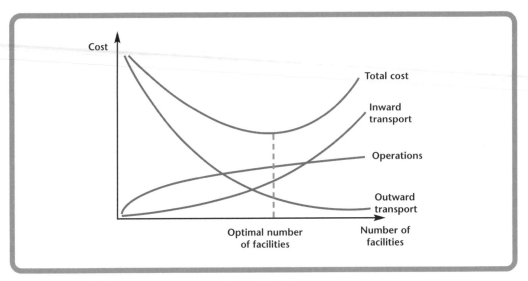

Figure 5.11 Finding the optimal number of facilities

⬤ Operating costs also vary with facility size, with larger facilities generally more efficient and giving economies of scale. Remember, though, that larger facilities do not necessarily give economies of scale, and there can be real 'diseconomies' caused by higher cost of supervision, co-ordination, communication and so on.

Figure 5.10 shows how these transport costs vary. If we plot transport and operating costs against the number of facilities we get the pattern shown in Figure 5.11. This has a clear minimum which corresponds to the optimal number of facilities. In practice, of course, before we make such a decision we have to consider many other factors, such as management costs, communications, fixed costs, employment effects, customer service, information flows, and so on.

Scoring models

Costing models can give useful comparisons, but they have weaknesses, including the difficulty of finding accurate costs, data that depends on accounting conventions, costs that vary over time, customer locations not being known in advance, order sizes not known in advance, factors that cannot be costed, and so on. It is often better to avoid these problems and use some other method for comparison. The most common alternative is a **scoring model**.

Scoring models emphasise the factors that are important for locations, but which cannot easily be costed or quantified. For example, an attractive lifestyle in one location would certainly benefit employees, reduce employee turnover and assist in recruiting – but we could not assign a realistic cost or measure to the lifestyle. This is a common problem and Andel[4] quotes a commercial estate agent's view that, 'More often than not, the decision on site selection is based upon factors you can't always put in a matrix or express quantitatively.'

Even if we cannot quantify the important factors, we still need to identify them. Gooley[5] says that the important factors in location decisions are the infrastructure, proximity of suppliers and customers, political and tax considerations, and international trade conditions. A more complete list of factors includes:

- *In the region and country*
    - availability, skills and productivity of workforce
    - local and national government policies, regulations, grants and attitudes
    - political stability
    - economic strength and trends
    - climate and attractiveness of locations
    - quality of life – including health, education, welfare and culture
    - location of major suppliers and markets
    - infrastructure – particularly transport and communications
    - culture and attitudes of people.

- *In the city or area*
    - population and population trends
    - availability of sites and development issues
    - number, size and location of competitors
    - local regulations and restrictions on operations
    - community feelings
    - local services, including transport and utilities.

- *In the site*
    - amount and type of passing traffic
    - ease of access and parking
    - access to public transport
    - organisations working nearby
    - total costs of the site
    - potential for expansion or changes.

Although we cannot quantify these factors directly, we can move in this direction by giving each a score. This is what happens with hotels: you cannot measure the quality of an hotel, but when you see that one has been awarded five stars you know that it is very good. This is the basis of scoring models, which have the following five steps:

Step 1   decide the relevant factors in a decision
Step 2   give each factor a maximum possible score that shows its importance
Step 3   consider each location in turn and give an actual score for each factor, up to this maximum
Step 4   add the total score for each location and find the highest
Step 5   discuss the result and make a final decision.

WORKED EXAMPLE

Williams-Practar considered five alternative locations for a new warehouse for their music distribution business. After many discussions they compiled a list of important factors, their maximum scores, and actual scores for each site. What is the relative importance of each factor? Which site would you recommend?

EXAMPLE
continued

Factor	Maximum score	A	B	C	D	E
Climate	10	8	6	9	7	5
Infrastructure	20	12	16	15	8	13
Accessibility	10	6	8	7	9	9
Construction cost	5	3	1	4	2	1
Community attitude	10	6	8	7	4	8
Government views	5	2	2	3	4	3
Closeness to suppliers	15	10	10	13	13	10
Closeness to customers	20	12	10	15	17	10
Availability of workforce	5	1	2	4	5	3

Solution

The most important factors are the available infrastructure and closeness to customers, with 20 points each. The closeness of suppliers is a bit less important with up to 15 points, and then come climate, accessibility and community attitude with up to 10 points each. Construction cost, government views and availability of workforce are least important.

Adding the scores for each location gives:

Location	A	B	C	D	E
Total Scores	60	63	77	69	62

These scores suggest that location C is the best. The company should now consider all other relevant information before coming to a final decision.

Rather than changing the maximum score for each factor, some people prefer to give each factor the same maximum score, but multiply the actual score by a weight to show its importance. In the example above we might give each factor a score out of ten, and then multiply the scores for climate by 1.0, the scores for infrastructure by 2.0, the scores for accessibility by 1.0, the scores for construction cost by 0.5 and so on.

Important factors for scoring models

The list of important factors and weight given to each obviously depends on the circumstances. Manufacturers look for economies of scale by building large facilities that are often near to raw materials. Then decisions about the location for a new factory are dominated by:

- availability of a workforce with appropriate skills
- labour relations and community attitudes
- environment and quality of life for employees
- closeness of suppliers and services

- quality of infrastructure
- government policies toward industry.

On the other hand, services cannot be kept in stock, so they look for smaller locations that are near to customers. Their decisions about location put more weight on:

- population density
- socio-economic characteristics of the nearby population
- location of competitors and other services
- location of other attractions such as retail shops
- convenience for passing traffic and public transport
- ease of access and convenient parking
- visibility of site.

The objectives in locating factories and services are clearly different, which is why town centres have shops but no factories, and industrial estates have factories but no shops.

LOGISTICS IN PRACTICE

Intel in Costa Rica

Deloitte & Touche Fantus developed a list of factors that high-tech industries consider in their location decisions. This includes:

Essential factors:
- skilled and educated workforce
- proximity of research institutions
- attractive quality of life
- access to venture capital.

Important factors:
- reasonable cost of doing business
- established technology industry
- adequate infrastructure
- favourable business climate and regulations.

Desirable factors:
- established suppliers and partners
- community incentives.

Intel Corporation is the world's leading producer of semiconductor devices. In the mid 1990s it was planning a new expansion, and Costa Rica was keen to get the development. To encourage Intel, Costa Rica offered eight years free of income tax, followed by four years at half rate, duty-free import of materials, and unrestricted movement of money into and out of the country. In addition, they granted licenses to foreign airlines to increase the number of international flights, built a new power sub-station for the site, reduced their cost of electricity by 28%, and reduced the liability for corporation tax.

Intel decided to locate a $300 million semiconductor testing and assembly plant near to San José, which started work in 1998 and, within two years, employed 2000 people.

Chuck Mulloy, a spokesman for Intel, said: 'When we are considering a site we use a multifaceted set of criteria. Incentives are part of this.'

Sources: Wall Street Journal Special Report, 25 September 2000, and website at www.interactive. wsj.com

NETWORK MODELS

Sometimes it is difficult to relate the two approaches we have described to actual road layout and geographic features. There are, however, many databases of road networks that automatically find the best routes between two points, such as Microsoft AutoRoute Express and Softkey Journey Planner. Typically, you supply the postcode of starting and finishing locations, and the package finds the shortest, fastest or cheapest route, or route with some other features. Then it gives details of the journey, locations and any other relevant information. Such systems can be put into vehicles, and combined with global positioning and traffic monitoring systems to find the best route from any current position to an endpoint.

These electronic maps of road networks allow another approach to location, which is based on actual road layouts. A huge number of models have been built for this kind of analysis, so we will illustrate typical approaches by two standard models, known as the single median problem and the covering problem.

Single median problem

Imagine a network of towns connected by roads. There are demands for some product in each town, and you want to locate a depot to deliver to these towns. In principle the best location could be anywhere on the network, and might be on a roadside rather than in one of the towns. However, a standard analysis[6] shows that the best location is always in a town. This makes the problem much easier, as we only have to compare locations in each town and identify the one that gives the best value for some measure of performance. A common measure is average travel distance or time, and finding the shortest is called the **single median problem**.

The easiest way to find the single median starts with a matrix of the shortest distances between towns. In practice, we can find this from route planning software, or using some surrogate measure such as the straight-line or rectilinear distance. To find the shortest average distance, we have to combine these distances with the loads carried. So we multiply the distances by the demands at each town, to get a matrix of the weight-distances. Then we add these for each town, and find the lowest overall value.

WORKED EXAMPLE

Ian Bruce delivers goods to eight towns, with locations and demands as shown in Figure 5.12. He wants to find the location for a logistics centre that minimises the average delivery time to these towns. Where should he start looking?

Solution

This is a single median problem, so we start with a matrix showing the minimum distances between each town, as shown in Figure 5.13. This matrix also shows the weight to be moved in column B. If we take one column, say C, this shows the distance from a centre located in AL to each other town. If we multiply this distance by the corresponding weight in column B, we get the weight-distance for each town. Then adding these down the column gives the total weight-distance for a logistics centre in AL, shown in Row 12.

EXAMPLE
continued

Weight-distance of a centre at AL = $(10 \times 0) + (15 \times 15) + (25 \times 22) + (20 \times 24)$
$\qquad + (20 \times 31) + (10 \times 28) + (10 \times 32) + (15 \times 36) \qquad = 3015$

Repeating this calculation for each of the other towns allows us to compare the costs across Row 12. As you can see, town EN has the lowest total cost, and is the single median. Ian should start looking for a location around this town.

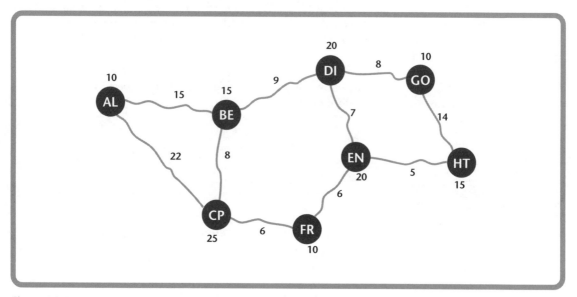

Figure 5.12 Map of Ian Bruce's problem

	A	B	C	D	E	F	G	H	I	J
1										
2		Weight	AL	BE	CP	DI	EN	FR	GO	HT
3	AL	10	0	15	22	24	31	28	32	36
4	BE	15	15	0	8	9	16	14	17	21
5	CP	25	22	8	0	17	12	6	25	17
6	DI	20	24	9	17	0	7	13	8	12
7	EN	20	31	16	12	7	0	6	15	5
8	FR	10	28	14	6	13	6	0	21	11
9	GO	10	32	17	25	8	15	21	0	14
10	HT	15	36	21	17	12	5	11	14	0
11										
12	Totals	125	3015	1475	1485	1330	1275	1395	2080	1690

Figure 5.13 Spreadsheet of calculations for Ian Bruce

Covering problem

Sometimes the average distance or time to a facility is less important than the maximum time. Classic examples of this are fire engines and ambulances which try to respond to emergencies within a maximum time. In the same way, suppliers often guarantee deliveries within one working day. This is an example of the **covering problem**.

There are two versions of the covering problem. In the first version, we are looking for the single location that gives the best service to all towns – in other words we want the location that gives the lowest value for the maximum time needed to reach any town. If, say, we choose location A the longest time to reach any customer is 4 hours, but if we choose location B the longest time to reach any customer is only 3 hours – so location B is clearly better. To solve this problem we simply compare the longest journey times from each location, and choose the location with the shortest of these.

The second version of the covering problem specifies a level of service that must be achieved. This might need an ambulance to arrive within ten minutes, or a parcel to be delivered within four hours. The problem is then to find the number of facilities needed to achieve this, and their best locations.

For both of these problems the best location might, in principle, be at any point of the road network. However, we can again use the standard finding that the best location is always in one of the towns. This is a common result for network problems, and it makes them much easier to solve.

WORKED EXAMPLE

Figure 5.14 shows part of a road network, with the travel time (in minutes) shown on each link. Where would you locate a depot to give best customer service? How many depots would be needed to give a maximum journey of 15 minutes?

Solution

We could, of course, do the calculations for this covering problem, finding the maximum time for each town and identifying the best, and then finding the combination of towns that gives service times of less than 15 minutes. There is no need for this, as a lot of software solves network problems and Figure 5.15 shows a printout from a simple package. As you can see, if a single location is needed the package recommends town C, giving a maximum journey of 25 minutes. If this is too much, facilities at A and I will reduce the maximum journey to 15 minutes.

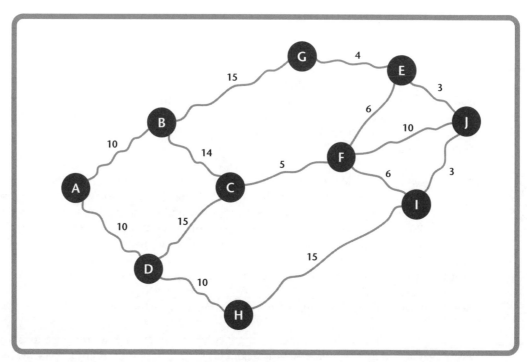

Figure 5.14 Road network showing travel time in minutes between locations

	A	B	C	D	E	F	G	H	I	J	K
1	Covering problem										
2											
3	Distance matrix										
4											
5		A	B	C	D	E	F	G	H	I	J
6	A	0	10	24	10	29	29	25	20	35	32
7	B	10	0	14	20	19	19	15	30	25	22
8	C	24	14	0	15	11	5	15	25	11	14
9	D	10	20	15	0	26	20	30	10	25	29
10	E	29	19	11	26	0	6	4	23	8	3
11	F	29	19	5	20	6	0	10	21	6	10
12	G	25	15	15	30	4	10	0	27	12	7
13	H	20	30	25	10	23	21	27	0	15	20
14	I	35	25	11	25	8	6	12	15	0	5
15	J	32	22	14	29	3	10	7	20	5	0
16	Maximum	35	30	25	30	29	29	30	30	35	32
17											
18	Single location			C							
19	Maximum time			25							
20											
21	Two locations			A	I						
22			A	0							
23			B	10							
24			C		11						
25			D	10							
26			E		8						
27			F		6						
28			G		12						
29			H		15						
30			I		0						
31			J		5						
32	Maximum time			10	15						

Figure 5.15 Solution to the covering problem

LOCATION PLANNING

We have described several approaches to location, but these are by no means the only ones. Useful models range from simple rules of thumb (such as, 'locate near to a similar operation that is already working successfully') through to more complex methods (such as mathematical programming). Whichever methods you choose, they need not work in isolation. We could, for example, use an infinite set approach to find the best general area, followed by a finite set approach to compare available sites nearby. A more formal procedure has the following five steps:

Step 1   Identify the features needed in a new location, determined by the business and logistics strategies, structure of the supply chain, aims, customers, and other relevant factors. Look for regions and countries that can best supply these.

Step 2   Within the identified region, use an infinite set approach – such as the centre of gravity or similar model – to find the best area for locations.

Step 3   Search around this area to find a feasible set of available locations.

Step 4   Use a feasible set approach – such as a costing model or scoring model – to compare these alternatives.

Step 5   Discuss all available information and come to a decision.

Locating facilities is always difficult, and it is important enough for organisations to look at every available analysis before reaching a conclusion. An important point is that this hierarchy of location decisions should fit into the logistics strategy. If the logistics strategy calls for short delivery times, then facilities must be in locations that can achieve this; if the strategy calls for low costs, facilities will probably be centralised to get economies of scale.

We can describe a useful approach for co-ordinating location decisions with other decisions about the supply chain. For this, we start by recalling what we want the supply chain to do, then examine the current supply chain's performance, identify any problems and design ways of overcoming these. To be more specific, we can use the following procedure:

1.   *Examine the overall aims,* looking at the logistics strategy and other plans to identify the aims and goals of logistics in terms of customer service, costs, timing, and so on.

2.   *Do a logistics audit,* describing the details of the current logistics system, including the location of facilities, network connecting these, measures of performance, and industry benchmarks.

3.   *Identify mismatches,* where there are differences between the aims (from step 1) and actual performance (from step 2).

4.   *Examine alternatives for overcoming the mismatch,* looking in general terms to see where and how the structure of the supply chain can be improved.

5.   *Location decisions,* having set the general features of the supply chain, look in detail at the facilities needed. Use appropriate models to find the best locations and sizes for these facilities.

6.   *Confirm the locations,* making sure that the locations identified in step 5 really are best, and work with the structure identified in step 4.

7.   *Implement and monitor the solutions,* doing whatever is needed to execute the changes and continuing to check performance.

In this procedure you can see that part 4 designs the general features of the supply chain. Then part 5 adds some details by finding the best locations – using the five-step procedure described above. As with most planning, this is more complicated than it seems, and we usually need to iteratively revise the plans until we find a satisfactory solution. By part 6 we have confirmed that the locations are good, and continue to implement the results. We return to this theme of planning in the next chapter.

CHAPTER REVIEW

❑ Location decisions find the best geographical positions for the facilities in a supply chain. These are important, strategic decisions with long-term effects on an organisation's performance.

❑ A location decision is needed whenever an organisation expands, contracts, or there are major changes to its operations. The choice of best location depends on many different factors.

❑ There is a hierarchy of location decisions. This starts with a decision about the region or country to work in, which is influenced by the logistics strategy. Following decisions identify the best area, town and eventually the specific site.

❑ Infinite set approaches use geometrical arguments to show where the best location would be in principle. We illustrated this with the centre of gravity method.

❑ Finite set approaches compare a limited number of feasible locations and find the best. We illustrated this by costing and scoring models.

❑ Sometimes it is better to consider location in the context of a network of towns and roads. There are many models for this, which we illustrated by the median and covering problems.

❑ Finding the best location must fit in with broader business and logistics plans. We described a general approach to planning which brings these different ideas together.

CASE STUDY — *Brenner Refrigeration Sales*

John Brenner had worked for the same domestic appliance retailer for over twenty years when he saw an advertisement from an East European manufacturer which wanted to start selling its brand of appliances in the UK. John answered the advertisement and spent a year preparing and negotiating with the manufacturer.

The manufacturer was not keen to have all its distribution done by a new and untried company. In the end John agreed to set up a company called Brenner Refrigeration Sales, and the manufacturers agreed to give him exclusive rights to

CASE STUDY   *continued*

distribute their products throughout Britain for two years. The agreement would be reviewed after a year and renegotiated after two years.

John invited three other directors to join the company. Their first problem was to find a location for the head office and main logistics centre. This centre would receive appliances directly from the manufacturer, and deliver them to retailers around the country. The directors realised that their future success depended on this site, but found it difficult to agree on a location.

They considered passing the problem to a firm of management consultants, but one of the directors discovered that similar companies paid up to £50,000 for an initial report and £125,000 for a more detailed study. The directors felt that this was too expensive and they would have to solve the problem themselves. The following summary gives an idea of their discussions.

- *Stefan Maior worked as a service repairman for many years before being promoted to service manager. He is now 54 years old and is looking for an opportunity to make some money for his retirement. Stefan argues that the location should be in Leeds. The appliances could be shipped to Liverpool or Hull, and then brought to Leeds by train. Leeds has a good transport system and it is a major population centre. Two of the directors live in Leeds and they understand local conditions.*

- *Pradesh Gupta has a degree in mechanical engineering, and has worked as an economic consultant in eastern Europe. He knows the manufacturer and is impressed by their progressive attitudes. Pradesh is critical of Stefan's approach as being old fashioned and relying more on where he feels at home than on any business criterion. He says that the sale of appliances is likely to depend on the population so they should look at a map of Britain, see where the main centres of population are, see how many appliances they expect to sell in each of these, and then do some fairly straightforward analyses to find the best location.*

- *Fiona McGregor worked in a retail bank, specialising in consumer loans. She is now 32 years old and is ambitiously looking for a long-term career that is both challenging and financially rewarding. She does not like the idea of only opening a logistics centre, but says that they should become more directly involved in sales to final customers. They would need a head office – probably in London – a central receiving area near to a port, and showrooms around Britain. The fastest way of doing this is to take over an existing retailer, or several retailers, to give coverage throughout the country.*

C A S E   S T U D Y   *continued*

■ *John Brenner says that Fiona McGregor's scheme is too ambitious, while the other two put the convenience of the company above the customers. He says there is only one way to sell appliances and that is to give customers a product they want, in a location they can get to. John's idea is to open a logistics centre to serve retailers, combined with a cash-and-carry warehouse for sales direct to customers. To find the best location for this, they should see where successful distributors already work, and open their facilities nearby. They would need a large dominating location that customers can see from a long way off, that they pass frequently, where they regularly visit to shop, and where other distributors have traditionally been able to sell.*

The time is now getting short for a decision. The directors are concerned that if they delay any longer the manufacturer will consider them indecisive, and they will not have time to give a good showing at their first year's review. To build entirely new premises could take a year. Alternatively they could find existing premises that are empty, or they could rent temporary premises until the company finds more suitable, permanent premises.

C A S E   S T U D Y

Questions

- If you were a director of Brenner Refrigeration Sales, what would you do now?
- What kind of facilities does Brenner need? What factors are important for the location?
- What location – or locations – would you recommend?

P R O J E C T

Poor Locations

Find an example of an organisation that has opened facilities in the wrong location, and see why their decisions went wrong. You might find a shop that seems to change hands surprisingly quickly, or a closed factory on an industrial estate. Unfortunately, you can find many recent examples, as well as historical ones (such as the Hillman car plant outside Glasgow, and Victorian railway stations built for towns that never developed).

P R O B L E M S

1. Mai Lao Industries manufacture 70 tonnes of goods a week in factory A and 50 tonnes a week in factory B. The map co-ordinates of these factories are (14,11) and (54,48) respectively. These goods are delivered to 14 main customers whose average weekly requirements and co-ordinates are shown below. The company wants to improve its customer service and decides to open a logistics centre. There are four possible locations, each with the same operating costs, located at (20,8), (61,19), (29,32) and (50,22). Which of these locations is best?

Customer	Demand	Co-ordinates	Customer	Demand	Co-ordinates
1	4	(11,16)	8	16	(12,69)
2	11	(30,9)	9	2	(27,38)
3	8	(43,27)	10	4	(51,6)
4	7	(54,52)	11	6	(43,16)
5	17	(29,62)	12	3	(54,16)
6	10	(11,51)	13	12	(12,60)
7	15	(8,10)	14	18	(12, 3)

2. A new electronics factory is planned in an area that is encouraging industrial growth. There are five alternative sites. A management team is considering these sites and has suggested the important factors, relative weights and site scores shown below. What is the relative importance of each factor? Which site appears best?

Factor	Maximum Score	A	B	C	D	E
Government grants	10	2	4	8	8	5
Community attitude	12	8	7	5	10	5
Availability of engineers	15	10	8	8	10	5
Experienced workforce	20	20	15	15	10	15
Nearby suppliers	8	4	3	6	3	2
Education centres	5	5	4	1	1	5
Housing	5	2	3	5	3	2

3. Find the centre of gravity of the data in question 1. What would be the transport cost of a distribution centre located there? Can you find a cheaper solution?

4. An assembly plant is planned to take components from four suppliers and send finished goods to eight regional warehouses. The locations of these and the amounts supplied or demanded are shown in the following table. Where would you start looking for a site for the assembly plant?

Location	X,Y co-ordinates	Supply/Demand
Supplier 1	7,80	140
Supplier 2	85,35	80
Supplier 3	9,81	120
Supplier 4	11,62	70

P R O B L E M S

continued

Location	X,Y co-ordinates	Supply/Demand
Warehouse 1	12,42	45
Warehouse 2	60,9	65
Warehouse 3	92,94	25
Warehouse 4	8,79	45
Warehouse 5	10,83	60
Warehouse 6	59,91	35
Warehouse 7	83,49	50
Warehouse 8	85,30	85

5. Pierre Malpasse is opening a logistics centre for his French clothing operations. If the likely demand is proportional to the population, where should he start looking for locations?

6. Figure 5.16 shows part of a road network and population of nine towns. Where would you start looking for a location for a new warehouse?

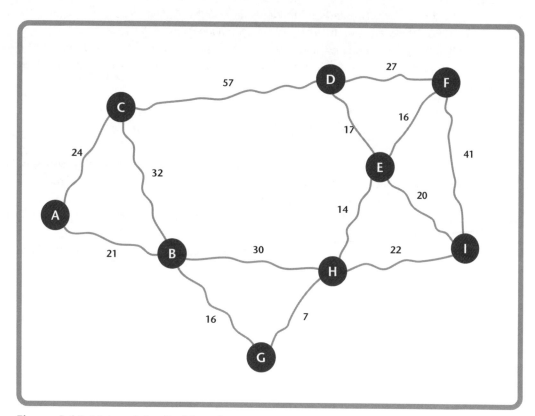

Figure 5.16 Network for Problem 6

DISCUSSION QUESTIONS

1. If a company chooses a poor site it can always move to a better one. Such change is an unavoidable part of business. Do you think this is true?
2. Which areas of the world do you think will have the fastest economic development over the next twenty years? How will this affect location decisions?
3. What costs should be considered in a location decision? Is cost always an important factor? What other factors should be considered? What effect do government grants have?
4. Mathematical models for location take a simplified view and they only include the few factors that can most easily be quantified. So how useful are they for real decisions?
5. What features would you expect to see in computer software that helps with location decisions? Do a survey of relevant packages. How do they work, and what analyses do they do?
6. Different cultures are the main problem of locating facilities in different countries. They make it impossible to standardise procedures, have consistent operations, compare performance, or anything else. Do you think this is true?

REFERENCES

1. Hoover E.M. (1948) *The Location of Economic Activity*, McGraw-Hill, New York.
2. Haley K.B. (1963) Siting of depots, *International Journal of Production Research*, **2**, 41–5.
3. Eilon S., Watson-Gandy C.D.T. and Christofides N. (1971) *Distribution Management*, Griffin, London.
4. Andel T. (1996) Site location tools, *Transport and Distribution*, June, 77–81.
5. Gooley T.B. (1998) The geography of logistics, *Logistics Management Distribution Report*, 37(1), 63–6.
6. Ahituv N. and Berman O. (1988) *Operations Management of Distributed Service Networks*, Plenum Press, New York.

Further reading

Drezner Z. (1995) *Facility Location: A Survey of Applications and Methods*, Springer-Verlag, Secausus, NJ.

Harrington J.W. and Warf B. (1995) *Industrial Location: Principles and Practice*, Routledge, London.

Hayter R. (1997) *The Dynamics of Industrial Location*, John Wiley, Chichester.

Salvaneschi L. and Akin C. (eds) (1996) *Location, Location, Location: How to Select the Best Site for Your Business*, Oasis Press, Central Point, OR.

Schriederjans M.J. (1999) *International Facility Acquisition and Location Analysis*, Quorum Books, Wesport, CT.

Waters C.D.J. (1999) *Global Logistics and Distribution Planning*, Kogan Page, London.

CHAPTER 6

Planning Resources

CONTENTS

- Aims of the chapter
- Types of planning
- Capacity planning
- Adjusting capacity
- Tactical planning
- Short-term schedules
- Chapter review
- Case study – Primal Autoparts
- Project – Network planning
- Discussion questions
- References
- Further reading

AIMS OF THE CHAPTER

After reading this chapter you should be able to:

- DISCUSS the role of planning in logistics
- MEASURE the capacity of a supply chain
- USE a standard approach to capacity planning
- DISCUSS some practical difficulties with capacity planning
- SEE how to design medium-term tactical plans
- EXPAND the tactical plans into short-term schedules

TYPES OF PLANNING

The last two chapters looked at the design of a supply chain. They considered the structure, based on the type and number of facilities, and the best locations for these facilities. Now we are going to see how to use the chain and how materials actually move through it. The next two chapters look at questions of planning. We see how activities along the supply chain are planned, and how resources are controlled.

All activities have to be planned – which means that we design timetables to show when they will be done. Delivery plans, for example, might show the planned schedules for deliveries over the next month. If an organisation does not plan for the future, it can only work from hour-to-hour, without any continuity, and in constant danger of meeting unexpected circumstances that it cannot cope with. Planning lets us face the future with some confidence, rather than descending into chaos.

Planning the supply chain starts with the logistics strategy, which gives the overall aims. More details are added, and we get long-term plans which show how these aims will be achieved. These plans are, in turn, expanded with more details added. The plans move down through the organisation, where they are continually expanded and described in more detail. You can see this approach to planning in Capital Trains Corporation. Their business strategy gives a general description of their products, which provide public transport around Washington. The logistics strategy shows how they run a network of train services for commuters. The next level of planning forecasts demand for these services, and then makes sure that there

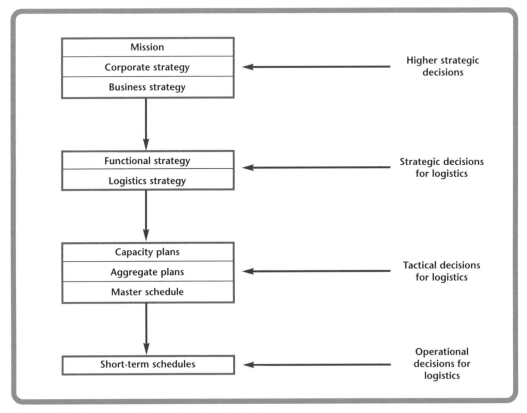

Figure 6.1 An approach to planning logistics

is enough capacity to meet this. In other words, they buy enough trains and hire enough staff to meet forecast demand. Then they move on to more detailed plans, which give their timetable of services, saying which routes their trains will serve and when they will arrive. Capital then expand these timetables into detailed schedules for individual trains and drivers, inspectors, materials, and any other resources they need.

As you can see, Capital Trains move down from strategic policies, through capacity plans, medium-term schedules of operations, and on to detailed timetables for all their resources. This is the usual approach to all planning (shown in Figure 6.1). People use different terms to describe these levels of planning, but the most common are:

● *Capacity plans*, which make sure there is enough capacity to meet long-term demand.
● *Aggregate plans*, which give summaries of the work done in related activities, typically by month at each location.
● *Master schedules*, which show a detailed timetable for all activities, typically by week.
● *Short-term schedules*, which show detailed timetables for jobs and resources, typically by day.

In this chapter we look at each of these in turn.

CAPACITY PLANNING

Definitions

The capacity of an operation is its maximum throughput in a specified time. All operations have some limit on their capacity: a factory has a maximum number of units it can make a week, a university has a maximum intake of students; an aeroplane has a maximum number of seats, and a lorry has a maximum weight it can carry. Sometime the stated capacity has an explicit reference to time, such as a maximum number of customers that can be served in a day. Even when it is not mentioned explicitly, every measure of capacity refers to time. The number of seats on an aeroplane sets the capacity as a maximum number of passengers on a particular flight; the number of rooms in a hotel sets the maximum number of guests who can stay each day.

Sometimes the capacity seems obvious – such as the number of seats on a bus or volume of a tanker. At other times the capacity is not so clear. How, for example, can you find the capacity of a supermarket, airport or train network? The usual answer has a surrogate measure, such as the maximum number of customers per square metre of floor space in a shopping mall, or the minimum distance between planes. Such measures come from discussion and agreement rather than any physical limit.

Capacity is an important concept for logistics, as it defines the maximum flow through the supply chain in a given time.

> The **CAPACITY** of a supply chain sets the maximum amount of product that can be delivered to final customers in a given time.

Most organisations do not like to work at full capacity, as this puts pressure on resources and people. Instead they work at a lower level that they can sustain over time. We allow for this disparity by defining different kinds of capacity. If you imagine a supply chain that is working in ideal conditions with no disruptions or problems of any kind, then the maximum throughput is its **designed capacity**. In reality, you seldom find such ideal conditions, and a more realistic measure is the **effective capacity**. This is the maximum throughput that can be sustained under normal conditions, and allows for disruptions, variations in performance, breakdowns, maintenance periods, and so on.

DESIGNED CAPACITY is the maximum possible throughput in ideal conditions.

EFFECTIVE CAPACITY is the maximum realistic throughput in normal conditions.

ACTUAL THROUGHPUT is normally lower than effective capacity.

Bottlenecks

Not all parts of a supply chain have the same capacity. There must be some part that limits overall throughput, and this forms a bottleneck. If you want to move some bulky materials from Johannesburg to Amsterdam, you might find a bottleneck at the docks in Cape Town. This part of the supply chain is working at full capacity, but other parts have spare capacity that is not used. The bottlenecks in a supply chain limit its overall capacity (as shown in Figure 6.2).

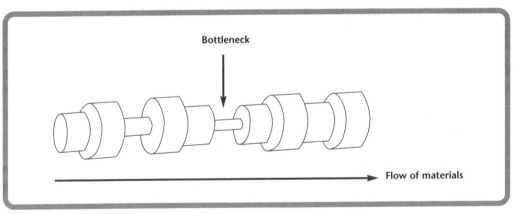

Figure 6.2 The bottleneck of a supply chain limits the capacity

WORKED EXAMPLE

The main bottling plant at J&R Softdrinks has a capacity of 80,000 litres a day, and works a seven-day week. It fills standard bottles of 750 ml, and these are passed to a packing area which can form up to 20,000 cases a day with 12 bottles each. The packing area

EXAMPLE
continued

works a five-day week. The cases are taken to warehouses by a transport company whose 8 lorries can each carry 300 cases, and make up to 4 trips a day for 7 days a week. There are two main warehouses, each of which can handle up to 30,000 cases a week. Local deliveries are made from the warehouses by a fleet of small vans that can handle everything passed to them by the warehouse. What is the capacity of this part of the distribution system? How can J&R increase the capacity?

Solution

We have information about five parts of the supply chain, and can use this to find the capacity of each part in consistent units, say bottles a week.

- The bottling plant has a capacity of 80,000 litres a day, or:

    $7 \times 80,000/0.75 = 746,666$ bottles a week

- The packing area has a capacity of 20,000 cases a day, or:

    $5 \times 12 \times 20,000 = 1,200,000$ bottles a week

- The transport company's lorries can handle 300 cases on each journey, so their capacity is:

    $7 \times 4 \times 8 \times 300 \times 12 = 806,400$ bottles a week

- Each warehouse can handle 30,000 cases a week, giving a capacity of:

    $2 \times 30,000 \times 12 = 720,000$ bottles a week

- We only know that the capacity of the delivery vans is greater than the capacity of the warehouses.

The capacity of this part of the supply chain is the smallest of these separate capacities, and you can see from Figure 6.3 that this is 720,000 bottles a week in the warehouses.

J&R can only increase capacity by expanding the warehouses. Improving other parts of the supply chain will have no effect at all. Of course, when one bottleneck is removed another is formed, and this will probably be at the bottling plant.

We have made a number of assumptions here about working days, reliability, and so on These factors would obviously have to be taken into account before any real decisions are made.

It is obvious that you can only increase the capacity of a supply chain by adding more capacity at the bottleneck. Unfortunately, you often see cases where this is not done. Transport companies, for example, that recruit more managers to give leadership, when they are actually short of drivers; bus stations increase the size of waiting rooms, when congestion in the arrivals bay is limiting the number of buses; airlines using bigger aeroplanes when passenger terminals are already over-crowded. Identifying and overcoming bottlenecks is clearly not as easy as it seems.

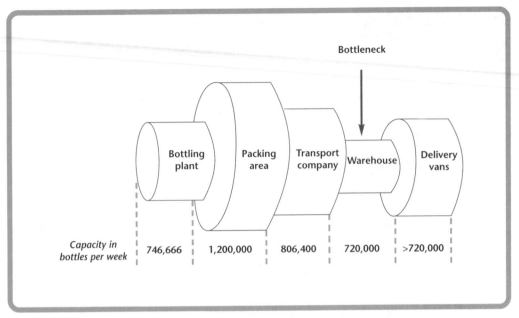

Figure 6.3 Capacity of distribution at J&R Softdrinks

Matching capacity and demand

The aim of capacity planning is to match the available capacity of facilities to the demands put on them. Any mismatch can be expensive. If capacity is less than demand, bottlenecks restrict the movement of materials, and customer service declines; if capacity is greater than demand, the organisation can move all its materials but it has spare capacity and underused resources. You can see these effects in shops. When you go into some shops there are not enough people serving and you have to wait. The capacity of the shop is less than demand, and you probably go to a competitor where the queues are shorter. In other shops there are many people waiting to serve customers – so there are no queues, but the cost of paying these underused people is added to your bill.

Thankfully, there is a standard approach to capacity planning that we can illustrate in the following worked example.

WORKED EXAMPLE

Anne Jenkins has a contract to deliver 100 computer systems a week to schools in South Wales. The systems have customised software installed, which takes an hour to test before delivery. The testing is done by trained staff, who achieve an average efficiency of 75%. They work a single eight-hour shift five days a week, but could move to double shifts or have overtime at weekends. How many testers should Anne employ?

WORKED EXAMPLE
continued

Solution

Each tester is available for $8 \times 5 = 40$ hours a week. Average efficiency is 75%, so their useful time is $40 \times 0.75 = 30$ hours a week. Each computer takes 1 hour to test, so each employee can test 30 systems a week. This is equivalent to saying:

- designed capacity = 40 units a tester a week
- effective capacity = 30 units a tester a week

There are several ways of meeting the demand of 100 units a week:

- Working a single shift on weekdays would need $100/30 = 3.33$ testers. If Anne only employs full-time testers, she has to round this up to 4. Then the utilisation of each would be $3.33/4 = 0.83$ or 83%.
- Employing 3 testers full-time, and one part-time tester for 1/3 time would meet all capacity with 100% utilisation.
- Using overtime at the weekends would need 3 full time testers who are willing to finish 10 tests at the weekend (working $10 / 0.75 = 13.3$ hours).

We could continue like this, suggesting alternative plans, adding allowances for holidays, problems, varying demand, and so on. Anne now needs to complete her capacity planning by comparing these alternatives and implementing the best.

From this example, you can see that the main steps in capacity planning find the resources needed, compare these with the resources available, and then look at alternative plans for overcoming any differences. To be more specific, we:

1. examine forecast demand and translate this into a capacity needed
2. find the capacity available in present facilities
3. identify mismatches between capacity needed and that available
4. suggest alternative plans for overcoming any mismatch
5. compare these plans and find the best
6. implement the best and monitor performance.

This is a standard approach to all kinds of planning, which is sometimes called **resource requirement planning**. Unfortunately, taking the steps in this straightforward sequence does not usually work. There can be a huge number of potential plans to consider, and it is impossible to look at them all in detail. It is also difficult to compare the alternatives, as there may be competing objectives and non-quantifiable factors. A more realistic view replaces the single procedure with an iterative one. This designs a plan and sees how close it gets to achieving its objectives; if it performs badly, the plan is modified to find improvements. In effect, steps 4 and 5 are repeated until they give a reasonable solution. This iterative procedure recognises that it is rarely possible to find the single 'best' plan, and we are really looking for one that is generally accepted.

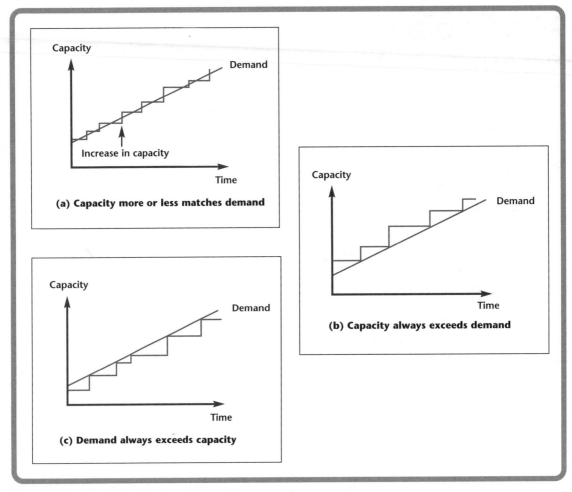

Figure 6.4 Alternative timing of capacity expansion

ADJUSTING CAPACITY

Problems with capacity planning

There are several practical problems with capacity planning. You can see one of these in the last worked example, where demand comes in small quantities and can take almost any value, while capacity comes in large discrete amounts. Typically, capacity can be increased by opening another shop, employing another person, using another vehicle, building another warehouse, and so on.

Suppose that the throughput of a supply chain rises steadily over time. Capacity should be increased at some point, but the increase will come as a discrete step. There is no way of exactly matching the discrete capacity to a continuous demand, so we have to use one of three basic strategies (as shown in Figure 6.4).

(a) more or less match capacity to demand, so that there is sometimes excess capacity and sometimes a shortage

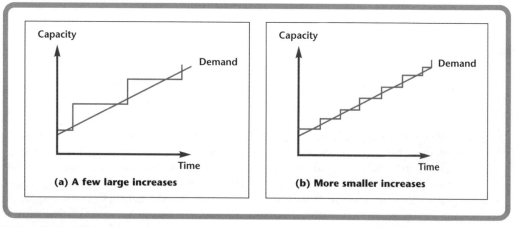

Figure 6.5 Alternative size of capacity expansion

(b) make capacity at least equal to demand by early expansion, which needs more investment in facilities and gives lower utilisation

(c) only add capacity when the additional facilities would be fully used, which has lower investment and high utilisation, but restricts throughput.

Each of these strategies is best in different circumstances. Factors that encourage an early increase in capacity include high cost of shortages, widely variable demand, varying efficiency, and low cost of spare capacity. The capacity of a large furniture shop, such as MFI, is largely set by the number of sales people. The nature of demand and relative costs, mean that the shop is likely to increase capacity early and make sure that there are always enough staff to serve customers. The main factor that encourages a delay before increasing capacity is the capital cost. New motorways are expensive and controversial, so expansions are delayed for as long as possible, and they are crowded as soon as they open.

A related question about changing capacity concerns the size of any changes. If you want to hire four new people over the next few months, should you recruit them all in one big campaign, or is it better to add them in smaller steps. Any change in capacity is likely to cause some disruption, so it might be better to have a few large increases rather than more smaller ones (as shown in Figure 6.5).

The benefits of large increases include longer periods without disruptions, less risk of not meeting unexpected demand, and the expansion might give economies of scale. On the other hand, there is not such a close match to demand, disruptions may be more serious, capital costs are higher, utilisation is low, and there are risks if demand changes.

Short-term adjustments to capacity

Capacity planning is largely a strategic function. Organisations can increase the overall capacity of a supply chain by opening a warehouse, designing a new process, opening new offices, or moving to a new location. They can reduce excess capacity by closing warehouses, shutting down a plant, or transferring facilities to other products. These are strategic decisions with long-term consequences. But an organisation can also adjust capacity by leasing extra space, working overtime, employing temporary staff, or sub-contracting parts of their work.

These are clearly tactical and operational decisions. It is fairer to say, then, that capacity planning includes decisions at all levels; strategic plans give the overall picture, modified by shorter term adjustments.

There are two ways of making these short-term adjustments to capacity:

- **capacity management** adjusts capacity to match demand
- **demand management** adjusts demand to match available capacity.

Imagine a wholesaler that runs a 12,000 square metre warehouse. This sets the normal capacity. If there is a temporary increase in business because of orders from a nearby construction site, the wholesaler can use capacity management and rent extra space for the duration of the construction project. Alternatively, there may be some reason why the wholesaler does not want to increase capacity, so it can use demand management to increase prices and reduce demand to match the existing capacity.

An obvious way of making short-term adjustments to capacity is to change the hours worked, by working overtime to increase capacity or undertime to reduce it. Ways of adjusting capacity include:

- *changing the work pattern* to match demand
- *employing part-time staff* to cover peak demands
- *using outside contractors*
- *renting or leasing extra facilities*
- *adjusting the speed of working*
- *rescheduling maintenance periods*
- *making the customer do some work*, such as packing their own bags in supermarkets.

Such adjustments cannot be done too often or too severely, as they can have significant effects on employees, operations and customers. The alternative is to adjust demand, and the obvious way of doing this is to change the price. There is, however, only a certain amount of flexibility here. Prices must be high enough to cover costs, low enough to be competitive, and not change too many times to confuse customers. Ways to adjust demand include:

- *vary the price*
- *limit the customers served*, by demanding specific 'qualifications'
- *change the marketing effort*
- *offer incentives to change demand patterns*, such as off-peak travel rates
- *change related products to encourage substitution*, such as holiday destinations
- *vary the lead time*
- *use a reservation or appointment system*
- *use stocks to cushion demand.*

Changing capacity over time

So far we have assumed that capacity is constant over time. In practice, the effective capacity of a supply chain can change quite markedly. Even if there are no changes to the operations, there are short-term variations due to staff illness, interruptions, breakdowns, weather, enthusiasm of employees, and so on. Imagine a group of people moving heavy materials about a warehouse. At the end of an eight-hour shift they will be tired and their effective capacity will be much lower than at the beginning of the shift, even though there has been no change to their work.

There are, however, other more systematic changes in capacity. One of the most obvious is the effect of a **learning curve**. The more often you repeat something, the easier it becomes and the faster you can do it (as shown in Figure 6.6). A common shape for a learning curve has the time taken to do an operation falling by a fixed proportion – typically around 10% – every time the number of repetitions is doubled. If you take 10 minutes to do a job for the first time, the second time takes only 90% of this, or 9 minutes; the fourth time takes 90% of the time for the second repetition, and so on. The following table shows the times for repetitions with this '90% learning curve'.

Number of repetitions	Time for the last (mins)
1	10.0
2	9.0
4	8.1
8	7.29
16	6.56
32	5.90
64	5.31
128	4.78

Another reason for systematic changes in capacity comes from ageing equipment and facilities. As equipment gets older its effective capacity declines as it breaks down more often, develops more faults, gives lower quality, slows down, and generally wears out. Sometimes the changes are slow – like the fuel consumption of a car, which rises steadily with age. Sometimes the change is very fast, like a bolt, which suddenly breaks.

This declining performance is by no means inevitable, and there are many things – ranging from mobile telephones to tea services – whose performance stays the same for long periods. Even if performance does decline, there are ways of slowing its effects, such as **preventive maintenance** and rational **replacement policies**.

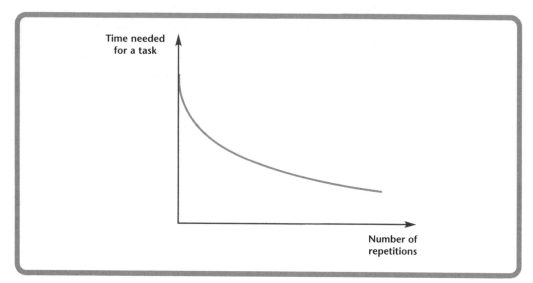

Figure 6.6 A typical learning curve

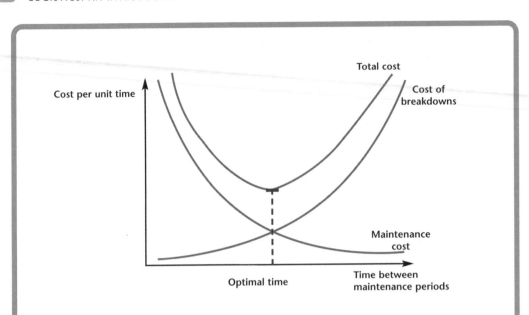

Figure 6.7 Cost of maintenance

With preventive maintenance, equipment is inspected and vulnerable parts are replaced after a certain period of use. By replacing bits that are worn – or are most likely to wear – the equipment is restored to give continuing, satisfactory performance. But how often should we do this maintenance? If it is done too often, the equipment runs efficiently but the maintenance costs are too high; if it is not done often enough, the maintenance costs are low but the equipment still breaks down. One way of finding the best compromise is to add together the costs of maintenance and expected failure. If we plot these against the frequency of maintenance, we get a U-shaped curve that has a distinct minimum. This minimum cost shows the best time between maintenance periods (as shown in Figure 6.7).

Even with regular maintenance there comes a point when repairs become too expensive and it is cheaper to buy new equipment. These replacement decisions can be expensive when building, say, a new logistic centre or shopping mall. There are many ways of tackling replacement decisions, but a common one extends the approach of preventive maintenance. In other words, we add the cost of operating equipment over a number of years and divide this by the age at replacement to give an average annual cost.

WORKED EXAMPLE

Juanita Princepio has recorded the costs of an automatic guided vehicle (AGV) that moves materials around an assembly hall. The longer the AGV works without maintenance, the higher are the expected failure costs (shown below). The maintenance also affects the resale value, giving a varying capital charge. Preventive maintenance can be done at a cost of £1000 and this brings the AGV back to new condition. What is the best time between maintenance periods?

EXAMPLE
continued

Months since maintenance	0	1	2	3	4	5
Cost of breakdowns in month	0	50	150	200	1600	3000
Capital charge	100	200	400	500	800	1200

Solution

We can find the total monthly cost of running the AGV over some period by adding the total costs of maintenance, capital and breakdowns, and dividing this by the number of months in the period. If the machine is maintained every month there is no cost for break-downs, but maintenance costs of £1000 and capital charge of £100, give a total of £1100 each month. If the machine is maintained every two months the expected cost of break-downs is £0 in the first month plus £50 in the second month, capital charge is £200 and maintenance costs £1000, giving a total of £1250 every two months, or £625 a month. If the machine is maintained every three months the expected cost of breakdowns is £0 in the first month, plus £50 in the second month, plus £150 in the third month, capital charge is £400 and maintenance is £1000, giving a total of £1600 for three months or £533 a month. Repeating this gives the following values, which suggest a minimum cost of £475 a month when maintenance is done every four months.

Months between maintenance	1	2	3	4	5	6
Maintenance cost	1000	1000	1000	1000	1000	1000
Cost of breakdowns in month	0	50	150	200	1600	3000
Cumulative cost of breakdowns	0	50	200	400	2000	5000
Capital charge	100	200	400	500	800	1200
Total cost	1100	1250	1600	1900	3800	7200
Average cost per month	1100	625	533	475	760	1200

LOGISTICS
IN PRACTICE

Capacity of Heathrow Airport

BAA run seven airports in the UK, including the three London airports at Heathrow, Gatwick and Stansted. In the year to April 2000, BAA handled 118 million passengers, an increase of 4.7% over the previous year. Passenger demand is particularly strong in the south-east of England, where the number of passengers is forecast to double over the next 15 years. To meet this rising demand, BAA has a continuing programme of airport expansion.

London Heathrow is the world's biggest international airport, and handled over 62 million passengers in 2000. This rise of 2% a year is modest compared with other airports around London. Stansted handled 10 million passengers, a rise of 33%, Gatwick grew at 3% to 30 million passengers, Luton airport is doubling its capacity to 10 million passengers a year, and the smaller London City Airport is growing by 9% a year to 2 million passengers.

The reason for Heathrow's relatively slow growth is that the runways and, more obviously, the four terminals are already working at full capacity. A fifth terminal, due to increase passenger capacity to 85 million a year, has been delayed by a public enquiry lasting four years – the longest-ever hearing for a development project in the UK. If everything goes smoothly, the earliest possible opening date is 2006. There are continuing improvements to facilities to give smaller increases in capacity, including an express rail link to Paddington, a second express rail link to St Pancras, improved access roads, extension to the London Underground Piccadilly Line, and £1 million a day spent on upgrading the existing four terminals. Discussions have also started into reducing the gap between aeroplanes and allowing more take-offs and landings.

Realistically, the congestion at Heathrow is likely to continue for the foreseeable future. This has forced growth at other airports. British Airways switched its African services to Gatwick in 1996, and its South American services in 1997. By 1998, Gatwick was serving 276 destinations – more than any other European gateway, including Heathrow. It spent £500 million to increase its capacity from 27 million to 30 million passengers, and is currently expanding to a capacity of 40 million. Stansted is expanding from 8 million to 15 million passengers a year. Luton has spent £170 million on new facilities to become London's fourth airport.

Sources: Ellson C. (1998) London's airports set for expansion, *The Times*, 30 April; Skapinker M. (1999), BAA plans to expand capacity at Gatwick, *Financial Times*, 31 May and websites

TACTICAL PLANNING

Aggregate plans

Tactical plans bridge the gap between longer term strategic plans and operational details. They show how the capacity will be used, and develop medium-term timetables for activities. Different names are used for this level of planning, but the most common are **aggregate plans** and **master schedules**.

Aggregate planning takes the forecast demand for logistics and uses this to design plans for each type of activity for, typically, each of the next few months. Suppose that Proctor Transport forecasts demand of 800 tonnes of materials to be delivered to Scandinavia over the next year. Capacity plans make sure that there are enough resources to deliver this. Then aggregate plans design an outline schedule for resources, perhaps planning deliveries of 100 tonnes in each of the first eight months. Aggregate plans only look at families of activities and are not concerned with details. They might show the number of cases moved through a logistics centre, but do not break this down into types of case or contents.

AGGREGATE PLANNING makes the tactical decisions that translate forecast demand and available capacity into schedules for families of activities.

Aggregate plans try to meet forecast demand, while using capacity as efficiently as possible. They typically aim at low costs, high customer service, stable throughput, full utilisation of resources, or some other objectives. To achieve this, they can adjust the values of several variables. They may, for example, change the number of people employed, the hours worked, the amounts of stock, the amount subcontracted, demand, and so on. Essentially, aggregate planners are looking for answers to questions, like:

● Should we keep throughput at a constant level, or change it to meet varying demand?
● How should we use stocks to meet changing demand?
● Should we vary the size of the workforce with demand?
● Can we change work patterns to meet changing demand?
● Should we use subcontractors or outside organisations to cover peak demands?
● Can we allow shortages, perhaps with late delivery?
● Can we smooth the demand?

At the end of the aggregate planning, an organisation has schedules for its major types of activity, typically for each month, at each location. The next stage is to add more detail, and this is done in the **master schedules**.

A master schedule 'disaggregates' the aggregate plan and shows the planned activities for, typically, each week over the next few weeks. The aggregate plan of Proctor Transport might show deliveries of 100 tonnes to Scandinavia next month. Then the master schedule gives more details, perhaps showing 2 deliveries of 9 tonnes to Denmark in week one, 3 deliveries of 7 tonnes to Sweden in week two, and so on.

The **MASTER SCHEDULE** gives a timetable for activities, typically for each week. Its aim is to achieve the activities described in aggregate plans as efficiently as possible.

Overall approach of tactical planning

Master schedules are more detailed than aggregate plans, so they tend to be more complicated and messy. For both of them, however, we can use the general procedure that we described earlier as **resource requirement planning.** Remember that this has six steps:

Step 1   translate forecasts and other information into a demand for resources
Step 2   find the resources currently available
Step 3   identify mismatches between resources needed and available
Step 4   suggest alternative plans for overcoming any mismatches

Step 5   compare these plans and find the best
Step 6   implement the best plan and monitor performance.

We can use this approach (which is illustrated in Figure 6.8) for all types of planning. Remember that steps 4 and 5 are usually repeated until a reasonable solution is found. This iterative adjustment can be done many times, but it must stop at some point when the plans become final. At this point, the planners can move on to the next level of detail.

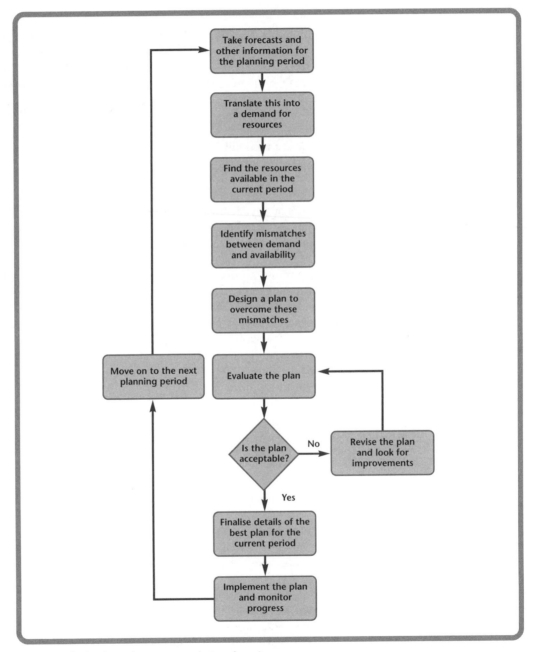

Figure 6.8 An iterative approach to planning

E X A M P L E

A&B Coaches

A&B Coaches of Blackpool plan their capacity in terms of 'coach-days'. They classify their business as either 'full day', which are long distance journeys, or 'half day' which are shorter runs. Forecasts show expected annual demands for the next two years to average 400,000 full-day passengers and 750,000 half-day passengers.

A&B have 61 coaches, each with an effective capacity of 40 passengers a day for 300 days a year. Breakdowns and other unexpected problems reduce efficiency to 90%. They employ 86 drivers who work an average of 220 days a year, but illness and other absences reduce their efficiency to 85%.

If there is a shortage of coaches the company can buy extra ones for £110,000 or hire them for £100 a day. If there is a shortage of drivers they can recruit extra ones at a cost of £20,000 a year, or hire them from an agency for £110 a day.

How can the company approach its tactical planning?

Solution

We can approach this problem using the first five steps of the six-step procedure outlined above.

Step 1   Translate forecasts and other information into a demand for resources

■ 400,000 full-day passengers are equivalent to 400,000/40 = 10,000 coach days a year, or 10,000/300 = 33.33 coaches.

■ 750,000 half-day passengers are equivalent to 750,000 / (40 × 300 × 2) = 31.25 coaches.

■ Adding these two gives the total demand as 64.58 coaches. Each coach needs 300/220 drivers, so the company needs a total of 88.06 drivers.

Step 2   Find the resources currently available

■ The company has 61 coaches, but the efficiency of 90% gives an availability of 61 × 0.9 = 54.9 coaches.

■ There are 86 drivers, but an efficiency of 85% reduces this to 86 × 0.85 = 73.1 drivers.

Step 3   Identify mismatches between resources needed and available

Without details of the timing, we can only take overall figures. There is a total shortage of 64.58 – 54.9 = 9.68 coaches and 88.06 – 73.1 = 14.96 drivers.

Step 4   Suggest alternative plans for overcoming any mismatches

Assuming that A&B do not want to reduce demand, they can either buy or hire coaches, and employ drivers or hire them from an agency. The only information we have about these alternatives are some costs.

- To buy 10 coaches would cost £1,100,000. To hire coaches to make up the shortage would cost $9.68 \times 300 \times 100 = £290,400$ a year. There is, of course, the alternative of buying some coaches and hiring others.

- To hire 15 drivers would cost £300,000 a year, while using temporary drivers from an agency would cost $14.96 \times 220 \times 110 = £362,032$ a year. There is also the option of hiring some drivers and making up shortages from an agency.

Step 5　Compare these plans and find the best

We do not have enough information to make the final decisions, and we have only outlined some of the alternatives. This very limited analysis might suggest a reasonable solution of buying eight coaches and making up any shortages by hiring, and hiring 12 drivers and making up the shortage from the agency.

When these plans are finalised, A&B can start looking at more detailed plans. The next stage would develop aggregate plans for types of journeys each month, perhaps showing the number of continental journeys each month, and so on. Then they could break the aggregate plans into master schedules of journeys each week, perhaps showing the number of journeys to the Netherlands in the first week, and so on.

Generating alternative plans

The last worked example illustrates the general approach of planning, but you can see that there are many practical difficulties. One of the most important concerns the way that alternative plans are generated and compared. There are usually so many possible plans that we cannot even list them all, let alone compare their merits. There are also so many competing objectives and non-quantifiable factors that it is difficult to find any plan that satisfies everyone, let alone identify the 'best'.

There are many ways of generating alternative plans, ranging from simple intuition through to sophisticated mathematical models. The most appropriate depends on several factors, the most obvious being the balance between the cost of planning and the expected benefits. If you are moving huge quantities of oil in tankers and pipelines, costs are high and it is worth putting a lot of effort into a sophisticated model that guarantees good results. On the other hand, a small business is unlikely to have the resources for this, and will use a simple method that will give reasonable results with a lot less effort. The following list shows the most common methods of generating plans.

1.　*Negotiations:* Planning is so complicated that the best approach is often to negotiate a solution among the people most closely concerned. This may not give the best technical answer, but it should have the support of everyone concerned.

2.　*Adjust previous plans:* Demands on logistics may not change much from one period to the next, so a useful approach is to take previous plans that worked successfully and update them in the light of current circumstances. This has the benefit of being relatively easy and giving stable operations. Unfortunately, the results can be of variable quality, they may take a long time to design, and they rely on the skills of the planner.

3. *Other intuitive methods:* These include a range of methods that rely on the skills, knowledge and experience of planners. They typically use a series of heuristic rules that have been successful in the past.

4. *Graphical methods:* Planners often find it easier to work with some kind of graphs or diagrams. A popular format uses a graph of cumulative demand over time, and the corresponding line of cumulative supply. The aim is to get the cumulative supply line nearly straight – giving constant throughput – and as close as possible to the cumulative demand line (as shown in Figure 6.9). There are many different formats for such diagrams.

5. *Spreadsheet calculations:* One of the most popular approaches to planning uses spreadsheets. Data can be presented in a variety of formats that show the effects of plans, and they can be easily manipulated in a series of 'what-if' analyses.

6. *Simulation:* Simulation imitates real operations over some typical period. Suppose you want some information about a logistics network; you could simply stand and watch the network for some time to see what was happening. Unfortunately, this takes a long time to get results and things may not work normally while you are watching. An alternative is to simulate the process, based on a computer model of the network. Once this has been designed, the computer can generate typical jobs and follow their progress through the model, so that any number of real situations can be simulated.

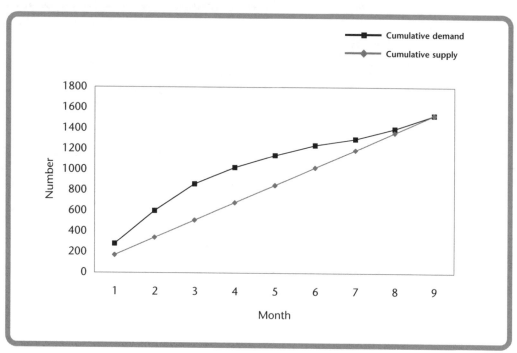

Figure 6.9 Graphical approach to planning – plotting cumulative demand and supply

7. *Expert systems:* These specialised programs allow computers to duplicate the methods of skilled planners. The basic skills, expertise, decisions and rules used by experts are collected in a knowledge base. A user of the system passes a problem to an inference engine, which analyses the problem, relates this to the knowledge base and decides which rules to use for a solution. Expert systems have been developing for many years, and a growing number of organisations report useful results.

8. *Mathematical models:* Most of the approaches we have described so far rely, at least to some extent, on the skills of a planner. More formal mathematical approaches give optimal solutions without any human intervention. The most common approach uses mathematical programming. This can be complicated and needs considerable expertise. In practice, aggregate plans include so many subjective and non-quantifiable factors, that optimal solutions in the mathematical sense do not necessarily give the best answers for the organisation.

Planning cycles

As you can see from Figure 6.8, planning is not a job that is done once and is then finished. It is continuous, and as plans for one period are finalised and implemented, planning moves on to the next period. The usual way of organising this is to work on plans for several periods at the same time; plans for the near future are fixed, while those for the more distant future are still tentative. Planning is then done in cycles. In one cycle an organisation might finalise plans for the next period and make provisional plans for the following period, and outline plans for the period after that. This gives the pattern of planning shown in Figure 6.10. It is

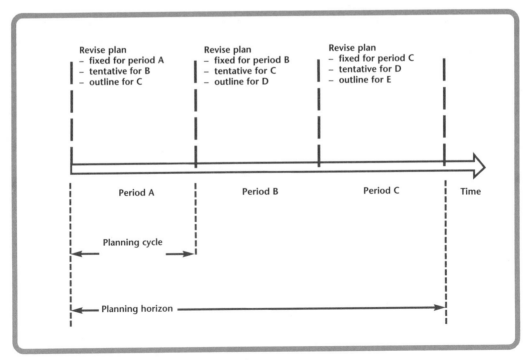

Figure 6.10 Revision of plans during cycles

difficult to generalise, but strategic plans might cover the next four years and be updated annually; aggregate plans might cover the next year and be updated every quarter; master schedules may cover the next three months and be updated monthly. This pattern of repeated cycles actually makes planning a lot easier. Most operations are relatively stable, so the plans for one period can be used as the basis for plans in following periods.

LOGISTICS IN PRACTICE

Piotr Hucek Transport

Wiesiek Tomac is the Logistics Manager of Piotr Hucek Transport in Prague, Czech Republic. Every month he designs, or updates, the aggregate plan to cover the next 6 months. He starts with forecasts of monthly demand for different types of transport, and collects other relevant information to design outline schedules for each type of transport for each month. At the beginning of 2001 he had the following information for one type of transport.

Month	Jan	Feb	Mar	Apr	May	June
Forecast	80	100	125	130	150	75

These figures are in nominal 'truck journeys', and the company uses euros for internal costs. These main costs are:

- Spare transport that is not used = €1000 a unit held at the month end
- Shortage of transport = €10,000 a unit at the month end
- Cost of moving an employee to this function from other jobs = €1000 per employee
- Cost of moving an employee from this function to other jobs = €700 per employee

At the beginning of the period 16 people were employed, each of whom can make 5 journeys a month.

Wiesiek has a spreadsheet to help with aggregate planning. He looks at the existing plans, and then makes adjustments to allow for changing circumstances. The spreadsheet does the associated calculation, but little else. Figure 6.11 shows how he developed an initial idea.

As you can see, Wiesiek started by looking at a smooth supply, set at the average demand over the six months. This needed six more employees, so there were costs for transferring people into the function in the first month. Other costs came from the unused demand in the first four months and shortage in month five. The shortage cost was particularly high, so Wiesiek kept looking for alternative plans until he had a reasonable solution. His obvious next move was to reduce availability of vehicles in the first four months, and then increase it later.

When he finalised an aggregate plan, Wiesiek moved on to design the master schedule. This showed the supply of vehicles of each type by week. Finally, short-term schedules were designed to show what each individual vehicle and driver would be doing each day.

Source: company reports

	A	B	C	D	E	F	G	H	I
1									
2	Line	Description	1	2	3	4	5	6	Total
3	1	Forecast demand	80	100	125	130	150	75	660
4	2	Cumulative forecast demand	80	180	305	435	585	660	660
5	3	Supply rate	110	110	110	110	110	110	660
6	4	Cumulative supply	110	220	330	440	550	660	660
7	5	Unused supply	30	40	25	5	0	0	100
8	6	Shortage of supply	0	0	0	0	35	0	35
9	7	Cost of unused supply	30000	40000	25000	5000	0	0	100000
10		(Line 5 × €1000)							
11	8	Cost of shortage	0	0	0	0	350000	0	350000
12		(Line 6 × €1000)							
13	9	Number of employees	22	22	22	22	22	22	
14	10	Cost of moving employees	6000	0	0	0	0	0	6000
15	11	Total cost	36000	40000	25000	5000	350000	0	456000
16		(Line 7 + Line 8 + line 10)							

Figure 6.11 Spreadsheet to help with planning in Piotr Hucek

SHORT-TERM SCHEDULES

Definitions

The master schedule gives a timetable for different activities, typically for each week. But this is not the end to planning, as we still have to design detailed timetables for jobs, equipment, people, materials, facilities and all other resources that are needed by the master schedule. This is the purpose of short-term scheduling.

SHORT-TERM SCHEDULES give detailed timetables for jobs, people, materials, equipment and all other resources.

Short-term schedules give the sequences of activities, and the times when they should be done. 'Sam the Fridge' runs a repair service and his daily schedule lists the customer to visit (with the order and time of each job) and the resources needed (the repair people, tools, spare parts, vans and so on needed for the jobs). The aim of these schedules is to organise the resources needed for the master schedule, giving low costs, high utilisations, or achieving some other measure of performance.

Designing these operational schedules is one of the most common problems in any organisation. As it is so common, you might think that short-term scheduling is easy – but in practice it is notoriously difficult. To start with there are so many possible schedules to consider. Imagine that you have ten jobs that you must finish today. In how many different ways can you arrange the ten jobs? You can choose the first job as any one of the ten; then the second job can be any one of the remaining nine, the third job can be any one of the remaining eight, and so on. This gives the number of possible schedules as:

$$10 \times 9 \times 8 \times 7 \times 6 \times 5 \times 4 \times 3 \times 2 \times 1 = 3,628,800$$

If you have a real problem with hundreds or thousands of jobs, you have a huge number of possible schedules to consider. Each of these has different features, and performs well by some criteria, but badly by others. You have to balance each type of performance, and take into account the complications of real problems, such as the amount and type of equipment, number and skills of people assigned to jobs, materials needed, patterns of work flow through equipment, different priority of jobs, objectives of the schedulers, and so on.

The result is that apparently simple scheduling jobs are actually very difficult to solve. Eilon et al.[1] noted that this type of problem 'has become famous for its ease of statement and great difficulty of solution'.

Approach to scheduling

You can imagine a typical scheduling problem in terms of a set of jobs waiting to use equipment. You want to organise the jobs to achieve some objective. The master schedule shows when jobs have to be finished, so the short-term schedules must take these dates into account. There are two ways of doing this:

- *Backward scheduling*, where schedulers know when a job has to be finished. Then they can work back through all the activities to find the date when the job must be started.
- *Forward scheduling*, where schedulers know when a job can start. Then they can work forward through all activities to find the date when the job will be finished.

Suppose you are giving a talk in three weeks time and want some photographs to illustrate this. It will take one week to prepare the photographs. With backward scheduling you know that the photographs must be ready in three weeks, so you can prepare them in two weeks time. With forward scheduling, you prepare the photographs as early as possible – starting now and finishing next week.

These two approaches suggest general principles, but we need some way of finding the best order for jobs. The available methods are basically variations on the list given above for tactical plans, and range from negotiation through to mathematical programming. The more complicated methods are usually too difficult and time-consuming for short-term schedules, and most organisations use simple methods, often based on **scheduling rules**. You see an example of a scheduling rule in banks which schedule customer service at their tellers in the order 'first come, first served'.

If you have a number of jobs waiting to use a single piece of equipment, the total processing time is fixed regardless of the order in which the jobs are scheduled (providing the set-up time for each job is constant, regardless of the job that was done previously). But the order of taking jobs does change other measures of performance. You can see this in the following four scheduling rules.

1. *First come, first served:* This is the most obvious scheduling rule and simply takes jobs in the order they arrive. It assumes no priority, no urgency, or any other measure of relative importance. Its drawback is that urgent jobs may be delayed while less urgent ones are being processed.

2. *Most urgent job first:* This rule assigns an importance, or urgency, to each job and they are processed in order of decreasing urgency. Emergency departments in hospitals, for example, treat those who are most seriously in need first. The benefit of this rule is that more important jobs have higher priority. Unfortunately, jobs that have low priority may be stuck at the end of a queue for a very long time.

3. *Shortest job first:* A useful objective is to minimise the average time spent in the system, where:

   time in the system = processing time + waiting time

   If a job needs one day of processing but it waits in the queue for four days, its time in the system is five days. Taking the jobs in order of increasing duration minimises the average time spent in the system. It allows those jobs that can be done quickly to move on through the system, while longer jobs are left until later. The disadvantage is that long jobs can spend a long time waiting.

4. *Earliest due date first:* This sorts jobs into order of delivery date, and the ones that are due earliest are processed first. This has the benefit of minimising the maximum lateness of jobs, but again some jobs may wait a long time.

WORKED EXAMPLE

Zambrucci Transport has to schedule the following six jobs for a heavy lift crane. How can it design a reasonable schedule?

Jobs	A	B	C	D	E	F
Duration in days	12	8	4	16	2	10
Target completion (days from now)	12	40	44	48	4	20

Solution

The simplest way of tackling this problem is to use some decision rules. Using 'first come, first served' gives the schedule:

Job	Duration	Start	Finish
A	12	0	12
B	8	6	20
C	4	10	24
D	16	12	40
E	2	20	42
F	10	21	52

The jobs are finished by day 52. Every sequence of jobs is going to give this same completion time, but they will perform differently when judged by other measures. We can,

EXAMPLE
continued

for example, minimise the average time in the system by taking jobs in order 'shortest first'. This gives the schedule:

Job	Duration	Start	Finish
E	2	0	2
C	4	2	6
B	8	6	14
F	10	14	24
A	12	24	36
D	16	36	52

The average time in the system (which is the same as the average finish time) is 134/6 = 22.3 days, compared with 190/6 = 31.7 days for 'first come, first served'. By day 36 this schedule has finished five journeys, while the previous schedule had only finished three.

We do not have enough information to schedule the jobs in order of urgency, but we can minimise the maximum lateness by taking jobs in order of due date. This gives the following schedule.

Job	Duration	Start	Finish	Due date	Lateness
E	2	0	2	4	0
A	12	2	14	12	2
F	10	14	24	20	4
B	8	24	32	40	0
C	4	32	36	44	0
D	16	36	52	48	4

This gives a maximum lateness of 4 days for jobs D and F, and an average lateness of 10/6 = 1.7 days.

These are only three scheduling rules, and we could use many others to achieve different objectives.

LOGISTICS
IN PRACTICE

Scheduling at Bombay Taxis

Bombay Taxis have a fleet of 170 cars working around greater Bombay. They employ 210 full-time drivers, and a varying number of part-time drivers. Usually there are around 100 of these, but at busy times there can be up to 200. Their aim is to keep the taxis in use for almost 24 hours a day.

The taxis are maintained in the com-

LOGISTICS
IN PRACTICE
continued

pany's garage. This has six bays, ten full-time mechanics, four part-time mechanics and eight apprentices. Bombay also employ 17 controllers. These take telephone calls from customers, schedule the work, and pass instructions on to taxis. The controllers keep a continuous check on the location and work of each taxi.

You can already see that Bombay have to do a range of scheduling. They start by scheduling the hours worked by cars, so that there are always enough taxis on the road to meet demand from customers. Then they schedule the drivers to make sure that there are enough drivers for the cars. The controllers design routes for each cab, starting with customers who make advance bookings and a list of regular cus-

tomers who have block bookings. These routes are continually modified as customers telephone in with new jobs (which are assigned to the nearest car with free time), or the cars pick up passengers who hail them on the streets.

As well as scheduling the cars, drivers and routes, the controllers design schedules for the maintenance and repair of cars, other internal work in the garage, work for external customers of the garage, hours worked by all other staff, purchase of parts and materials, cleaning and maintaining the building, staff training, and all other operations of the business.

Source: Chandrasekar J., (2001) Where are the taxis? Western Operations Seminar, Toronto and company reports

CHAPTER REVIEW

❑ The logistics strategy gives the general shape of the supply chain. After this, tactical and operational plans are needed to manage the flow of materials. Planning is essential, as it gives timetables for all the activities and resources in the supply chain.

❑ Capacity is an important feature of a supply chain, as it sets the maximum amount of products that can be delivered to final customers in a given time. The capacity of the whole chain is set by a bottleneck.

❑ Capacity planning matches the available capacity to demand. Resource requirement planning gives a standard procedure which iteratively searches for a reasonable solution.

❑ There are many practical difficulties with organising the capacity, including discrete capacity size and changing capacity over time.

❑ Capacity plans focus on the longer term, but with shorter term adjustments. They set the scene for more detailed tactical and operational planning.

CHAPTER REVIEW *continued*

❑ Tactical aggregate plans describe timetables for families of activities over the medium term. Master schedules add more details, giving plans for individual activities. Both of these can use the approach of resource requirement planning, with plans actually designed by different methods ranging from negotiation through to mathematical programming.

❑ Short-term schedules give timetables for the resources that support the tactical plans. The most common approach to short-term scheduling uses simple rules to get reasonable solutions.

CASE STUDY — *Primal Autoparts*

Primal Autoparts is a supplier of car parts to customers in south-western USA. It sources these from its own manufacturing plants and from other manufacturers, primarily in south-east Asia. It plans to extend its operations to include customers in north-western USA and the western provinces of Canada. George Havering is a senior partner for Mayer, Jones and Armanti, and has been given the job of designing realistic alternatives for Primal's additional logistics requirements. Whatever alternative he suggests must be integrated with the existing distribution system.

George's problem is that he does not know much about Primal's existing operations. He knows that they work as wholesalers, keeping stocks in warehouses until delivered to customers. These customers are mainly mechanics working in repair workshops. They have to repair cars in the shortest time possible, so Primal must give at least overnight delivery, with parts available at the start of the next working day. The demand for any part is variable and difficult to forecast. Some demand is seasonal, such as radiators which are vulnerable during severe winters.

At present Primal's main warehouse is near San Francisco, with smaller depots in Los Angeles, Phoenix and Salt Lake City. The largest parts they supply are bodies, which can easily be carried by road, rail or air. The most reasonable approach for George would be to study the existing distribution system and look for ways of expanding. Then Primal can use their existing skills and resources to serve a wider customer base, and spread their fixed costs.

CASE STUDY
Questions

● If you were George Havering, how would you start your study? What steps would you follow, and what would you aim to put in your report to Primal?

● What type of logistics systems might you consider? How would you compare these alternatives?

● What information would you need for this study, and how would you collect it?

PROJECT
Network Planning

Consider an organisation that has a well-established logistics network. You might take a local company or a national one such as a supermarket, airline, or car manufacturer. Describe the main features of the network. What is the capacity of the main facilities? How do you think these capacities were chosen? How does the company plan the flow of materials through its supply chain?

PROBLEMS

1. A purchasing department sends out about 100 routine orders a day. Each person in the department can deal with three orders an hour, but has to do associated paperwork that takes an average of 40 minutes an order. Each person also loses about 20% of their time doing other things. The standard working day is from 0900 to 1600 five days a week, with an hour off for lunch. How many employees do you think the department should employ?

2. Sean Higgins estimates that his periodic plant maintenance costs €50,000. If he does not close the plant and do this maintenance, his breakdown costs rise as shown below. How often should he maintain the plant?

Time since last maintenance (years)	0	1	2	3	4	5
Annual cost of breakdowns (€000)	0	10	40	80	150	240

3. A warehouse has to meet the demand for a product shown below. Each unit of stock remaining at the end of a month has a notional holding cost of £20. If there are shortages, 20% of orders are lost at a cost of £200 a unit, and the rest are met by back orders, at a cost of £50 a unit. A production department sends the product to the warehouse. Designed capacity of this department is 400 units a month, but utilisation seldom exceeds 80%. Every time the production rate is changed it costs £15,000. How would you set about designing an aggregate plan for the product?

Month	1	2	3	4	5	6	7	8
Aggregate demand	310	280	260	300	360	250	160	100

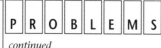

P R O B L E M S

continued

4. Eight jobs are to be processed on a single machine, with processing times as follows:

Job	A	B	C	D	E	F	G	H
Processing time	2	5	3	8	4	7	2	3
Due date	13	7	8	30	14	20	2	36

How could you design short-term schedules for the jobs?

DISCUSSION QUESTIONS

1. Capacity is the most important decision in the design of a supply chain, as it affects the amount of materials that can be moved. Do you find this argument convincing?
2. Tactical plans – such as aggregate plans and master schedules – are useful for manufacturing, but they are not so relevant for logistics. Do you think that this is true? What happens if there is no tactical planning for a supply chain?
3. What decisions are involved in tactical planning for logistics?
4. Mathematical models can find optimal solutions for planning and scheduling problems. By definition, these solutions are the best. If an organisation uses any other methods, it is accepting poor results. What do you think of this view?
5. There must be better ways of scheduling jobs than by using simple scheduling rules. What methods are available, and what are their advantages and weaknesses?

REFERENCES

1. Eilon S., Watson-Gandy C.D.T. and Christofides N. (1971) *Distribution Management*, Griffin, London.

Further reading

Comel J.G. and Edson N.W. (1995) *Gaining Control: Capacity Management and Scheduling*, John Wiley, New York.

Dauzere-Peres S. and Lasserve J.B. (1994) *An Integrated Approach to Production Planning and Scheduling*, Springer Verlag, Berlin.

Klammer T.P. and Klammer T. (1996) *Capacity Management and Improvement*, Irwin, Homewood, IL.

Menasse D. (1993) *Capacity Planning: A Practical Approach*, Prentice Hall, Englewood Cliffs, NJ.

Morton T.E. and Penticto D.W. (1993) *Heuristic Scheduling Systems*, John Wiley, New York.

Proud J.F. (1999) *Master Scheduling* (3rd edn), John Wiley, New York.

Vollman T.E., Berry W.L. and Whybark D.C. (1996) *Manufacturing Planning and Control Systems* (4th edn), Richard Irwin, Homewood, IL.

Waters D. (2001) *Operations Management*, Financial Times/Prentice Hall, London.

CHAPTER 7

Controlling Material Flow

AIMS OF THE CHAPTER

After reading this chapter you should be able to:

- DESCRIBE the distinctive approach of material requirements planning

- USE MRP to timetable orders and deliveries

- DISCUSS the benefits and disadvantages of MRP

- EXTEND the MRP approach along the supply chain

- DESCRIBE the principles of just-in-time operations

- DESIGN *kanban* systems for controlling JIT

- DISCUSS the benefits and disadvantages of JIT

- EXTEND JIT along the supply chain for efficient consumer response

MATERIAL REQUIREMENTS PLANNING

Introduction

In the previous chapter we described an approach to planning logistics based on resource requirement planning. This takes the logistics strategy and continually adds more details to get capacity plans, aggregate plans, master schedules and short-term schedules. The result is a set of timetables showing what all the facilities, equipment, people and resources should do at any time.

This seems a reasonable approach, but it does have drawbacks. It is, for example, fairly rigid and can be slow to react to changing conditions. If a customer urgently wants a delivery, we cannot tell them to wait until we fit them in to the next planning cycle. Another concern arises from the reliance on forecasts. Essentially planners take forecasts of demand for logistics, and then plan the supply to meet this. The problem, of course, is that forecasts are often wrong.

A way of getting around these problems is to match the supply of logistics to actual demand. In other words, we want some way of finding the known, actual demand rather than using unreliable forecasts. This might seem rather optimistic, but there are several circumstances when we know the actual demand in advance. We can illustrate the first of these with **material requirements planning** (MRP). This uses the master schedule to give a timetable for the delivery of materials.[1]

Dependent and independent demand

The conventional approach to planning assumes that overall demand for a product is made up of individual demands from many separate customers. These demands are independent of each other, so the demand from one customer is not related to the demand from another customer. If you are selling Nike shoes, the overall demand comes from hundreds of separate customers, all independently asking for a pair of shoes. This gives an **independent demand**, where planning is done using the standard methods we described in Chapter 6.

There are, however, many situations where demands are not independent. One demand for a product is not independent of a second demand for the product; or demand for one product is not independent of demand for a second product. When a manufacturer uses a number of components to make a product, the demands for all components are clearly related, since they all depend on the production plan for the final product. This gives **dependent demand**. The characteristic approach of MRP is that it 'explodes' a master schedule to plan the deliveries of related materials.

■ **MATERIAL REQUIREMENTS PLANNING** uses the master schedule, along with other relevant information, to plan the supply of materials.
■ It is used for dependent demand.

You can see the differences between the traditional approach and MRP in the way that restaurant chefs plan the ingredients for a week's meals. With the traditional approach, the chefs see what ingredients they used in previous weeks, use these past demands to forecast future demands, and then make sure there is enough ingredients in the pantry to cover these

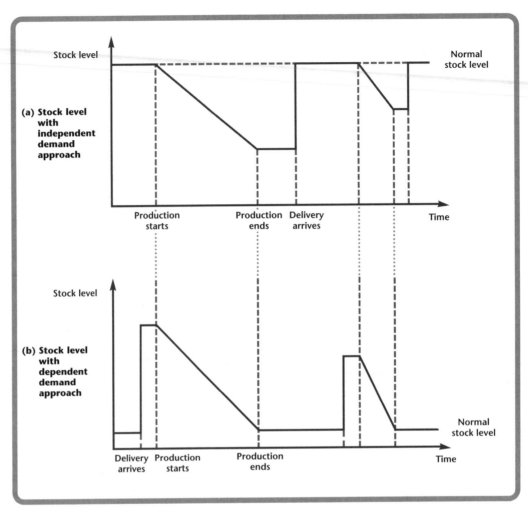

Figure 7.1 Comparison of stock levels

forecast demands. With the alternative MRP approach, chefs look at the meals they are going to cook each day, analyse these to see what ingredients they need, and then order the ingredients to arrive at the right time.

An important difference between the two approaches is the pattern of material stocks. With independent demand systems, stocks are not related to production plans so they must be high enough to cover any likely demand. These stocks decline during operations, but are soon replaced to give the pattern shown in Figure 7.1(a). With MRP, stocks are generally low but rise as orders are delivered just before operations starts. The stock is then used during production and declines to its normal, low level. This pattern is shown in Figure 7.1(b).

The MRP approach

MRP uses a lot of information about schedules, products and materials. This comes from three main sources:

● *master schedule*, giving the number of every product to be made in every period
● *bill of materials*, listing the materials needed for every product
● *inventory records*, showing the materials available.

A bill of materials is an ordered list of all the parts needed to make a particular product. It shows the materials, parts and components – and also the order in which they are used. Suppose a company makes tables from a top and four legs. Then each top is made from a wood kit and hardware; the wood kit has four oak planks, side panels, and so on. The bill of materials for this is shown in Figure 7.2. You can see that every item has a 'level' number that shows where it fits into the process, and figures in brackets show the numbers needed to make each unit. The finished product is level 0; level 1 items are used directly to make the level 0 item, level 2 items are used to make the level 1 items, and so on.

A full bill of materials keeps going down through different levels until it reaches materials that the organisation always buys in from suppliers. By this time, there might be hundreds or even thousands of different materials. MRP uses this bill of materials, along with the master schedule, to get a timetable for the delivery of each of the materials.

Suppose a master schedule shows that the company plans to make 10 tables in February. It obviously needs 10 tops and 40 legs ready for assembly at the beginning of February. In practice, these are the **gross requirements**. The company may not have to order them all, as it may already have some in stock, or have outstanding orders that are due to arrive shortly. If we subtract these from the gross requirements we get the **net requirements** for materials. The company needs 40 table legs by the beginning of February, but if it already has 8 in stock and an order of 10 that is due to arrive in January, the net requirement is for $40 - 8 - 10 = 22$.

Net requirements = gross requirements – current stock – stock on order

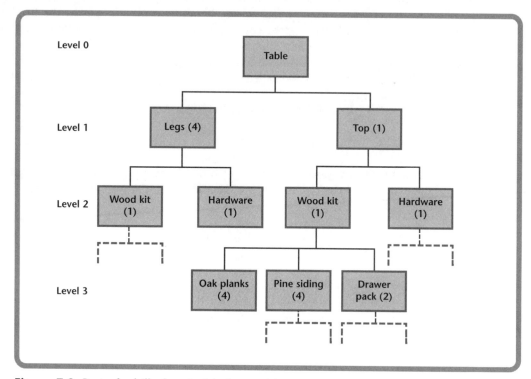

Figure 7.2 Part of a bill of materials for a table

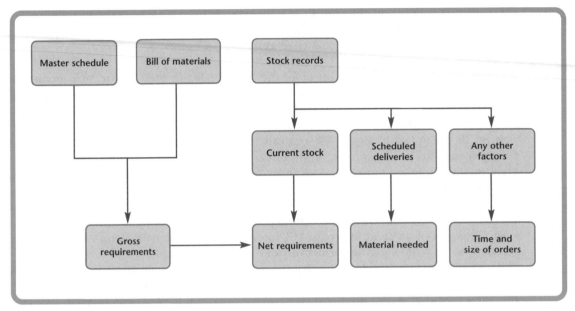

Figure 7.3 Summary of MRP procedure

Now we know the quantities to order, and when these orders should arrive. The next step is to find the time to place the order. For this we need the lead times – and we place orders this lead time before the materials are actually needed. If the company buys tabletops and legs from suppliers who give a lead time of four weeks, it needs to place orders at the beginning of January. These orders will arrive by the end of January just before assembly is due to start.

Finally, we have to consider any other relevant information, such as minimum order sizes, discounts, minimum stock levels, variation in lead time, and so on. When the company takes all of this into account it gets a detailed timetable for orders. This procedure is shown in Figure 7.3.

We can summarise this MRP procedure by the following steps:

● *Step 1:* Use the master schedule to find the gross requirements of level 0 items.

● *Step 2:* Subtract any stock on hand and orders arriving to give the net requirements for level 0 items. Then schedule production, with starting times to meet these net requirements.

● *Step 3:* Take the next level. Use the bill of materials to translate the net requirements from the last level into gross requirements for this level.

● *Step 4:* Take each material in turn and:
  ● subtract the stock on hand and scheduled deliveries to find the materials needed
  ● use the lead time and any other relevant information to give the size and timing of these orders.
  Then if there are more levels of materials, go back to step 3.

● *Step 5:* Finalise the timetable, adding any specific adjustments.

Semple-Brown assemble kitchen tables using bought-in parts of four legs and a top. These have lead times of two and three weeks respectively, and assembly takes a week. The company receive orders for 20 tables to be delivered in week 5 of a planning period and 40 tables in week 7. It has current stocks of 2 complete tables, 40 legs and 22 tops. When should it order parts?

Solution

The orders give the following production schedule for finished tables – shown as the gross requirements for level 0 items. Subtracting the current stock of finished tables gives the net requirements. Then allowing a week for assembly gives the start times.

Level 0 – kitchen tables

Week	1	2	3	4	5	6	7
Gross requirements					20		40
Opening stock	2	2	2	2	2		
Net requirements					18		40
Start assembly				18		40	
Scheduled completion					18		40

The 'scheduled completion' shows the number of units that become available in a week, which is the number started the lead time earlier.

We have already described the bill of materials for this example as the first two levels in Figure 7.2. We can use this, together with the assembly plans, to find gross requirements for level 1 items – which are legs and tops. In week 4 there is a net requirement of 18 tables, which translates into a gross requirement of $18 \times 4 = 72$ legs and $18 \times 1 = 18$ tops. So we can find the gross requirements for level 1 materials as:

- legs: $18 \times 4 = 72$ in week 4, and $40 \times 4 = 160$ in week 6
- tops: 18 in week 4, and 40 in week 6.

Subtracting the stock on hand from these gross requirements gives the net requirements. To make sure the parts arrive on time, they must be ordered the lead time in advance – which is 2 weeks for legs and 3 weeks for tops.

Level 1 – legs

Week	1	2	3	4	5	6	7
Gross requirements				72		160	
Opening stock	40	40	40	40			
Net requirements				32		160	
Place order		32		160			
Scheduled deliveries				32		160	

EXAMPLE
continued

Level 1 – tops

Week	1	2	3	4	5	6	7
Gross requirements				18		40	
Opening stock	22	22	22	22	4	4	
Net requirements						36	
Place order			36				
Scheduled deliveries						36	

There are no more levels of materials, so we can finalise the timetable of events as:

- week 2: order 32 legs
- week 3: order 36 tops
- week 4: order 160 legs and assemble 18 tables
- week 6: assemble 40 tables.

Benefits of MRP

Traditional, independent demand systems forecast likely demand for materials, and then hold stocks that are high enough to meet these. To allow for the inevitable errors in their forecasts, organisations hold more stocks than they really need. These extra stocks give a measure of safety, but they also increase the inventory costs. MRP avoids these costs by relating the supply of materials directly to demand. Benefits that come from this direct link include:

- lower stock levels, with savings in capital, space, warehousing, and so on
- higher stock turnover
- better customer service – with no delays caused by shortages of materials
- more reliable and faster delivery times
- less time spent on expediting and emergency orders
- MRP schedules can be used for planning other logistics activities.

MRP can also give early warning of potential problems and shortages. If the MRP schedules show that some materials will arrive too late, the organisation can speed up deliveries or change the production plans. In this way MRP improves the wider performance of the organisation – measured in terms of equipment utilisation, productivity, customer service, response to market conditions, and so on.

Disadvantages of MRP

There are also some problems with MRP, the most obvious being the amount of information and calculation that it needs. The basic information comes from a detailed master schedule, so

MRP cannot be used when there is no master schedule, the master schedule is not designed far enough in advance, it is inaccurate and does not show what actually happens, or when plans are changed frequently.

Other requirements of MRP include a bill of materials, information about current stocks, orders outstanding, lead times, and other information about suppliers. Many organisations simply do not record this information. Others find that their information does not have enough detail, or is in the wrong format, or is not accurate enough. Accuracy is particularly important, as large numbers of small stock transactions can introduce errors. Ordinarily these errors are small enough not to matter, as there is enough stock to give cover until the errors are detected. MRP, however, does not have these reserve stocks, so there is no room for errors. Another problem with MRP is its inflexibility. The only materials available are those needed for the specified master schedule, so this cannot easily be adjusted. Some general disadvantages of MRP include:

● reduced flexibility to deal with changes
● needs a lot of detailed and reliable information
● systems can become very complex
● the order sizes suggested by MRP can be inefficient
● MRP may not recognise capacity and other constraints
● can be expensive and time consuming to implement.

LOGISTICS IN PRACTICE

British Airways plc

British Airways (BA) is one of the world's largest airlines, with flights to 150 destinations over 1200 routes. You can imagine the amount of materials that it has to move just to serve 50 million meals a year to passengers. Kitchens at Heathrow and Gatwick prepare 250 tonnes of chicken and 40,000 cases of wine, but third party suppliers around the world provide most of the food. BA is, however, responsible for all the non-food items, such as crockery, wine, dry foods, cutlery, and so on. A typical Boeing 747 flight carries around 45,000 items.

BA is a 'full service' airline, which means that it emphasises service rather than lowest possible price. Nonetheless, in 1997 it announced plans to save £1 billion over five years by improving efficiency, and looked for even further savings following a drop in business in 2001/2. As part of this, BA Catering reviewed its services and cost, reduced the length of its supply chains and more positively managed links with supply chain partners. It also effectively introduced MRP for several million items from 300 suppliers. Passenger bookings provide the master schedule, and these are used to co-ordinate the airlines stock levels and deliveries. By matching supply to known demand – thereby eliminating waste and reducing stocks – BA saves around £4 million a year. The company's original investment was repaid within the first year.

Reduced costs are only one benefit of the new system. Less storage space was

LOGISTICS
IN PRACTICE

continued

needed at airports, lead times were reduced, there was less wastage, control of materials was improved, shortages were reduced, and so on. More reliable information became available, and by recording every item demanded by every route, flight and even customer, BA has a means of significantly increasing customer service.

Sources: Collinge P. and Reynolds P. (1997) Food for thought, *Logistics Focus*, 5(9), 2–8; Jones C. (1998) Making the missing link, *Logistics Focus* 6(7), 2–6; and website at www.ba.com

EXTENDING THE ROLE OF MRP

Initial ideas

We have outlined the basic approach of MRP and now can look at ways of improving the results. For example, the basic procedure might suggest a series of small, frequent orders. It may be cheaper and more convenient to combine several of these small orders into one larger one. This is called **batching**. There are four common methods of batching:

1. **Lot-for-lot** – where you order exactly the net requirement suggested by MRP for each period. This has the advantage of minimising the amount of stock, but can give high ordering, delivery and administration costs.

2. **Fixed-order quantity** – where you find an order size that is convenient, such as a truckload, a container load, or an economic order quantity (which we describe in Chapter 9). When you want a delivery, you always order this amount, and put any spare in stock.

3. **Periodic orders** – where you combine the requirements over some fixed period, and place regular orders for different quantities. You might, for example, place a weekly order for the amount of materials needed in the following week. Working to a regular timetable is simple and makes ordering routine.

4. **Batching rules** – which uses a specific procedure to calculate the best pattern of orders. Typically they look for the combination of orders that gives the lowest overall cost. In practice, this can be quite a difficult scheduling problem.[2]

Another improvement comes when the same material is used for different products. Then we combine the demands from all products to give the overall gross requirement. Similarly, when several materials are ordered from the same supplier, it obviously makes sense to add them all to a single order. Now the batching rules have to extend to cover different products, and different materials from the same source.

A more significant extension to MRP adds feedback for planning. MRP uses the master schedule to generate orders for materials, and this schedule usually has some variation. But we saw in Chapter 2, that this variation can be magnified in the supply chain to give widely

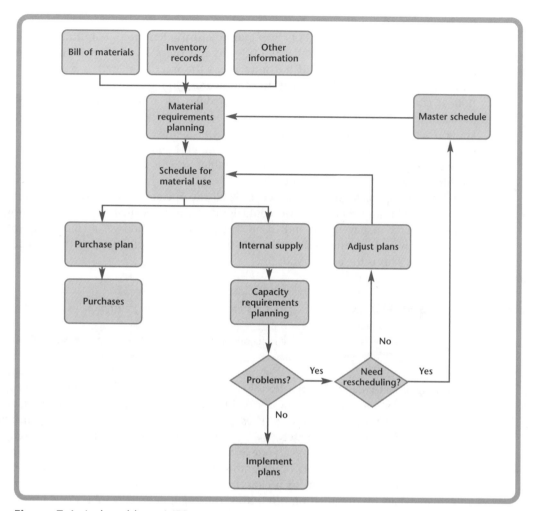

Figure 7.4 A closed-loop MRP system

varying demands for upstream suppliers. Their operations may not be able to deal with this varying demand, particularly during the peaks. It is obviously better to anticipate such problems during the planning stage, so that schedules or capacity can be adjusted before the plans are finalised. In other words, we introduce feedback from MRP to capacity planning. This linking of capacity planning to MRP is called **capacity requirements planning**. Overall systems with feedback of this kind are called **closed-loop MRP**, with one system summarised in Figure 7.4.

Moving to MRP II

You can see how capacity requirements planning extends the MRP approach further into the organisation. We started by using MRP to schedule the delivery of materials, and can now use it in capacity planning. But we need not stop here. Materials are only one resource, and organisations have to schedule others, including people, equipment, facilities, finances, transport, and so on. Surely we can use the same MRP approach to consider these other resources. This thinking has led to a major extension of MRP into **Manufacturing Resources Planning**, or **MRP II**.

Imagine an organisation that uses MRP to get a timetable for purchasing materials and preparing materials internally. If it knows when the internal materials have to be ready, it knows when to start preparing them. In other words, MRP can give schedules for the production of components. But we can use the schedules for components to get timetables for production equipment, people working on it, raw materials, and other resources. And if we know when the raw materials are needed, we can schedule inward transport, drivers, quality checks, and so on. Continuing in this way, we could build an integrated system that would 'explode' the master schedule to give timetables for all the jobs, equipment, operators, machines, and facilities needed to achieve it.

With this approach, MRP would schedule all the operations. However, there is no reason why we should stop there, and we could look at the associated finance, marketing, sales, human resource management, and so on. Eventually we would get a completely integrated system that would use the master schedule as the basis for planning all the resources in an organisation. This is the aim of MRP II.

■ **MRP II** gives an integrated system for synchronising all functions within an organisation.
■ It connects schedules for all functions and resources back to the master schedule.

Linking all activities to the master schedule can give very efficient logistics. There are no late deliveries or shortages, no stocks of work in progress accumulate, and products move smoothly through the whole process. These benefits have encouraged many organisations to move towards MRP II. Unfortunately, there can be serious practical difficulties. To start with, it is difficult to get schedules that everyone accepts as being good and workable. A more serious problem, though, is the difficulty of integrating all functions and systems. Many organisations have asked if the rewards from such close integration are worth the effort. MRP tends to be inflexible, so a whole organisation run in this way might become cumbersome, unwieldy, slow to respond to changing conditions.

Because of these difficulties, many organisations have moved towards MRP II, but have not implemented complete systems. Often different names are used for these partial systems, and you might hear about **distribution resource planning** or **logistics resource planning**, where the MRP approach is used to plan logistics. Unfortunately, such terms are used rather inconsistently. Some people, for example, use distribution resource planning to describe more limited systems where the demand does not come from a production plan, but from received customer orders.

Working with other organisations

MRP II can generate plans for all activities and material movements within an organisation. But this is still not the end of the story. Following the trend for integrating the supply chain, we can extend the planning to other organisations. This gives the basis of **Enterprise Resource Planning** (ERP).

Suppose a manufacturer's MRP system finds that it needs a delivery of 100 units of some material at the beginning of June. It uses this information to schedule its purchases.

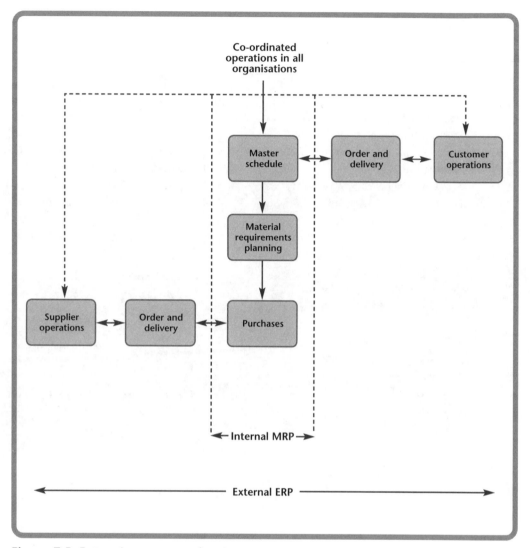

Figure 7.5 Enterprise resource planning

However, EDI (electronic data interchange) can link the MRP system to the supplier's system, so the supplier knows in advance when it has to deliver this material, and it can start scheduling operations to make sure that it is ready in time. If second tier suppliers are linked to the MRP system of the first tier supplier, they can also start their preparations. In this way, the message moves backwards through the supply chain, giving integrated planning (illustrated in Figure 7.5).

In principle, the free flow of information needed by ERP is relatively easy to organise with EDI, EFT, the Internet and other tools of e-business. However, it might be difficult to get such complete trust between organisations, even when they are prepared to form alliances. You can also imagine the complexity of systems needed, and the practical problems that arise. Nonetheless, this approach has considerable potential, and is leading to the next stage of 'virtual enterprise resource allocation'.[3]

LOGISTICS
IN PRACTICE

SAP AG

ERP software has been available since the 1990s and the market has grown very quickly. Estimates of world sales value vary widely, but it probably reached $10 billion a year before 2000.

SAP was founded in Walldorf, Germany in 1972, and is the world's largest 'inter-enterprise' software company. It employs 25,000 people, in more than 50 companies and has '10 million users; 30,000 installations; 1,000 partners'. You can see how quickly its market has grown from the following revenues for ERP in the mid 1990s.[4]

Year	1994	1995	1996	1997
ERP licence revenue ($ million)	692	1350	1730	2370

Many other companies supply such integrated software, including BAAN, JD Edwards, SSA, and PeopleSoft. Their very large systems have an average installation cost of $15 million. Of this, 17% is for software, 14% for hardware, 46% for professional services and 23% for internal staff costs. The time to implement the systems vary from under 18 months to over 30 months. After this, benefits begin to appear in about a year and it takes around five years to break even.

Peter Burris of META Group summarises these results[5] with the comment:

To say that implementing ERM/ERP solutions requires an enormous commitment is an understatement. They are expensive, are time-consuming, and require change in virtually every department in the enterprise.

Sources: Brace G. and Rzevski G. (1998) Elephants rarely pirouette, *Logistics Focus*, 6(9), 14–18; Anon (1999) *ERM Solutions and Their Value*, Meta Group, Stamford, CT; and websites at www.SAP.com and www.metagroup.com

PRINCIPLES OF JUST-IN-TIME

Principles and definitions

Just-in-time (JIT) offers another way of planning. It organises all activities so they occur at exactly the time they are needed. They are not done too early (which would leave materials hanging around until they were actually needed) and they are not done too late (which would give poor customer service). You can see this effect when you order a taxi to collect you at 08:00. If the taxi arrives at 07:30 you are not ready and it wastes time sitting and waiting; if it arrives at 08:30 you are not happy and will not use the service again. When the taxi arrives at 08:00 – just-in-time for your trip – it does not waste time waiting, and you are pleased that the service arrives exactly when you wanted it.

JIT seems an obvious idea, but it can have a dramatic effect on the way that materials are organised. You can see this with stocks of raw materials. The traditional approach buys materials early and keeps them in stock until they are needed. MRP reduces stock by co-ordinating the arrival of materials with the demand. But JIT aims at delivering materials directly to operations and virtually eliminating stock.

Companies such as Toyota[6,7] spent years developing JIT through the 1970s. Their methods were so successful that all major organisations now use some elements of JIT. We can start describing the principles by looking at the effect on stock, and then generalise the approach to other areas.

The main purpose of stock is to give a buffer between operations. Stocks are built-up during good times, to be used when there are problems. Then if some equipment breaks down, or a delivery is delayed, or demand is unexpectedly high, everything continues to work normally by using the stocks. The traditional view of managers is that stocks are essential to guarantee smooth operations. They allow for any mismatches between the supply and demand for materials.

Inventory control systems (which we describe in Chapter 9) define stock levels that are high enough to cover likely problems. Unfortunately, with widely varying demand or potential problems, these stock levels can be very high – and expensive. MRP reduces the amount of stock by using the master schedule to match the supply of materials more closely to demand. In practice, the batching rules of MRP add some stock, and they keep some more to allow for uncertainty and problems. However, the principle is clear – the more closely we can match the supply of materials to demand, the less stock we need to carry. If we can completely eliminate any mismatch, we need no stocks at all. This is the basis of just-in-time systems (illustrated in Figure 7.6).

■ **JUST-IN-TIME** systems organise materials to arrive just as they are needed.
■ By co-ordinating supply and demand, they eliminate stocks of raw materials and work in progress.

You can see an example of just-in-time operations with the fuel in a lawnmower. If a lawnmower has a petrol engine, there is a mismatch between the fuel supply that you buy from a garage, and demand when you actually mow the lawn. You allow for this mismatch by keeping stocks of fuel in the petrol tank and spare can. This is the traditional approach to inventory control, where stocks are high enough to cover any likely demand. If a lawnmower has an electric motor the supply of electricity exactly matches demand and there are no stocks of fuel. This is a just-in-time system.

So what happens when there really is a mismatch between supply and demand? What does a supermarket do when it sells loaves of bread one at a time, but gets them delivered by the truckload? The traditional answer is to hold enough stock to cover the mismatch – the supermarket puts the truckload of bread on its shelves until it is sold or goes stale. JIT says that this is a mistake. There is an alternative, which is to remove the mismatch. The supermarket might approach this by using smaller delivery vehicles, or opening a small bakery on the premises.

Now we can summarise JIT's view of stock:

● Stocks are held to cover short-term mismatches between supply and demand.
● These stocks serve no useful purpose – they only exist because poor co-ordination does not match the supply of materials to the demand.
● As long as stocks are held, there are no obvious problems and no incentive for managers to improve the flow of materials.
● Then operations continue to be poorly managed, with problems hidden by stocks.
● The real answer is to improve operations, find the reasons for differences between supply and demand, and then take whatever action is needed to overcome the differences.

As you can see, JIT is based on very simple principles. Instead of holding stocks to allow for problems, you identify the problems and solve them. Unfortunately, this often puts new pressures on logistics. With deliveries of bread to a supermarket, for example, logistics managers have to design new systems that can deliver small, frequent quantities of fresh bread.

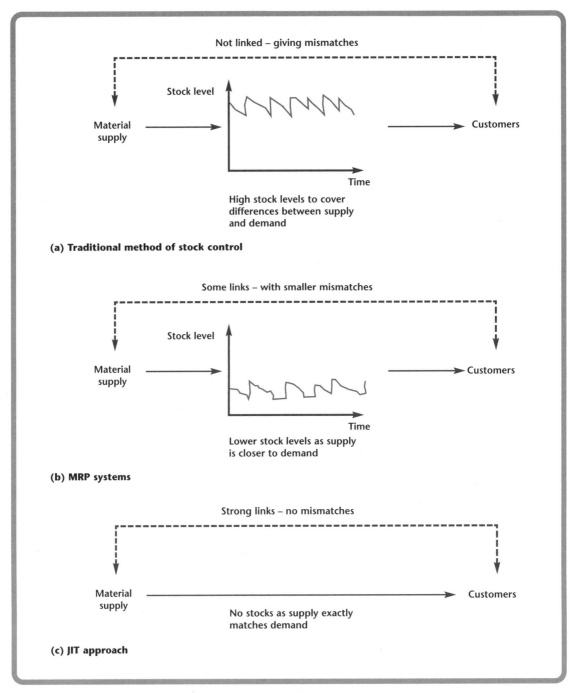

Figure 7.6 Stock levels with different types of control

Wider effects of JIT

We have introduced JIT as a way of reducing stock levels, but it is much more than this. JIT involves a change in the way an organisation looks at all its operations. Its supporters describe it as 'a way of eliminating waste', or, 'a way of enforced problem solving'. In this wider sense, JIT sees an organisation as having a series of problems that hinder efficient operations. These problems include long lead times, unreliable deliveries, unbalanced operations, constrained capacity, equipment breakdowns, defective materials, interruptions, unreliable suppliers, poor quality, too much paperwork and too many changes. Managers try to get around these problems by holding large stocks, buying extra capacity, keeping back-up equipment, employing 'trouble-shooters', and so on. But these methods only hide the symptoms of problems. A much more constructive approach is to identify the real problems – and solve them. This approach leads to a number of changes in viewpoint.

- *Stocks:* As we have seen, organisations hold stocks to cover short-term differences between supply and demand. JIT assumes that these stocks actually hide problems. Organisations should find the reasons for differences between supply and demand, and then take whatever action is needed to remove them.

- *Quality:* Organisations have defined some arbitrary level of acceptable quality, such as, 'we will accept one defect in a hundred units'. JIT recognises that all defects have costs, and it is better to find the cause and make sure that no defects are produced (supporting the view of total quality management).

- *Suppliers:* JIT relies totally on its suppliers – so it supports the view of customers and suppliers working closely together in long-term partnerships pursuing common objectives.

- *Batch size:* Operations often use large batch sizes, as they reduce set-up costs and disruptions. But if demand is low, the products made in large batches sit in stock for a long time. JIT looks for ways of reducing the batch size so that it more closely matches demand.

- *Lead times:* Long lead times encourage high stocks, as they have to cover uncertainty until the next delivery. JIT aims for small, frequent deliveries with short lead times.

- *Reliability:* JIT is based on continuous, uninterrupted production, so all operations must be reliable. If, say, equipment breaks down, managers must find the reasons and make sure it does not happen again.

- *Employees:* Some organisations still have a friction between 'managers' and 'workers'. JIT argues that this is a meaningless distinction, as the welfare of everyone depends on the success of the organisation. All employees should be treated fairly and equitably.

By now, you can see that JIT is not just a way of minimising stocks. By co-ordinating all activities, it increases efficiency and eliminates waste.

Just-In-Time at Guy La Rochelle International

Guy La Rochelle International is one of Europe's leading manufacturers of cosmetics and toiletries. It has a major production plant near Lyon that employs more than 700 people.

One of the problems with La Rochelle's market is the speed at which customers' tastes change. To maintain its market share and meet these changing demands, La Rochelle has to be flexible. It has improved its response to customers and reduced costs by introducing just-in-time manufacturing. This has small batch sizes, short production runs, low stocks, fast changeover between products, reliable delivery from suppliers, efficient shipment of goods to customers, and fast response to changing customers' tastes. Now customers are guaranteed products that have been made within the past few days and have not spent weeks sitting on a warehouse shelf.

When La Rochelle reduced its stock of lipstick by $1 million it saved $250,000 a year. Their Baby Soft bath oil has changed from a production run of 60,000 units every 30 days, to 10,000 units every 5 days; the run of 200,000 units of lipstick every 65 days has changed to 60,000 units every 20 days.

The conversion to JIT is well-supported and liked by La Rochelle employees. Every employee now has a variety of skills, and works in a team rather than as an individual.

Source: company reports

Key Elements in JIT

One problem with JIT is that it only works well in certain types of organisation. The most successful users of JIT are large-scale assembly plants, which make virtually identical products in a continuous process. You can see why this is, from the following arguments:

● Every time there are changes to a process, or it switches from making one product to making another, there are delays, disruptions and costs. JIT says that these changes waste resources and should be eliminated. In other words, JIT needs a stable environment where a process makes large numbers of a standard product, at a fixed rate, for a long time.

● This stable environment can reduce costs by using specialised automation. Then JIT works best with high volume, mass production.

● The level of production must allow a smooth and continuous flow of products through the process. Each part of the process should be fully utilised, so the process is likely to be a well-balanced assembly line.

● Deliveries of materials are made directly to the assembly line at just the time they are needed. Suppliers must be able to adapt to this kind of operation. It would be impractical to bring each individual unit from suppliers, so the next best thing is to use very small batches.

● If small batches are used, reorder costs must be reduced as much as possible or the frequent deliveries will be too expensive.

● Lead times must be short or the delay in answering a request for materials becomes too long. This means working closely with suppliers, and encouraging them to build facilities that are physically close.

● As there are no stocks to give safety cover, any defects in materials would disrupt production. Suppliers must, therefore, be totally reliable and provide materials that are free from defects.

● If something goes wrong, people working on the process must be able to find the cause, take the action needed to correct the fault, and make sure that it does not happen again. This needs a skilled and flexible workforce that is committed to the success of the organisation.

ACHIEVING JUST-IN-TIME OPERATIONS

Push and pull systems

The success of JIT is not solely based on its idea of organising activities at just the time they are needed, but on its description of how to achieve this. It works by 'pulling' materials through the process.

In a traditional process, each operation has a timetable of work that must be finished in a given time. Finished items are then 'pushed' through to form a stock of work in progress in front of the next operation. Unfortunately, this ignores what the next operation is actually doing – it might be working on something completely different, or be waiting for a different item to arrive. At best, the second operation must finish its current job before it can start working on the new material just passed to it. The result is delays and increased stock of work in progress.

JIT uses another approach to 'pull' work through the process. When one operation finishes work on a unit, it passes a message back to the preceding operation to say that it needs another unit to work on. The preceding operation only passes materials forward when it gets this request. As you can see, this kind of process does not have earlier operations **pushing** work through, but has a later operation **pulling** it through. You can see the difference in a takeaway sandwich bar. With the traditional push system, someone makes a batch of sandwiches and delivers them to the counter where they sit until a customer buys them. With a JIT pull system, a customer asks for a particular type of sandwich, and this is specially made and delivered – thus eliminating the stocks of work in progress. You can also see that there is inevitably some lead time between an operation requesting material and having it arrive. In real JIT systems, messages are passed backwards this lead time before they are actually needed. Materials are also delivered in small batches rather than continuous amounts, so JIT still has some stocks of work in progress. These stocks are as small as possible, so it would be fairer to say that JIT minimises stocks rather than eliminates them.

Scandinavian Health Products

Scandinavian Health Products (SHP) sell a range of 280 products to customers in northern Europe. They deliver products by post, with orders received by e-mail, telephone, fax and post. Their main products are vitamin pills, mineral supplements, oil capsules, herb extracts and a range of other natural products that foster good health.

Operations in SHP centre on four sections:

■ At the beginning of each day the receipt section looks at all new orders, checks the details and sends orders down to the warehouse.

■ The warehouse section looks at each order, collects the products requested in a box and passes this to the finishing section.

■ The finishing section checks the contents of each box against the order, checks the bill, adds some promotional material and seals the box.

■ The transport section consolidates and wraps the boxes, and each afternoon at 4pm they take the day's orders to a national parcel delivery service which guarantees delivery by the following morning.

This process should work smoothly, but the finishing section always complained that they had to work late, and orders often missed the post. Kurt Brandt, the logistics manager, identified the problem as the trolleys used to move boxes between the warehouse and finishing. These trolleys carried over a hundred boxes. People in the warehouse section loaded up a trolley, and when it was full they used a forklift truck to push it through to the finishing section.

On most days the finishing section would get a surge of work at the end of the day as the warehouse section cleared their orders before going home, and pushed through two or three trolleys just before the four o'clock deadline. Finishing could not deal with these in time, but worked on some during overtime at the end of their working day, and left the remainder until the next morning.

Kurt Brandt found a simple solution to the problem. He reduced the working day of people in the finishing section so that they arrive 15 minutes later than those in the warehouse. In return, rather than wait for the trolleys to be delivered, they go to collect them whenever they run out of work. The big trolleys were replaced with small ones that only carry five boxes and which can be pushed by hand. People in the warehouse make sure that there are always three or four of the new trolleys filled and waiting for the finishing section to collect.

Sources: company reports and Brandt K (2002) *Using JIT, Practice Seminar,* Logistics Quest, Oslo

Kanbans

JIT needs some way of organising the flow of materials that are pulled through the process. The simplest system moves materials between two stages in containers. When a second stage

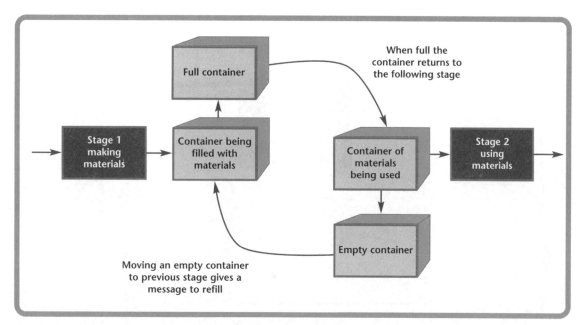

Figure 7.7 The simplest form of message for JIT

needs some materials, it simply passes the empty container back to the previous stage as a signal to fill it (see Figure 7.7).

This method is not reliable enough for most operations, so the usual alternative uses *kanbans*. 'Kanban' is the Japanese for a card, or some form of visible record.

■ *KANBANS* are cards that control the flow of materials through JIT operations.
■ They arrange the 'pull' of materials through a process.

There are several ways of using *kanbans*. The most common system (shown in Figure 7.8) uses two distinct types of card, a *production kanban* and a *movement kanban*.

● All material is stored and moved in standard containers – with different containers for each material.

● A container can only be moved when it has a movement *kanban* attached to it.

● When one stage needs more materials – that is when its stock of materials falls to a reorder level – a movement *kanban* is attached to an empty container. This gives permission to take the container to a small stock of work in progress.

● A full container is found in this stock, which has a production *kanban* attached.

● The production *kanban* is removed and put on a post. This gives a signal for the preceding workstation to make enough to replace the container of materials.

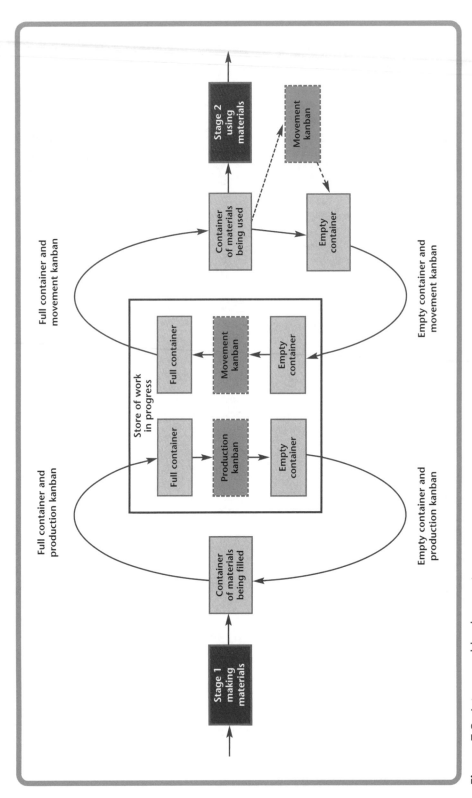

Figure 7.8 A two-card kanban system

● The movement *kanban* is attached to the full container, giving permission to move it back to the operation.

Although this system has a stock of work in progress, this stock is small. When a full container is removed, it is usually the only container in stock – and materials are not replaced until the previous workstation makes them. JIT almost always uses a product layout – such as an assembly line – so this stock of work in progress is really a small amount that is kept in the line, and there is no actual movement.

Each full container in the store has a production *kanban* attached to it, so the number of these *kanbans* effectively fixes the amount of work in progress. If there is only one production *kanban*, it means that the stock of work in progress is limited to at most one container of items. If there are two production *kanbans*, this doubles the stock of work in progress, and more *kanbans* would give even higher stocks. The aim of JIT is to work with minimum stocks and, therefore, a minimum feasible number of *kanbans*.

The main features of such *kanban* systems are:

● A message is passed backwards to the preceding workstation to start production, and it only makes enough to fill a container.

● Standard containers are used which hold a specific amount. This amount is usually quite small, and is typically 10% of a day's needs.

● The size of each container is the smallest reasonable batch that can be made, and there are usually only one or two full containers at any point.

● A specific number of containers and *kanbans* is used.

● The stock of work in progress is controlled by the size of containers and the number of *kanbans*.

● Materials can only be moved in containers, and containers can only be moved when they have a *kanban* attached. This gives a rigid means of controlling the amount of materials produced and time they are moved.

● While it is simple to administer, this system makes sure that stocks of work in progress cannot accumulate.

JIT has developed into many different forms. A common one replaces the manual *kanbans* with electronic signals. Then a control system monitors movements of materials using bar codes or other item coding, and it sends a message backwards to signal when it is time to prepare more materials.

Benefits and disadvantages of JIT

We introduced JIT as a way of lowering stocks, and some organisations have reduced these by 90%.[8] This gives a number of related benefits, such as reduction in the space needed (up to 40% less), lower procurement costs (up to 15%), less investment in stocks, and so on. In general, JIT gives the following benefits:

● lower stocks of raw materials and work in progress
● shorter lead times
● shorter time needed to make a product
● higher productivity

- higher equipment capacity and utilisation
- simplified planning and scheduling
- less paperwork
- improved quality of materials and products
- less scrap and wastage
- better morale and participation of the workforce
- better relations with suppliers
- emphasis on solving problems in the process.

Unfortunately, some of these benefits can only be bought at a high price. Making high quality products with few interruptions by breakdowns, for example, can mean buying better quality, more expensive equipment. Reduced set-up times usually need more sophisticated equipment. Small batches can increase production costs. Higher skills in the workforce increase training costs and the subsequent wage bill. Equipment must respond quickly to changing demands, so there must be more capacity.

One of the main problems with JIT is its inability to deal with unforeseen circumstances. Accidents or breakdowns, for example, can interrupt supplies and cause problems in the supply chain. Early in 2001 fuel supplies in the UK were disrupted by industrial action. Companies working with JIT felt the effects immediately when their materials were not delivered, while those with higher stocks kept working normally.

Some specific problems listed by JIT users include:

- high risks of introducing completely new systems and operations
- initial investment and cost of implementation
- long time needed to get significant improvements
- reliance on perfect quality of materials from suppliers
- inability of suppliers to adapt to JIT methods
- need for stable production when demand is highly variable or seasonal
- reduced flexibility to meet specific, or changing, customer demands
- difficulty of reducing set-up times and associated costs
- lack of commitment within the organisation
- lack of co-operation and trust between employees
- problems linking JIT to other information systems, such as accounts
- need to change layout of facilities
- increased stress in workforce
- inability of some people to accept devolved responsibilities.

LOGISTICS IN PRACTICE

JIT at Harley-Davidson

Harley-Davidson was one of the first companies to notice the effects of JIT. In the 1960s many countries had domestic manufacturers of motorcycles who met most of the local demand. These included Harley-Davidson in America, BSA in Britain and BMW in Germany. But in the 1970s the industry changed dramatically, and many

LOGISTICS
IN PRACTICE
continued

well-established companies went bankrupt. Their problem was the sudden new competition from the Japanese companies of Honda, Yamaha, Suzuki and Kawasaki.

These four companies could supply motorcycles anywhere in the world with higher quality and lower cost than competitors. In 1978 Harley-Davidson in America tried – but failed – to prove that the Japanese companies were dumping motorcycles on the market at less than the cost of manufacture. During these hearings it was shown that the Japanese companies' operating costs were 30% lower than Harley-Davidson's. One of the main reasons was their use of JIT manufacturing.

Harley-Davidson recognised that it could only compete by using the same methods, and adopted JIT in 1982. They stuck to their 'materials as needed' programme – their version of JIT – through initial difficulties and are now thriving in a very competitive market. In a five-year period Harley-Davidson reduced machine set-up times by 75%, warranty and scrap costs by 60%, and work in progress stocks by $22 million. During the same period productivity rose by 30%.

Source: company reports, www.HarleyDavidson.com

EXTENDING JIT ALONG THE SUPPLY CHAIN

Efficient consumer response

JIT forces suppliers to change the way they work, with fast deliveries, perfect quality, small batches, and complete reliability. The easiest way for them to meet these requirements – which also reinforces the idea of an integrated supply chain – is to adopt JIT methods themselves. Then second tier suppliers adopt JIT to support first tier suppliers, and so on. This ensures that the whole supply chain is working together with the same aims and principles. This extension of JIT along the supply chain is known by a variety of names, including **quick response** (QR), **continuous replenishment planning** (CRP) and more commonly **efficient consumer response** (ECR).

> **EFFICIENT CONSUMER RESPONSE** pulls materials through tiers of organisations in the supply chain.

Early work in ECR was done in the fashion industry. This had severe problems with its stockholdings, largely caused by the traditional planning of production around four seasons. At the start of, say, the summer season, shops had to be full of new products in the latest styles. Then shops needed high stocks to give customers a wide choice, and wholesalers needed high stocks to re-supply the shops at short notice. To make sure that these stocks were in place, peak manufacturing occurred some time before the start of the season. If demand for a product was particularly high, there would be shortages as manufacturers had already moved on to making their autumn and winter collections. If demand was low, shops could not reduce their purchases as the clothes were already sitting on their shelves and in wholesalers. At the end of each season there were major sales as wholesalers and retailers tried to get rid of their less popular items, and major restocking in preparation for the next season.

The industry realised that it could get huge savings if it smoothed its operations. The way to do this was not to have huge stocks sitting in the supply chain, but to move items quickly, and respond to customer demands by more flexible manufacturing. Now they use just-in-time operations and link information systems so that they can 'pull' materials through the supply chain. When a retailer sells an item, their cash register automatically sends a message to the wholesaler requesting a replacement. In turn, the wholesaler's system sends a message to the manufacturer asking for a delivery. The manufacturer is not bogged down in making excessive amounts of items that are later sold at discounts, but responds quickly to the demand and replaces garments that have actually been sold.

With ECR, a message passes backwards through the supply chain, and each organisation co-operates in moving materials forwards. In 1985 the US retailer J.C. Penney formed one of the world's first ECR partnerships with Burlington (a fabric manufacturer) and Lanier Clothing (a garment maker). As a result, they increased sales by 22% and reduced stocks by 50%.[9] Interest in ECR has grown since the mid 1990s. The grocery trade was quick to see the potential benefits, and when you buy a packet of biscuits in a supermarket the till automatically sends a message back to the supplier to send a replacement, and the supplier's system sends a message to its own supplier, and so on back through the chain.

ECR extends the benefits of JIT to the whole supply chain. So it brings lower stocks, better customer service, lower costs, more responsive operations, improved space utilisation, less paperwork, and so on. Organisations introducing ECR in the 1990s reported a string of benefits. Quaker Oats, for example, reported a threefold increase in stock turnover, 65% lower stocks and 77% reduction in paperwork.[10] Integrated Systems Solutions reported 3–4% increase of service level, 40–50% reduction in stock and 2–3 times increase of stock turnover.[11]

Features of ECR

It is not necessarily physical transport that slows the flow of materials through a supply chain, but the associated flow of information. It might take a month for an organisation to prepare the details for a purchase, collect information, send orders, arrange payments, and so on, while delivery only takes a day. So ECR only became feasible when a practical method of control was designed. With JIT this came with *kanbans*; with ECR it came with EDI.

ECR relies on a string of 'enablers', many of which we have already met. For a start, ECR only really works when organisations and their suppliers are working together in partnerships. This allows full EDI including purchase orders, invoices, planning information, point-of-sales data, fund transfer, and so on. Each organisation's control system sends a message to suppliers and signals the need for more materials using an 'electronic *kanban*'. Some systems go further and hand over more responsibility to the supplier in **vendor managed inventory**. Then the supplier becomes responsible for maintaining stocks at their customers' operations, checking the availability, organising deliveries and all other aspects of inventory control that make sure stocks are available when needed.

There is no point in having a sophisticated signalling system if the physical delivery of materials is slow. So ECR relies on very fast movement of materials. To some extent, this needs efficient transport, but we have already noted Beesley's comment[12,13] that: 'In typical UK manufacturing supply chains at least 95% of the process time is accounted as non-value adding.' Then material movement can be made more efficient by removing non-value adding steps and, in particular, reducing the time spent in storage. Karabus and Croza[9] say that: 'product should never be warehoused or stored, but should continually be in movement, with the least possible number of handling steps'. Cross-docking – which co-ordinates materials movement so that they are transferred from the arrival bay directly to the departure bay without ever going into storage – can give much faster delivery and reduce costs to less than half. Luton summarises this by saying that: 'Efficient consumer response requires cross-docking'[14] and he suggests that an efficient terminal should aim for turning over stock at least daily, or 250 turns a year. These ideas are consolidated in **flow through logistics**, which aims at a smooth, continuous and uninterrupted flow of materials.

In different circumstances there can be many other enablers for ECR. These include integration of the whole supply chain, transparency (so that all organisations can see what is happening and how this affects them), understanding the operations of other organisations (particularly the conditions and constraints they work with), flexible operations that can deliver materials with short lead times, balanced resources to give a smooth flow of materials, and so on.

Introducing ECR

ECR is a deceptively simple idea. Like JIT, though, it needs substantial changes to operations and can only be used in certain circumstances. If the supply chain starts with potatoes, they are grown in a particular season and farmers cannot suddenly grow a crop at short notice. Another problem comes with the length of the supply chain, as a single organisation that does not want to be involved – or cannot adapt – will disrupt the flow. If the supply chain crosses a slow international border, or includes an area where productivity is low, or hits other problems, the delays become unacceptable and ECR cannot work.

Introducing JIT can be a huge undertaking, fundamentally changing the way an organisation works. When JIT is extended to ECR, implementation becomes an even bigger issue. This is probably why organisations have seemed slow to introduce it. By 1997 almost no organisations had a fully established ERC system.[15] Nonetheless, interest was clearly growing, and Szymankiewicz said that: 'If the massive increase in ECR activity predicted ... becomes a reality, it will become the main catalyst for developments in supply-chain thinking. ... ECR could well become the basis for supply-chain management.'[16]

The following list includes some key stages for an organisation implementing ECR:

● design a logistics strategy based on responsive replenishment
● understand the principles of ECR and how this will affect operations
● define the aims of ECR for the organisation and measures of performance from partnerships with organisations that can match the organisation's aims
● introduce comprehensive EDI with suppliers and customers
● build 'flow through' logistics, where materials are moved as efficiently as possible
● benchmark other operations and continue to improve.

This is, of course, only a partial list, and it seems deceptively simple. Forming partnerships, for example, is not easy, so integrating an entire supply chain is extremely difficult. If it were easy to get an efficient flow of materials with 'flow through' logistics, more organisations would already be working like this. Despite these cautions ECR can, when working properly, give dramatic improvements. Estimates suggest a typical return on investment of 250% over the first three years of use.[9]

CHAPTER REVIEW

❑ The traditional approach to planning is based on forecasts of demand. When actual demand is known, we can use approaches based on 'dependent demand'.

❑ Material requirements planning is a dependent demand system which 'explodes' a master schedule to give timetables for the delivery of materials. By relating deliveries to actual requirements, MRP can both reduce costs and improve customer service.

❑ There are several extensions to MRP, such as closed-loop MRP which gives feedback for capacity planning. MRP II extends the idea of MRP to other functions, so that all plans within an organisation are related back to the master schedule.

❑ Enterprise resource planning extends the MRP approach to suppliers. It co-ordinates the movement of materials along the supply chain.

❑ Just-in-time aims at eliminating waste from an organisation. It does this by organising operations to occur just as they are needed. This needs a new way of thinking, which solves problems rather than hides them.

❑ JIT matches the supply of materials to the demand by 'pulling' materials through the process. *Kanbans* give a simple, practical method of controlling this flow.

❑ Efficient consumer response extends the ideas of JIT, by pulling materials through an integrated supply chain. There are several enablers for ECR, including EDI and 'flow through' logistics.

C A S E   S T U D Y — *JIT at Pentagon Plastics*

Pentagon Plastics make small injection-moulded parts for a number of manufacturers. A few years ago, they faced a new problem with one of their best selling parts, which was used by an instrument maker and eventually put into Ford cars. When Ford expanded their quality management programme all their suppliers – including those who were several tiers up the supply chain – had to change their habits. In particular, they had to introduce total quality management and just-in-time operations.

C A S E   S T U D Y   continued

Jaydeep Julami was the production manager at Pentagon, and he was wondering how to meet the new demands on his operations. There were 30 main products and 120 minor ones, and the plant worked a single shift for five days a week. Their current production planning was based on a regular six-week cycle. The first 15 days of this cycle were spent making the main products, and the next 15 days making minor products. This schedule was designed to reduce the disruption of changing production from one product to another. Each change usually took less than an hour, but could take up to four hours if things went wrong.

A dashboard instrument panel was typical of Pentagon's main products. This was made in batches of 25,000 and sent to a store of finished goods. When customers ordered the panel there was a minimum order quantity of 4000. Most orders were met from stock, but if Pentagon did not have enough stock to meet an order, they would reschedule production. This might give a week's delay, as well as upsetting the schedules of other products.

Transport was arranged with a local company, who picked the parts up from Pentagon and delivered them directly to customers, usually within two weeks.

Jaydeep was reading an article about Hewlett-Packard's introduction of JIT. This said that they introduced JIT in seven stages. They:

1. designed an efficient mass production process
2. implemented total quality management
3. stabilised production quantities
4. introduced kanbans
5. worked with suppliers
6. continually reduced stocks
7. improved product designs.

Jaydeep thought about how he could use Hewlett-Packard's experience in his own plant. He knew roughly what was involved, but still was not confident they could make JIT work.

C A S E   S T U D Y
Questions

- Describe in detail the steps that Hewlett-Packard used to introduce JIT.
- From the limited information available, do you think that Pentagon Plastics should consider JIT? What benefits could they get?
- How might Pentagon set about introducing JIT?

P R O J E C T
Planning in Practice

One of the main differences between MRP and JIT is their reliance on computer systems. MRP needs specialised software, often using huge systems. Do a survey to see what programs you can find for MRP and compare their features. On the other hand, JIT looks for simple systems. Restaurants use a simple form of *kanban* when waiters pass messages back to cooks, telling them what to prepare. What other examples of JIT can you find? How do they send messages back through the supply chain?

DISCUSSION QUESTIONS

1. MRP was developed to plan the supply of parts at manufacturers, so it cannot really be used in other types of organisation. Do you think this is true?
2. MRP II seems a good idea in theory, but it would be difficult to plan logistics, let alone finance and marketing, from a master schedule. The systems would also be so unwieldy that they could never work properly. Even if they did work, operations would be too inflexible to cope with agile competitors. What do you think of these views?
3. What are the main difficulties of using ERP?
4. If you were in hospital and needing a blood transfusion, would you rather the transfusion service used a traditional system of holding stocks of blood, or a just-in-time system? What does your answer tell you about JIT in other organisations?
5. What are the most significant changes that JIT brings to the planning of logistics in an organisation? What happens if an organisation wants to introduce JIT, but finds that its suppliers cannot cope with the small batches and frequent deliveries?
6. What are the problems of using ECR? How can these problems be overcome?

REFERENCES

1. Orlicky J. (1974) *Materials Requirement Planning*, McGraw-Hill, New York.
2. Waters C.D.J. (1992) *Inventory Control and Management*, John Wiley, Chichester.
3. Brace G. and Rzevski G. (1998) Elephants rarely pirouette, *Logistics Focus*, **6**(9), 14–18.
4. Sharp A.E. (1998) quoted in 'Better routes for decision makers', *Financial Times*, 1/7/98.
5. Burris P. (1999) Study dispels common myths about ERP/ERM, Press release by META Group, 01/01/99.
6. Monden Y. (1994) *Toyota Production System* (2nd edn), Chapman & Hall, London.
7. Shingo S. (1981) *Study of Toyota Production System from an Industrial Engineering Viewpoint*, Japanese Management Association, Tokyo.
8. Hay E.J. (1988) *The Just-in-time Breakthrough*, John Wiley, New York.
9. Karabus A. and Croza M. (1995) The keys to the kingdom, *Materials Management and Distribution*, May, 21–2.
10. Boden J. (1995) A movable feast, *Materials Management and Distribution*, November, 23–6.

11. Margulis R.A. (1995) Grocers enter the era of ECR, *Materials Management and Distribution*, February, pp. 32–3.

12. Beesley A. (1995) Time compression – new source of competitiveness in the supply chain, *Logistics Focus*, 3(5), 24–5.

13. Beesley A. (2000) Time compression in the supply chain, Chapter 11 in Waters D. (ed.) *Global Logistics and Distribution Planning*, Kogan Page, London.

14. Luton D. (1995) Efficient consumer response requires cross-docking, *Materials Management and Distribution*, April, p. 15.

15 P-E Consulting (1997) *Efficient Customer Response*, P-E Consulting/Institute of Logistics, Surrey.

16. Szymankiewicz J. (1997) Efficient customer response, *Logistics Focus*, 5(9) 16–22.

Further reading

Cheng T.C.E. and Podolsky S. (1996) *Just in Time Manufacturing* (2nd edn) Chapman & Hall, London.

Hutchins D. (1999) *Just in Time* (2nd edn), Gower, London.

Louis R.S. (1997) *Integrating Kanban with MRP II*, Productivity Press, Cambridge, MA.

Luscombe M. (1993) *MRP II: Integrating the Business*, Butterworth Heinemann, London.

Sandras W.A. (1995) *Just in Time*, Oliver Wight Publications, Williston, VT.

Schniederjans M.J. and Olson J.R. (1999) *Advanced Topics in Just in Time Management*, Quorum Books, New York.

Turbide D.A. (1993) *MRP+*, Industrial Press, New York.

CHAPTER 8

Measuring and Improving Performance

AIMS OF THE CHAPTER

After reading this chapter you should be able to:

- RECOGNISE the importance of measuring performance
- DESCRIBE different measures of supply chain performance
- DISCUSS the best measures and their use
- USE benchmarking
- ANALYSE a supply chain using different charts
- DESCRIBE different approaches to improving logistics

MEASURING PERFORMANCE

The last few chapters have described the design and planning of a supply chain. At this point, we have set the structure of the supply chain, and shown how to organise the movement of materials. However, the supply chain is not fixed, but continues to evolve. So we need some way of saying how well it works at the moment, and how it can be improved. For this we have to answer four questions:

1. *What are we doing now?*
   Analysing the current methods, aims and operations of logistics.

2. *What do we want to do in the future?*
   Giving new aims and clear objectives for improvement.

3. *What is the best way to get there?*
   Looking at options and implementing the best.

4. *How do we know that we are getting there?*
   Measuring performance, comparing actual results with expectations.

We have already answered question 2, as the strategy and following plans say what logistics should do in the future. In this chapter we can look at the other questions, starting with measures of logistics performance (for question 4). Then we describe some methods of analysing current operations (for question 1), and suggest some approaches to improvement (for question 3).

Measures for logistics

Managers in every organisation have to measure the performance of logistics. If they do not take measures, they have no idea how well they are doing, whether things are improving or getting worse, whether they meet targets, or how they compare with competitors. An old maxim says, 'what you can't measure, you can't manage'. The problem, of course, is finding what to measure and how to measure it.

There is a huge number of possible measures of logistics. Some of these are indirect measures and often relate to finance, such as the return on assets, payback period, or contribution to profits. Financial measures are popular, as they are easy to find, sound convincing, give a broad view and allow comparisons. However, they also have weaknesses as they concentrate on past rather than current performance, are slow to respond to changes, rely on accounting conventions, and do not record important aspects of logistics. Financial performance can show that something is wrong, but it does not show what is wrong or how to correct it. This is like a doctor finding that you have a fever – it shows that something is wrong, but does not show how to get better.

In practice, it is much better to use direct measures of logistics, such as the number of tonnes delivered, stock turnover or distance travelled. Again, there are many possible measures. We will start by looking at general ones for capacity, utilisation and productivity.

Keystone-Gunterbach

Keystone-Gunterbach offers a range of transport and warehousing services around Berlin. For several years the major shareholders felt that the company was under-performing, and in 2000 they appointed a new chief executive, with an explicit goal of improving results. The chief executive started a restructuring and cost-cutting exercise, and by 2001 could report some progress. The annual report showed that the company's performance was now generally comparable with the industry. The table shows an extract of some key indicators.

At the annual meeting three shareholders who had worked for the original Gunterbach transport company asked for some clarification. They felt that the company's long-term survival depended on its being competitive. They could see the financial performance, but did not know how well the company was running its logistics.

Actually, the company was having trouble with competition in the developing markets of central Europe. They tried to compete on the quality of their service, but delivery times were getting longer, there were increasing problems with reliability, lack of investment was making their systems outdated, and customer satisfaction was declining. In the first quarter of 2002 their business fell by 15% and they appointed a new chief executive.

Performance indicator	Value	Change in year
Return on capital	12.4%	+2.4%
Return on assets	6.1%	+2.0%
Pre-tax margin	3.3%	+0.1%
Return on shareholders' funds	21.2%	+6.5%
Equity gearing	28.9%	−4.2%
Debt gearing	43.7%	−6.3%
Interest cover	2.5 times	−0.2
Current ratio	1.27 times	−0.3

Source: company annual reports

Capacity and utilisation

In Chapter 6 we defined the capacity of a supply chain as the maximum amount that can be moved through it in a specified time. This is a basic measure of supply chain performance. Each part of a supply chain has a different capacity, and the overall capacity is set by the bottlenecks.

It might seem strange to describe capacity as a measure of performance, rather than a fixed value or constraint on the throughput. There are two answers to this. First, we can say that the capacity depends on the way that resources are used. Two organisations can use identical resources in different ways, and get different throughputs. Then the capacity gives a direct measure of performance and management skills. Second, we can point out that capacity is not fixed, but varies over time. At the start of the day a team of people might be able to move 500 cases an hour; at the end of the day the same team are tired and can only move 400 cases an hour. The operations seem to be exactly the same, but the capacity has declined.

To allow for these effects, we define difference types of capacity. **Designed capacity** is the maximum possible throughput in ideal conditions; **effective capacity** is what we can actually achieve over the long term; **actual throughput** shows what we actually achieved. The designed capacity of Ellison's call centre is 1000 telephone calls an hour. They can achieve this for a short period, but after taking into account different types of calls, staff schedules, holidays, faults with equipment and other factors the effective capacity is 850 calls an hour. In one typical hour Ellison actually handled 710 calls. This shows that they were working below capacity and have not fully used their resources.

Utilisation shows the proportion of designed capacity that is actually used. Suppose you have a vehicle fleet that is designed to deliver 100 tonnes of materials a week. This is its designed capacity. If the fleet only delivers 60 tonnes in one week:

$$\text{utilisation} = \frac{\text{amount of capacity used}}{\text{designed capacity}} = \frac{60}{100} = 0.6 \text{ or } 60\%$$

The designed capacity of a supply chain is not the same throughout its length, but different parts have different utilisation. You might, for example, find that a transport fleet is under-utilised, while the warehouse it is delivering to is working flat out. Figure 8.1 shows an illustration of some typical calculations.

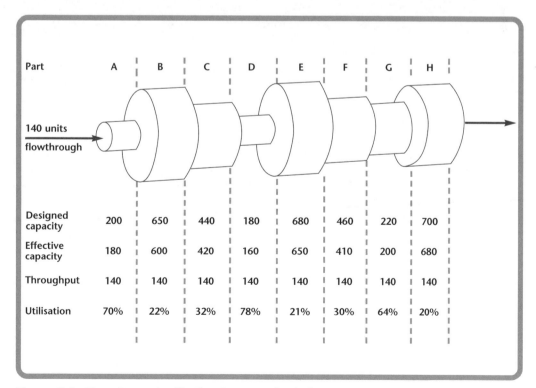

Figure 8.1 Capacity and utilisation in a supply chain

LOGISTICS IN PRACTICE

Ying-Chua Associates

In July 2000, Ying-Chua Associates had ten people organising 1000 specialised insurance policies for dangerous goods movements. In theory they could process 1250 policies a month but breaks, interruptions, holidays, schedules and other factors limited this to about 1150. The direct costs of this operation were £115,000.

Demand for the service was growing, and in September the company did a small reorganisation. After this they employed eleven people, who could deal with a maximum of 1600 policies a month, but with a more realistic limit of 1300. They were a little disappointed to find that in the following month they only processed 1200 policies, with direct costs of £156,000. Some measures of this performance are given in the table.

As you can see, even these simple measures have to be interpreted with some care.

	Before reorganisation	After reorganisation
Number of policies processed per person	1000/10 = 100	1200/11 = 109
Direct costs per policy	115,000/1000 = £115	156,000/1200 = £130
Designed capacity	1250	1600
Effective capacity	1150	1300
Utilisation	1000/1250 = 80%	1200/1600 = 75%

Ying-Chua's reorganisation increased the number of policies processed per person, but they also increased the direct costs per policy. The capacity has risen, but the utilisation has declined. Whether performance has improved, or not, depends on the objectives of the company.

Source: company reports

Productivity

Productivity is one of the most widely used measures of performance. Unfortunately, people often confuse its meaning, assuming that it is the amount of work done by each person. There are really several kinds of productivity. The broadest picture comes from **total productivity**, which relates throughput of a supply chain to the amount of resources used.

$$\textbf{TOTAL PRODUCTIVITY} = \frac{\text{total throughput}}{\text{total resources used}}$$

Unfortunately, this definition has a number of drawbacks. Throughput and resources must use consistent units, so they are normally translated into units of currency. This depends on the accounting conventions used – so we no longer have an objective measure. Another problem is finding values for **all** the inputs and outputs. This is particularly difficult for intangible inputs (such as sunlight, the environment and reliability) and outputs (such as pollution, waste prod-

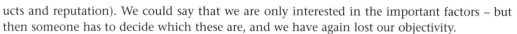

ucts and reputation). We could say that we are only interested in the important factors – but then someone has to decide which these are, and we have again lost our objectivity.

Because of these practical difficulties, hardly any organisations measure total productivity, preferring to use **partial productivity**, or **single factor productivity**. This relates the throughput of a supply chain to a single type of resource.

$$\text{PARTIAL PRODUCTIVITY} = \frac{\text{total throughput}}{\text{units of a single resource used}}$$

There are four types of partial productivity relating the throughput to different types of resource:

- *equipment productivity* – such as the number of customer visits per van, weight moved per forklift, or miles flown per aeroplane
- *labour productivity* – such as the number of deliveries per person, tonnes moved per shift, or orders shipped per hour worked
- *capital productivity* – such as the amount stored for each pound of investment, deliveries per unit of capital, or throughput per dollar invested in equipment
- *energy productivity* – such as the number of deliveries per litre of fuel, amount stored per kilowatt–hour of electricity, or the value added for each pound spent on energy.

Productivity can be a very useful measure of performance. But when an organisation simply reports its 'productivity' you have to look very carefully at what they mean. If an automated warehouse increases its labour productivity, this might be much less important than changes to its equipment or capital productivities.

WORKED EXAMPLE

The van der Perlitz Corporation runs a number of warehouses in southern Africa. Over the past two years they collected data about logistics, using standard units for throughput and converting values into South African rand.

	2001	2002
weight of materials moved	1000	1200
selling price	R100	R100
raw materials used	5100 kg	5800 kg
cost of raw materials	R20,500	R25,500
hours worked	4300	4500
direct labour costs	R52,000	R58,000
energy used	10,000 kWh	14,000 kWh
energy cost	R1000	R1500
other costs	R10,000	R10,000

How can you describe the productivity?

continued

Solution

From the information given we can use several measures of productivity.

■ The total productivity in 2001 was:

$$\frac{\text{total throughput}}{\text{total resources used}} = \frac{100 \times 1000}{20{,}500 + 52{,}000 + 1{,}000 + 10{,}000} = 1.2$$

By 2002 this had risen to 120,000/95,000 = 1.26, which is a rise of 5%

■ Units of throughput per kilo of raw material in 2001 was 1000/5100 = 0.196. In 2002 it was 1200/5800 = 0.207 which is a rise of 5%

■ Some other measures are:

	2001	2002	% increase
total productivity	1.20	1.26	5.0
units/kg of raw material	0.196	0.207	5.6
units/R of raw material	0.049	0.047	−4.1
units/hour	0.233	0.267	14.6
units/R of labour	0.019	0.021	10.5
units/kWh	0.100	0.086	−14.0
units/R of energy	1.000	0.800	−20.0

In general, labour productivity has risen, raw materials productivity has stayed about the same, and energy productivity has fallen.

Other measures

Capacity, productivity and utilisation give general measures of logistics performance, but we can use many more specific ones. For example, some common measures of transport performance include:

● Reliability of delivery
● Total travel time and distance
● Delivery cost
● Customer satisfaction
● Frequency of service
● Loss and damage
● Availability of special equipment

● Helpfulness of drivers
● Time to load and unload
● Total weight moved
● Number of errors in deliveries
● Errors in processing and administration
● Size and capacity of vehicles
● Skills of drivers
● Utilisation of vehicles.

Although we describe these as 'measures', some are clearly more difficult to quantify than others. Nonetheless, they may all be important, so we have to find ways of assigning numerical values. Sometimes we can use surrogate measures, perhaps measuring customer satisfaction by the number of complaints received. More often we use notional scales, so we might ask customers to rate some factor on a scale of one to five. But remember that when we use these methods to judge 'customer satisfaction', 'staff morale', 'management leadership', or some intangible concept, we are trying to give numerical values to essentially non-quantifiable factors, and should treat the results with caution.

Warehouses have a range of different performance measures, often related to the rate of stock turnover or utilisation of space. Some measures are based on the value of stock held. This varies over time – often quite widely – so we use average or typical values. The average value of stock of a single product is the average number of units held multiplied by the unit value. When this is summed for all products, we get an average total inventory value.

Average total inventory value = $\sum$ (average number of units held × unit value)

Managers can track this value over time and look for trends. If the value of stock is rising, it might be a cause for concern. More useful measures relate the amount of stock to the demand. Then an organisation can report the number of weeks' supply held in stock.

$$\text{Weeks' supply} = \frac{\text{average total inventory value}}{\text{average weekly throughput}}$$

Ideally this should be as low as possible, suggesting that stocks are being kept to a minimum. Some manufacturers hold 10 weeks' supply or more, particularly if supply is uncertain or demand is variable; companies using just-in-time operations only hold a few hours' supply.

A slightly different view measures the **stock turnover**, or **turn**. This shows how quickly materials move through the supply chain.

$$\text{Stock turnover} = \frac{\text{annual throughput}}{\text{average total inventory value}}$$

If the annual throughput of a warehouse is $1 million and the average total inventory value is $200,000, the turnover is 5. This means that materials are replaced an average of five times a year, and the average stock level is 1/5 years or 10 weeks' supply.

Other common measures of warehouse performance include:

● Average stock value
● Changes in stock value
● Utilisation of storage area and volume

⬤ Proportion of orders met from stock
⬤ Proportion of demand met from stock
⬤ Weeks of stock held
⬤ Stock turnover
⬤ Order cycle time
⬤ Number of orders processed
⬤ Cost of each stock transaction
⬤ Customer services
⬤ Errors in order picking
⬤ Damage and loss
⬤ Special storage facilities.

These lists are obviously not complete, and in different circumstances many other measures might be important. We could also make similar lists for other functions of logistics. With procurement, for example, we could measure the performance by the cost per transaction, cost as a percentage of purchase value, time to submit orders, value of materials bought, discounts achieved, number of transactions per person, number of errors, proportion of automatic orders, and so on.

There is clearly no shortage of measures, but we should ask which ones are actually used. A survey by Harrison and New[1] found that most organisations use some formal means of assessing supply chain performance – but 20% of their respondents did no assessment at all (as you can see from the following table).

Means of assessing supply chain performance	Percentage of companies
No formal means	20
Limited formal means	29
Some formal means	39
Extensive formal means	12

On the positive side it seems that 80% of organisations use some measures of logistics performance. Ferreira[2] said that the ten most common measures are quality, lead time, order fulfilment (which measures the proportion of orders that are delivered as expected), on-time delivery, responsiveness to demand, technical support, warranty and service, consolidation of deliveries, payment terms and ordering systems. Again some of these seem difficult to measure, but a more interesting point is that none of these measures contains an explicit reference to cost. Measures like 'service' have an implicit reference, but it seems that cost is not always a major concern. This view is supported by Harrison and New[1] who found the most common measures of logistics performance are customer delivery performance (86%), inventory turn (76%), supplier performance (66%), days of inventory (57%), order fulfilment (54%), lead time (52%), customer returns (52%), and supplier costs (48%). Less than half of companies reported using cost as a measure of performance. Other surveys report similar findings, such as Lennox,[3] who suggests that important factors are order fulfilment (68%), delivery errors (57%), damage (50%) and lead time (40%).

Balancing different measures

One problem is that the different measures give different – and often conflicting – views. If a truck is driven faster than usual, the miles per hour goes up, but the miles per litre of fuel go down; when a shop is renovated its sales per square metre go up, but its sales per pound invested go down; increasing the amount of automation in a warehouse gives higher labour productivity but lower capital productivity. To get a reasonable picture of logistics we have to take a balanced view of measures. But which measures are most important?

We can start answering this with the obvious comment that measuring the performance of a supply chain is not an end in itself. The measures give basic information for managers to use in their decisions, and they show how well the supply chain is achieving its goals. If the goal is to have a fast flow of materials through the chain, managers should measure this speed of flow and not bother so much about, say, productivity; if the aim is to minimise costs, managers should measure different aspects of cost, but not worry so much about utilisation. Unfortunately, managers often ignore this advice and use inappropriate measures that are easiest to find, support their views, have always been used in the past, or show them in the best light. Some consequences of this are warehouses full of goods because managers' status is judged by the amount of investment they control, rushed service because servers are judged by the number of clients they speak to and not the quality of their service, double booked seats because airlines are judged by seat occupancy, speeding trucks because drivers are judged by the number of deliveries they make in a day.

To give a reasonable view of logistics, a measure must:

- relate to the objectives of the supply chain
- focus on significant factors
- be measurable
- be reasonably objective
- look at current performance, not historical
- allow comparisons over time and with other organisations
- be easy to understand by everyone concerned
- be difficult to manipulate to give false values
- be useful in other analyses.

LOGISTICS IN PRACTICE

Delivering frozen food

Figure 8.2 outlines the structure of the UK frozen food industry. An important feature of this is the dominant role of the retail multiples. The three largest supermarket chains sell a third of all food, and buy from several hundred manufacturers and importers.

A problem, which is common for many industries, is that manufacturers and retailers use different criteria to judge performance. The main requirements of manufacturers' logistics can be summarised as:

- allowing them to focus on core operations of manufacturing
- standard distribution through a single contractor
- automated order processing
- integrated stock management system
- single stockholding point near to production
- low production and distribution costs
- long lead times and production runs.

The retailers' requirements from logistics include:

- no stock-outs in shop displays
- small, frequent, reliable deliveries
- deliveries made at any requested time
- short lead times
- linked systems based on efficient customer response
- direct movement of goods arriving onto display
- lower stock in stores
- no errors or damage in deliveries
- influence in the supply chain aiming at lower distribution costs
- opportunities to backhaul returnables.

There is clearly a lot of agreement here, but there are some areas where the two groups judge success in different ways. For example, manufacturers want third party contractors to take responsibility for logistics, while supermarkets want a more positive say, with greater influence over costs and operations.

One area where manufacturers and retailers agree is that delivery vehicles should move quickly and give a reliable service. A survey[4] of 11,900 trips, delivering 206,000 pallets of food and covering 1.16 million km found that 25% of journeys were delayed. The main causes of the delays were problems at the delivery point (31%) and traffic congestion (23%). This survey also found that trucks spent 21% of their time idle.

Activity of trucks	Percentage of time
Running on the road	35
Idle (empty and stationary)	21
Loading/unloading	16
Waiting for loading or departure	12
Maintenance and repair	6
Delayed on the road	6
Delayed while loaded	4

Sources: Lindfield G. (1998) *Logistics Focus*, **6**(1), 2–8; McKinnon A. (2000) Measuring the efficiency of road freight transport operations, *Logistics and Transport Focus*, **2**(8), 26–7

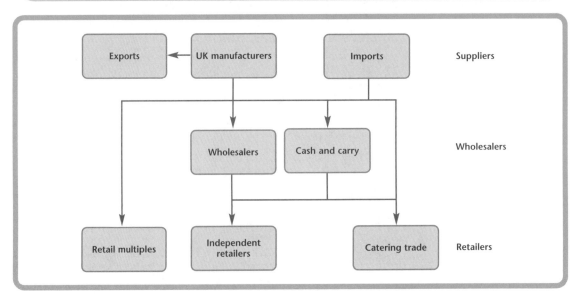

Figure 8.2 Structure of the UK frozen food industry

COMPARING PERFORMANCE

Standards for comparison

We have already said that measures of performance are not an end in themselves, but they help managers make decisions about the supply chain. In particular, measures can be used to:

- see how well objectives are being achieved
- compare the current performance of logistics with performance in the past
- make comparisons of logistics with other organisations
- compare the performance of different parts of the supply chain
- make decisions about investments and proposed changes
- measure the effects of changes to the supply chain
- help with other internal functions, such as wage negotiations
- highlight areas that need improving.

As you can see, many of these involve comparisons. This is because absolute measures often have little real meaning. If you know that a shop has annual sales of $1200 per square metre, you cannot say whether this is good or bad until you know the sales in comparable shops. There are basically four ways of judging performance, using comparisons with:

1. *Absolute standards* – which give the best performance that can ever be achieved. This is an ideal performance that operations might aspire to – such as the target of zero defects in total quality management.

2. *Target performance* – which is a more realistic target that is agreed by managers, who want to set tough, but attainable, goals. The absolute standard for the number of customer complaints received each week is zero, but a more realistic target might be four.

3. *Historical standards* – which look at performance that was actually achieved in the past. As organisations are always looking for improvement, we can regard this as the worst performance that might be accepted.

4. *Competitors' standards* – which looks at the performance actually being achieved by competitors. This is the lowest level of performance that an organisation must achieve to remain competitive. Federal Express deliver packages 'absolutely, positively overnight' so other delivery services must achieve this standard to compete.

There are many ways of making these comparisons. Some are very informal, and when warehouse managers visit another warehouse they automatically look for ideas they can use. Often a more formal method is better, and the most common uses **benchmarking**.

Benchmarking

With benchmarking, an organisation compares its performance with a competitor. There is no point in comparing performance with some random competitor, so benchmarking compares an organisation's performance with the best results achieved in the industry. To be blunt, organisations use benchmarking to find ideas for logistics that they can copy or adapt.

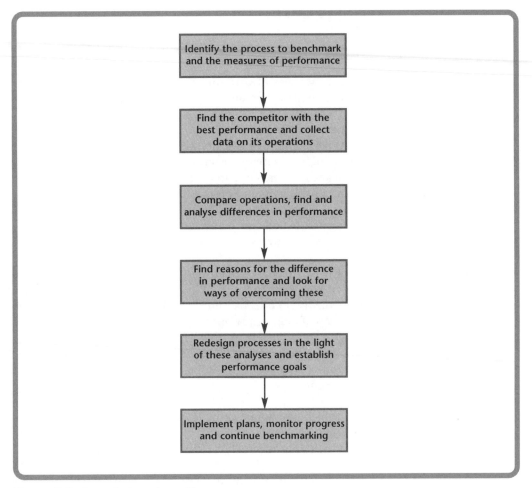

Figure 8.3 Steps in benchmarking

There are several steps in benchmarking. These start with an organisation recognising the need to improve its logistics. Then it has to define the most appropriate measures of performance, identify the leading competitor in the industry, and examine their logistics to see how they achieve this superior performance (as shown in Figure 8.3).

The easiest benchmarking to organise is internal, with one division of a company comparing its operations with another division. However, managers should take a broad view, and look for possible improvements anywhere they get the chance. You might think that organisations are reluctant to give details of their operations to competitors. In practice it can be fairly easy to get this information, and fears that it will be exploited are largely groundless. Everyone knows how to deliver parcels, serve food, run a shop, provide a taxi service – but thousands of organisations work very successfully in these industries, despite the fact that everyone knows all about their operations. Organisations in the same industry will share information when they can benefit from the results – as even the best performers can learn things that make them even better. When Sainsbury's benchmarked the operations at their depot in Buntingford, they contacted 45 companies who had agreed to take part in the exercise. More than half returned useful information, and Sainsbury's made follow-up visits to ten particularly useful operations.[5]

Sometimes, however, it is difficult to find a direct competitor for benchmarking, and then it is useful to look at organisations that are not in the same industry. BP is not a direct competitor of Tate & Lyle, but they both run fleets of tankers and may learn from each other's transport operations. Sometimes it is possible to learn from completely different types of organisation. Train operators, for example, might find improvements from bus operators, airlines, or other companies that are not involved in transport but give high customer service, such as supermarkets.

LOGISTICS IN PRACTICE

Charles Friderikson Car Rentals

When Charles Friderikson Car Rentals (CFCR) started a business in Copenhagen, there were already many competitors in the market. In general, the major international companies tended to compete by service, including Hertz ('Call the world's No. 1'), Avis ('We try harder'), Eurodollar ('Rent from the best'), Europcar ('All around – a better service'), Ford ('A big name in rental'), Thrifty ('World class service at your doorstep'). The smaller, local companies tended to compete on price, such as Economy ('The lowest prices around'), Capital ('Competitive rates, best value'), and Harald ('Lowest rates in town').

CFCR decided that they would compete by giving a good, personal service at a reasonable price. They obviously could not give the scale of service offered by the international companies, but they learnt a lot from their operations. For example, CFCR automated their administration, so that after their first visit a customer can pass a plastic card through a reader and pick up a car immediately.

At the same time, CFCR recognised that private customers were more interested in price, so they looked at the operations of the smaller companies to see how they reduce operating costs. For example, they do not use expensive locations like airport arrival lounges, keep their cars for rather longer, and have more flexible pricing.

CFCR effectively benchmarked their operations against international companies when looking at the quality of service, and local companies when looking for low costs. The important point about their benchmarking is that it identified better performance and it showed how this was achieved.

Source: Friderikson C. (2000) *Benchmarking Car Rentals*, Western Operations Group, London

ANALYSING A SUPPLY CHAIN

Process charts

Suppose that we benchmark a competitor's purchasing system, and find that it is ten per cent cheaper than ours. Now we have to look at the system and see exactly how it works, and where it makes the savings. In other words, we need some way of describing the detailed operations in the supply chain; we want some means of listing the individual activities and showing the relationships between them. The easiest way of doing this is with a **process chart**.

There are several types of process chart, but they all start by breaking down a process into separate activities. Suppose we look at our process for submitting an order. We could describe the main activities as:

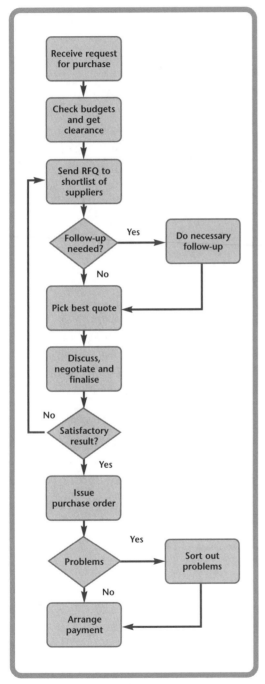

- receive request to purchase materials
- check departmental budgets and get clearance to purchase
- make a short list of possible suppliers and send a request for quotations
- examine quotations received and pick the best
- discuss, negotiate and finalise terms and conditions
- issue a purchase order for the materials
- do any necessary follow-up and expediting
- arrange payment of the supplier's invoice.

We can draw an informal process chart for this in the form of a flow chart (shown in Figure 8.4).

This informal chart gives a general view of the process, but it does not give many details. A better approach starts by describing all the activities as:

- *operation*: where something is actually done
- *movement*: where products are moved
- *storage*: where products are put away until they are needed
- *delay*: where products wait for something to happen
- *inspection*: to test the quality.

Then we can track a series of activities and describe exactly what happens. For this, we use the following six steps.

Step 1: List all the activities in their proper sequence from the start through to the finish.
Step 2: Classify each activity as an operation, movement, inspection, delay or storage. Find the time taken and distance moved.
Step 3: Summarise the activities by adding the number of activities, total times, rate of doing each activity, and any other relevant information.
Step 4: Critically analyse each activity, asking questions like, 'Why is it done this way?', 'Can we eliminate this activity?', 'How can we improve this activity?', 'Can we combine activities?'.

Figure 8.4 An informal process chart

Step 5: Now revise the process to give fewer activities, shorter times, less distance travelled, and so on.

Step 6: Check the new procedures, prepare the organisation for changes, train staff, and so on and implement the changes.

The first three steps give a detailed description of current activities, and an example of the format for a chart is shown in Figure 8.5.[6,7] Steps 1 and 2 are usually done by observation, while Step 3 is a calculation. The last three steps look for improvements.

Process chart									
Number	Description	Operation	Move	Store	Delay	Inspect	Time	Distance	Comment
1	Activity 1	X					10		
2	Activity 2		X				45	120	Into stores
	etc								
	.								
	Totals						55	120	

Figure 8.5 Format for a process chart

WORKED EXAMPLE

Draw a chart of the process involved when a lorry makes a delivery to a supermarket

Solution

Details of the process, and particularly the time, vary considerably. Figure 8.6 shows the start of a chart from one supermarket. When this chart is completed in as much detail as we need, we can start looking for improvements. Why, for example, do we have to move 100 metres to move goods to storage – can we reduce this somehow? Why does it take 30 minutes to put goods onto the shelves – can we do this faster?

Process chart								
Number	Description	Operation	Move	Store	Delay	Inspect	Time	Distance
1	Get details of delivery	X					10	
2	Unload lorry	X					45	
3	Check goods					X	25	
4	Move to storage		X				15	100
5	Store			X			450	
6	Take from store	X					15	
7	Move to consolidation		X				10	75
8	Wait for check				X		20	
9	Check goods					X	15	
10	Move to shelves		X				12	110
11	Put onto shelves	X					30	
	Totals						647	285

Figure 8.6 Part of a process chart for deliveries at a supermarket

Precedence diagrams

Another format for describing a supply chain uses a **precedence diagram**. This consists of a network of circles (representing activities) and arrows (representing the relationships between them). Suppose a very simple operation has two activities A and B, and A must finish before B can start. We can represent the activities by two circles and the relationship by an arrow, as shown in Figure 8.7. Then we can extend this method to more complex supply chains, as illustrated in the following example.

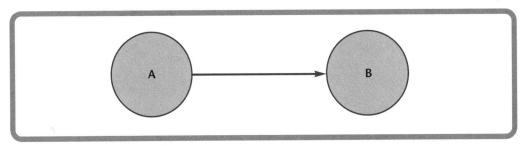

Figure 8.7 Precedence diagram, with activity B following activity A

WORKED
EXAMPLE

A supply chain has 11 activities with the precedence shown in the following table. Draw a precedence diagram of the chain.

Activity	Must be done after
1	–
2	1
3	1
4	2, 3
5	4
6	4
7	4
8	5
9	6, 7
10	8, 9
11	10

Solution

Activity 1 can be done right at the start. When this is finished both activities 2 and 3 can start. Activity 4 can be done after both activities 2 and 3, and so on. Continuing with this logic gives the diagram shown in Figure 8.8. When we have drawn this network, we can start looking for improvements.

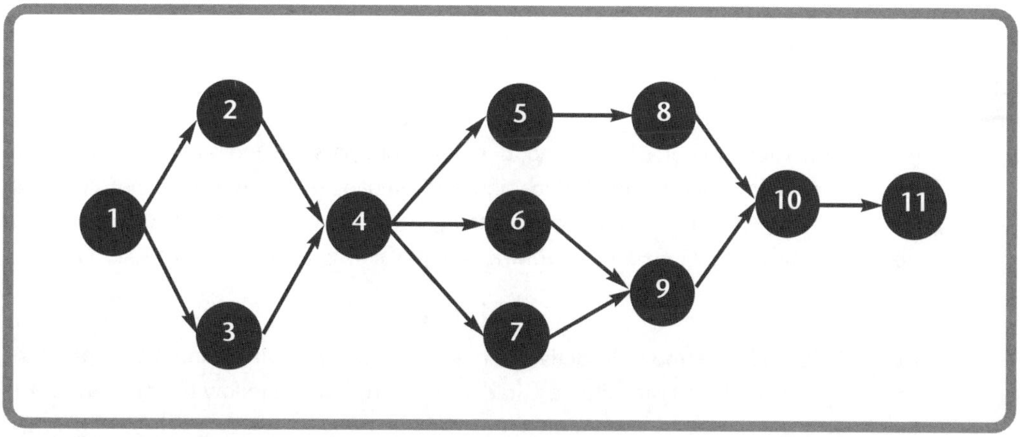

Figure 8.8 Precedence diagram for worked example

Multiple activity charts

It is often useful to see what each person or piece of equipment, is doing at any time. We can do this most easily with a **multiple activity chart**. This has a time scale down the side of the diagram, with all the participants listed across the top. The time each participant works on the process is blocked off (as shown in Figure 8.9).

This chart is for two people working in a small warehouse. When they get an order they go around and put the goods in a trolley, then they take them to a packing machine. The participants in the process are two people, two trolleys and the packing machine. The chart shows what orders (A to E) each participant is working on during 5-minute time slots. As you can see, each order takes 15 minutes to collect and 5 minutes to pack. We can see exactly what each participant is doing at any time, and we can look at the pattern of work to identify bottlenecks and idle periods.

Multiple activity chart					
Time	Person 1	Trolley 1	Person 2	Trolley 2	Packing machine
5	A	A	B	B	
10	A	A	B	B	
15	A	A	B	B	
20		A			A
25	C	C		B	B
30	C	C	D	D	
35	C	C	D	D	
40		C	D	D	C
45	E	E		D	D
50	E	E			
55	E	E			
60		E			E
Totals	54	60	30	35	25

Figure 8.9 Example of a multiple activity chart

One operator is currently assigned to each of three packing machines. The machines work a cycle with 6 minutes for loading, 6 minutes for operating and 4 minutes for unloading. An operator is needed for the loading and unloading, but the machines can work without any supervision. The warehouse manager plans to make savings by using two people to operate the three machines. Draw a multiple activity chart to see if this is feasible.

Solution

Figure 8.10 shows a multiple activity chart for three machines and two operators, assuming all people and machines are idle at the start, and we follow the process for the first hour.

Multiple activity chart

Time	Operator 1	Operator 2	Machine A	Machine B	Machine C
2	Load A	Load B	Load	Load	
4	Load A	Load B	Load	Load	
6	Load A	Load B	Load	Load	
8	Load C		Operate	Operate	Load
10	Load C		Operate	Operate	Load
12	Load C		Operate	Operate	Load
14	Unload A	Unload B	Unload	Unload	Operate
16	Unload A	Unload B	Unload	Unload	Operate
18	Load A	Load B	Load	Load	Operate
20	Load A	Load B	Load	Load	
22	Load A	Load B	Load	Load	
24		Unload C	Operate	Operate	Unload
26		Unload C	Operate	Operate	Unload
28		Load C	Operate	Operate	Load
30	Unload A	Load C	Unload		Load
32	Unload A	Load C	Unload		Load
34	Load A	Unload B	Load	Unload	Operate
36	Load A	Unload B	Load	Unload	Operate
38	Load A	Load B	Load	Load	Operate
40	Unload C	Load B	Operate	Load	Unload
42	Unload C	Load B	Operate	Load	Unload
44	Load C		Operate	Operate	Load
46	Load C	Unload A	Unload	Operate	Load
48	Load C	Unload A	Unload	Operate	Load
50	Unload B	Load A	Load	Unload	Operate
52	Unload B	Load A	Load	Unload	Operate
54	Load B	Load A	Load	Load	Operate
56	Load B	Unload C	Operate	Load	Unload
58	Load B	Unload C	Operate	Load	Unload
60		Load C	Operate	Operate	Load
Totals	52	52	60	56	50

Figure 8.10 Multiple activity chart for worked example

WORKED EXAMPLE
continued

The process starts with operators 1 and 2 loading machines A and B respectively. These machines start working, while operator 1 loads machine C. The operators unload machines A and B as soon as they are finished, and then they reload the machines. Machine C has to wait to be unloaded until an operator is free. The chart follows these activities for the first hour, at which point both operators have been idle for 8 minutes, and the three machines have been idle for 0, 4 and 10 minutes. Some of this idle time was needed to get things going at the start of the day, so it does look as if the new arrangement will work. We could confirm this by following the activities for a longer period.

IMPROVING PERFORMANCE

Benefits of better performance

Organisations work with continual change. Products, competitors, costs, markets, locations, infrastructure, employees, customers, the economy, the business environment, company objectives, technology, shareholders, and just about everything else changes over time. If organisations do not respond to these changes, they get left behind by more flexible competitors. The argument is that competitors are always trying to get an advantage by improving their own supply chains, so every organisation has to keep improving just to stay in the same place. So the main benefits of better logistics include:

- long-term survival
- lower costs
- increased profits, wages, real income, and so on
- improved competitiveness and growth
- better job security and staff involvement
- better use of available skills
- less waste of resources
- realistic targets for improving performance
- monitoring improving performance
- allowing comparisons between operations
- measuring management competence.

But how do we make sure that our logistics continue to change and improve? The best answer is to develop an organisational commitment to improvement – accepting that continual change is inevitable, necessary and beneficial. We develop a culture that welcomes and encourages improvement. Of course, a supportive culture does not necessarily generate new ideas, so we still need some way of looking at the supply chain and finding ways to improve it.

It might seem fairly easy to spot ways of improving a supply chain. As you look around, you continually see things that could be done better – poor road layouts, enquiry desks with long queues, transport that is not punctual, products that are too expensive, staff who are poorly trained, long waits for appointments, unhelpful service, and so on. Organisations could easily improve these. In principle, managers should seize every chance for improvement, but they seem happy to continue with their old, inefficient methods. Why is this? In practice there are many explanations. Managers may have tried to improve things in the past, failed, become disillusioned and not want to repeat similar experiences. More often there is no incentive for them to change, or they lack authority to push through reforms. They may not have the time for the necessary investigation, or not see the need, or not like change, or not know how to improve things, or think that changes would be too expensive and difficult to implement, or claim that they cannot measure performance. This probably accounts for Robert Townsend's observation that[8] 'All organisations are at least 50% waste – waste people, waste effort, waste space and waste time.' Beesley[9–11] goes further and says that: 'In typical UK manufacturing supply chains at least 95% of the process time is accounted as non-value adding.' This certainly suggests that there are opportunities to make things better.

Finding improvements

There are numerous suggestions for improving logistics. As we saw when designing a logistics strategy, many of these adopt general themes, such as total quality management, increasing technology, lean operations, emphasising human resources, timely operations, controlling materials flow, alliances, improved communications, and so on.

One clear point from these themes is that the old fashioned idea of 'getting people to work harder' has very little to do with performance. A hard-working person with a spade is far less productive than a lazy person with a bulldozer. About 85% of performance is set by the system that is designed by management; only 15% is under the control of individual employees. If things are going well, it is largely because the managers are doing a good job: if things are going badly, it is probably the managers who are to blame.

We have already suggested using benchmarking and process charts to highlight areas for improvement. Another obvious approach is to ask people most closely involved in logistics for their suggestions. They may already have a string of suggestions, or could quickly find some. Unfortunately, these people may be reluctant to suggest improvements. They may be so closely involved with the details of their job that they simply do not notice better options. And if they do find improvements, there is the unpleasant suggestion that they have been doing things badly in the past. A more pressing problem is that people who know how to make improvements do not have the authority to make the changes themselves, and are never asked for their opinion by those who could change things. In principle 'empowerment' and related ideas should overcome this problem.

Often simple rules of thumb can improve logistics. These make general suggestions, like, 'reduce the frequency of delivery', 'charge a premium for small deliveries', 'do value adding activities for customers', 'use the Web', 'use third parties for non-core business', 'reduce stock levels', 'make sure the warehouse is tidy', and so on. These can focus on areas that commonly cause problems in logistics. We have met this approach before, with the experience of Toyota who found that the following six areas caused most concern.[12]

- *Quality* – that is too poor to satisfy customers
- *Production level* – making products, or having capacity, that is not currently needed

🔵 *Processing* – having unnecessary, too complicated or time-consuming operations

🔵 *Waiting* – for operations to start or finish, for materials, repairs, and so on

🔵 *Movement* – with products making unnecessary, long, or inconvenient movements during operations

🔵 *Stock* – too much stock that needs storing and raises costs.

A different view comes from Devonshire[13] who suggests that information processing is the key, saying that, 'there is a direct link between the performance of supply chains and the quality of available information – indeed, in some approaches to making supply chains more efficient, stock is said to be replaced by information.'

These suggest specific areas to find improvements (like Emmett[14]), but it might be better to use a more general approach and talk about principles. For example, Sordy[15] suggests that logistics can be improved by aiming for five principles:

1. *Balance*, giving a smooth flow of materials through the chain
2. *Location*, with all operations in the best positions
3. *Minimise*, using the least amount of handling, distance travelled and cost
4. *Simplify*, to make everything as simple as possible
5. *Communicate*, as a good information flow gives good material flow.

Wheatley[16] uses a slightly different approach, giving the general advice to reduce the number of participants in logistics (number of suppliers, and so on), eliminate activities and resources that do not add value, use EDI, focus on customer needs, use the Internet, benefit from collaboration and develop the supply chain into a virtual factory.

Wherever we look for improvements, we need some general procedure for tackling the problems. In other words, we need to design a structure for our logistic improvement projects. We have already mentioned one possible structure in Chapter 4 when we described a plan–do–check–act cycle. This has a team of people whose job is to go around and positively search for things that could be done better, using the cycle:

🔵 *plan* – looking at the existing logistics, collecting information, discussing alternatives, and suggesting a plan for improvement

🔵 *do* – where the plan is implemented, and data is collected on performance

🔵 *check* – which analyses the performance data to see if the expected improvements actually appeared

🔵 *act* – if there are real improvements the new procedures are made permanent, but if there are no improvements, lessons are learnt and the new procedures are not adopted.

The team is continuously looking for improvements, and at this point they return to the beginning of the cycle, and start looking for more improvements. Other people use different approaches. A reasonable one for most problems has the following steps:

1. Make everyone aware that changes are needed to the supply chain, describing the reasons, alternatives and likely effects.
2. Examine current practices, identify their aims, see how well they achieve these and identify problem areas and weaknesses.
3. Use benchmarking and other comparisons to identify potential improvements and improved methods.
4. Design better procedures using the knowledge, skills and experience of everyone concerned.

5. Discuss the proposals widely and get people committed to the new methods.
6. Design a detailed plan for implementing the improvements, anticipating likely problems rather than waiting for them to happen.
7. Make any necessary changes to the organisation's structure, systems, facilities, and so on.
8. Give appropriate training to everyone involved.
9. Set challenging, but realistic, goals for everyone, and make it clear how these can be achieved.
10. Have a specific event to start the new methods.
11. Establish milestones and monitor progress to make sure they are achieved.
12. Give support and encouragement to everyone concerned.
13. Have continuing discussions about progress, problems, adjustments, and so on.
14. Monitor and control progress to make sure that everything continues to go as planned, remain committed to the new methods while they are giving improvements, and update them as necessary.
15. Accept that the new methods are only temporary, and continually look for further improvements.

This seems a rather formal list, but it is based on simple principles – analysing where we want to go and how we can get there. An important point is that the procedure uses continuous improvement. When new methods are introduced, we have to recognise that they are only temporary, and will be replaced again in the future. This generally – but not inevitably – involves a stream of relatively minor changes that can easily be absorbed by the organisation, give few disruptions, and cause no major problems. There is little risk, as any small change that does not work can easily be reversed.

This incremental approach to change builds a momentum for improvement, and makes sure that logistics is always getting better. Remember, though, that the incremental approach has critics who say that continually tinkering with the supply chain is counter-productive. They are more likely to recommend a radical approach such as business process re-engineering.

LOGISTICS IN PRACTICE

Hebblethwaite Ltd

George Hebblethwaite runs a small warehouse and transport company distributing a range of camping equipment in northern Britain. He was keen to improve company performance and collected data (see table) on costs for transport and warehousing.

Fixed costs	%	Variable costs	%
Wages	35	Fuel	54
Depreciation	27	Maintenance	19
Management	22	Tyres	24
Insurance	12	Oil	5
Licences	4		

(a) Transport fleet operations

George easily identified the areas where he could look for improvements. He got paid for moving vehicles, but his costs were largely fixed – so his first study looked for improvements in the activities for which he got no pay. Specifically, he looked for improvements in the loading, unloading

LOGISTICS
IN PRACTICE
continued

and idle times (as trucks spend an average of 58% of their time idle).[17] The other area he focused on was vehicle routes. In general, the variable costs rise with distance, but they also vary with conditions such as congested, urban and hilly areas that reduce speeds and increase fuel consumption.

(b) Warehouse operations:

Wages	58%
Buildings	23%
Equipment	19%

The cost of wages in the warehouse was particularly high, so George analysed people's activities and found the proportion of their time that they spent doing certain activities.

Total time	%	Of picking time	%
Receiving materials	18	Travel	58
Putting on shelves	11	Picking	31
Picking	39	Checking	8
Despatching	23	Other	3
Other	9		

Picking was clearly most time consuming, and then more than half of the picking time was spent moving around. George felt that this was another place with large potential savings.

Sources: company reports; Hebblethwaite G. (2001) Western Operations Group, Leeds

CHAPTER REVIEW

❏ Organisations must continually improve their logistics to remain competitive. This means that managers in every organisation have to measure the performance of their supply chains.

❏ Without these measures managers have no idea how well their logistics is working, how they compare with competitors, how performance has changed over time or what can be improved.

❏ There is a huge number of possible measures for the supply chain. Many of these are indirect and based on finance. It is, however, important to have some direct measures of logistics.

❏ General measures include capacity, utilisation, and productivity. There are many other specialised measures for transport, warehousing and other parts of logistics. An organisation has to take a balanced view of these to get an overall view.

❏ Performance measures are often used for comparisons. This is the basis of benchmarking, which compares an organisation's logistics with the best performance in the industry.

continued

❑ We can describe the activities in a supply chain using a variety of different charts. These highlight areas that need improving.

❑ There are several ways that an organisation can approach improvement. It might focus on specific areas that commonly cause problems, or it might use a particular procedure. We described a general approach to improvement.

C A S E   S T U D Y   *Ed's Drive-through Bottle Shop*

Ed's Drive-through Bottle Shop sells alcoholic drinks in Brisbane, Australia. The prices are low and the 'drive-through' shop is busy. Customers accept some delays to get cheap drinks, but at busy periods the manager saw that he was losing customers.

The basic plan of the shop has a single line of cars driving past a service window (customers can park and visit the shop as normal, but relatively few do this). The obvious way of reducing the delays is to have more service windows working in parallel, but the site is rather long and narrow, so this is difficult.

The manager decided to try a number of improvements, such as dividing the service into several parts. He found the distributions of times for various operations, and then used a spreadsheet to simulate a number of options.

Figure 8.11 gives an idea of his approach. For this he put three servers in series. The first server, A, took the customer's order, the second, B, looked after the bill and payment, and the third, C, delivered the goods. The spreadsheet follows ten customers through the process. It generates times for each activity (randomly gener-ated to follow actual distributions), and shows how the process performs during a typical short period.

Behind the shop is an area of bulk storage. Most orders are delivered by eight wholesalers, who generally make one delivery a week. Sometimes stocks run low, and the manager arranges a special delivery. Another twenty smaller suppliers deliver special goods or make special deliveries when there are problems. To make administration easy, the manager always uses a standard order for each supplier. Every week he takes the standard orders, adjusts them if there has been any unusual demand, and prepares for special events such as local football matches. Then he faxes the orders to suppliers, and the invoices are delivered with the goods.

	A	B	C	D	E	F	G	H	I	J
1	Customer	A			B			C		
2		Join queue	Start service	Leave	Join queue	Start service	Leave	Join queue	Start service	Leave
3										
4	1	8.45	8.47	8.51	8.52	8.55	9.00	9.01	9.02	9.04
5	2	8.45	8.51	8.53	8.53	9.00	9.01	9.02	9.04	9.07
6	3	8.58	8.58	9.01	9.02	9.07	9.09	9.10	9.10	9.13
7	4	9.00	9.01	9.04	9.05	9.09	9.10	9.11	9.13	9.16
8	5	9.05	9.05	9.06	9.06	9.10	9.13	9.13	9.16	9.18
9	6	9.20	9.20	9.21	9.21	9.21	9.23	9.23	9.23	9.25
10	7	9.20	9.21	9.24	9.25	9.25	9.28	9.29	9.29	9.33
11	8	9.22	9.24	9.26	9.27	9.28	9.30	9.30	9.33	9.35
12	9	9.25	9.26	9.29	9.30	9.30	9.34	9.35	9.35	9.38
13	10	9.25	9.29	9.32	9.33	9.35	9.38	9.39	9.39	9.44
14										
15	Analysis									
16	Number of customers		10							
17	Time in queue A		2.10			Service time A			2.50	
18	Time in queue B		6.30			Service time B			-1.90	
19	Time in queue C		1.20			Service time C			2.40	
20										
21	Time in queues		6.00			Time being served			7.40	
22						Time in system			15.20	

Figure 8.11 Part of a simulation for Ed's Drive-through Bottle Shop

CASE STUDY
Questions

● How do you think the manager can measure the performance of the shop?
● Where should he start looking for improvements?
● How can he describe the details of the operations?

PROJECT
Quality of Logistics

Take a critical look around you and see if you can see examples of poor logistics. You might find, for example, that a train is cancelled, a bus arrives at the wrong time, a delivery of goods arrives after the promised time, a shop runs out of a product that you want, a town centre is poorly laid out, and so on. What could you do to improve these operations? Why do you think that no one has made these obvious improvements?

P R O B L E M S

1. In two consecutive years a warehouse had the following characteristics:

	Year 1	Year 2
Weight of materials moved	5000 tonnes	6500 tonnes
Number of orders satisfied	1650	1820
Number of stock-outs	87	53
Average value stocked	£254,000	£287,000
Cost of administration	£60,000	£76,000
Hours worked	12,000	15,000
Direct costs	£115,000	£173,000
Energy used	20,000 kWh	24,000 kWh
Energy cost	£2000	£3000

What can you say about the performance of the warehouse

2. The activities of an insurance broker can be described by the following table. Draw a precedence diagram of the process.

Activity	Must be done after
1	–
2	1
3	1
4	1
5	2, 3
6	4
7	2
8	5
9	6
10	7, 8
11	9, 10

3. Quality inspectors in a company take random samples of materials arriving from suppliers. An inspection involves three separate tests, each of which uses a different type of machine. There are two machines of each type. Each test takes six minutes for assessment, followed by four minutes for fine adjustment. There are three inspectors working in the area. Draw a process chart for the inspection area. How many units can be inspected each hour?

DISCUSSION QUESTIONS

1. 'What you can't measure you can't manage.' To what extent do you think this is true?
2. Managers can be tempted to use the easiest measures of performance, or those that show themselves in the best light. What are the consequences of this? Can you give examples of problems this creates?

3. What are the most appropriate measures of performance for a supply chain?
4. Performance measures can give conflicting views – changes that improve some measures, make others worse. How can you decide whether the overall effect is beneficial or not?
5. It is easy to find improvements in any supply chain. So why have the managers not already made them?
6. Continuous improvement is not really useful as it just tinkers with existing operations and does not look for significant gains. To what extent do you think this is true?

REFERENCES

1. Harrison A. and New C. (2002) The role of coherent supply chain strategy and performance management in achieving competitive advantage, *Journal of the Operational Research Society*, **53**(3), 263–71.
2. Ferreira J.A. (1993) Re-engineering the materials and procurement function, *APICS – The Performance Advantage*, October, 48–53.
3. Lennox R.B. (1995) Customer service reigns supreme, *Materials Management and Distribution*, January, 17–19.
4. Cold Storage and Distribution Federation (2000) *Key Performance Indicators*, CSDF, Bracknell.
5. Chaplen A. and Wignall J. (1997) Sainsbury's checks out benchmarking, *Logistics Focus*, **5**(9), 13–14.
6. Waters D. (2001) *Operations Management*, Financial Times/Prentice Hall, Harlow.
7. Brunt D. (1999) Value stream mapping tools, *Logistics Focus*, **7**(2), 24–31.
8. Townsend R. (1970) *Up the Organisation*, Coronet Books, London.
9. Beesley A. (1995) Time compression – new source of competitiveness in the supply chain, *Logistics Focus*, **3**(5), 24–5.
10. Beesley A. (1995) Time compression tools, *Logistics Focus*, **3**(7), 17–20.
11. Beesley A. (2000) Time compression in the supply chain, Ch. 11 in Waters D. (ed.) *Global Logistics and Distribution Planning*, Kogan Page, London.
12. Monden Y. (1983) *Toyota Production System*, Industrial Engineering and Management Press, Norcross, GA.
13. Devonshire R.M. (1996) Supply chain information, *Logistics Focus*, **4**(5), 29–31.
14. Emmett S. (2000) Improving freight transport and warehouse operations, *Logistics and Transport Focus*, **2**(2), 30–4.
15. Sordy S. (1997) Do you have any principles?, *Logistics Focus*, **5**(8), 19.
16. Wheatley M. (1998) Seven secrets of effective supply chains, *Management Today*, June, pp. 78–87.
17. McKinnon A. (1999) The effect of traffic congestion on the efficiency of logistical operations, *International Journal of Logistics Research and Applications*, **2**(2).

Further reading

Armistead C. and Roland P. (1996) *Managing Business Processes: BPR and Beyond*, John Wiley, Chichester.
Berry L.G. (1995) *Great Service*, Free Press, New York.
Hammer M. (1996) *Beyond Reengineering*, HarperCollins, New York.
Leibfried K.H.J. and McNair C.J. (1992) *Benchmarking: A Tool for Continuous Improvement*, HarperCollins, New York.

Activities in the Supply Chain

This book is divided into three parts. Part I gave a general introduction to the subject of supply chain management; Part II discussed the planning needed for a supply chain; and Part III focuses on some specific functions of logistics.

There are five chapters in Part III, each of which describes a major activity in the supply chain. Chapter 9 looks at the procurement of materials. Materials are kept in stock, so Chapter 10 describes inventory management, while Chapter 11 discusses some questions of warehousing. Chapter 12 describes the transport of materials and Chapter 13 looks at issues of international logistics.

This is the last part of the book, which relates to our earlier discussions on specific activities in the supply chain.

CHAPTER 9

Procurement

CONTENTS

AIMS OF THE CHAPTER

After reading this chapter you should be able to:

- DEFINE the role of procurement

- APPRECIATE the importance of procurement in the supply chain

- CHOOSE an appropriate supplier

- DISCUSS the steps in a procurement cycle

- DESCRIBE e-procurement and its advantages

- TALK about different arrangements for purchasing

DEFINITIONS

Purchasing and procurement

In previous chapters we have described the planning of a supply chain. This starts with strategic aims, and moves down to organise the flow of materials, makes sure that resources are available, and continually looks for better methods. But we have not really discussed the mechanism for initiating the flow of materials. This is provided by **purchasing** or **procurement**.

In a supply chain, each organisation buys materials from upstream suppliers, adds value, and sells them to downstream customers. As each organisation, in turn, buys and sells, the materials move through the whole supply chain. The trigger that initiates each move is a **purchase**. This is basically a message that an organisation sends to a supplier, saying, 'we have agreed on terms, so send us materials and we will pay you'.

PURCHASING gives a mechanism for initiating and controlling the flow of materials through a supply chain.

Purchasing is the function responsible for acquiring all the materials needed by an organisation. Many of these transactions are not standard purchases, but include rental, leasing, contracting, exchange, gifts, borrowing, and so on. This is why some people prefer to talk about the 'acquisition of materials' or the more common term of **procurement**. 'Procurement' and 'purchasing' are often taken to mean the same thing. Usually, though, purchasing refers to the actual buying, while procurement has a broader meaning. It can include different types of acquisition (purchasing, rental, contracting, and so on) as well as the associated work of selecting suppliers, negotiating, agreeing terms, expediting, monitoring supplier performance, materials handling, transport, warehousing and receiving goods from suppliers.

■ **PROCUREMENT** is responsible for acquiring all the materials needed by an organisation.
■ It consists of all the related activities needed to get goods, services and any other materials from suppliers into an organisation.

Procurement does not usually move materials itself, but it organises the transfer. It gives the message that materials are needed, and arranges the change of ownership and location. But it is another function, such as transport, that actually delivers them. So procurement is largely concerned with information processing. It collects data from various sources, analyses it, and passes information to the supply chain.

Importance of procurement

You can easily see why procurement is important. If we take a broad view, procurement forms an essential link between organisations in the supply chain, and it gives a mechanism for co-ordinating the flow of materials between customers and suppliers. At every point in the supply chain, procurement passes messages backwards to describe what customers want, and it passes messages forwards to say what suppliers have available. Then it negotiates terms and conditions for delivery.

If we take a more limited view, procurement is clearly an essential function within every organisation. We know that every organisation needs a supply of materials, and procurement is responsible for organising this. If procurement is carried out badly, materials do not arrive, or the wrong materials are delivered, in the wrong quantities, at the wrong time, with poor quality, at too high price, low customer service, and so on.

You can get a feel for the importance of procurement from the following example. In the first half of the twentieth century farmers in the US prairies could be fairly isolated. Sears Roebuck introduced a new way of buying that gave farmers the same access to products as the rest of the population.

LOGISTICS IN PRACTICE

Sears Roebuck

Sears Roebuck is a major retailer in the United States. Founded in 1886 it now has annual revenues of over $40 billion. Much of its early growth was based on delivering goods to farmers in the remote prairies. In 1913 its catalogue contained 1500 pages, with thousands of items ranging from boxes of matches to complete houses. People in any location could post their orders or send them to agents, and have goods delivered by post or train. Their customers were always satisfied, as the company gave a comprehensive guarantee on their catalogue cover:

If for any reason whatsoever you were dissatisfied with any article purchased from us, we expect you to return it to us at our expense. We will then exchange it for exactly what you want or will return your money, including any transportation charges you have paid.

They have maintained this tradition, and still advertise, 'Satisfaction guaranteed or your money back'.

According to Ackerman and Brewer[1] this kind of mail order business has some important features for logistics:

- logistics providers have direct contact with customers
- this direct contact allows more precise ordering
- an efficient system for exchanging information is essential
- orders are smaller than normal
- customers are more demanding and want better service
- transport is more complicated.

Sources: promotional material, company reports and website at www.sears.com

Not only is procurement essential, but it is also responsible for a lot of expenditure. For a typical manufacturer, 60% of its spending goes on materials, with companies like General Motors spending over $50 billion a year. So procurement is directly responsible for most of a company's spending, and a relatively small improvement can give substantial benefits. Suppose that a company buys raw materials for €60, spends €40 on operations and then sells the product for €110. It clearly makes a profit of $110 - (60 + 40) = €10$ a unit. Now suppose that procurement negotiates a 5% discount on materials. Materials now cost $60 \times 0.95 = €57$, and with the same selling price the €3 saving goes straight to profit. The profit on each unit now jumps to €13, so a 5% decrease in materials costs raises profit by 30%.

WORKED EXAMPLE

Last year Wiesiek Limited had total sales of £108 million. Their direct costs were £58 million for materials, £27 million for employees and £12 million for overheads. What is the effect of reducing the cost of materials by 1%? If materials costs are not reduced, how much would sales have to increase, or overheads fall, to get the same effect?

Solution

■ The actual profit last year was $108 - (58 + 27 + 12) = £11$ million.

■ If the cost of materials drops by 1%, it falls to $58 \times 0.99 = £57.42$ million. Then the profit rises to $108 - (57.42 + 27 + 12) = £11.58$ million. A 1% decrease in materials costs increases profits by 5.3%. Profit as a percentage of sales rises from 10.2% to 10.7%.

■ If materials costs do not change, and assuming that other costs remain the same proportion of sales value, then sales would have to rise by 5.3% to £114 million to get the same increase in profit.

■ To get the same extra profit the fixed costs would have to fall by £0.58 million or 4.8%.

In recent years there has been wider recognition of procurement's position as an essential function that can control most of an organisation's expenditure. As a result, the function has received a lot more attention. It used to be considered little more than a clerical job, buying materials as they were requested. Now it is recognised as an important management function in its own right. This trend has been encouraged by changing patterns of procurement. Supply chains are getting shorter as more customers use the Web or avoid different tiers of suppliers; alliances are reducing the number of suppliers used by each organisation; amounts purchased are increasing as companies focus on their core activities and outsourcing more; customers are more demanding of products and conditions of purchase. These, and other factors, turn a spotlight on procurement. With this context, it is not surprising that procurement is treated as a senior management role.

Aims of procurement

The overall aim of procurement is to guarantee that an organisation has a reliable supply of materials. With this overriding aim, we can develop the following list of more immediate goals:

- organising a reliable and uninterrupted flow of materials into an organisation
- working closely with user departments, developing relationships and understanding their needs
- finding good suppliers, working closely with them and developing beneficial relationships
- buying the right materials and making sure that they have acceptable quality, arrive at the time and place needed, and meet any other requirements
- negotiating good prices and conditions
- keeping stocks low, considering inventory policies, investment, standard and readily available materials, and so on
- moving materials quickly through the supply chain, expediting deliveries when necessary
- keeping abreast of conditions, including pending price increases, scarcities, new products, and so on.

Organisation of procurement

The way that procurement is organised clearly depends on the type and size of the organisation. In a small organisation, a single buyer might be responsible for all purchases, policy and administration. A medium-sized organisation might have a department with buyers, expeditors, storekeepers, and clerks. A large organisation might have hundreds of people co-ordinating huge amounts of purchases.

Usually procurement is organised as a single department to get the benefits of **centralised purchasing**. These benefits include:

- consolidation of all orders for the same, and similar, materials to get quantity discounts
- co-ordinating associated activities to reduce costs of transport, stockholding and administration
- eliminating duplicated effort and haphazard practices
- having a single point of contact for suppliers and giving them consistent information and service
- developing specialised skills and improving procurement operations
- allowing other people to concentrate on their own work without diverting into purchasing
- concentrating responsibility for procurement, making management control easier.

These benefits can be considerable, but centralised purchasing has its critics. If you work in an office in Leeds, it seems nonsensical to contact your purchasing department in Milton Keynes (450 km away) to buy materials from a supplier in Bradford (20 km away). Nonetheless, this system should give overall benefits. However, organisations that work over a wide geographical area are aware of the problems of centralised purchasing, and may use local purchasing. This can, of course, bring its own benefits. Local offices are likely to have better knowledge of local conditions and culture, better relations with suppliers, more flexible operations, lower transport costs, and so on.

LOGISTICS IN PRACTICE

CN Railway

Canadian National Railways (CN) used to have a traditional purchasing and materials management department. At the beginning of the 1990s this employed 1400 people in 60 locations. The department had been successful in lowering prices (by up to 35%) through alliances and volume purchasing. Despite this, the company felt that it could improve procurement performance. Bob Gallant, head of supply management at CN, said that there was a strong push for better performance at the railway and that: 'Purchasing is one of the most powerful ways to enhance economic performance.'

CN's traditional approach was to buy each material from the best supplier, negotiating for the lowest price. But they found that they could get lower overall costs by purchasing from a few main distributors, rather than from separate companies. In September 1994, for example, they stopped dealing individually with 500 geographically dispersed suppliers in western Canada. Instead, they formed an alliance with Acklands, a major distributor who became responsible for co-ordinating these supplies. CN replaced 6000 annual invoices by a single monthly bill and reduced costs by C$1.2 million a year.

They chose Acklands, and other distributors, by forming a shortlist of companies who could supply all their main purchases, and then comparing the companies' ability to form productive partnerships. Bob Gallant explained that they were 'looking for a supplier that could provide us with a total package. We also wanted to work with a company that had a common view and management commitment'.

The transition to new procurement and changing culture was difficult for a department that served 23,000 employees. They changed the department's name, ran a series of seminars and workshops to explain the new philosophy, hired outside people, formed alliances and actively searched for new ideas. The most difficult part was convincing people that they were aiming for the lowest overall cost, rather than the cheapest immediate price.

By 1995 CN had reduced their supply management department to 280 people in 25 locations, the total cost of materials purchased by C$14 million and stocks by C$4 million. The following year they looked for reductions of C$40 million in costs and C$34 million in stock, with similar improvements in 1997.

Source: Anon. (1996) Buying power, *Materials Management and Distribution*, February, 43–5

CHOOSING SUPPLIERS

Qualified suppliers

Arguably, the most important part of procurement is finding the right supplier. There is no point in having a well-designed product, if the supplier cannot actually deliver it. Imagine that you are working on a project and want to buy some important materials – perhaps a prefabricated bridge for a construction project. You will look for two factors. First, a product design that satisfies your needs. Second, a supplier who can guarantee to deliver the product as designed. In other words, the supplier must be capable of doing the work, giving high quality, working to a schedule, with acceptable costs, and so on. An advertised time of four hours for a train journey might seem a good service, but it has less value if the train operator cannot actually deliver this.

Procurement starts, then, by finding a **qualified supplier**. This is one who can actually deliver the materials needed. In general, organisations look for suppliers who:

● are financially secure with good long-term prospects
● have the ability and capacity to supply the necessary materials
● accurately deliver the requested materials
● send materials of guaranteed high quality
● deliver reliably, on time with short lead times
● quote acceptable prices and financing arrangements
● are flexible to customers' needs and changes
● are experienced and have expertise in their products
● have earned a good reputation
● use convenient and easy procurement systems
● have been used successfully in the past and can develop long-term relationships.

In different circumstances, many other factors might be important, such as convenient location, ability to deal with variable demand, and so on.

Most organisations have a list of approved suppliers who have given good service in the past, or who are otherwise known to be reliable. If there is no acceptable supplier on file, the organisation has to search for one. Suppliers for low value items can probably be found in trade journals, catalogues or through business contacts. More expensive items need a thorough search, and this can be very time consuming. A useful approach for choosing the best supplier for a product has the following steps:

● Look for alternative suppliers
● Build a long list of qualified suppliers who can deliver the products
● Compare organisations on this long list and eliminate those who are, for any reason, less desirable
● Continue eliminating organisations until you have a shortlist (usually four or five) of the most promising suppliers
● Prepare an enquiry, or request for quotation, and send it to the shortlist
● Receive bids from the shortlist
● Do a preliminary evaluation of bids and eliminate those with major problems
● Do a technical evaluation to see if the products meet all specifications
● Do a commercial evaluation to compare the costs and other conditions
● Arrange a pre-award meeting to discuss bids with the remaining suppliers
● Discuss condition bids, which are specific conditions that have to be agreed
● Choose the supplier that is most likely to win the order
● Arrange a pre-commitment meeting to sort out any last minute details
● Award orders to the preferred supplier.

This is clearly a time-consuming procedure, but remember that a poor supplier can cause more problems than poor materials. The whole procedure is only used for major purchases, and if you are buying pencils the shop next door is probably as good as any other supplier. Normally, an organisation will spend little time looking at alternative suppliers if:

- it is buying low value materials
- there is only one possible supplier
- there is already a successful arrangement with a supplier
- there is not enough time for extended negotiations
- the organisation has a policy of selecting specific types of supplier.

Sometimes, particularly with government work, procurement has to be visibly fair, and all potential suppliers must be given an opportunity to submit quotations. Rather than forming a shortlist of qualified suppliers, an organisation will widely advertise that it is seeking quotations for particular work or materials. The organisation compares all the bids submitted and chooses the one that best meets the prescribed criteria. This is called **open tender**. A variation reduces the administrative effort by putting some qualifications on suppliers, perhaps based on experience, size or financial status. This gives **limited tender**.

As you can see, we are talking about customers selecting suppliers – and assume that suppliers are happy to serve all the customers they can find. This is usually the case, but sometimes suppliers have more power and effectively choose their customers. This might happen when a supplier has a monopoly, or near monopoly, of some material. It might also happen when there is a temporary shortage of some commodity, such as oil, and suppliers choose the customers they will supply, perhaps giving preference to larger customers, those who pay more, or those who have long-term agreements. In these cases the supplier has more power, as shown in Figure 9.1.[2]

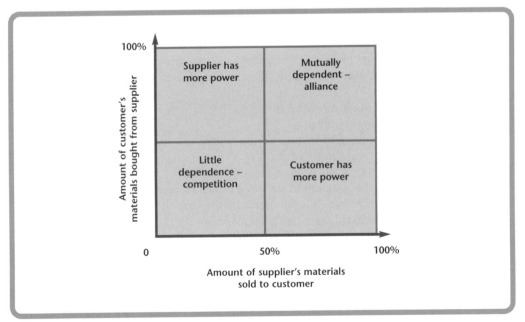

Figure 9.1 Relative power of a customer and a supplier

Number of suppliers

We have already discussed the trend towards long-term alliances and partnerships. This inevitably moves organisations towards single suppliers, either for each material, or for a range of different materials. Some organisations say that this **single sourcing** leaves them vulnerable to the performance of an individual company, and they have severe problems if something goes wrong. If the single supplier of a vital component hits financial problems, an organisation may, through no fault of its own, have to stop production. To avoid this, some organisations have a policy of buying the same materials from a number of competing suppliers. They might use rules of thumb such as 'never let a manufacturer account for more than 20% of total revenue; never let a customer absorb more than 50% of total resources'.[3] The choice must depend on individual circumstances, but we can list some advantages of policy:

- *Advantages of single sourcing:*
    - a stronger relationship between customers and suppliers, often formalised in alliances or partnerships
    - commitment of all parties to the success of the relationship
    - economies of scale and price discounts with larger orders
    - easier communication, reduced administration and simpler procedures for regular orders
    - less variation in materials and their supply
    - easier to keep requirements, conditions and so on, confidential.

- *Advantages of multi-sourcing:*
    - competition between suppliers reduces prices
    - there is less chance of disrupted supplies, as problems can be avoided by switching suppliers
    - can deal more easily with varying demands
    - involving more organisations can give access to wider knowledge and information
    - is more likely to encourage innovation and improvement
    - does not rely on trusting one external organisation.

Organisations use more suppliers when they want to avoid potential problems. Another way of doing this uses **forward buying**. In its simplest form, this happens when an organisation orders more materials than it currently needs and keeps the excess in stock. Another form uses contracts to deliver materials at specific points in the future. Both of these bring two benefits. First, they guarantee supplies for some period in the future and minimise the effect of possible disruptions. Second, the price of materials is fixed, avoiding the effects of future price rises or uncertainty. Of course, things can still go wrong. A company that signs a long-term contract can still go out of business, or a warehouse can burn down, but the chances of a problem are much smaller. It is probably safest for an organisation to hold spare stock itself, but this has higher costs; agreeing a contract for future deliveries gives lower costs, but does not eliminate so much risk (and it is also a poor arrangement when material prices might fall).

Monitoring supplier performance

Most organisations monitor their suppliers to make sure that they continue to give satisfactory service. This is called **supplier rating** or **vendor rating**. Often this is done informally by a subjective review; sometimes there are complex measures for every aspect of performance. Most organisations use a compromise that gives a reasonable view of performance, and needs a reasonable amount of effort. One common approach uses a checklist of important factors and checks that the supplier meets an acceptable standard in these. The checklist might ask whether the supplier is financially sound; whether it delivers on time; if material quality is high enough; if there is technical support; whether the price is competitive; about relevant trends, and so on. If the supplier does not meet any criterion the customer has to discuss improvements or look for new sources. The aim is not really to replace existing suppliers, but to monitor performance, identify areas that need improving and agree the best way of achieving these improvements. Only as a last resort should an organisation start looking for new suppliers.

A more useful approach to rating gives the supplier a score for different aspects of performance. They might, for example, give each supplier a score out of ten for on-time delivery, and if a supplier's score drifts down below eight the customer can discuss ways of improving performance. Although this approach sounds convincing, there can be considerable difficulties. How, for example, can you identify the most important factors of supplier performance, the relative importance of each, the actual performance, and the lowest acceptable performance? Each of these is likely to come from a combination of discussion and agreement, rather than from more precise measurement. The result is a subjective view that may be useful, but contains little objective measurement.

LOGISTICS IN PRACTICE

Philips Semiconductors, Stadskanaal

Philips Semiconductors' plant in Stadskanaal, the Netherlands, makes millions of diodes a year. These are made on an automated assembly line, using just-in-time operations. Materials (such as glass, wires and connectors) have to be delivered at exactly the right time, with any delays interrupting the process.

Over 65% of the plant's cost is materials, and Philips puts exacting demands on its suppliers. It only tolerates a few defects per million parts, and typically demands decreases in price of 7% a year. To monitor supplier performance, Philips introduced a Supplier Rating System which measures five criteria for 12 main suppliers each month. The criteria measured are as follows.

Criteria	Performance required
Delivery performance	99.5% delivered on time, with average deliveries twice a week
Quality	less than 3–5 parts per million defective
Price	expected to fall by 7% a year
Responsiveness	supplier feedback within two hours for critical problems
Audit score	compiled score according to Philips audit system

This system plays a key role in Philips keeping its leading position in an increasingly competitive market.

Sources: Philips Semiconductors, Stadskanaal, *Purchasing Annual Report* (1998) and *Supplier Rating System*, manual (1998)

PROCUREMENT CYCLE

Steps in the cycle

Once it has chosen a supplier, an organisation has to follow some procedure for arranging purchases. Imagine that you want to buy something expensive, like a new computer. You probably approach this in several stages, listing the facilities you want, searching for systems that can provide these, identifying suppliers, developing a shortlist of options, comparing these, and choosing the best. Your aim is to find the combination of products and suppliers that best satisfies your needs. The procurement function in an organisation does exactly the same, and follows a specified procedure for each purchase. This procedure is different in every organisation, and varies with the type of thing being purchased. You would not expect an organisation such as the US army, which buys millions of items a day, to work in the same way as the directors of Real Madrid football club when they acquire a new striker. And the US army would not approach its decision to buy pencils in the same way as its decision to buy helicopters.

Despite these inevitable differences in detail, we can suggest a general approach to procurement. This has a series of common steps, which start with a user identifying a need for materials and end when the materials are delivered. Figure 9.2 shows an outline of these steps, while a more detailed view of a typical **procurement cycle** has the following steps (with key documents in bold).

1. *A user department:*
   - identifies a need for purchased materials
   - examines materials available and prepares **specifications**
   - checks departmental budgets and gets clearance to purchase
   - prepares and sends a **purchase request** to procurement.

2. *Then procurement:*
   - receive, verify and check the purchase request
   - examine the material requested, looking at current stocks, alternative products, production options, and so on – and after discussions with the user department confirm the decision to purchase

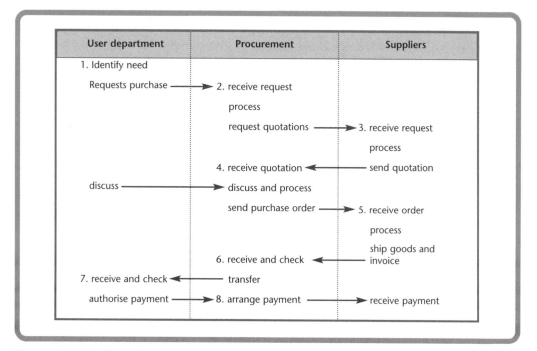

Figure 9.2 Outline of steps in a procurement cycle

● make a shortlist of possible suppliers, from regular suppliers, lists of preferred suppliers, or those known to meet requirements
● send a **request for quotations** to this shortlist.

3. *Then each supplier:*
   ● examines the request for quotations
   ● checks the customer's status, credit, and so on
   ● sees how it could best satisfy the order
   ● sends a **quotation** back to the organisation, giving details of products, prices and conditions.

4. *Then procurement:*
   ● examine the quotations and do commercial evaluations
   ● discuss technical aspects with the user department
   ● check budget details and clearance to purchase
   ● choose the best supplier, based on the details supplied
   ● discuss, negotiate and finalise **terms and conditions** with the supplier
   ● issue a **purchase order** for the materials (with terms and conditions attached).

5. *Then the chosen supplier:*
   ● receives, acknowledges and processes the purchase order
   ● organises all operations needed to supply the materials
   ● ships materials together with a **shipping advice**
   ● sends an **invoice**.

6. *Then procurement:*
   ● acknowledge receipt
   ● do any necessary follow-up and expediting
   ● receive, inspect and accept the materials
   ● notify the user department of **materials received**.

7. *Then the user department:*
   ● receives and checks the materials
   ● authorises transfer from budgets
   ● updates inventory records
   ● uses the materials as needed.

8. *Then procurement:*
   ● arrange payment of the supplier's invoice.

The first three steps sort out the materials and supplier, and then comes the crucial point with the issue of a purchase order in step 4. At this point the organisation agrees to buy specified materials from a supplier, and the purchase order triggers the supply (along with necessary production planning, transport arrangements, finance, and so on). The purchase order is part of a legal contract between the organisation and its supplier. The remaining steps finalise the details of delivery.

This procedure seems complicated, and involves many steps and documents. If you are buying something expensive, this effort is certainly worthwhile – and you may actually follow a much more complicated procedure to fix product specifications, select the supplier and negotiate terms. But if you are making small purchases, if there are existing relationships with suppliers, or there is only one qualified supplier, it is clearly not worth going through this whole expensive, procedure. Then you will look for more routine methods. For these, a rule of thumb suggests £80 as the cost of processing a basic, simple order, while Allen quotes figures of $115 to $150.[4] Even this is too expensive for very low value items, where the procurement would cost more than the materials. Then you will look for even simpler, automatic or ad hoc procedures.

Apart from its cost, another problem with the formal procurement procedure is the time that it takes. It is too slow to make quick purchases. Paul Sigarro buys material to make designer dresses for l'Haute Vision in Stockholm, and found that a delivery of materials typically took one day to arrive from the supplier in Nice, but organising this delivery often took five weeks.[5] This supports an earlier survey in the USA[6] which found the following average times for processing orders at manufacturers.

Part of procurement	Average days
From customer placing order, to supplier receiving it	1.9
From supplier receiving order, to finishing administration	2.1
From finishing administration, to shipping order	2.2
From supplier shipping order, to customer receiving it	4.1
Total	**10.3**

Using a traditional, paper-based system took an average of 10.3 days for a customer to get materials delivered from a manufacturer's stock. If there were problems such as shortages, special products that needed some work, special transport or delivery arrangements, difficult negotiations of conditions, or any similar problems, this time was considerably longer.

In recent years a lot of work has been done to reduce both the cost and time for procurement. Some of these methods are fairly simple. **Blanket orders**, for example, use a single order to cover regular deliveries of materials over some specified time in the future. **Value analysis** uses a team of people from different functional areas to find substitute materials that are lower in price but equally as good as the original.

None of these adjustments tackle one of the basic problems with paper-based procurement, which is its unreliability. Purchasing staff typically spend a third of their time dealing with problems that occur when the procurement process fails in some way.[7,8] Some of these problems with paper-based procurement include:

● taking a long time to go through the whole procedure
● relying on a lot of forms and paperwork which move around different locations
● needing a lot of people to complete, analyse, process, store and generally deal with all the paper
● having other people to supervise, manage and control the administrative procedures
● inevitable errors with so many documents and people involved
● not giving attention to related systems, such as stock control.

A major step in improving procurement came with electronic purchasing. Electronic data interchange (EDI) has been used since the 1980s, and this allows automated procurement. An organisation links its information system to a supplier's, and when it is time to place an order the system automatically sends a message. This works well for small, regular, repeat orders and most organisations readily adopted the principles. There are several variations on automated procurement, all of which are considered under the general heading of **e-procurement**.

e-procurement

Most organisations already use some form of e-procurement. Surveys[7,8] suggest that over 60% of UK companies used e-procurement by 2002, and 80% of European managers soon expect to use it extensively. Some of the advantages this brings are:

● allowing instant access to suppliers anywhere in the world
● creating a transparent market where products and terms are readily available
● automating procurement with standard procedures
● greatly reducing the time needed for transactions
● reducing costs, typically by 12–15%[7,8]
● outsourcing some procurement activities to suppliers or third parties
● integrating seamlessly with suppliers' information systems.

There are basically two types of e-procurement which are described as B2B (where one business buys materials from another business) and B2C (when a final customer buys from a business). Most of us are more familiar with B2C transactions, where we buy books, music, software or travel from websites. Between 1999 and 2002 the number of Internet shoppers in the UK rose from 2 million to 6 million.[9] Nonetheless, many of these sites have hit financial troubles with the bursting of the 'dot-com bubble', and there have been a number of widely publicised bankruptcies. In 1996 Anderson Consulting predicted that on-line shopping would soon account for 20% of UK groceries, but by 2002 the figure was still less than 1%.[9] Verdict, a retail research agency, then predicted that on-line sales would rise to 6% of all grocery sales by 2006. It is clearly difficult to get reliable figures in this area, but there is a general feeling that B2C will continue to grow strongly.

One problem, of course, is that people do not necessarily like e-procurement. If you want to buy a book, you can use various websites, fill in the forms for your purchase, and get the book delivered within a day. But if you go to your nearest bookshop, you might use less sophisticated technology, but pick up the book immediately and without the delivery charge. B2C can hit difficulties because people actually like going to look at things before they buy. Some evidence for this comes from the USA, where only 1% of car purchases are made through the Web, but before buying 75% of people do on-line searches to compare prices and specifications.[9]

A more important factor is that most e-procurement is actually B2B. The Gartner Group have produced the following estimates of B2B trade.[10,11]

Year	Value of B2B procurement ($ billion)
1998	43
1999	219
2000	433
2001	919
2002	1900
2003	3600
2004	6000
2005	8500

The attractions of e-procurement are so great that most organisations will continue to move in this direction. One major software company estimated the following savings from e-procurement (values are in € per transaction). The system gave a return on investment of 400% a year.

Process step	Original cost	Cost with e-procurement
1. Create detailed requirement	17.2	9.3
2. Approval process	5.5	2.7
3. Check requirements	20.2	0
4. Order processing	54.4	6.8
5. Receiving	10.3	2.9
6. Internal delivery	35.0	13.0
7. Payment process	23.6	0.6
Total	**166.2**	**35.3**

Many people are enthusiastic about the growth of e-procurement, but they often forget an important point. If we organise e-procurement very efficiently, it gives much better communications – but it does not necessarily improve the physical flow of materials. This only happens when organisations in the supply chain use the communications to find better ways of moving materials. As Doerflinger et al. say, 'The real barrier to (B2B) entry is the back-end – fulfilment – not the website itself'.[12] Perhaps the main effects of e-procurement are not the speed of purchasing but the effects it has on the supply chain. Customers can now buy from a range of suppliers who might be geographically remote. They also have the option of buying directly from manufacturers or primary suppliers, and can use the increasing number of specialised Web retailers. Merrill Lynch[13] suggest that the main changes that this will bring are:

- growing use of the Internet for procurement will change patterns of logistics
- e-commerce will change buying patterns, but will probably not generate much new business
- organisations will have to improve customer service by, for example, home delivery services.

LOGISTICS IN PRACTICE

Amazon.com

The traditional way of buying books is to visit a bookshop, or perhaps join a book club. In 1995 Jeff Bezos went a step further and started an on-line book retailing business from his garage. His mission was 'to use the Internet to transform book buying into the fastest, easiest, and most enjoyable shopping experience possible'. His aim of stocking every book in print soon made Amazon.com the world's largest book retailer. In its first full year of operation its sales were $15.7 million, and rose by 34% a month. Stock was turning over 150 times

a year, compared with three or four times a year for a normal bookshop. To develop their logistics, Amazon looked at the best practices and recruited the Vice President of logistics (and 15 other staff) from Wal-Mart.

At the heart of Amazon's operations is a sophisticated system to guide customers through the steps of making their purchases. This system basically records customer orders, gets the payment, and arranges delivery. However, it does far more than this and can search for material in different ways, list similar books and other people's purchases, recommend books, give reviews from other readers, authors and publishers, supply information about authors, tell you about new books that are being released, send newsletters, let you track an order, and a whole range of other functions.

Amazon use their efficient operations to give low overheads, so they get substantial economies of scale, and use their size to negotiate discounts from publishers. As a result, they can give discounts of up to 50% on the publishers' price of best sellers. This combination of customer service, wide choice, efficient delivery and low costs has attracted 25 million customers in 160 countries. Net sales for the first quarter of 2000 were US$578 million, an increase of 84% on the previous year. They have expanded beyond their original operations in Seattle, with major operations in the UK, Germany and France. They have expanded beyond books – first into associated areas of CDs and videos, and then into toys, games, garden furniture, gifts, hardware, kitchen equip-

ment, auctions and so on. They have also formed partnerships with on-line pharmacies, sporting goods suppliers, grocers, and so on. As a result, they offer 18 million distinct products. Their UK branch, for example, lists 1.2 million British books, 250,000 US books, 220,000 CDs and 23,000 videos and DVDs. In July 2000 when *Harry Potter and the Goblet of Fire* was published, Amazon put in the biggest ever advance order of 410,000 copies, 250,000 of which were delivered by Federal Express on the first day of sales.

Despite its impressive performance, Amazon is not immune from the pressures and share price fluctuations of e-business. In 2000 it was making a net loss of around $200 million a quarter. The first quarter of 2002 saw its first operating profit.

Sources: company annual reports and website at www.amazon.com; Kotha S. (1998) Competing on the Internet, *European Management Journal*, April

TYPES OF PURCHASE

Different approaches for different products

When we described a formal procedure for procurement, we said that it can be very complicated and time consuming. It would be expensive and unnecessarily complicated to use this procedure for every purchase, and nobody wants to spend six months buying a packet of envelopes. On the other hand, major purchases need much more information and analysis. This is why organisations vary the details of their procurement procedures, matching the methods to the types of materials. Generally speaking, the higher the cost of materials and the more complicated the requirements, the more time and effort procurement needs.

Organisations often set rules for the effort put into procurement, perhaps using ad hoc procedures for low-value routine supplies, a simple, automatic procedure for purchases up to

£20,000, a more rigorous procedure for purchases up to £150,000, and special, detailed analyses for bigger purchases. Van de Vliet[14] describes a variation on this at 3M, where the procurement effort depends on the importance of materials:

- *non-critical materials* have low profits with little risk in supply, and need basic, simple procedures for purchasing
- *bottleneck materials* have low profits but have more risk in supply, and need long-term contracts with alternative sources to avoid potential problems
- *strategic materials* with higher profits need more formal relationships with suppliers over the long term, possibly developing into alliances and partnerships.

Once such rules are established, a management control system can monitor purchases and make sure they are done in the best way. It can see how purchases have been made, if the outcome is satisfactory, if the effort is reasonable in relation to the costs and importance, and if the procedure can be improved for the future.

An important point here is the difference between routine, repeat orders and new ones. If a supplier has given good service over some extended time, an organisation might avoid almost all the procurement cycle and put minimal effort into administering future orders. Ordering becomes routine and the organisation effectively sends a message to say, 'send another order like the last one'. With non-routine purchases, an organisation has to be more careful and put more effort into the choice of supplier, and conditions of purchase.

If an order is repeated often enough, an organisation might consider the 'make-or-buy' decision. In other words, it has to choose those materials that it can make itself, and those that are best met by outside suppliers. In its simplest form, this asks whether an organisation can get materials more cheaply from a supplier than it can make them. Efficient operations and economies of scale often mean that specialised suppliers can deliver materials at lower prices than other organisations can produce them. There are, however, many other factors to consider. Making parts internally can be more reliable, give greater control over supply, tailor products, have shorter lead times, use spare resources, protect designs, keep value-adding oper-ations, increase the size of the company, and so on. On the other hand, buying them from suppliers can get the benefits of specialisation, give access to greater expertise, get economies of scale, reduce stock levels, transfer some risk, maintain flexibility, and so on.

The Department of Trade and Industry[15] suggests that the three main criteria for such deci-sions are:

- financial factors – relating to the costs
- operational factors –relating to responsiveness, flexibility, reliability, and so on
- strategic factors – relating to the long-term implications of the decision for the organisation.

In practice, the perceived benefits of outsourcing are increasing and more organisations are happy to concentrate on their core functions and use specialised suppliers for materials.

Terms and conditions

Although we have talked in general terms about 'placing an order', there are several different types of order. Organisations typically talk about 'placing an order' for goods, but 'signing a contract' for services and 'leasing' equipment. To a large extent, these are different ways of saying the same things, but there may be legal differences. For example, with hire purchase the materials remain the property of the supplier until they are fully paid for, while credit financing gives ownership to the organisation which becomes responsible for servicing a debt. We have already mentioned some specific types of order, with the following being most common:

- *Purchase orders* are used in the standard approach to procurement that we described above. It is essentially a letter from one organisation to another, giving details of the materials it wants to purchase and its conditions of purchase. This is usually a response to a quotation from a qualified supplier, giving the materials it can supply and its conditions of trade.

- *Blanket orders* give a simple system for cheap, standard items, such as stationery. An organisation places a single order for all the materials that it will need over some period, such as a year. Then the supplier delivers batches of materials when requested during the year.

- *e-Procurement* uses EDI or the Internet to simplify purchases by replacing paper-based procedures with electronic ones. This gives a fast and efficient method for repeat, or straightforward, orders.

- *Contracts* give detailed descriptions of an agreement between an organisation and a supplier; they describe exactly the responsibilities, work and services for each, together with all relevant terms and conditions. Many organisations use contracts instead of purchase orders for extended services, so they sign a contract for a supply of electricity. In the same way, organisations sign a contract for a specific piece of work, such as a construction company building a length of road.

- *Sub-contracts:* when a supplier signs a contract with an organisation, it may not do all the work itself, but prefers to pass on some work to a sub-contractor. Then, there are two agreements – the contract between the organisation and the supplier, and the sub-contract between the supplier and sub-contractor. For big projects, there can be several more layers of sub-contracting.

- *Leases and rental agreements* again present the terms and conditions of acquiring materials. They are generally used for buildings or equipment that is returned to the owner after some period of use. You can rent or lease a car, for example, and when you have finished with it, you return it to the owner.

The different types of purchase suggest another problem with procurement. There can be so many different terms and conditions that it is surprisingly difficult to compare them. Suppose that you are buying some standard commodity, such as electricity. Many competitors offer the same product so the best is the one that offers the lowest price. Often, however, there are different conditions of purchase. If you want a telephone service, all suppliers give essentially the same product, but the pricing structure, discounts and offers can make significant differences. Then it is the conditions of purchase that show the best supplier.

In practice, there can be many factors other than cost to consider. Hill suggests[16] that decisions about purchases are made in two stages. In the first, available products are examined and those with 'qualifying' factors get onto a shortlist. Then 'order winning' factors identify the best product from the shortlist. Cost is likely to be one of the qualifying factors, but is only likely to be an order winning factor with commodities. Quality is particularly important, which is the reason why total quality management says that the lowest price does not necessarily give the best deal.[17]

Pricing is a very complicated issue. It is certainly not in an organisation's long-term interest to force suppliers to give unrealistically low prices, or they will go out of business and not be there next time they are needed. Supermarkets in parts of the European Union have followed

consumer pressure to reduce food prices. While this benefits their customers – and presumably the broad population – it means paying less to farmers who grow the crops. If farmers go out of business, there is a major impact on rural communities and the countryside, more reliance on imported food, an effect on the balance of trade, and so on. In general, there are four ways of setting a price for materials:

1. *Price lists* – where suppliers quote fixed prices. Book publishers, for example, quote a selling price that they expect retailers to use. They can give discounts for large or special purchases, but one organisation essentially fixes the price.

2. *Special quotation* – where suppliers quote prices to each customer, particularly for non-standard materials. Customers submit a request for a quotation, and the supplier returns a price and conditions that it is willing to offer.

3. *Negotiation* – when there is some flexibility in price and conditions. A supplier might give a quote, but is willing to negotiate if it can get some benefit such as repeat orders. Similarly, customers can negotiate if they want special conditions, such as fast delivery.

4. *Commodity pricing* – for commodities such as oil, coffee, gold and wheat, market forces set the going rate that is used by all suppliers. You can see many such figures in, say, financial futures markets.

Even when the basic price has been agreed there can be other difficulties with conditions. Who, for example, pays for transportation to the final location and who accepts the risks for the journey? Several standard conditions are used (shown in Figure 9.3) and for historical reasons they seem to be phrased in terms of shipping:

-   *Ex-works:* The purchaser accepts materials 'at the factory gate' and takes over all responsibility for transport, documentation, customs clearance, insurance, risk and so on. This type of contract is best when the supplier has little experience of moving materials through the relevant area, or the purchaser has a lot of experience. If neither has the necessary experience, they can sub-contract the actual movement to third party specialists.

-   *Free alongside* (FAS): Here the supplier moves materials to a specified 'port' and delivers them 'alongside a ship'. The customer takes over the loading on a vessel and movement onward.

-   *Free on board* (FOB): This is a variation of FAS, where the supplier also takes care of the loading onto the vessel, and then the customer is responsible for onward transport. This might seem like a small adjustment to FAS, but loading might involve heavy lifts, risk of damage, or use of lighters (which are small vessels used to move materials out to a larger vessel moored in deeper water).

-   *Delivered ex-ship:* Where the goods are available on the ship (or quayside) but the customer has to arrange for customs clearance, duty, and so on.

-   *Cost and freight* (C&F): Here the supplier arranges transport to an agreed point, but the customer accepts any risk and arranges insurance for the journey.

-   *Cost, insurance and freight* (CIF): Where the supplier delivers to an agreed point, and also arranges insurance for the journey.

-   *Delivered:* Where the supplier is responsible for all aspects of the transport up to delivery to the customer.

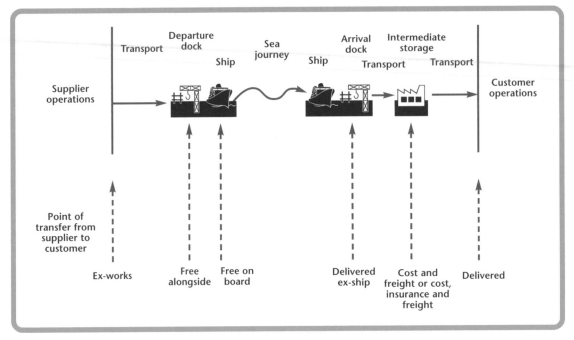

Figure 9.3 Some arrangements for delivery

TT&G

TT&G make a range of prefabricated buildings for use in the Russian and Canadian arctic. Over the past three years they have moved towards single sourcing, developing informal partnerships with preferred suppliers. They have not analysed the costs of these arrangements, but have found significant reductions in the times needed for certain activities. The following table gives a comparison of their current partnering and previous approach of competitive bidding:

	Partnering (weeks)	Bid process (weeks)
Bid review	2–3	4–6
Drawing preparation	4–5	7–10
Drawing approval	1	2–3
Manufacturing time	10–12	18–24
Test time	1	2–3
Total	17–22	33–46

Source: company reports

CHAPTER REVIEW

❏ Purchasing gives a mechanism for initiating the movement of materials from one organisation to another. Procurement is a broader term which includes a series of related activities.

❏ Procurement is responsible for acquiring all the materials needed by an organisation. It consists of all the activities needed to organise an inward flow of materials from suppliers.

❏ Procurement is an essential function in every organisation. It is often responsible for the greatest part of expenditure, and a small improvement can bring significant benefit.

❏ The first step in procurement is finding the right supplier. This decision can be as important as getting the right products.

❏ Procurement usually works in a cycle with a number of distinct steps. There are many variations on this basic model.

❏ Traditional approaches to procurement can be expensive and time consuming. Many organisations have moved towards e-procurement, which can bring considerable benefits.

❏ Different types of purchase need different conditions, with the amount of effort generally related to the product value.

❏ Total cost is often important in purchasing decisions, but there can be many other factors. It is often surprisingly difficult to compare the terms and conditions.

CASE STUDY — *Arnold Haralson*

For many years Arnold Haralson worked in the port of Bergen. In 1997 he had his 55th birthday and took early retirement. He had a number of projects he wanted to work on, including writing a history of Norse influence on Russian cultural development. He finished the book in two years and published it through Norgeldt, a specialist local publisher. It sold 300 copies in the first year, and Arnold was soon working on a second book discussing the links between Norse mythology and Russian folklore.

Arnold had considerable expertise in his field and planned to continue his series of books. He recognised that they did not have broad appeal, but there was a steady demand in this specialised market. Norgeldt seemed happy to consider his new proposals.

CASE STUDY — *continued*

Although he enjoyed writing books, Arnold was troubled by the marketing. Norgeldt only really worked in Norway and Sweden, where they estimated a continuing demand for his type of book at around 200 copies a year. Arnold felt that there were large Scandinavian populations in the USA, Australia and other countries, who were not being reached, and there were almost no sales in Russia. Although he was not expecting a great return from his books he was disappointed by the size of his royalty cheques. His books retailed for 1000 NKr, but his royalties were calculated from 6% of the publisher's selling price, which depended on the discounts offered but was usually less than 700 NKr.

Arnold was unlikely to get his books published by any of the major, international companies, but there were other alternatives. He could, for example, approach a 'vanity publisher' who would charge a fee for publishing the book, but return more of the income generated. A more attractive option might be to use the Web. Arnold could simply set up a website to advertise his current books more widely. But if he set up a website, he might as well bypass the retailer and sell copies directly to customers. When Arnold started to think along these lines, he thought that he could also bypass the publisher. Then he could either produce the book himself and sell it through his website, or avoid the paper version and allow customers to pay a fee to access an electronic version.

CASE STUDY
Question

- Arnold clearly has to think hard about publishing his books. What options do you think he has? What would be the benefits and problems with each? What route would you recommend him to follow?

PROJECT
How to Buy

Imagine that you want to buy something relatively expensive, such as a car. What alternative sources are there? Describe the steps you would follow in making the purchase. Now compare these with the steps followed by a company making a similar purchase. Is it difficult to get information about the procedure that an organisation uses for procurement?

DISCUSSION QUESTIONS

1. Some people say that you should always look for quotations, even for repeat orders, as this encourages competition and keeps prices low. Other people say that you should form an alliance with one supplier so that you understand each other's needs. Which of these views do you think is more persuasive?

2. Everyone is talking about the benefits of purchasing through the Internet. What are these? How will e-procurement affect wider operations? What other changes will there be in the future?

3. What features would make an ideal supplier?

4. Forward purchasing has many advantages – as demonstrated by the huge market in financial futures. What are these benefits? If these are so obvious, why are many organisations ignoring them and using just-in-time?

5. Do you think an organisation should always negotiate hard with suppliers to get the cheapest prices and best conditions it can?

6. In October 2000 The Trading and Standards Institute in London made test purchases in 102 retail websites. There were problems with 37% of these, 38% arrived later than promised and 17% did not arrive at all.[9] What does this tell you about e-procurement?

REFERENCES

1. Ackerman K.B. and Brewer A.M. (2001) Warehousing: a key link in the supply chain, Ch. 14 in Brewer A.M., Button K.J. and Hensher D.A. (eds) *Handbook of Logistics and Supply Chain Management*, Pergamon, Oxford.

2. Scott C. and Westbrook R. (1991) New strategic tool for supply chain management, *International Journal of Physical Distribution and Logistics Management*, **21**(1), 23–33.

3. Perry R. (1998) Quoted in Lawless J. 'Challenges of going global', *Sunday Times*, 26/4/98.

4. Allen S. (2001) Leveraging procurement: the quiet e-business, *Logistics and Transport Focus*, **3**(4), 29–30.

5. Sigarro P. (2001) Speeding up procurement, Western Operations Seminar, Nice.

6. LaLonde B.J. and Zinszer P.H. (1976) *Customer Service*, National Council of Physical Distribution Management, Chicago.

7. Cummings N. (2002) UK leading the world in e-procurement, *OR Newsletter*, March.

8. Website at www.BarclaysB2B.com.

9. Rushe D. (2001) www.basketcase, *Sunday Times*, 2 September, p. 5.

10. Anon. (2001) *The Economic Downturn is Not an Excuse to Retrench B2B Efforts*, Gartner, Stamford, CT.

11. The Gartner Group (2001) Website at www.gartner.com.

12. Doerflinger T.M., Gerharty M. and Kerschner E.M. (1999) The information revolution wars, *Paine-Webber Newsletter*, New York.

13. Merrill Lynch (1999) *E-commerce: Virtually There*, Merrill Lynch, New York.

14. Van de Vliet A. (1996) When the gaggling has to stop, *Management Today*, June, pp. 56–60.

15. Department of Trade and Industry (2001) *Logistics and Supply Chain Management*, Website at www.dti.gov.uk.

16. Hill T. (1993) *Manufacturing Strategy* (2nd edn), Macmillan – now Palgrave Macmillan, Basingstoke.

17. Deming W.E. (1986) *Out of the Crisis*, MIT Press, Cambridge, MA.

Further reading

Arnold J.R.T (1996) *Introduction to Materials Management* (2nd edn) Prentice Hall, Englewood Cliffs, NJ.

Baily P., Farmer D., Jessop D. and Jones D. (1998) *Purchasing Principles and Management* (7th edn), Pitman, London.

Gattorna J.L and Walters D.W. (1996) *Managing the Supply Chain*, Macmillan – now Palgrave Macmillan, Basingstoke.

Leenders M.R. and Fearon H.E. (1996) *Purchasing and Supply Management*, McGraw-Hill, New York.

Saunders M. (1997) *Strategic Purchasing and Supply Chain Management* (2nd edn), Financial Times/Prentice Hall, London.

CHAPTER 10

Inventory Management

AIMS OF THE CHAPTER

After reading this chapter you should be able to:

- UNDERSTAND why organisations hold stocks

- ANALYSE the costs of holding stock

- CALCULATE economic order quantities

- CALCULATE associated lead times, costs and cycle lengths

- DEFINE 'service level' and DO related calculations for safety stock

- DESCRIBE periodic review systems and CALCULATE target stock levels

- DO ABC analyses of inventories

REASONS FOR HOLDING STOCK

Aggregate stockholdings

In the last chapter we saw how procurement organises the flow of materials into an organisation. But we did not ask when an organisation should buy materials, or how much it should buy. In this chapter we discuss these questions, and relate them to the broader policies on inventory management.

Ideally, materials move smoothly and continuously through a supply chain. In practice, there are always delays – and when materials stop moving they form stocks. All organisations hold stocks of some kind, whether it is a shop that stocks goods for customers to look at, a chef with stocks of ingredients in the pantry, or a market research company with stocks of information in a database.

STOCKS are supplies of goods and materials that are held by an organisation. They are formed whenever the organisation's inputs or outputs are not used at the time they become available.

An **INVENTORY** is a list of things held in stock.

In Chapter 7 we discussed material requirements planning and just-in-time. In their different ways, both of these assume that stocks are a waste of resources that should be eliminated, or at least minimised. From their arguments you might get the impression that every organisation is getting rid of its stocks and moving to 'stockless' operations. There is certainly a trend in this direction. Surveys by, for example, the Institute of Grocery Distribution[1] found that stock levels fell by as much as 8.5% in a year, while the Institute of Logistics[2] found that in 1999 UK companies, 'managed to almost halve the stockholding requirements since the 1995 survey'. We can get a broader picture from government figures.[3-5] The easiest measure takes the ratio of aggregate stock to gross domestic product (GDP). This does not give an absolute measure of performance, but it allows reasonable comparisons over time. Figure 10.1 shows the book value of aggregate stock held in the United Kingdom as a percentage of GDP from 1949 to 1998.[6]

At the end of the 1940s and into the early 1950s there was a rapid decline in stocks as the economy returned to normal after the Second World War. From the early 1950s right through to the present day there has been a steady decline, which we can attribute to improving inventory management. There are, of course, some unexpected movements, such as the sudden change in the early 1970s that was caused by the rapid increase of oil prices and the economic disruption that followed. These can, however, be viewed as a short–term fluctuation on the underlying downward trend.

The steady fall in stocks clearly suggests improving inventory management, but there may well be other factors, such as the changing structure of industry, the move towards services, international competition, economic cycles, inflation, changing GDP, currency value and increasing mobility. Inventories clearly respond to such external influences. If you look at a business cycle, for example, it might start with industry being over-optimistic about the future – they expect sales to rise and increase production to meet this higher demand. Inventories build up as sales lag behind production, and at some point industry loses confidence and cuts back on production to use the excess stocks. This causes a decline in the economy,

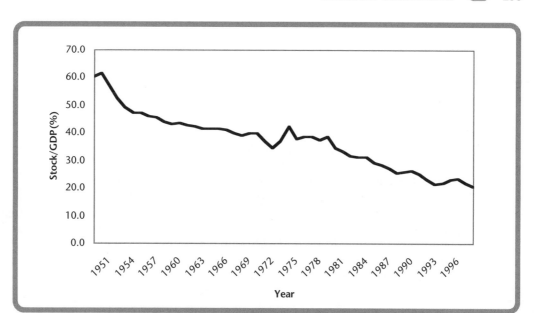

Figure 10.1 Aggregate stock as a percentage of GDP for the UK

which only picks up again when stocks are lower and production is not meeting current demand. Because it is relatively easy to change inventory levels – much easier than, say, adjusting production levels – they tend to fluctuate more than the business cycle itself.

In the UK manufacturing contributes less than 20% of the GNP, but it holds 40% of the stocks. There are roughly equal amounts of materials, work in progress and finished goods (about £20 billion of each). The amount of stock held by manufacturers has fallen much faster than other sectors of industry, suggesting that they have been at the forefront of stock reduction – and also that they are in the best position to reduce stocks. Organisations further down the supply chain have to pay more attention to their final customers and react quickly to demands – a lead time of one day is very good for a manufacturer, reasonable for a wholesaler, but not good enough for a retailer.

Buffering supply and demand

Despite the clear trend towards lower stocks, many organisations cannot reduce them. Farmers grow one crop of hay a year, and then store it to feed animals throughout the year. A distiller stores whisky in barrels for at least three years before selling it. A video store buys copies of videos and keeps them in stock until people want to hire them. These organisations do not want to eliminate stocks, but they want to control them properly.

The main reason for holding such stocks is to give a buffer between variable – and uncertain – supply and demand. Imagine the food being delivered to a supermarket. This is delivered in large quantities – perhaps a truckload at a time – but it is sold in much smaller quantities to individual customers. The result is a stock of goods that is replenished with every delivery, and is reduced over time to meet demand. The stocks give a cushion between supply and demand. They allow the supermarket to continue working efficiently, even when delivery vehicles are delayed, or there is unexpectedly high demand from customers.

> ■ The main purpose of **STOCKS** is to act as a buffer between supply and demand.
> ■ They allow operations to continue smoothly and avoid disruptions.

To be more specific, stocks:

- act as a buffer between different parts of the supply chain
- allow for demands that are larger than expected, or at unexpected times
- allow for deliveries that are delayed or too small
- take advantage of price discounts on large orders
- allow the purchase of items when the price is low and expected to rise
- allow the purchase of items that are going out of production or are difficult to find
- allow for seasonal operations
- make full loads and reduce transport costs
- give cover for emergencies
- can be profitable when inflation is high.

IN PRACTICE

Stock holdings

Tesco

Tesco is the largest food retailer in the UK, where it has 16% of the market. It also operates in central Europe and the Far East. Its annual report for 2000 showed:

Total sales	£20,385 million
Fixed assets	£8527 million
Number of stores	845
Total sales area	24.0 million square feet
Stocks	£744 million

IBM

For many years IBM has been a leader in the computer industry. In 2000 its revenue was $87.5 billion, and it held £3.7 billion of stocks of work in progress and $1.2 billion of stocks of finished goods.

ICI

ICI is a major chemical company, with four major divisions – National Starch, Quest, Industrial Specialities and Paints. In the first half of 2000 it reported a trading profit of £275 million, on a turnover of £3.8 billion. Its assets were valued at £7.3 billion, of which £920 million were stocks.

L.T. Francis

L.T. Francis is a manufacturer of pre-cast concrete fittings for the building trade. Its 2000 annual report showed sales of £14 million and total stocks £2.4 million.

As you can see, these organisations hold large stocks. In Tesco the stock is around 4% of sales, in IBM about 7% in total, in ICI it is 11% for the full year, and in L.T. Francis it is 17%. Many organisations have very high stocks, and it is not unusual for manufacturers to hold 25% of annual sales.

Sources: company annual reports and websites www.tesco.com, www.ICI.com and www.ibm.com

Types of stock

Just about everything is held as stock somewhere, whether it is raw materials in a factory, finished goods in a shop or tins of baked beans in a pantry. We can classify these stocks as:

- ⬤ **Raw materials** – the materials, parts and components that have been delivered to an organisation, but are not yet being used.
- ⬤ **Work in process** – materials that have started, but not yet finished their journey through the production process.
- ⬤ **Finished goods** – goods that have finished the process and are waiting to be shipped out to customers (see Figure 10.2).

This is a fairly arbitrary classification, as one company's finished goods are another company's raw materials. Some organisations, notably retailers and wholesalers, have stocks of finished goods only, while others, like manufacturers, have all three types in different proportions. Nationally, around 30% of stocks are raw materials, 40% work in progress and 30% finished goods.[6] Some stock items do not fall easily into these categories, and we can define two additional types:

- ⬤ **Spare parts** for machinery, equipment, and so on
- ⬤ **Consumables** such as oil, fuel, paper, and so on.

In Chapter 7 we described material requirements planning as a **dependent demand system**, where the demand for an item is found directly from a master schedule. The alternative

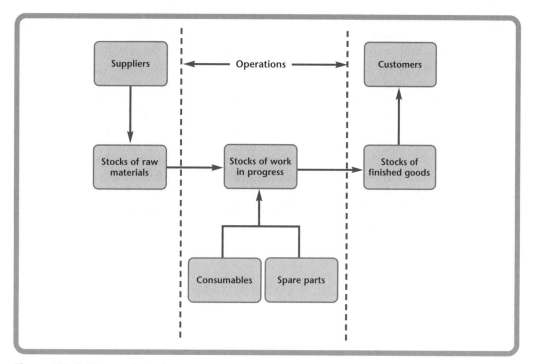

Figure 10.2 Types of stock

approach looks at an **independent demand system**, where the total demand for an item is made up of lots of separate demands that are not related to each other. The overall demand for bread in a supermarket, for example, is made up of lots of demands from separate customers who act independently. Independent demand systems control stocks by finding the best balance between various costs. In particular, they look for answers to three basic questions:

1. *What items should we stock?* No item, however cheap, should be stocked without considering the costs and benefits. This means that an organisation should stop unnecessary, new items being added to stock, and it should make regular searches to remove obsolete or dead stock.

2. *When should we place an order?* This depends on the inventory control system used, type of demand (high or low, steady or erratic, known exactly or estimated), value of the item, lead time between placing an order and receiving it into stock, supplier reliability, and a number of other factors.

3. *How much should we order?* Large, infrequent orders give high average stock levels, but low costs for placing and administering orders: small, frequent orders give low average stocks, but high costs of placing and administering orders.

The first of these questions is a matter of good housekeeping, simply avoiding stock that is not needed. The following section looks for answers to the last two questions.

Costs of carrying stock

The total cost of holding stock is typically around 25% of its value a year. A reasonable objective is to minimise this cost. You might think – especially after the lessons of just-in-time – that minimising costs is the same as minimising stocks. But this is not necessarily true. If a shop holds no stock at all, it certainly has no inventory costs, but it also has no sales; it effectively incurs another cost of losing customers.

Lambert[7] describes one approach which looks at the costs of capital (for borrowing, opportunity, and so on), inventory service (insurance, taxes, and so on), storage space (rent, heating, and so on) and inventory risk (obsolescence, damage, and so on). We will use a slightly different approach that divides the overall costs of stock into four separate components.

1. **Unit cost:** the price for an item charged by the supplier, or the cost to the organisation of acquiring one unit of the item. It may be fairly easy to find this by looking at quotations or recent invoices from suppliers, but it is more difficult when there are several suppliers offering slightly different products, or offering different purchase conditions. If a company makes the item itself, it may be difficult to give a reliable production cost or set a transfer price.

2. **Reorder cost:** the cost of placing a repeat order for an item. This might include allowances for preparing an order, correspondence, receiving, unloading, checking, testing, use of equipment and follow-up. Sometimes, costs such as quality control, transport, sorting and movement of received goods are included. In practice, the best estimate for a reorder cost often comes from dividing the total annual cost of the purchasing department by the number of orders it sends out.

3. **Holding cost**: the cost of holding one unit of an item in stock for a unit period of time – for example, the cost to Air France of holding a spare engine in stock for a year. The obvious cost is tied-up money. This is either borrowed (in which case there are interest payments) or it is cash that could be put to other uses (in which case there are opportunity costs). Other holding costs are for storage space, loss, handling, special treatment, such as refrigeration, administration and insurance. Another problem is obsolescence, which refers to stock that has been kept in storage so long that it has little or no value, such as spare parts that are no longer needed or food that is past its sell-by date. There is a trend for products to have shorter life cycles, so the amount of obsolescence might increase. On the other hand, we are moving materials much more quickly through supply chains, so in many circumstances the amount of obsolescence is declining.

It is difficult to give typical values for these, but a guideline for annual costs as a percentage of unit cost, has:

	% of unit cost
cost of money	10–15
storage space	2–5
loss and obsolescence	4–6
handling	1–2
administration	1–2
insurance	1–5
Total	**19–35**

4. **Shortage cost**: occurs when an item is needed but it cannot be supplied from stock. In the simplest case a retailer loses direct profit from a sale. But the effects of shortages are usually more widespread and include lost goodwill, loss of reputation, and loss of potential future sales. Shortages of raw materials for production can cause disruption, rescheduling of production, re-timing of maintenance periods, and laying off employees. Shortage costs might also include payments for positive action to remedy the shortage, such as expediting orders, sending out emergency orders, paying for special deliveries, storing partly finished goods or using more expensive suppliers.

It can be difficult to get figures for any inventory costs, but shortage costs are a particular problem. These can include so many intangible factors, such as lost goodwill, that it is difficult to agree a reasonable value. Most organisations take the view that shortages are expensive, so it is generally better to avoid them. In other words, they are willing to pay the relatively lower costs of carrying costs to avoid the relatively higher costs of shortages. As you can imagine, this tends to increase the amount of stock held, particularly when there is uncertainty.

WORKED EXAMPLE

Janet Long is a purchasing clerk at Overton Travel Group. She earns £16,000 a year, with other employment costs of £3000, and has a budget of £6200 for telephone, communications, stationery and postage. In a typical month Janet places 100 orders. When goods arrive there is an inspection that costs about £15 an order. The cost of borrowing money

EXAMPLE
continued

is 9%, the obsolescence rate is 5% and insurance and other costs average 4%. How can Overton estimate their reorder and holding costs?

Solution

The total number of orders a year is 12 × 100 = 1200 orders.

■ The reorder cost includes all costs that occur for an order. These are:
   ■ salary = £16,000/1200 = £13.33 an order
   ■ employment costs = £3000/1200 = £2.50 an order
   ■ expenses = £6200/1200 = £5.17 an order
   ■ inspection = £15 an order

So the reorder cost is 13.33 + 2.50 + 5.17 + 15 = £36 an order.

■ Holding costs include all costs that occur for holding stock. These are:
   ■ borrowing = 9%
   ■ obsolescence = 5%
   ■ insurance and taxes = 4%

So the holding cost is 9 + 5 + 4 = 18% of inventory value a year.

It is even difficult to agree a value for basic figures like the value of stock held. Is it worth the amount you actually paid for it, the amount you would pay to replace it, the amount you can sell it for, or some other value? In practice, the most common costing is based on the amount paid and can use:

● *FIFO* – first in, first out, which assumes that stock is sold in the order it was bought, so the remaining stock is valued at the current replacement cost
● *LIFO* – last in, first out, which assumes that the latest stock is used first, so the remainder is valued at earlier acquisition costs
● *Average cost* – which uses a moving average cost over some period.

WORKED
EXAMPLE

A company bought the following numbers of an item. In July it had 8 units in stock. What was the value of this stock?

Month	Jan	Feb	Mar	Apr	May	Jun
Number bought	6	4	5	8	3	2
Unit price	21	19	18	22	24	26

EXAMPLE
continued

Solution

There is no right answer to this, as it depends on the conventions that we choose to use.

■ FIFO assumes that the remaining units are the last that were bought, and the value of the last eight units is $(2\times26) + (3\times24) + (3\times22) = 190$

■ LIFO assumes that the first units bought are still in stock, and the value of these first eight units is $(6\times21) + (2\times19) = 164$

■ Current replacement cost gives a value of $(8\times26) = 206$

■ A three-month moving average gives a smoothed unit price of $(22+24+26)/3 = 24$, and a value of $(8\times24) = 192$.

ECONOMIC ORDER QUANTITY

Finding the order size

The **economic order quantity** (EOQ) was developed early last century[8–10] and has remained a dominant theme for the control of independent demand systems. It remains the best way of tackling a wide range of inventory problems. It is flexible and easy to use, and gives good guidelines for a wide range of circumstances.

Imagine a single item, held in stock to meet a constant demand of D per unit time. Assume that unit cost (U), reorder cost (R) and holding cost (H) are all known exactly, while the shortage cost is so high that all demands must be met and no shortages are allowed. The item is bought in batches from a supplier who delivers after a constant lead time. We want to find the best order quantity, Q, and always place orders of this size. There is no point in carrying spare stock, so we time orders to arrive just as existing stock runs out. Then we get a series of **stock cycles**, with the saw-tooth pattern shown in Figure 10.3.

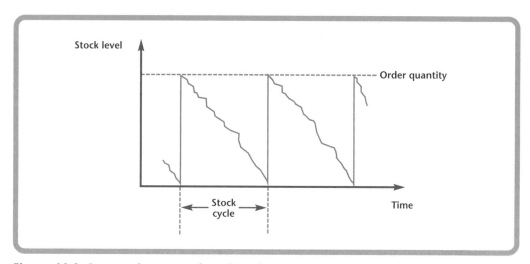

Figure 10.3 Repeated pattern of stock cycles

At some point an order of size Q arrives. This is used at a constant rate, D, until no stock is left. We can find the total cost for the cycle by adding the four components of cost – unit, reorder, holding and shortage. No shortages are allowed, so we can ignore this cost, and the cost of buying the item is constant regardless of the ordering policy, so we can also leave the unit cost out of the calculations. Then we can show that the cost per unit time is:

$$C \;=\; \text{total reorder costs} + \text{total holding costs}$$
$$=\; RD/Q + HQ/2$$

If we plot these two parts separately against Q, we get the results shown in Figure 10.4.
From this graph you can see that:

● the total holding cost rises linearly with order size
● the total reorder cost falls as the order quantity increases
● large infrequent orders give high total holding costs and low total reorder costs
● small frequent orders give low total holding costs and high total reorder costs
● adding the two costs gives a total cost curve that is an asymmetric 'U' shape with a distinct minimum
● this minimum cost shows the optimal order size – which is the **economic order quantity, EOQ**.

A standard analysis shows that the economic order quantity is found from the following equation:

$$\text{Economic order quantity, } Q \;=\; \sqrt{\frac{2RD}{H}}$$

where   D = demand
        R = reorder cost
        H = holding cost

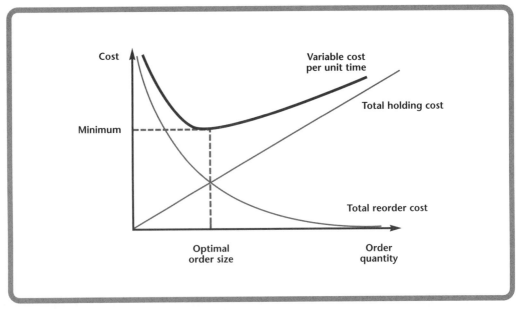

Figure 10.4 Variation of cost with order size

WORKED EXAMPLE

John Pritchard buys stationery for Penwynn Motors. The demand for printed forms is constant at 20 boxes a month. Each box of forms costs £50, the cost of processing an order and arranging delivery is £60, and holding cost is £18 a box a year. What are the economic order quantity, cycle length and costs?

Solution

Listing the values we know in consistent units:

D = 20 × 12 = 240 units a year

U = £50 a unit

R = £60 an order

H = £18 a unit a year.

■ Substituting these values into the economic order quantity gives:

$$Q = \sqrt{\frac{2RD}{H}} = \sqrt{\frac{2 \times 60 \times 240}{18}} = 40 \text{ units}$$

■ Then the variable cost is:

C = total reorder costs + total holding costs = RD/Q + HQ/2
= 60 × 240/40 + 18 × 40/2 = 360 + 360 = £720 a year

You can see that the total reorder costs equal the total holding costs. This is always true if we order the economic order quantity, so we can simplify the calculation to twice the total holding cost or:

C = HQ = 18 × 40 = £720

■ We also have to consider the fixed cost of buying boxes, which is the number of boxes bought a year, D, times the cost of each box, U. Adding this to the variable cost above, gives the total cost of stockholding:

total cost = UD + C = 50 × 240 + 720 = £12,720 a year

■ We buy 40 boxes at a time, and use 20 boxes a month, so the stock cycle length is 2 months. In general, we can find the stock cycle length from T = Q/D:

T = Q/D = 40/240 = 1/6 years or 2 months

The best policy – with total costs of £12,720 a year – is to order 40 boxes of paper every 2 months.

Finding the time to place orders

When an organisation buys materials, there is a **lead time** between placing the order and having the materials arrive in stock. This is the time taken to prepare an order, send it to the supplier, allow the supplier to make or assemble the materials and prepare them for shipment, ship the goods back to the customer, allow the customer to receive and check the materials and put them into stock. Depending on circumstances, this lead time can vary between a few minutes and months or even years.

Suppose the lead time, L, is constant. To make sure that a delivery arrives just as stock is running out, we have to place an order a time L earlier. The easiest way of finding this point is to monitor current stock and place an order when there is just enough left to last the lead time. With constant demand, D, this means that we place an order when the stock level falls to LD, and this point is called the **reorder level**.

Reorder level = lead time demand = lead time × demand

ROL = LD

In practice, the inventory control system keeps a continuous record of the stock on hand, updating this with every transaction and sending a message when it is time to place an order. Ordinarily, this message is sent to a purchasing department; with e-procurement or some form of alliance the message is sent directly to the supplier; with ECR systems the message is sent to the supplier and other organisations down the supply chain.

This calculation works well provided the lead time is less than the length of a stock cycle. In the next example the lead time is two weeks and the stock cycle is 50/20 = 2.5 weeks. Suppose the lead time is raised to three weeks. The calculation for reorder level then becomes:

Reorder level = lead time × demand = LD = 3 × 20 = 60 units

WORKED EXAMPLE

Demand for an item is constant at 20 units a week, the reorder cost is £125 an order and holding cost is £2 an unit a week. If suppliers guarantee delivery within 2 weeks what is the best ordering policy for the item?

Solution

Listing the variables in consistent units:

D = 20 units a week

R = £125 an order

H = £2 a unit a week

L = 2 weeks

Substituting these gives:

$$Q = \sqrt{\frac{2RD}{H}} = \sqrt{\frac{2 \times 125 \times 20}{2}} = 50 \; units$$

Reorder level = lead time × demand = LD = 2 × 20 = 40 units

The best policy is to place an order for 50 units whenever stock falls to 40 units.

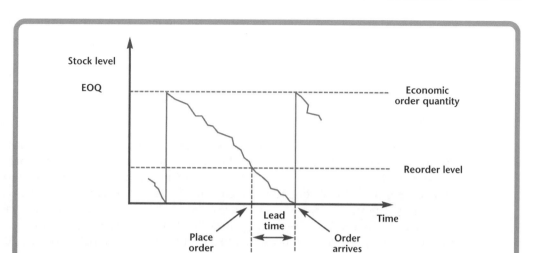

Figure 10.5 Using a reorder level to time orders

The problem is that the stock level never actually rises to 60 units, but varies between 0 and 50 units. The way around this problem is to recognise that the calculated reorder level refers to both stock on hand and stock on order. Then the reorder level equals lead time demand minus any stock that is already on order. In the example above, the order quantity is 50 units, so a lead time of three weeks would have one order of 50 units outstanding when it is time to place another order. Then:

Reorder level = lead time demand – stock on order = LD – Q
= 3 × 20 – 50 = 10 units

An order for 50 units should be placed whenever actual stock declines to 10 units. Because the lead time is longer than the stock cycle, there will always be at least one order outstanding, as shown in Figure 10.6.

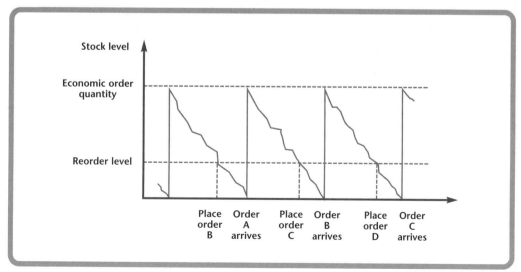

Figure 10.6 Order patterns when lead time is longer than stock cycle

One problem, of course, is that the lead time may not be constant. We know how long the lead time has been in the past, and we know the current target, but there may be some variability and the supplier might not always achieve this target. As well as forecasting demand, we also have to forecast the lead time, so the reorder level is actually based on two forecasts.

Sensitivity analysis

One problem with the economic order quantity is that it can give awkward order quantities. It might, for example, suggest buying impossible figures, such as 88.39 tyres. We could round this to 88 tyres, but might prefer to order 90 or even 100. But does this rounding have much effect on overall costs? In practice, the total cost curve is always shallow around the economic order quantity. The amount we order can increase to 156% of the economic order quantity or fall to 64% and only raise variable costs by 10%. Similarly, the order quantity can increase to 186% of the economic order quantity or fall to 54% and only raise variable costs by 20%. This is one reason why the EOQ analysis is so widely used – although the calculation is based on a series of assumptions and approximations, the total cost rises slowly around the optimal. EOQ gives a good guideline for order size in a wide range of circumstances (see Figure 10.7).

W O R K E D
E X A M P L E

Cheng Tau Hang notices that demand for an item his company supplies is constant at 500 units a month. Unit cost is $100 and shortage costs are known to be very high. The purchasing department sends out an average of 3000 orders a year, and their total operating costs are $180,000. Any stocks have financing charges of 15%, warehouse charges of 7% and other overheads of 8% a year. The lead time is constant at one week.

Find a good ordering policy for the item. What is the reorder level if the lead time increases to 3 weeks? What range of order size keeps variable costs within 10% of optimal? What is the variable cost if orders are placed for 200 units at a time?

Solution

Listing the values we know and making sure the units are consistent:

D = 500 × 12 = 6000 units a year

U = $100 a unit

$R = \dfrac{\text{annual cost of purchasing department}}{\text{number of orders a year}} = \dfrac{180,000}{3000} = \$60$ an order

H = (15% + 7% + 8%) of unit cost a year = (0.3) × U = $30 a unit a year

L = 1 week

■ We can find the best ordering policy by substituting these values into the equations:
  ■ order quantity,

$$Q = \sqrt{\frac{2RD}{H}} = \sqrt{\frac{2 \times 60 \times 6000}{30}} = 154.9 \text{ units}$$

W O R K E D
E X A M P L E
continued

- ■ cycle length, T = Q/D = 154.9/6000 = 0.026 years or 1.3 weeks
- ■ variable cost a year = HQ = 30 × 154.9 = $4647 a year
- ■ total cost a year = UD + variable cost = 100 × 6000 + 4647 = $604,647 a year.

■ The lead time is less than the stock cycle, so:

Reorder level = LD = 1 × 6000/52 = 115.4 units

The optimal policy is to order 154.9 units whenever stock falls to 115.4 units.

■ If the lead time increases to 3 weeks, there will be 2 orders outstanding when it is time to place another. Then:

Reorder level = lead time × demand − stock on order
= LD − 2Q = 3 × 6000 / 52 − 2 × 154.9 = 36.4 units.

■ To keep variable costs within 10% of optimal, the quantity ordered can vary between 64% and 156% of the economic order quantity, which is 99.1 units to 241.6 units.

■ If fixed order sizes of 200 units are used the variable costs are:

C = total reorder costs + total holding costs
= RD / Q + HQ / 2 = 60 × 6000 / 200 + 30 × 200 / 2 = $4800 a year

We are not using the economic order quantity, so the variable cost is higher and the total reorder costs no longer equal the total holding costs.

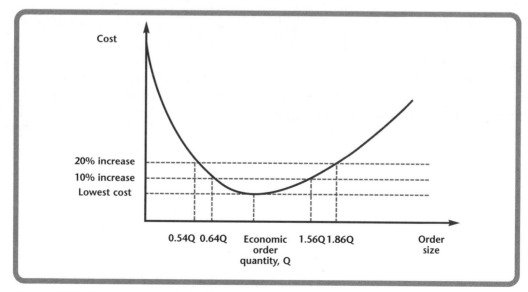

Figure 10.7 The cost curve is shallow around the economic order quantity

Weaknesses of this approach

The economic order quantity has been used for almost a century, and is still the basis for most independent demand inventory systems. It has a number of advantages, such as:

● easy to understand and use
● giving good guidelines for order size
● finding other values such as costs and cycle lengths
● easy to implement and automate
● encouraging stability
● easy to extend, allowing for different circumstances.

On the other hand, there are a number of weaknesses, as it:

● takes a simplified view of inventory systems
● assumes demand is known and constant
● assumes all costs are known and fixed
● assumes a constant lead time and no uncertainty in supplies
● gives awkward order sizes at varying times
● assumes each item is independent of others
● does not encourage improvement, in the way that JIT does.

We can overcome some of these problems by, for example, developing more complicated models. In the next section we will show one step in this direction.

LOGISTICS IN PRACTICE

Montague Electrical Engineering

Montague Electrical Engineering (MEE) is a small electric motor manufacturer with annual sales of £8 million. Robert Hellier is the operations manager. He read the monthly inventory report and was surprised to find total stocks had jumped from £2.2 million to £2.6 million in the past month.

Robert noticed there were very high stocks of part number XCT45, which is a 3 cm diameter bearing. MEE used these steadily, at a rate around 200 a week. The bearings cost £5 each and Robert had been buying 2500 units at a time. There were many such items in the report, and Robert realised that he had been ordering parts without taking any notice of the inventory costs. The accountant calculated the cost of inventory as 30% a year and the ordering costs were about £15 an order. Based on these figures Robert adjusted his purchase pattern and reduced orders for XCT45 to 500. One year later, stocks had fallen to less than £1 million, customer service had improved, emergency orders were almost eliminated and MEE was saving over £0.5 million a year.

Source: Robert Hellier (2000) Presentation to Western Operations Group, September

UNCERTAIN DEMAND AND SAFETY STOCK

The basic economic order quantity assumes that demand is constant and known exactly. In practice demand can vary widely and have a lot of uncertainty. A company selling a new CD, for example, does not know how many copies will sell in advance, or how sales will vary over time. When the variation is small, the EOQ model still gives useful results, but they are not so good when demand varies more widely. There are several ways we can deal with variable and uncertain demand, and we will illustrate one approach where the demand is normally distributed.

You can see easily why our previous calculations do not work with a variable demand. We used a reorder level found from the mean demand in the lead time. But if demand in the lead time is above average, stock will run out before the next delivery arrives and there will be shortages. Unfortunately, when demand is, say, normally distributed, it is above the mean in 50% of cycles. Most organisations would not be happy with shortages in 50% of stock cycles.

An alternative is to hold additional stocks – above the expected needs – to add a margin of safety. Then organisations increase their holding costs by a small amount, to avoid the higher shortage costs. These **safety stocks** are used if the normal working stock runs out. They have no effect on the reorder quantity – which is still defined by the EOQ – but do affect the time when an order is placed (shown in Figure 10.8). In particular, the reorder level is raised by the amount of the safety stock to give:

REORDER LEVEL = lead time demand + safety stock = LD + safety stock

Higher safety stocks obviously give a greater cushion against unexpectedly high demand, and better customer service. Of course, the costs of holding larger stocks are also higher, so we have to balance these two effects. The problem is that shortage costs are so difficult to find that they are little more than guesses. An alternative approach relies on managers' judgement

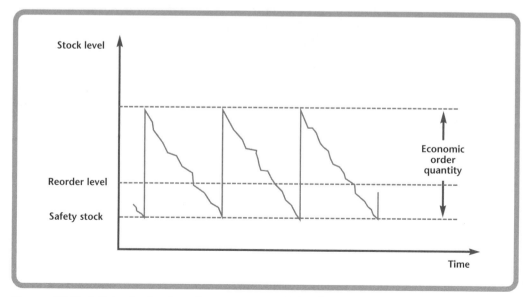

Figure 10.8 Safety stock raises the average stock level

to set an appropriate **service level**. This is the probability that a demand is met directly from stock. An organisation typically gives a service level of 95%. This means that it meets 95% of orders from stock – and accepts that 5% of orders cannot be met from stock. The service level needs a positive decision by managers, based on their experience, objectives, competition, and knowledge of customer expectations.

There are several ways of defining service level, but we will take it as the probability of not running out of stock in a stock cycle. This is the **cycle-service level**.

Suppose that demand for an item is normally distributed with a mean of D per unit time and standard deviation of σ. If the lead time is constant at L, the lead-time demand is normally distributed with mean of LD. The lead-time demand has a variance of $\sigma^2 L$ and standard deviation of $\sigma\sqrt{L}$. We get this result from the fact that variances can be added, and if:

● demand in a single period has mean D and variance σ^2,

then

● demand in two periods has mean 2D and variance $2\sigma^2$,
● demand in three periods has mean 3D and variance $3\sigma^2$,

and

● demand in L periods has mean LD and variance $L\sigma^2$.

The size of the safety stock depends on the service level. To be specific, when lead-time demand is normally distributed the safety stock is:

SAFETY STOCK = Z × standard deviation of lead-time demand = $Z\sigma\sqrt{L}$

As usual, Z is the number of standard deviations away from the mean, and probabilities can be found from a statistics package or tables. To give some examples:

● Z = 1 gives a stock-out in 15.9% of stock cycles
● Z = 2 gives stock-outs in 2.3% of stock cycles
● Z = 3 gives stock outs in 0.1% of stock cycles.

If demand varies widely, the standard deviation of lead-time demand is high – and very high safety stocks are needed to give a service level anywhere close to 100%. Usually, organisations choose lower service levels that reflect the importance of each item. Then very important items have service levels close to 100%, while less important ones are around 85%.

WORKED EXAMPLE

Associated Kitchen Furnishings runs a retail shop to sell a range of kitchen cabinets. The demand for cabinets is normally distributed with a mean of 200 units a week and a standard deviation of 40 units. The reorder cost, including delivery, is £200, holding cost is £6 per unit a year and lead time is fixed at 3 weeks. Describe an ordering policy that gives the

EXAMPLE
continued

shop a 95% cycle-service level. What is the cost of holding the safety stock in this case? How much does the cost rise if the service level is set at 97%?

Solution

Listing the values we know:

D = 200 units a week = 10,400 units a year
σ = 40 units
R = £200 an order
H = £6 a unit a year
L = 3 weeks

- ■ Substituting these values gives:
  - ■ $Q = \sqrt{(2RD/H)} = \sqrt{(2 \times 200 \times 200 \times 52/6)} = 833$ (to the nearest integer)
  - ■ Reorder level = LD + safety stock = 600 + safety stock

- ■ For a 95% service level Z = 1.64 standard deviations from the mean. Then:
  - ■ safety stock = $Z\sigma\sqrt{L} = 1.64 \times 40 \times \sqrt{3} = 114$ (to the nearest integer)

The best policy is to order 833 units whenever stock falls to 600 + 114 = 714 units. On average orders will arrive when there are 114 units left.

The safety stock is not usually used, so the holding cost is simply:

= safety stock × holding cost = 114 × 6 = £684 a year

- ■ If the service level is set at 97%, Z becomes 1.88 and:
  - ■ safety stock = $Z\sigma\sqrt{L} = 1.88 \times 40 \times \sqrt{3} = 130$

The cost of holding this is:

= safety stock × holding cost = 130 × 6 = £780 a year

LOGISTICS
IN PRACTICE

Wiesiek Teknika

Wiesiek Teknika (WT) market a range of diagnostic equipment for clinical laboratories and blood banks. They are the Polish branch of a Dutch parent company, and have been open for 25 years. A summary of their activities includes:

- ■ Marketing equipment
- ■ Customising equipment to customer needs
- ■ Installing it in customers' premises
- ■ Training customers to use the equipment

■ Maintaining a 24-hour help and advice desk

■ Preventive maintenance

■ Emergency repairs.

WT currently support 33 types of equipment, guaranteeing a repair within 48 hours. For this they need stocks of parts and consumables, and currently hold 22,000 items valued at 300,000 Zl (based on internal transfer prices). These are ordered from the parent company with a normal lead time of 14 days, but rush orders can arrive in five days. Up until 2001, the amount of stock held was determined by the parent company. WT recorded transactions and every month placed an order to replace the parts that had been used in the previous month. This system had a number of disadvantages, with:

■ no attempt to minimise or reduce costs

■ time-consuming procedures to check transaction records and prepare orders

■ no check that all items held were actually needed

■ no guarantee that stock levels were appropriate

■ occasional shortages needing rush orders

■ no records of stock performance

■ stock levels rising by 60% in the previous four years.

In 2001 the parent company encouraged its branches to review and improve their inventory control. WT looked at some standard programs, but decided to get tailored software from the company that had installed their information system. This set stock levels according to company policy, but related purchases to actual use, forecast demand, and analyses of lead times. Using the current supplier had the advantages of:

■ using existing systems to do some of the necessary analyses

■ integrating the new system easily with existing systems

■ giving a customised system for the stock analyses

■ building on WT's experience with current systems

■ having a software supplier that has proved reliable and helpful

■ having lower development and operating costs.

The key parts of the new system are improved data entry (based on international bar codes), analysis of demand (with forecasts, monitoring customer service, and so on), order generation (automatically generating and transmitting orders to the parent company) and order tracking (checking progress of each order, timing, costs, and so on). The benefits of the new system include lower stock levels, costs, time spent on administration and shortages.

Source: company reports

PERIODIC REVIEW SYSTEMS

The EOQ analysis uses a **fixed order quantity** for purchases, so an order of fixed size is placed whenever stock falls to a certain level. A heating plant may order 25,000 litres of oil whenever the amount in the tank falls to 2500 litres. Such systems need continuous monitoring of stock

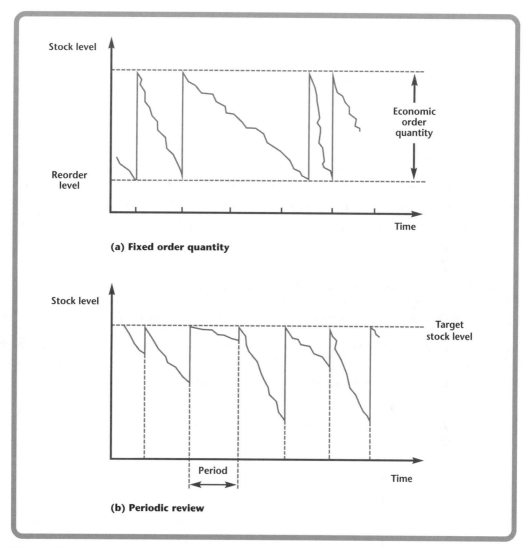

Figure 10.9 Alternative approaches to ordering

levels and are best suited to low, irregular demand for relatively expensive items. But there is an alternative **periodic review** approach, which orders varying amounts at regular intervals. A supermarket may refill its shelves every evening to replace whatever it sold during the day. The operating cost of this system is generally lower and it is better suited to high, regular demand of low value items. (See Figure 10.9).

If the demand is constant these two systems are the same, but differences appear when demand varies. We can show this by extending the last analysis, and looking at a periodic review system where demand is normally distributed. Then we are looking for answers to two questions. First, how long should the interval between orders be? This can be any convenient time, and organisations typically place orders at the end of every week, or every morning, or at the end of a month. If there is no obvious cycle we might aim for a certain number of orders a year or some average order size. One approach is to calculate an economic order quantity, and then find the period that gives orders of about this size. This decision is largely a matter for management judgement.

Second, what is the **target stock level**? The system works by looking at the stock on hand when an order is due, and ordering an amount that brings this up to a target stock level.

---

order quantity = target stock level – stock on hand

At the end of a month a company might have ten units remaining of an item with a target stock level of 40, so it orders 30 more units.

We can find the target stock level by extending our previous analyses. Suppose the lead time is constant at L. When an order is placed, the stock on hand plus this order must last until the next order arrives. As you can see from Figure 10.10:

next order arrives after a time = order interval + lead time = T + L

Again, we will assume that the demand for each period is normally distributed with a mean D and standard deviation σ, and that both the order period and lead time are fixed at T and L respectively. Then:

● demand in one period has mean D and variance σ^2
● demand over two periods has mean 2D and variance $2\sigma^2$
● demand over (T + L) periods has mean D(T+L), variance of $(T + L)\sigma^2$

The standard deviation in demand over (T + L) is $\sigma\sqrt{(T + L)}$, so we can define a safety stock as:

safety stock = Z × standard deviation of demand over (T+L) = $Z\sigma\sqrt{(T+L)}$

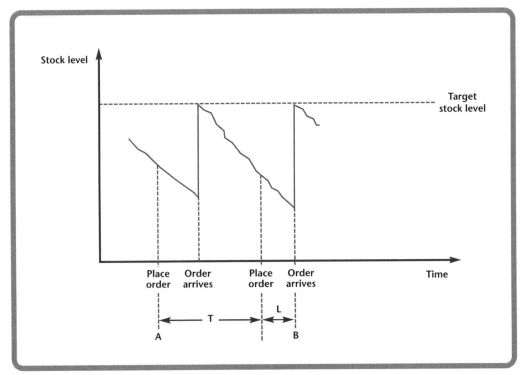

Figure 10.10 Order placed at A has to cover demand until B

Then:

target stock level = mean demand over (T+L) + safety stock
$$= D(T+L) + Z\sigma\sqrt{(T+L)}$$

Supermarkets traditionally use periodic review, and with EDI you can imagine a store where the tills pass messages every night to replenish products that were used during the day. But the system becomes more responsive and reduces stock levels, if it sends messages, say, two or three times a day. Suppliers consolidate these orders and send deliveries as often as necessary.

WORKED EXAMPLE

Demand for an item has a mean of 200 units a week and standard deviation of 40 units. Stock is checked every four weeks and lead time is constant at two weeks. Describe a policy that will give a 95% service level. If the holding cost is £2 a unit a week, what is the cost of the safety stock with this policy? What is the effect of a 98% service level?

Solution

Listing the values given:

D = 200 units
σ = 40 units
H = £2 a unit a week
T = 4 weeks
L = 2 weeks

■ For a 95% service level, Z is 1.64 (which you can find from a standard package or tables). Then:
  ■ safety stock = $Z\sigma\sqrt{(T+L)}$ = 1.64 × 40 × $\sqrt{6}$ = 161 (to the nearest integer)
  ■ target stock level = D(T+L) + safety stock = 200 × 6 + 161 = 1361.

When it is time to place an order, the policy is to find the stock on hand, and place an order for:
  ■ order size = target stock level – stock on hand = 1361 – stock on hand.

If, for example, there are 200 units in stock, we place an order for 1361 – 200 = 1161 units.

■ The safety stock is not normally used, so the holding cost:
  = safety stock × holding cost = 161 × 2 = £322 a week.

■ If the service level is increased to 98%, Z = 2.05. Then:
  ■ safety stock = $Z\sigma\sqrt{(T+L)}$ = 2.05 × 40 × $\sqrt{6}$ = 201 units
  ■ target stock level = D(T+L) + safety stock = 200×6 + 201 = 1401 units
  ■ cost of the safety stock is safety stock × holding cost = 201 × 2 = £402 a week.

But why stop at two or three messages a day, when the tills can send messages every time they make a sale? This is the approach of **continuous replenishment**, which has reduced stocks in Tesco by 10%, while increasing availability by 1.5% and significantly increasing productivity.[11]

EFFORT OF STOCK CONTROL

ABC analysis

Even the simplest and most highly automated inventory control system needs some effort to make it run smoothly. For some items, especially cheap ones, this effort is not worthwhile. Very few organisations include, for example, routine stationery or nuts and bolts in their stock control system. At the other end of the scale are very expensive items that need special care above the routine calculations. Aircraft engines, for example, are very expensive, and airlines have to control their stocks of spare engines very carefully.

An **ABC analysis** puts items into categories that show the amount of effort worth spending on inventory control. This is a standard Pareto analysis or 'rule of 80/20', which suggests that 20% of inventory items need 80% of the attention, while the remaining 80% of items need only 20% of the attention. ABC analyses define:

⬤ A items as expensive and needing special care
⬤ B items as ordinary ones needing standard care
⬤ C items as cheap and needing little care.

Typically an organisation might use an automated system to deal with all B items. The system might make some suggestions for A items, but decisions are made by managers after reviewing all the circumstances. C items might be excluded from the automatic system and controlled by ad hoc methods.

An ABC analysis starts by calculating the total annual use of each item by value. We find this by multiplying the number of units used in a year by the unit cost. Usually, a few expensive items account for a lot of use, while many cheap ones account for little use. If we list the

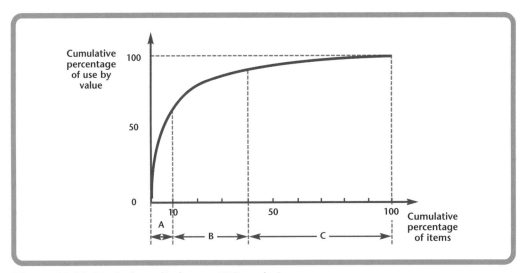

Figure 10.11 Typical results for an ABC analysis

items in order of decreasing annual use by value, A items are at the top of the list, B items are in the middle and C items are at the bottom. We might typically find:

Category	% of items	Cumulative % of items	% of use by value	Cumulative % of use by value
A	10	10	70	70
B	30	40	20	90
C	60	100	10	100

Figure 10.11 shows typical results of plotting the cumulative percentage of annual use against the cumulative percentage of items.

You have to be careful with ABC analyses as they can give misleading advice. The annual value of a material's use is often a poor measure of its importance. Essential safety equipment, for example, has to be present even if it is never used. An assembly line only keeps going if all materials have the same, high service level, regardless of their cost.

WORKED EXAMPLE

A small store has ten categories of product with the following costs and annual demands:

Product	P1	P2	P3	P4	P5	P6	P7	P8	P9	P0
Unit Cost (€)	20	10	20	50	10	50	5	20	100	1
Annual demand ('00s)	2.5	50	20	66	15	6	10	5	1	50

Do an ABC analysis of these items. If resources for inventory control are limited, which items should be given least attention?

Solution

The annual use of P1 in terms of value is 20 × 250 = €5000. Repeating this calculation for the other items gives the following results:

Item	P1	P2	P3	P4	P5	P6	P7	P8	P9	P0
% of items	10	10	10	10	10	10	10	10	10	10
Annual use (€'000s)	5	50	40	330	15	30	5	10	10	5

Sorting these into order of decreasing annual use gives the following results:

Product	P4	P2	P3	P6	P5	P8	P9	P1	P7	P0
Cumulative % of items	10	20	30	40	50	60	70	80	90	100
Annual use (€'000s)	330	50	40	30	15	10	10	5	5	5
Cumulative annual use	330	380	420	450	465	475	485	490	495	500
Cumulative % annual use	66	76	84	90	93	95	97	98	99	100
Category	<–A–><————B————><—————————C—————————>									

The boundaries between categories of items are often unclear, but in this case P4 is clearly an A item, P2, P3 and P6 are B items and the rest are C items.

The C items account for only 10% of annual use by value. If resources are limited, these should be given least attention.

Vendor managed inventory

If an organisation is trying to reduce the amount of effort it puts into inventory control, one option is to leave the whole problem to someone else and use third parties. We have already seen that outsourcing parts of logistics can bring advantages, and one option is to use a third party to keep all stock. Another option is to have another organisation look after the stock control, without them actually holding the stock. Perhaps the most common arrangement of this kind is **vendor managed inventory**. You can imagine this is a department store, which holds stocks of, say, shoes. Ordinarily the store controls its own stocks, and orders more from a wholesaler when it wants them. With vendor managed inventory, the wholesaler controls the stocks, and sends more along when they are needed. The benefits of such arrangements are that the supplier can co-ordinate stocks over a wider area, use optimal inventory policies, organise transport more efficiently, increase integration in the supply chain, collect more information about demand patterns, and give a consistent customer service.[12] The drawbacks include more reliance on a supplier who may have different objectives, less clear responsibility for stock, need for more sophisticated information systems, and less flexibility.

LOGISTICS IN PRACTICE

BHP and Nalco/Exxon Energy Chemicals

Every day BHP offshore produces 70,000 barrels of oil and 300 million cubic feet of gas. Since 1995 they have had an alliance with Nalco/Exxon Energy Chemicals to supply specialty chemicals. In 1998 they looked for improvements to the supply chain, a key section of which is shown in Figure 10.12. This had several problems including:

■ very large safety stocks
■ poor order policies
■ no single point of responsibility for stocks
■ poor management practices
■ barriers and delays to orders.

The companies decided to introduce a single inventory system, based on vendor management. Local operations gave up their stocks and relied on the supply from Nalco/Exxon, removing stages 2, 3, 4 and 6 from the supply chain in Figure 10.12. Although the companies already had a working alliance, this was a significant step. The new system was launched after a lot of preparation in 1999, and reduced costs by 28% – or $300,000 a year – with no reduction in customer service. There have also been numerous intangible benefits, such as the redeployment of scarce resources to more profitable area.

Source: Jones A. (2001) Vendor managed inventory, *Logistics and Transport Focus*, 3(5), 31–5

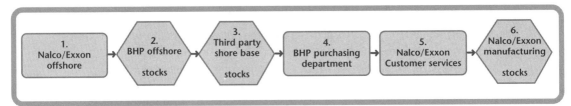

Figure 10.12 Original supply chain for Nalco/Exxon

❑ Stocks are the materials that organisations keep in store until they are needed. Every organisation holds stocks of some kind, to give a buffer between supply and demand. Their main purpose is to allow for uncertainty and variation.

❑ There are many types of stocks and arrangements for their storage. This is always expensive and organisations look for methods of control that achieve some specific purpose. They usually look for a balance between the different costs.

❑ Most independent demand inventory systems are based on an economic order quantity. This is the order size that minimises the total cost of a simple inventory system. The reorder level shows the times to place orders.

❑ If demand varies widely we can add a safety stock to achieve a specified service level. There are many other extensions to the basic models.

❑ An alternative approach uses a periodic review system that places regular orders to bring stocks up to a target level.

❑ There are several ways of allocating reasonable effort to stock control. One uses an ABC analysis; another outsources part of the function, perhaps using vendor managed inventory.

C A S E   S T U D Y — *Lennox Wholesale Group*

Brisbane is the main city of Queensland, Australia. To the north are a series of coastal towns that are growing very quickly. In 1988 George Lennox opened a distribution centre in Cairns to supply pharmaceuticals and related products to retail pharmacies, hospitals, dispensing doctors and a few other outlets. In the past, deliveries of pharmaceuticals in this remote area had been made directly by manufacturers, but the growing population had encouraged wholesalers to open. Now there is a mature industry giving an efficient delivery service from centralised warehouses.

As more pharmaceutical wholesalers arrived the market has become increasingly competitive. George Lennox's company has grown into the Lennox Wholesale Group (LWG) and is one of the main companies in the area. It is now classified as a medium-sized private company which is run efficiently and gives a good service to customers. The three main activities of LWG are:

■ *order taking and processing*
■ *stock holding and control*
■ *delivery to customers.*

To ensure his company's continuing success, George Lennox is always looking for improved performance. A short while ago he was concerned that the cost of deliveries to customers was rising. The distribution system had been reviewed occasionally as the company grew, but it was essentially designed for a much smaller operation. George hired a management consultant to give advice on improving the transport operations. The consultant did some work which suggested areas for improvement, and his final report suggested that the company look at its stock holding policies.

George looked at the stock control system, which was based on standard software provided by CyborgExceler seven years earlier. This had been updated and expanded twice, and still seemed to work quite well. Unfortunately, a close examination showed that stock levels had actually been drifting upwards for some time. The purchasing department explained that the company was successful because it had a reputation for reliability and service. A customer could e-mail, fax or telephone an order and delivery would be guaranteed during the next working day. Unfortunately LWG had occasionally run out of stock and had let down customers (their own lead time from manufacturers averaged about a week). To make sure this happened rarely, the purchasing department had adopted a policy of keeping two weeks' demand in reserve stock, but for some reason this seemed to be drifting up to three weeks' demand.

The same ordering procedure was used for all items. This was based on the purchasing department's view that the most important factor was average demand over the past five weeks. This value was used as a forecast of future demand. Then a reorder level was set as:

Reorder level = Forecast × (lead time + safety stock) × Factor

where Factor is a variable between 1 and 2 to give a subjective view of the item's importance and the supplier's reliability.

Order quantities are really set by the number of staff in the purchasing department. Three people work in the department, each processing up to sixty orders a day. In 200 working days a year they can process 36,000 orders. As there were 4000 items in stock, each item can have an average of 9 orders a year. To add another element of safety, each order was made big enough to last about eight weeks.

The system was largely automated, and nobody really checked its performance. Items were usually in stock when they were needed, so managers did not look at the details of the operations. Unit costs varied between one dollar and several hundred dollars, and no one had calculated cost of stock holding or purchasing. As an experiment, George collected some information for a small sample of nine items.

CASE STUDY   *continued*

Week	Item 1	2	3	4	5	6	7	8	9
1	53	284	252	27	145	1235	567	121	987
2	64	301	260	32	208	1098	664	87	777
3	82	251	189	23	177	987	548	223	743
4	41	333	221	22	195	1154	602	304	680
5	73	276	232	27	211	1559	530	76	634
6	18	259	195	30	179	1209	650	377	655
7	40	242	217	31	205	993	612	156	598
8	53	310	225	23	187	1313	608	198	603
9	52	311	186	28	156	1405	596	94	621
10	21	336	265	23	182	1009	637	355	564
11	67	258	245	25	171	985	555	187	559
12	50	277	212	28	169	1237	589	209	519
13	22	263	224	31	210	1119	601	304	485
Reorder level	302	1220	1050	160	1120	6100	2520	900	4400
Order quantity	450	2000	1500	245	1450	7900	4500	1950	6400
Unit cost (A$)	45.25	10.20	8.75	32.60	12.25	6.50	28.50	36.00	4.20

CASE STUDY

Questions

- How well do you think the existing inventory control system works? What are its weaknesses?
- How could you improve the system?
- George Lennox is keen to make progress in this area. What would you advise him to do next?

PROJECT

National Stock Holdings

On a national scale, the amount of stock seems to be falling. Collect some figures to check this observation. How do these figures vary for different countries? What are the main factors that affect national stockholdings? What effect does this have on the economy? What other trends are there in inventory control?

PROBLEMS

1. The demand for an item is constant at 200 units a year. Unit cost is £50, cost of processing an order is £20 and holding cost is £10 per unit per annum. What are the economic order quantity, corresponding cycle length and costs?

2. Jean Jeanie spa. work 48 weeks a year to meet demand for jeans which is more or less constant at 200 units a week. They pay £20 for each pair of jeans and aim for a return of 20% on capital invested. Annual storage costs are 5% of the value of goods stored. The purchasing department costs £65,000 a year and sends out an average of 2000 orders. Find the optimal order quantity for jeans, the best time between orders and the minimum cost of stocking the item.

3. Demand for an item is steady at 40 units a week and the economic order quantity has been calculated at 150 units. What is the reorder level when the lead time is:

   (a) 1 week (b) 3 weeks (c) 5 weeks (d) 7 weeks?

4. Fenicci e Fantocca forecast demand for components to average 18 a day over a 200 day working year. Any shortages disrupt production and give very high costs. The holding cost for the component is 120,000 lire a unit a year, and the cost of placing an order is 240,000 lire an order. Find the economic order quantity, the optimal number of orders a year and the total annual cost of operating the system if the interest rate is 20% a year.

5. A company advertises a 95% cycle-service level for all stock items. Stock is replenished from a single supplier who guarantees a lead time of 4 weeks. What reorder level should the company adopt for an item that has a normally distributed demand with mean 1000 units a week and standard deviation of 100 units? What is the reorder level for a 98% cycle-service level?

6. Wolfgang Heinz stocks an item with a unit cost of $80, reorder cost of $100 and holding cost of $2 a unit a week. Demand for the item has a mean of 100 a week with standard deviation 10. Lead time is constant at 3 weeks. Design an inventory policy for the item to give a service level of 95%. How would you change this to give a 90% service level? What are the costs of these two policies?

7. Describe a periodic review system with an interval of two weeks for the company described in Problem 10.5.

8. A small store has ten categories of product and the following costs and annual demands:

Product	H1	P2	A3	X1	W2	P3	Z1	C2	C3	Z2
Unit Cost (Dm)	60	75	90	3	12	18	30	45	60	66
Annual demand ('00s)	3	2	2	10	8	7	30	20	6	4

   Do an ABC analysis of these items.

DISCUSSION QUESTIONS

1. What costs are incurred by holding stock? Some organisations try to reduce stocks by making to order, or guaranteeing delivery within a specified period. Do such methods really reduce inventory costs?

2. What factors in real inventory control are not included in the economic order quantity model? If the costs of holding stock are so difficult to find, how reliable are the results from this kind of analysis?

3. What should you consider when setting a service level? How can a hospital set a reasonable service level for its supplies of blood for transfusions?

4. We have now seen how stocks can be controlled by MRP, JIT and independent demand systems. When would you use each of these? Are there any other methods?

5. What features would you expect to see in an automated inventory control system? Look at some commercial packages and compare the features they offer.

6. Stocks are an inevitable. Methods like JIT only transfer stocks from one part of the supply chain to another. To what extent do you think this is true?

REFERENCES

1. Institute of Grocery Distribution (1998) *Retail Distribution 1998*, IGD, Herts.
2. Institute of Logistics (1998) *European Logistics: Comparative Survey*, Institute of Logistics, Corby.
3. Office for National Statistics (2001) *Annual Abstract of Statistics*, HMSO, London.
4. Office for National Statistics (2001) *UK Economic Accounts*, HMSO, London.
5. Office for National Statistics (2001) *Economic Trends*, HMSO, London.
6. Waters C.D.J. (2001) Inventory management, Ch. 12 in Brewer A.M., Button K.J. and Hensher D.A. (eds) *Handbook of Logistics and Supply Chain Management*, Pergamon, London.
7. Lambert D.W. (1976) *The Development of an Inventory Costing Methodology*, National Council for Physical Distribution Management, Chicago.
8. Harris F. (1915) *Operations and Cost*, A. Shaw & Co., Chicago.
9. Raymond F.E. (1931) *Quantity and Economy in Manufacture*, McGraw-Hill, Chicago.
10. Wilson R.H. (1934) A scientific routine for stock control, *Harvard Business Review*, No. XIII.
11. Tesco plc (2001) *Annual Review and Summary Financial Statement*. 2001.
12. Herring S. (2000) Inventory management into the 21st century, *Logistics and Transport Focus*, **2**(7), 43–5.

Further reading

Greene J.H. (1997) *Production and Inventory Control Handbook* (3rd edn), McGraw-Hill, New York.
Lewis C.D. (1997) *Demand Forecasting and Inventory Control*, Woodhead Publishing, Cambridge.
Silver E.A., Pyke D.F. and Peterson R. (1998) *Inventory Management and Production Planning and Scheduling* (3rd edn), John Wiley, New York.
Tersine R.J. (1994) *Principles of Inventory and Materials Management*, Prentice Hall, Englewood Cliffs, NJ.
Waters C.D.J. (1992) *Inventory Control and Management*, John Wiley, Chichester.
Waters C.D.J. (1998) *A Practical Introduction to Management Science* (2nd edn), Addison-Wesley Longman, Harlow.

CHAPTER 11

Warehousing and Material Handling

AIMS OF THE CHAPTER

After reading this chapter you should be able to:

- APPRECIATE the purpose and aims of warehouses

- DESCRIBE the main activities in a warehouse

- COMPARE the benefits of private and public warehousing

- SEE how to design good warehouse layouts

- CHOOSE the most appropriate type of equipment

- APPRECIATE the purpose of packaging

PURPOSE OF WAREHOUSES

Definitions

All organisations hold stocks. The last chapter looked at questions of controlling inventories to find the best patterns for orders, amount to stock, and so on. In this chapter we are going to look at the way stock is actually stored.

Stocks occur at any point in the supply chain where the flow of materials is interrupted. Most organisations arrange for stocks to be kept in **warehouses**. In practice, these warehouses might be open fields where raw materials like coal, ores or vegetables are heaped; or sophisticated facilities that give the right conditions for frozen or delicate materials; or databases that hold stocks of information; or people who have a stock of skills; or almost any other form that you can think of. To simplify things, we will simply refer to warehouses as any place for storing materials.

People use a number of different terms for warehouses, with the most common being **distribution centres** and **logistics centres**. Sometimes they describe distribution centres as storing finished goods on their way to final customers, while logistics centres store a wider mix of products at different points in the supply chain. Other names are used, such as 'transit centre', to show that the facility not only stores materials, but does a range of other jobs. To make things easy, we will use the general term 'warehouse' to cover all such facilities.

■ A **WAREHOUSE** is any location where stocks of material are held on their journey through supply chains.
■ As well as storage, warehouses can be used for a number of other activities.

Warehouses are an essential part of most supply chains. Olsen[1] comments that:

We have seen the demise of warehousing predicted again and again, especially with the evolution of the philosophies of just-in-time, quick response, efficient consumer response, direct store delivery, and continuous flow distribution.

As we have already seen, the reality is that every organisation holds stocks to give a buffer between supply and demand. As long as they need to hold stocks of materials, they need warehouses to hold them.

Most warehouses are designed for raw materials collected before operations, and finished goods during distribution to customers. To a lesser extent, they store work in progress, consumables and spare parts. In this chapter we are going to look at some of the main decisions relating to these stores.

When we talk about warehouses storing materials, this is really only part of the story. Many organisations are using warehouses as convenient locations for doing a range of related jobs. Obviously, they can be used to inspect, sort materials and break bulk (taking large deliveries and breaking them into smaller quantities). They might also be used for finishing products, labelling, packaging, making products 'store ready' for retailers, doing other aspects of postponement, servicing vendor managed inventories, and so on. The overall trend is for warehouses to do more tasks, positively adding value rather than being a pure cost centre.

Fitting into the logistics strategy

Warehouses are expensive to run and need careful planning. We have already looked at some of the key decisions for this. The logistics strategy sets the overall structure of the supply chain, including the role of warehouses; location decisions show where to open warehouses; capacity plans show the number of warehouses to build and best size for each; inventory management shows the materials to store and amounts of each to stock. Now we are going to look at some related decisions. What jobs should we do in the warehouses? Who should own them? What is the best layout? What equipment should we use to move materials? How do we measure performance?

As always, there is a hierarchy of decisions, with the strategy leading to a series of tactical and operational decisions. If, for example, the business strategy is based on high customer service, the logistics strategy will probably be based on more, smaller warehouses. At least in principle, warehouses located near to customers can give faster response and better levels of service. Apart from the obvious factor of total throughput, there are some other important factors in choosing the best size for a warehouse. These include:

- the number of products using the warehouse
- the type of demand for each product, how much it varies, average order size, and so on
- physical features of the products, particularly size and weight
- special storage conditions, such as climate control, packaging, and so on
- target customer service level
- lead times from suppliers and promised to customers
- economies of scale
- type of material handling equipment
- layout of storage and related facilities.

Most of these are fairly obvious, such as higher customer service level needing bigger warehouses to hold higher stocks, and longer lead times needing more safety stock to cover for the unexpected.

Warehouse operations have to contribute to the logistics strategy. So managers have to analyse this strategy, design warehouses that will support it, and then run these warehouses as effectively as possible. We can describe one approach to this with the following steps:[2]

1. analyse the logistics strategy – setting the context and finding what the warehouse has to achieve
2. examine current operations – to see the failings and how these can be overcome.
3. design an outline structure – finding the best main location, number of sub-depots, and so on
4. make detailed plans – finding the size of facilities, stock holdings, material handling equipment, systems to develop, people to employ, transport needs, and so on
5. get final approval – submitting the plans to senior managers to agree the funding
6. finalise building design – purchasing land, choosing contractors and building
7. finalise equipment design – choosing equipment, suppliers and purchasing
8. finalise systems design – designing the ordering, inventory control, billing, goods location, monitoring, and all other systems needed
9. fit out – installing all equipment, systems, staff and testing
10. open and receive stock – to test all systems, finish training and begin operations
11. sort out teething problems – to get things running smoothly
12. monitor and control – ensuring that everything works as planned, measuring performance, revising incentive schemes, and so on.

These steps need not be done in strict sequence, but they highlight some of the important decision areas. To go through this complete process takes some time, perhaps two or three years for a typical facility.

Daniel West Wholesale Ltd

Daniel West Wholesale (DWW) is a privately owned wholesaler of frozen fish and a range of fresh foods. It employs 85 people, receives goods from 52 suppliers, and delivers to 570 main customers in the north of England using a fleet of 26 vans. All its operations are based in a single warehouse in Gateshead.

DWW is successful in a highly competitive market, and it attributes its success to its outstanding customer service. This is judged by the five criteria of close personal relationships, flexibility to respond to individual needs, low prices enhanced by discounts, high stocks meeting 98% of orders off the shelf, and frequent deliveries, normally twice a day.

DWW's turnover is £35 million a year, with a gross margin of about 4.5%. All the costs are classified as acquisition (76%), storage (7%), distribution (4%) and others (13%).

Every morning the order-processing room in DWW checks orders that have been automatically sent by customer tills, e-mailed, faxed, or telephoned overnight.

Then they contact customers who have not sent orders, asking if they want anything. These orders are consolidated into 'customer requirement lists', which are sent to the warehouse. The goods for each order are picked from the shelves, assembled, put into a delivery box, checked, and taken to a departure bay. At the departure bay the materials have final packing and promotional material added.

The customer requirement lists are used to design routes for the vans. The drivers collect the schedule of customers to be visited, pick up the boxes to be delivered, and load them into the van in the specified order. Then they set off on their deliveries, visiting an average of 20 customers, travelling 110 miles a morning, and delivering £3000 of goods. This whole procedure is repeated on a slight smaller scale in the afternoon.

After each of the main delivery runs, DWW's purchasing system analyses the purchases, consolidates these into orders, and automatically transmits them to suppliers.

Source: West D. (2002) *Report to Shareholders,* Newcastle-upon-Tyne

ACTIVITIES WITHIN A WAREHOUSE

Basic activities

The basic function of a warehouse is to store goods. This means that they receive deliveries from upstream suppliers, do any necessary checking and sorting, store the materials until they are needed and then arrange delivery to downstream customers. We can add some details and get the following list of activities that are generally included in 'warehousing'.

- receiving goods from upstream suppliers
- identifying the goods, matching them to orders and finding their intended use
- unloading materials from delivery vehicles
- doing any necessary checks on quantity, quality and condition
- labelling materials (usually with bar codes) so they can be identified
- sorting goods as needed
- moving goods to bulk storage area
- holding them in stock until needed
- when necessary, moving materials from bulk storage to a smaller picking store
- picking materials from this store to meet orders
- moving the materials to a marshalling area
- assembling materials into orders
- packing and packaging as necessary
- loading delivery vehicles and dispatching the order
- controlling all communications and related systems, such as inventory control and finance.

This is obviously a general picture and some warehouses do not do all of the activities, while others do many more. You can get some idea of the costs involved from the following example.

LOGISTICS IN PRACTICE

Waldenmier TWL

Waldenmier TWL are specialists in transport between countries in central Europe and those in the former Soviet Union. To ensure a smooth flow of goods they run a series of logistics centres. Every year they review their operations to see how the costs of these centres vary in different countries. In 2001 they found that warehousing added an average of 3.8% to selling price. The breakdown of this cost was:

Employment (wages, benefits, compensation, training and so on)	36%
Storage (rent, depreciation, interest, local taxes, and so on)	22%
Material handling (fork lift trucks, pallets, packaging, and so on)	12%
Utilities (electricity, heat, and so on)	8%
Communication and control (Internet, telephone systems, and so on)	10%
Administration (management, insurance, security, and so on)	12%

Source: company annual reports

Other activities in warehouses

Traditionally warehouses were seen as places for the long-term storage of goods. Now organisations try to move materials quickly through the supply chain, so their role has changed.

They are now viewed more as staging points through which materials move as quickly as possible. As their role in long-term storage has decreased, they have become convenient locations to do a range of other jobs. They are, for example, the best place for sorting materials, packing and consolidating deliveries.

Imagine a customer who needs part loads of different materials from different suppliers. Part loads are amounts that do not fill the transport used, so a part load might be half a container or part of a full van. Transport operations are often divided into full load and part load – so you can hear of TL (truckload) and LTL (less than truckload) operators. As you would expect, the unit costs are higher for part loads. Our customer needs several part loads delivering, so it can reduce costs by consolidating these into full loads. Then it gets all the part loads delivered to a warehouse near the suppliers, consolidates them into full loads, and pays the lower costs of full-load transport to its operations (as illustrated in Figure 11.1). The extra cost of consolidation in a warehouse is more than recovered from the reduced cost of transport. This is the way that freight forwarders make their money.

A different form of consolidation occurs when a manufacturer makes, or buys, parts of a final product in different locations. Then it can arrange for all components to be sent to a warehouse which combines the parts into the final product, and arranges delivery to customers. A computer manufacturer, for example, might collect in a central warehouse a keyboard from Brazil, software from the USA, a monitor from the UK, speakers from Taiwan and the main box from Japan, and so on. The warehouse assembles the components into final systems and delivers them to customers.

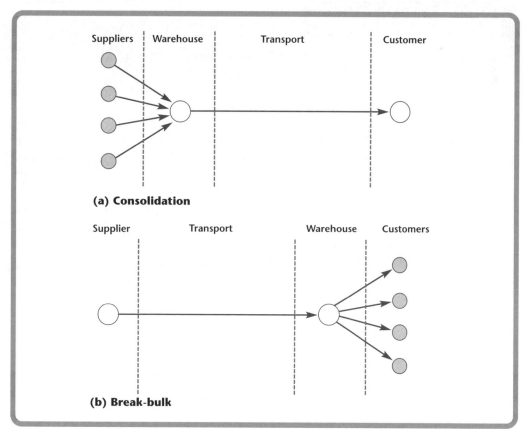

Figure 11.1 Using warehouses to reduce transport costs

This kind of consolidation can go further than simply bringing together materials from different sources. It might add the final packing and packaging to present a single product, or even do a limited amount of final manufacturing. This is the basis of **postponement**, where the final steps of production are left to the last possible moment. As we saw in Chapter 2, this has the advantage of reducing stocks and increasing flexibility to meet late changes in customer demands.

Warehouses also do the opposite of consolidation when they **break-bulk**. Here a supplier sends all the demand for a particular area in a single delivery to a local warehouse. The warehouse breaks this delivery into the separate orders and passes them on to each customer.

Warehouses are increasingly places for sorting and doing work on materials rather than storing them. In the extreme they do these associated jobs, but the materials are never put into storage. This is the basis of **cross-docking**. The arrival of materials at a warehouse is co-ordinated with its departures to customers, so that they are transferred directly from the arrival area to the loading area, and immediately sent for delivery to downstream customers. In practice, there might be some delay, but this is usually less than 24 hours. Some depots for cross-docking do not even have storage, but only organise the transfer of materials from, say, one truck to another. As well as reducing stock levels, this removes all the non-value adding activities of putting materials into storage, and later removing them. Dale Ross, Director of Logistics at Oshawa Foods in Toronto, estimates that: 'cross-docking full pallets of product can save 60% of a company's direct labour costs in a warehouse'.[3]

LOGISTICS IN PRACTICE

25 Canadian Forces Supply Depot

25 Canadian Forces Supply Depot opened in Montreal in 1995. This 60,000 square metre warehouse replaced three earlier facilities in Montreal, Toronto and Moncton. Its aim is to, 'receive, warehouse and issue everything needed to support bases, stations, ships and service battalions across eastern Canada and United Nations peacekeeping units around the world'.

The warehouse receives new materials from commercial suppliers and returns from Canadian Forces units. When a truck arrives, the documents are checked and the vehicle is directed to one of 11 receiving docks. There it is unloaded, bar codes on materials are scanned, and data is fed into the warehouse management information system (WMIS). Materials are then put onto conveyors, where each unit is automatically weighed and measured. When everything has been checked, and details confirmed, the materials are officially 'received'. Then WMIS prints a 'licence plate' bar code to identify each unit, and assigns a storage location. This location is set by the features of the unit, and is chosen to give the best use of storage space. WMIS then delivers the unit to its storage location, using fixed, hand-held and vehicle-mounted scanners around the warehouse to track and control movements. WMIS is also linked to other Canadian Forces systems to keep track of ordering, stocks, invoicing and related information.

WMIS has four different types of storage location:

■ Larger, palletised shipments are moved by forklift from the conveyor to one of

LOGISTICS
IN PRACTICE
continued

six stacker cranes which work in the high bay area. There are 18 aisles, 20 metres high, providing 140,000 locations for storage.

■ Smaller units are taken from the conveyor by a monorail system which delivers them to the mid-rise stacks. Four monorail trains, each with 8 trolleys, move on a 400 metre track and take units to delivery chutes. They are picked up by 10 wire-guided stock pickers which work in the 37 aisles, 10 metres high, providing 600,000 storage locations.

■ Larger units are taken from a special arrivals dock to the bulk storage area, which has space 6 metres high for free-standing goods.

■ Hazardous materials are taken from a special arrivals dock to a separate area for special treatment.

The warehouse was built using a developer-lease arrangement. With this, the developer paid for all major construction, retains ownership, and leases the warehouse to the Canadian Forces for C$6.6 million a year. Other costs came to C$31.8 million, including $4.4 for minor construction, C$13 million for warehouse equipment, C$4.8 million for the warehouse management information system, C$3.5 million to relocate stock, C$3.4 million for project support, and C$2.7 million contingency allowance. The savings of closing the older facilities came to C$33 million a year, so 25 Canadian Forces Supply Depot paid for itself in about three years.

Source: Brooker D. (1995) Forward march, *Materials Management and Distribution*, August, 19–21

Aims of warehousing

In general, the aims of a warehouse are to support the broader logistics function by giving a combination of high customer service and low costs. More specific aims include:

- providing necessary storage at key points in a supply chain
- giving secure storage of the type needed by materials
- keeping all materials in good condition and with minimal damage
- giving high customer service
- doing all necessary activities efficiently and with low costs
- getting high productivity and utilisation of resources
- controlling all movements of materials effectively and without errors
- sorting materials arriving and quickly transferring them into storage
- picking materials departing, quickly transferring them out of storage and consolidating deliveries
- being able to store the whole range of materials needed
- being flexible enough to deal efficiently with variations in stock levels
- allowing for special conditions, rotation of stock , and so on
- giving safe working conditions, and compliance with regulations.

OWNERSHIP

Many organisations own and run their own warehouses. But for small organisations this would be both difficult and expensive, so they use facilities provided by specialised warehousing companies. Even large companies can benefit from this arrangement, so they have a basic choice between **private** and **public warehouses**.

Private warehouses are owned or leased by an organisation as part of its own supply chains. The organisation runs its own warehouses to support its main operations. This gives greater control over a central part of logistics, and allows integration of warehousing with the broader activities of logistics. The warehouse can be tailored to the organisation's needs, being in the right location, right size, fitting in with customer service, and so on. Communications are easier with systems integrated throughout the organisation. It might also give lower costs (without the profit that would be needed by another organisation), with possible tax advantages and development grants. Another less tangible benefit comes from the corporate image, as private warehouses can give an impression of reliability and long-term dependability.

In Chapter 3 we mentioned that organisations often choose to concentrate on their core activities and contract out some of their logistics. In the last chapter we mentioned one aspect of this, where vendor-managed inventories transfer responsibility for inventory management to an outside organisation. Generally, stocks are still kept within the organisation, but they are managed by a supplier. A more common form of contracting has an organisation outsourcing parts of its warehousing. Then stocks are actually held by a third party in a public warehouse.

A public warehouse is run as an independent business, which makes money by charging users a fee. There are many types of public warehouse, including bonded warehouses, cold stores, bulk storage, tankers and various speciality stores. The facilities available are generally so flexible that an organisation can get, within reason, any facilities that it needs. There are also many arrangements for their use. At one extreme, an organisation might simply rent an area of empty space in a warehouse that it shares with many other organisations. The organisation still looks after all aspects of its warehousing and runs the necessary operations itself. At the other extreme, an organisation might contract out all its warehousing operations to a specialist third party. Then the organisation does none of its own warehousing, but specifies standards that must be met. The provider might meet these standards by using spare capacity in its existing facilities, or for large operations it might build and run special, dedicated facilities.

The main benefit of public warehouses is their flexibility. They can be used to cover short-term changes in demand without buying or disposing of facilities. Some other benefits include:

- flexibility to deal with changing demand, perhaps due to seasonality
- ability to supply skills and experience that the organisation does not have internally
- access to the latest equipment and practices
- avoiding large capital investment, giving higher return on investment
- easy access to a wider geographical area
- allowing short-term tests of working in new areas
- use of economies of scale to reduce warehousing costs
- consolidating loads with other organisations to reduce transport costs
- guaranteed high quality and efficient service

● flexibility to deal with changing conditions, removing risks from dated practices and technology.

These benefits have to be balanced against the loss of control. There is also some question of cost. Public warehouses might be efficient and large enough to get economies of scale, but they also have to make a profit and, by definition, generate more income than their costs. Careful analyses are needed to find the balance of these costs.

The trend in recent years has clearly been to use public warehouses.[4,5] This leaves organisations free to concentrate on their core operations and use the expertise of specialist warehousing companies. It might also form the basis of a policy of outsourcing other logistics services, such as transport.

The move towards contracting out warehousing means that the most common arrangement for warehousing is probably a mixture of private and public. An organisation uses private warehouses for basic, core needs and then tops this up with public warehousing as needed. As a rough guideline, a warehouse with enough capacity to meet peak demand will only work at full capacity for 75–85% of the time. So a sensible option is to have a private warehouse with enough capacity for this 75–85% of the time, and use public warehouses for the rest of the time. With such arrangements (illustrated in Figure 11.2) organisations can achieve occupancy rates of over 90%.[6]

The choice between private and public warehousing is often seen as another aspect of the 'make or buy' decision, and is often presented as a break-even analysis. Private warehouses have higher fixed costs but lower unit operating costs, while public warehouses have low fixed costs but potentially higher variable costs, as shown in Figure 11.3. This gives a very simple view, and many other factors should be included in such decisions. The basic question, of course, is whether a public warehouse can give the same (or better) service for the same (or lower) cost. If it can give a better service or lower cost then there are clear arguments for moving in this direction.

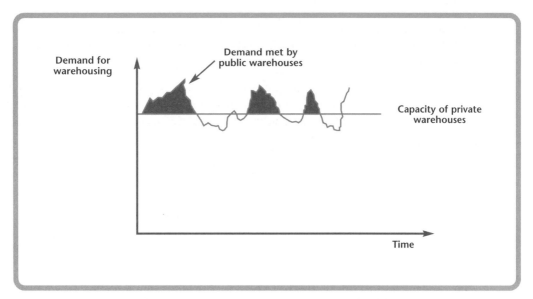

Figure 11.2 Meeting demand with a mixture of private and public warehouses

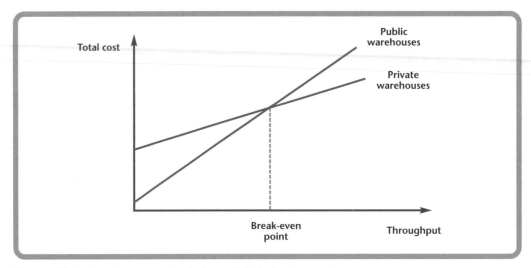

Figure 11.3 Break-even analysis for public/private warehouses

LAYOUT

General layout

One of the most important decisions when running a warehouse is its layout. This describes the physical arrangement of storage racks, loading and unloading areas, equipment, offices, rooms, and all other facilities. As you can imagine, this has a significant effect on the efficiency of operations. If a frequently used item is stored a long way from the delivery and departure bays, time is wasted every time a unit is put into, or taken from, stores. Stevenson[7] summarises this by saying that:

> Layout decisions are important for three basic reasons: (1) they require substantial investments of both money and effort, (2) they involve long-term commitments ... (3) they have significant impact on the cost and efficiency of short-term operations.

Every time you go into a supermarket you see a sort of warehouse. Materials are delivered at the back of the supermarket, they are sorted and put onto shelves in the middle, then customers pick the items they want and take them away from the front. This suggests that the essential elements in a warehouse (illustrated in Figure 11.4) are:

- an arrival bay, or dock, where goods coming from suppliers are delivered, checked and sorted
- a storage area, where the goods are kept as stock
- a departure bay, or dock, where customers' orders are assembled and sent out
- a material handling system, for moving goods around
- an information system, which records the location of all goods, arrivals from suppliers, departures to customers, and other relevant information.

There are many variations on this basic outline. The most common one – which is also used in most supermarkets – actually has two storage areas. Goods arrive and are put into a bulk store (the backroom in a supermarket) which is the main storage area. The packages in the bulk store are broken into individual units and moved to a smaller picking store that is used to

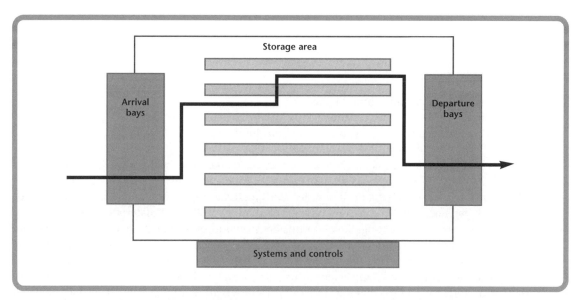

Figure 11.4 Basic layout of a warehouse

assemble orders (the shelves in a supermarket). When an order is received, the items needed are 'picked' from the smaller, picking store and brought together in a consolidation area, before moving to the departure bays. When stocks in the picking store run low, they are replenished from the bulk store. This gives the flow of materials from arrival bays, bulk store, picking store, consolidation area to departure bays, as illustrated in Figure 11.5.

You can see from this that supermarkets are not really typical warehouses, as they have fundamentally different aims. Warehouses want the picking to be as fast as possible, with goods moving quickly to the exit; supermarkets want their customers to pick goods slowly, as the longer they are in the shop the more they spend.

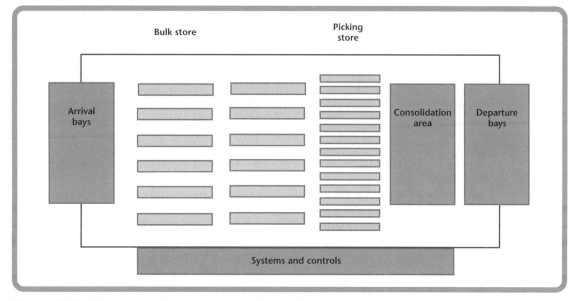

Figure 11.5 Schematic of a common warehouse layout

Layout of racking

In most warehouses, materials are stored in some form of shelving or racking. This can take many forms, leading to three basic questions:

- What type of racking should be used?
- What is the best layout for the racking?
- Where should different items be stored on the racks?

The basic type of storage is an area of floor space, marked out in a grid to identify different locations. Bulky or heavy items are put into a location, probably by a forklift truck. The next level of storage uses shelving built in aisles, with materials typically on pallets. A problem with this arrangement is that the shelves have to be shallow, so that all materials are within reach, and the aisles tend to be long. Smaller units are stored in bins, which are containers arranged in pigeonholes, so that materials are easy to find and remove. Flow racks can increase the density of storage by making the shelves much deeper. These are sloping shelves that are filled from the back, and as you remove a unit from the front, all the remaining units move forward. Other options for storage include horizontal carousels (bins on an oval track that rotate to bring materials to a picker), vertical carousels (shelves that rotate up and down to bring materials within reach), hanging racks for garments, silos and tanks for fluids, and a huge assortment of other arrangements.

Storage in a warehouse is almost inevitably arranged in aisles. To reduce the ground area needed, these aisles can be quite high. In practice, the details of the layout are determined by the existing building, architect's views, site available, height, or some physical constraint. Within these constraints, warehouse managers try to design the best layout for racking. This depends, to a large extent, on the type of goods being stored and the handling equipment used. If the goods are small and light, such as boxes of pills, they can be moved by hand, and the warehouse must have low shelving and be small enough to walk round. If the goods are large and heavy, such as engines, they need heavier handling equipment such as cranes and forklift trucks. Then the aisles must be big enough for these to manoeuvre. We will return to this theme in the next section.

One way of approaching the design is to:

- estimate demand for materials over the next five years or so
- translate this into forecast movements of materials into, through and out of the warehouse
- compare available equipment for handling these movements and choose the most appropriate
- find the space needed for storing and moving each item
- design a general layout for the racking
- see which materials should be close to each other (such as fast moving materials nearer to transport bays, chilled goods in the same area, high value goods in safe areas, and so on) and those that should be far apart (such as foods far away from chemicals)
- develop outline plans for the layouts and handling areas and choose the best (using appropriate analyses such as simulations)
- add details to give final plans.

In any particular circumstances there is not really a single 'best' layout, so organisations usually look for one that satisfies their requirements. Then, because of the wide variety of materials, locations, operations, objectives, and so on, it is difficult to go far beyond these general guidelines. Experience does, however, make some suggestions for good layouts. These include:

- plan the layout to give a smooth flow of materials into, through and out of the warehouse
- simplify movements, eliminating or combining separate movements where possible
- use high level storage where possible, as this reduces the overall area
- have offices outside the main warehouse area, as space above them is wasted
- consider using spare roof space for overhead movement of materials
- give appropriate space for aisles – as narrow as possible to reduce non-working space, but wide enough for equipment
- consider mezzanine floors for picking and administration
- have movements in straight lines on one floor.

Notice that several of these suggest using all of the available volume. The costs of warehousing often rise with the area, so there are advantages to having tall buildings, provided that the extra height is properly used. Rather than looking at turnover per square metre, warehouse efficiency is often judged on turnover per cubic metre.

Locating materials on shelves

Many costs of running a warehouse are fixed – such as rent, local taxes, utilities, and depreciation. Some of these fixed costs are set by management policy, such as the total investment in stock. The main variable cost comes from the details of the layout, and depends on the time needed to locate items and either add them to stock or remove them. When there are thousands of items in store, small differences in the way they are arranged can give markedly different service and costs.

WORKED EXAMPLE

A small store has a rack with nine colours of paint in five litre tins. At one end of the rack is an issue area where the storekeeper works. Weekly demand for the paint is as follows:

Colour	Red	Blue	White	Black	Brown	Green	Yellow	Grey	Pink
Tins	150	210	1290	960	480	180	360	60	90

If all paint is stored in bins that are 5 m wide, design a layout for the rack. Design a layout if the size of bins varies with the weekly demand.

Solution

A reasonable aim is to minimise the distance walked by the storekeeper, assuming that each tin of paint needs a separate journey. The paint should be laid out so that colours with highest demand are nearest the issue area, so the layout has paint in order white, black, brown, yellow, blue, green, red, pink and grey (as illustrated in Figure 11.6). Assuming that tins come from the middle of bins, the total distance moved by the storekeeper is:

$$= 2 \times (2.5 \times 1290 + 7.5 \times 960 + 12.5 \times 480 + 17.5 \times 360 + 22.5 \times 210$$
$$+ 27.5 \times 180 + 32.5 \times 150 + 37.5 \times 90 + 42.5 \times 60)$$
$$= 86{,}400 \text{ m}$$

If the size of bin is proportional to the weekly demand, and assuming that paint is taken from the middle of the bins, the paint can be stored equally well in any order.

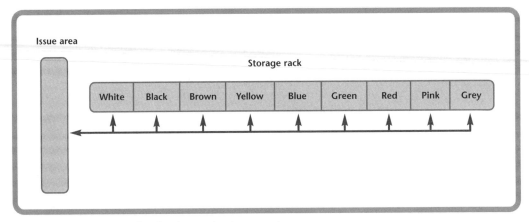

Issue area

Storage rack

| White | Black | Brown | Yellow | Blue | Green | Red | Pink | Grey |

Figure 11.6 Layout of paint in worked example

Turnaround time

Apart from the layout of the storage areas, the efficiency of a warehouse also depends on how quickly it deals with delivery vehicles. There are several measures of **turnaround time**, but the most common is the time taken between a vehicle arriving (either delivering materials or collecting them) and departing. Transport operators get paid for having their vehicles and drivers moving, so they do not want them sitting idly in a warehouse during loading or unloading. This is why airlines like passengers to disembark quickly, so that new passengers can be loaded and the plane can move on to its next journey. At the same time, there is limited docking space, so it must be freed up quickly to get a reasonable throughput.

It is, then, in everybody's interest to minimise the turnaround time. Three arrangements can help with this. First, orders can be assembled and waiting to move onto a vehicle – when the vehicle arrives it is loaded quickly and moved on. Second, special loading and unloading equipment can be used to speed operations. With, for example, rollers on vehicle floors a standard vehicle can be loaded and unloaded in five minutes or less. Third, the bays can be laid out carefully to minimise congestion.

LOGISTICS IN PRACTICE

Cornwall, Ontario

Wal-Mart operates 170 stores in Canada, where its logistics is managed by Tibbett & Britten. In 2000, they opened a new distribution centre in Cornwall, Ontario. This centre serves the 61 stores in eastern Canada, joining two other centres that serve the rest of the country. It also specialises in the supply of linen and shoes throughout Canada, as these need special inspections and finishing which are best centralised.

The Cornwall distribution centre covers 100,000 square metres, stocks 10,000 different items, with storage for 55,000 pallets and 10,000 cases.

An order management system analyses all demand met by the centre, forecasts

future sales, and places orders with suppliers. These deliveries are received in 80 docks, with bar codes added to each pallet and case to allow automatic movement. Most goods arrive on pallets and are put onto conveyors for movement into storage and there are 19 docks for articles that cannot use conveyors. There is some cross docking, with items going from the receiving area to the departure docks in 15 minutes. Sixty high-volume products are kept near to conveyors, and stay in stock for less than a day. The average stay for remaining items is two weeks.

The centre breaks pallet loads into cases, with a throughput of 115,000 cases a day.

Orders are automatically received from the stores' point-of-sales systems, the cases are picked, put onto a conveyor and sent to the departure docks (automatically guided by bar codes). There are 79 departure docks, so one dock with its conveyor is used for each store. This makes sorting very easy. Some goods that cannot go on the conveyors are handpicked and moved by forklift.

Independent carriers, or one of the centre's small fleet of vehicles, deliver to stores, usually within 24 hours of ordering.

Sources: Daudelin A. (2001) Supply chain management the Wal-Mart way, *Supply Chain and Logistics Journal*, Spring, and websites at www.walmart.com and www.infochain.org

MATERIALS HANDLING

A lot of the work in a warehouse moves materials from one location to another. Everything has to be taken from delivery vehicles, moved around the warehouse – often several times – and eventually put onto departing vehicles. The activities involved form part of **materials handling**.

> **MATERIALS HANDLING** is concerned with the movement of materials for short distances generally within a warehouse, or between storage areas and transport.

Every time an item is moved it costs money, takes time, and gives an opportunity for damage or mistake. Efficient warehouses reduce the amount of movement to a minimum, and make the necessary movements as efficient as possible. Some objectives of materials handling include:

- moving materials around a warehouse as required
- moving materials quickly, reducing the number and length of movements
- increasing storage density, by reducing the amount of wasted space
- reducing costs, by using efficient operations
- making few mistakes, with efficient material management systems.

These aims rely, to a large extent, on the choice of handling equipment. This can affect the speed of movement, type of materials that can be moved, costs, layout, number of people employed, and so on.

In some warehouses most of the materials handling is done by hand, with little equipment except, perhaps, for trolleys and baskets. Other warehouses have forklift trucks and cranes for moving heavy items. These suggest two levels of automation – manual and mechanised. A third level gives automated warehouses, where all materials handling is managed by a central computer. These three levels of technology give warehouses with completely different characteristics.

Manual warehouses

This is probably the easiest arrangement to imagine, and is still one of the most common. Items are stored on shelves or in bins. People go around and pick items from the shelves, and put them into some sort of container for movement – like a supermarket trolley. There may be some aids, like hand trucks for moving pallets, or carousels to bring materials to pickers, but essentially people control all aspects of movements. You can get an idea of these operations by looking around a supermarket, which is very similar to a manual warehouse.

Manual warehouses only work if the items are small and light enough to lift. Shelves must be low enough for them to reach and close together to reduce the distance walked. Materials are stored on shelves, or in bins, that are no higher than about two metres. The warehouse must be heated, lit and allow people to work comfortably.

Mechanised warehouses

Mechanised warehouses replace some of the muscle power of manual warehouses by machines. Typical examples of mechanised equipment are:

- reach trucks, which are usually electrically powered and move pallets and similar loads up to storage locations. A driver controls the truck, which can raise loads vertically to a considerable height. These trucks are quite small, slow, and with limited facilities, but they work well in confined spaces.

- order-picking machines are a variation on reach trucks, where the driver is lifted with the materials to pick, or deliver, at high locations.

- forklift trucks, come in many different versions and are the standard means of moving pallets and equivalent loads for short distances. They are very manoeuvrable, flexible, and can be adapted for many jobs. On the other hand, they need space to work, and are fairly expensive to use.

- cranes, which describe a family of vehicles used to lift materials.

- towlines, which are continuous cables that can move trailers around a fixed path, rather like ski lifts.

- conveyors, which are used to move large quantities of goods along fixed paths. You can see many examples of conveyor belts moving materials that range from iron ore to letters. An alternative uses roller conveyors.

● tractors or trains, which are power units that pull loads that have been put onto trailer units. The tractor delivers trailers to the place needed, rather like small articulated trucks or tugs and barges.

● carousels, which are basically a series of bins going round a fixed track. At some point on the journey items are put into a bin, and the bins are emptied when they pass another chute or collection point.

These warehouses can store heavier goods and may be much bigger. Some equipment needs wide aisles to manoeuvre, but racking can be higher – typically up to 12 metres with a forklift truck and higher with cranes or high-reach equipment.

Materials in these larger warehouses will probably not be put straight onto shelves, but are likely to be in 'unitised' loads. These are simply standard sized packages or containers that are used for all movements. The idea is that standard packages can be moved much more easily than a set of different sizes and shapes. The most common format, which we have already mentioned in passing, uses pallets. These are the wooden carriers that evolved into a standard 1.2 m by 1 m format in the 1960s. We will return to this theme in the next section.

A survey[8] found that forklifts were by far the most widely used equipment for moving materials from warehouses, being used by 94% of companies. Other widely used equipment included various manual trucks (55%), conveyors (40%), various 'man aboard' trucks (33%), horizontal carousels (26%), stacker cranes (23%) and vertical carousels (9%).

The key point about mechanised systems is that they are still under the control of an operator. Someone actually drives a forklift or controls the movement along a towline. The next alternative is to pass the control of movements to a computer.

Automated warehouses

Traditional warehouses, even mechanised ones, tend to have high operating costs. These operating costs can be reduced, as well as improving aspects of service, by using automation. Unfortunately, this needs a very high investment in equipment, and is only really worthwhile for very big stores that move large amounts of materials.

Automated warehouses work in the usual way, but they include the following components:

● storage areas that can be accessed by automatic equipment; these often use narrow aisles up to, say, 40 m tall to get a high density of materials and minimise the distances moved.

● equipment to move materials around the warehouse; these are usually automated guided vehicles (AGVs) which use guide wires in the floor, but might include conveyors, tractors, or a range of other moving equipment.

● equipment to automatically pick materials and put them into storage, including high speed stacker cranes that can reach any point in the narrow aisles very quickly.

● equipment to transfer materials between the different types of equipment; these automatic loaders and unloaders might include industrial robots.

● a warehouse management system to record material locations, and control all movements.

There can be considerable benefits to automation. Greenwood[9] suggests some of these as reduced errors, improved records of inventory, increased productivity, reduced paperwork, improved space utilisation, lower stocks, better control of movements, support of EDI, and better customer service. An obvious point is that no people work in the storage areas, so there is no need for heat and light.

Choice of equipment

In general, higher volumes of throughput use higher levels of automation. Warehouses for low volumes of throughput (like a shop) are usually manual, medium volumes of throughput (like a food warehouse) are mechanised, and high volume of throughput (like an e-mail book seller) are automated, as shown in Figure 11.7.

Although it is important, volume is only one factor in the choice of equipment. The final decision needs a lot of analysis, with the key factors likely to include:

● physical characteristics of loads – size, weight, and so on
● number of loads to be moved – from the throughput of the warehouse, plus any internal movements for sorting, checking, and so on
● distance to be moved – from the size of the warehouse
● speed of movement required – how quickly the warehouse has to respond to demands, and so on.

Most organisations move to higher technology systems to improve productivity[8] but other aims are improved customer service, reduced costs, safety, better stock control and more flexibility. Many analyses can help with this decision, including break-even points, return on investment, net present value, and measures of productivity.

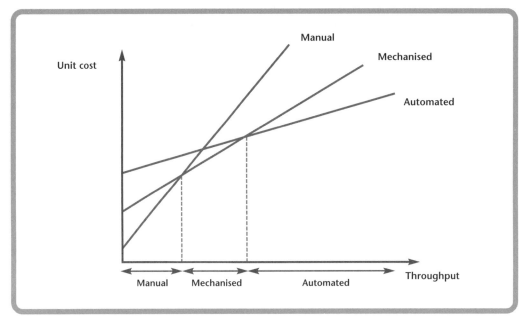

Figure 11.7 Choice of automation and warehouse size

Handemann Group

Handemann Group run a fairly standard warehouse for distributing materials for their gas and electricity supply business in areas of Austria and Germany. The warehouse is divided into a number of areas as shown in Figure 11.8.

- Goods in, 1200 square metres containing seven docks, and areas for checking, bulk breaking, re-packaging, quality assurance and returns.
- High bays, 2400 square metres with eight aisles 45 metres long and 2 metres wide. Pallet racking is 14 metres high, with space for 3580 pallets weighing up to a tonne. This is the main storage for appliances and bulk materials.
- Low bays, 1200 square metres with six aisles 35 metres long and 1.67 metres wide. Pallet racking is 8 metres high, providing space for 910 pallets weighing up to a tonne.

- Shelving, 600 square metres with three aisles 35 metres long and 1.5 metres wide. Shelves are 8 metres high, providing 8000 locations for packages of various sizes and weights up to 200 kg.
- Bins, 200 square metres, with one aisle giving 6000 locations for small, fast-moving items.
- Despatch area, 800 square metres containing ten docks and areas for sorting, assembling deliveries.

The materials handling equipment can change according to current needs, but uses a variety of trucks to move people and/or materials along aisles and up storage racks. Typical configurations have 12 electric trucks (based on forklifts but of various designs), 10 hand-operated trucks, 1 sweeper and 4 lorries for local deliveries.

Source: company reports

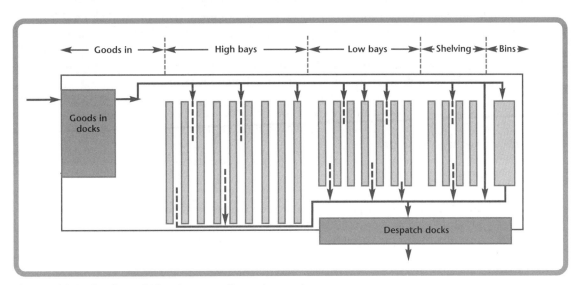

Figure 11.8 Outline of Handemann Group's warehouse

PACKAGING

Standard packages

We have already mentioned pallets (the standard wooden trays about four feet square that materials are put on to ease movement) and containers (the 20- or 40-foot metal boxes that are used to move a huge variety of goods around the world). Collecting together materials into these standard packages is called **unitisation** to form **unit loads**. It is much easier to move standard loads than it is to move a variety of different sizes and shapes. If a company always uses standard loads, it can set up all its handling equipment to move these efficiently. This is why deliveries to a supermarket have all the goods of different sizes put onto standard trolleys that are simply wheeled on and off trucks. Putting everything into containers means that a company only has to move the containers, rather than moving each item separately.

Another benefit of standard packages is that they can increase the density of storage. Imagine a company moving bicycles; the density of a load of finished bicycles is quite low, as the bicycles have bits that stick out and prevent them being packed closely together. The company could increase the density of the load and reduce freight charges by using standard crates for all the pedals, handlebars, saddles and other bits, while frames go into other standard crates.

You can see the benefits of standard packages whenever loads are being moved. If you get a removal company to help you move house, they put all your smaller items into standard sized cardboard boxes. These are often combined into pallet loads that are moved by forklift trucks. These in turn might be assembled into container loads for moving anywhere in the world by road, rail or ship. We will talk about containers in the next chapter.

So one of the obvious benefits of packaging is that it makes materials handling easier. This is why you take your clothes on holiday in a suitcase, rather than carry everything separately. But there are other reasons for using proper packaging.

Purpose of packaging

Many items need special protective packaging during moves, particularly delicate things like china and electronics. Sometimes the packaging can protect goods from harsh environments, such as rain or sun; sometimes it is needed to separate materials that would contaminate each other, such as sugar and petrol; sometimes it keeps the contents clean, such as foodstuffs and medicines. In general, packaging serves four basic functions as it:

- identifies the product and gives basic information
- protects items while they are being moved through the supply chain
- makes handling easier
- assists in marketing, promoting the product, advertising and giving information to customers.

The balance between these depends very much on the product. Bars of chocolate, for example, might put more emphasis on marketing, while boxes of ice cream might be more concerned with protection. There are also two types of packaging to consider. First, the interior, or **consumer packaging**, is designed for the customer and includes the marketing and promotional materials. This is the one that is brightly coloured and has cellophane and advertisements. Second, the exterior or **industrial packaging** that is designed to protect and make handling easier. This is the plain box or pallet that gives information to organisations in the supply chain.

This packaging can be made of many different materials, but the consumer packaging tends towards bright plastic, while the industrial packaging tends towards dull cardboard. Some perfumes and alcoholic drinks come in very elaborate bottles that cost a lot more to produce than the contents. With expensive consumer goods this might be acceptable, but it would certainly not work with basic products such as milk or sugar. So we have to consider the design and materials of the packaging carefully.

There are five main materials for packaging:

- *Glass* is easy to clean, reuse and recycle, but is fragile, relatively expensive and difficult to make
- *Plastic* is light, strong and easy to clean, but can be expensive and difficult to make or reuse
- *Cardboard* is light, cheap and can be recycled, but has little strength and poor durability
- *Wood* is strong, durable, easy to use and can be reused, but it is heavy, bulky and difficult to clean
- *Metal* is strong and durable, but it is heavy and can be expensive.

The choice of these – or other materials – depends largely on the type of products, movement and protection needed. This can be a difficult decision, balancing many factors. You would, for example, ordinarily expect liquids to delivered in some form of plastic bottles. But this would give the wrong image for wine which is generally delivered in glass bottles. Shrink-wrapped pallet loads give a lot of protection, but they would not be appreciated by JIT operations that want fast access to small quantities of parts.

Packaging waste

When you buy something, you might be surprised by the amount of packaging. Cakes and chocolates routinely have three layers of wrapping; sometimes you might find up to five layers. But remember that you only see the consumer wrapping, and there have probably been two more layers of industrial wrapping which has already been removed. There are growing concerns about the amount of packaging, its cost and disposal. The UK produces about eight million tonnes of packaging waste a year, and half of this comes from industrial packaging.[10]

Conventionally, industrial packaging is more likely to be reused and recycled than consumer packaging, because it is more robust, and can be collected from a few locations. Consumer packaging is more likely to be discarded, but some companies, such as Body Shop, have policies of reducing this by reusable containers. This is an important issue, as the European Union, and other areas are introducing limits on the amount of packaging waste that companies can discard. Several countries only allow glass containers if these are collected and reused, or at least recycled. There are similar regulations for metal containers, particularly aluminium cans. Perhaps more noticeable are the regulations on other packaging, which are increasingly forcing organisations to record the amount of packaging they use, and the amount they recycle. If they fail to achieve some target for recycling, they face heavy fines. The European Union has moved towards this scheme, with overall recycling targets of 50%.

Such trends have encouraged many organisations to switch away from packaging that is discarded after delivery to the final customer, and towards reuseable packaging and reverse logistics. Replacing cardboard containers by wood might seem expensive, but it can be used repeatedly and actually reduce overall costs – as well as contributing to a cleaner environment.[10]

❏ A warehouse is the general term for any place where materials are stored on their journey through a supply chain.

❏ The traditional function of a warehouse is to store materials. This involves a range of activities from receiving materials for storage, through to preparing deliveries for customers.

❏ The trend to move materials more quickly through a supply chain is changing the role of warehouses. Their role as long-term stores is declining, and they are increasingly seen as a convenient location for other jobs, such as consolidating part loads and postponement. They are developing value-adding activities, rather than being pure cost centres.

❏ One important consideration is the ownership of warehouses, with a choice between private and public operations. The trend is towards public warehousing, using specialist third-party providers.

❏ The layout of a warehouse has a significant effect on its operations. Each warehouse is essentially unique, but there are general guidelines for good layout.

❏ Many types of equipment are used in warehouses. We can classify these as manual, mechanised or automated. The choice determines the type of operations and features of the warehouse.

❏ Packaging is an important aspect of materials handling. It serves several purposes including protection, easing movement and passing on product information.

CASE STUDY — *Via Cendor*

Hungary had a centrally planned economy for over 50 years, with most economic activity controlled by the government. By the 1990s commercial and industrial organisations were inefficient, outdated and falling further behind competitors from other countries. Political and economic reforms started in the 1990s with the aim of transferring most organisations back to the private sector. Transport had been tightly controlled, but was substantially privatised and deregulated.

Janos Cendor was keen to take advantage of new developments, and started a trucking company. He took over an existing depot with all its facilities, with plans

CASE   STUDY   *continued*

for transforming this into a modern and competitive company. Initially, he had considerable problems. His facilities were decaying, his vehicles were falling apart, he was overstaffed, and working practices were outdated. In the past the depot had focused on trade with countries in the former Soviet bloc, and now had to look for other trading partners in the West.

By 1997 Janus was making progress, and was profiting from the huge increase in trade between Hungary and countries within the European Union. He had modernised his depot, replaced vehicles and was making progress with staff. In early 2001 he was planning a new warehouse near to the Austrian border to import consumer goods, and export agricultural produce. However, competition from other transport companies was increasing, and European operators were introducing new ideas. So Janus planned his new warehouse to play a leading role in moving his company forward; it would be a flagship operation that would have a clear advantage over competitors.

The problem facing Janus is that, like everyone else, he does not know exactly what the future will hold. He read reports[5] which suggested that warehouses of the future would concentrate on:

- better service to give complete customer satisfaction
- concentration of operations in fewer logistics centres
- reducing stocks by improved materials flow
- paperless electronic transactions
- flexibility giving customised operations
- cross-docking
- third-party warehousing
- automation of material movements
- more skilled employees to manage new operations.

CASE   STUDY
Questions

- How do you think the changing economic conditions in Hungary changed logistics in the region?
- If Janus asked for your advice on the facilities needed by his new warehouse, what kind of operations would you suggest? What are the benefits of the new operations? Would these give a sustainable competitive advantage?

PROJECT

Warehouse Options

Imagine that you have started a company to make some product, such as a new type of ice cream for sale in supermarkets. Your logistics system will include warehousing. How would you set about designing the number, size, location and facilities of the warehouses? Have a look around and see how companies actually handle this problem. Are there significant differences between the real companies and your model?

DISCUSSION QUESTIONS

1. If the flow of materials is properly co-ordinated there is no need for stock and, therefore, no need for warehouses. When do you think that warehouses will disappear from the supply chain?

2. Warehouses used to be places where goods were stored, often for long periods, until they were needed. A more recent view has warehouses as places where loads are reorganised on their journey through the supply chain. Do you think this is a real difference? If it is, what effect does this have on warehouse operations?

3. Many organisations are using specialist third party suppliers for warehousing. What are the benefits of this? What are the different types of arrangement for third party warehousing?

4. Why is the layout of warehouses important? Supermarkets are really one type of warehouse, so the same factors will be important in each. Is this true?

5. Automation is bound to give the most efficient warehouses, so everyone should move in this direction. Will all warehouses eventually be automated?

6. We are often told that packaging is a major problem for waste disposal. Why is there so much packaging, and how can the amount be reduced?

REFERENCES

1. Olsen D.R. (1996) Warehousing trends for the next generation, *Logistics Focus*, **4**(2), 6–8.
2. Waters C.D.J. (2001) *A Case Study in Warehouse Design*, Western Operations Group, London.
3. Robertson R. (1996) On the move, *Materials Management and Distribution*, May, p. 56.
4. Anon. (1999) The rise of the infomediary, *The Economist*, 351, 8215.
5. Hurdock B. (2000) Ten 21st century warehouse trends, *DSN Retailing Today*, **39**(15), 14.
6. Doerflinger T.M., Gerharty M. and Kerschner E.M. (1999) *The Information Revolution Wars*, Paine-Webber Newsletter, New York.
7. Stevenson W.J. (1993) *Production/Operations Management* (4th edn), Irwin, Homewood, IL.
8. McGillivray R. and Saipe A. (1996) Logging on, *Materials Management and Distribution*, January, pp. 19–23.

9. Greenwood P.N. (1997) How will a warehouse management system benefit me? *Logistics Focus*, **5**(4), 10–13.

10. Pihl A. (1997) Packaging re-use: how to meet legal obligations and cut costs, *Logistics Focus*, **5**(3), 8–13.

Further reading

Fernie J. and Sparks L. (eds) (1998) *Logistics and Retail Management*, Kogan Page, London.

Frazelle E. (2001) *World Class Warehousing and Materials Management*, McGraw-Hill, New York.

Mulcahy D.E. (1993) *Warehouse Distribution and Operations Handbook*, McGraw-Hill, New York.

Simchi-Levi D., Kaminski P. and Simchi-Levi E. (1999) *Designing and Managing the Supply Chain*, McGraw-Hill, New York.

CHAPTER 12

Transport

CONTENTS

- Aims of the chapter
- Introduction
- Mode of transport
- Intermodal transport
- Ownership of transport
- Routing vehicles
- Chapter review

- Case study – Mount Isa Mines
- Project – Toorvik Transport Consultants
- Discussion questions
- References
- Further reading

AIMS OF THE CHAPTER

After reading this chapter you should be able to:

- APPRECIATE the importance of transport

- COMPARE different modes of transport

- DISCUSS the use of intermodal operations

- COMPARE alternative forms of transport ownership

- LIST different organisations who offer services for transport

- APPRECIATE other operational problems, such as routing of transport

INTRODUCTION

Definition

When you talk about logistics, most people imagine lorries driving down a motorway. As we know, logistics has a far wider meaning, but transport is certainly one of its main components. In the last chapter we saw that materials handling is concerned with movements within a facility. Here we will look at **transport**, which is concerned with the movement of goods between facilities.

TRANSPORT is responsible for the physical movement of materials between points in the supply chain.

As we have already seen, e-commerce can have a major effect on an organisation's logistics. But remember that it is essentially part of the information system. When you look at a company's website you can see descriptions of its products, send an order and arrange payment – but you still need transport to deliver it. Sometimes, of course, you buy intangibles such as information, software or music, and the website can deliver it. But most products are more tangible, and they need transport. At the heart of logistics are transport vehicles moving goods between suppliers and customers. This is why transport in the UK employs 1.3 million people out of a workforce of 27 million[1] and, along with storage, generates 6% of the GDP.

Transport rate

If an organisation uses third-party transport, the price of moving a unit of material between locations is the **rate** or **tariff**. This is set by the cost of the service provided, value to the customer, the distance moved, weight, size and value of goods, complexity of journey, and so on. This rate is an important consideration for logistics, and can affect whole patterns of movement. If an item costs $20 to make in town A and $25 to make in town B, then the maximum rate worth paying to move from A to B is $5. If the rate is actually $3, producers in town A will export to B, customers in town B pay less for the item, price sensitive demand will rise, logistics companies grow to move the item, competition encourages producers in town B to look for cost savings, some producers in B may divert to other products that they can trade back to town A. Trade rises and everyone seems happy. If, however, the rate is actually $6, none of this happens, and everyone seems to lose out.

You can find many examples of this effect. The Czech Republic can brew beer more cheaply than countries in western Europe (which may explain why they have the highest beer consumption in the world). However, transport of heavy, relatively low-value loads across Europe is expensive, and these additional costs make the trade unattractive.

There is a common view that more expensive fuel, vehicles and drivers are making transport more expensive. The costs for particular journeys vary considerably with conditions, but it is fairer to say that the relative cost of transport is actually falling. This is largely due to more efficient operations and vehicles, but also due to changes in fuel prices and taxes. Partly as a result of this, the overall amount of trade is rising. Manufacturers in the Pacific Rim have efficient operations that give low unit production costs, and cheap transport to Europe means that they often compete on cost with local producers.

Relatively cheap transport also changes the shape of supply chains, as organisations can cover a wider area from a facility. A single logistics centre can deliver materials quickly and relatively cheaply to any destination in Europe. This has encouraged many companies to replace their national warehouses by regional ones that cover a wide area. In 1995, for example, Nike was selling $1 billion of goods in Europe, with deliveries through 25 warehouses. It replaced these with a single pan-European distribution centre in Belgium, and worked with four specialised transport companies. These companies gave efficient services which allowed transport costs to remain constant – with inbound transport costs falling slightly, and outbound transport costs rising slightly. Then Nike could benefit from the huge reduction in warehousing and inventory costs.[2]

The rate is clearly important, but service users seem to have little influence in setting it. A large organisation negotiating freely with a transport company may have some flexibility. The transport industry is very competitive, and large customers can get good deals. They also have the option of running their own fleets if external operators charge too much. Often, however, the rates are fixed by agreement between transport companies, government policies, or monopoly suppliers. Shipping conferences, for example, quote agreed rates between destinations, cartels of major transport operators use industry agreed rates, and government owned rail and road industries fix prices through their monopoly. Transport is one of the most expensive parts of logistics, but users often have little control over it.

In practice, organisations do have more influence, as they can make a series of decisions about the form of transport. What mode of transport is best? Should we run our own transport or use a third-party carrier? What kind of vehicles should we use? How do we deal with international transport? What routes should we use? Can we back-haul? Every organisation faces these questions, but they come to different answers that depend on particular circumstances. We can give some general advice, and will start by looking at the question of the transport mode.

MODE OF TRANSPORT

The **mode of transport** describes the type of transport used. There are basically five different options – rail, road, water, air and pipeline. Each mode has different characteristics, and the best in any particular circumstances depends on the type of goods to be moved, locations, distance, value and a whole range of other things. Sometimes there is a choice of mode, such as rail or ferry across the English Channel; road, rail or air between Rome and Geneva. Often, though, there is little choice. If you want to deliver coffee from Brazil to Amsterdam, you will use shipping; if you want to move gas from the Gulf of Mexico to Dallas, you use a pipeline; if you want an express parcel service across the Atlantic, you use air freight.

Overall, most goods travel by road. In the UK, 65% of all freight is moved by road, or about 160 billion tonne kilometres out of 240 billion tonne kilometres.[3,4] Figure 12.1 shows the amount of materials using each mode in the UK over the past ten years or so (the amount of air freight is too small to appear on this graph). There are some variations between countries, but this is a familiar pattern.

Rail

Rail transport is most commonly used for heavy and bulky loads over long land journeys. Trains can maintain a consistent, reasonably high speed, and can link with other modes to carry containers and bulk freight.

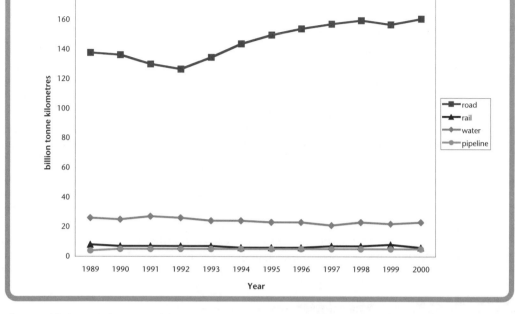

Figure 12.1 Freight moved by transport mode in the UK

Rail services are organised in different ways. They are almost invariably public carriers (giving a service to all other organisations) rather than private carriers (carrying goods for one organisation). This public service is often considered so important that it is run by the state. Even when the rail service is not nationalised, it is allowed a (near) monopoly. The number of carriers is inevitably small when compared with, say, road transport. The main reason for this is the large investments needed for tracks, rolling stock and terminals. A trucking company can start a service between, say, Paris and Zagreb by renting a truck and using public roads; a rail operator has to build its tracks and terminals and buy the trains before it can start work.

Costs can be reduced by sharing facilities. Some countries have several train operators using commonly owned tracks, or tracks owned by another company. Such arrangements are not common and they present obvious problems for operations.

One advantage of rail is that once the infrastructure is in place, it has very high capacity and low unit costs. This is another factor that discourages competition, as a track built by one organisation between two points, will generally have enough capacity to meet all demand, and it becomes unviable for a competitor to open parallel facilities. There is, for example, only one rail line under the English Channel, but this has enough capacity to meet demand on this very heavily used route for the foreseeable future. Historically there has been more competition in, for example, the USA but this has virtually disappeared.

Another advantage of rail is that the unit transport cost is low, so it can be used to move large volumes of relatively low-priced materials, such as coal and minerals. For this reason, rail transport is more common in the earlier, upstream, parts of the supply chain. You are more likely to see organisations using rail for inbound raw materials than outbound finished goods.

The main disadvantage of rail is its inflexibility. All train services have to be timetabled in advance, so that they can all fit onto the same tracks. This leaves little flexibility for last minute or emergency deliveries. Despite this, train operators can provide a number of different services, perhaps offering merry-go-round services (where a train continually moves between two locations, such as a port and a factory), full train services (where customers hire an entire train), full wagon load attached to scheduled services, container transport, or shared wagons on scheduled services.

A more obvious concern is that trains can only travel along specified routes between fixed terminals, and cannot stop at intermediary points. Most customers are some distance away from these terminals, so they have to transfer goods by road at both ends of the journey. These transfers add time, and they can leave rail as a fairly slow alternative. It is more useful for long distances, such as between Perth and Sydney in Australia, but is inefficient for small journeys, such as between Rotterdam and Arnhem in the Netherlands. In the UK the average journey length by rail is 180 kilometres, compared with 95 kilometres by road.[3]

The problem of limited access is common to several modes of transport, but there are ways of overcoming its effects. The most obvious is to locate facilities near to rail terminals (or ports, airports, container ports or appropriate terminals). If demand is big enough, it is worth building special facilities. A power station, for example, might find that it is cheaper to build a special rail line to a coal mine, than to use trucks. Another option is to use intermodal transport, which we discuss later in the chapter.

LOGISTICS
IN PRACTICE

DIRFT Ltd

The Channel Tunnel has given efficient rail links between the UK and European destinations. This has encouraged some companies to move their freight from heavy goods vehicles to the train. Daventry International Rail Freight Terminal (DIRFT) realised that such moves would create a growing demand for a logistics park near to Daventry with good connections to rail and road.

Construction started on the railport near the M1 in Northamptonshire in 1994. The first two million square feet of facilities opened in 1997, operated by Tibbett & Britten. This included facilities to unload three 750 metre trains simultaneously. English, Welsh and Scottish Railway runs 35 trains from the Channel Tunnel each week, largely from Germany, France and Italy.

Upgrading of the West Coast Main Line should make rail movements even more efficient.

The site is popular and has attracted major customers, such as Eddie Stobart and Tesco. Demand is strong for the next phase of four million square feet, which will need no further infrastructure. The Strategic Rail Authority are encouraging such developments. One problem, of course, is that not everyone is keen on the railport. It has already used 365 acres of green fields, and expansion plans may be questioned more closely.

Sources: Jones J. (2001) Success is not enough, *Logistics and Transport Focus*, **3**(6), 32–5; Strategic Rail Authority (2001) *A Strategic Agenda*, HMSO, London

Road

Road is the most widely used mode of transport and is used – at least somewhere – in almost all supply chains. Its main benefit is flexibility, being able to visit almost any location. Although the maximum speed on roads is limited, this ability to give a door-to-door service avoids transfers to other modes and can give a shorter overall journey time. You can see this effect if you want to travel between, say, Paris and Brussels. The plane travels faster, but when you add on the travel times to and from the airports, check-in and boarding, it is faster to catch a bus between the city centres. Nonetheless, travel speed can be an important consideration, especially as roads are becoming more congested and vehicles are likely to move even more slowly.

Road transport has the advantage of being able to use extensive road networks. Unlike rail, these already exist, so users do not have to build and maintain their own tracks. Also, vehicles do not have to keep to such rigid timetables, so they can go on journeys at short notice and with little planning.

In contrast to rail, where each operator is likely to have a (near) monopoly over some route, road transport is characterised by a large number of carriers working in the same areas. In the USA, for example, there are 40,000 public carriers and 600,000 private fleets. With so many operators competition is likely to be more intense and pricing more flexible.

There is a huge number of different types of road vehicle. Many of these are specialised, and designed for specific purposes, and there are different regulations in different countries. The following list mentions some of the more important types.

- *Delivery vans* are the small delivery vehicles which can carry a tonne or two in a sealed body. Smaller vans are based on car designs, while larger ones – such as Luton Box vans – are like small removal vans.

- *Flat-bed lorries* are basic, rigid vehicles with two or three axles, and a flat platform that is used to stack materials. Materials are tied on, or small sides are added.

- *Box-bodied lorries* are like the flat beds, except they have bodies added, traditionally with access from the rear. These give more protection than flat beds. In the 1970s Boalloy added curtain siding to give easier access to the load.

- *Articulated lorries*, are more manoeuvrable than rigid lorries, so they can be bigger, up to the legal weight limit. There are many variations on the theme of trucks that bend in the middle. A common format has a two- or three-axled tractor and a two- or three-axled trailer.

- *Lorry and trailer*, which combine a rigid lorry pulling a two-axle trailer. This gives greater capacity than an articulated lorry, but maintains some of its manoeuvrability.

Many different formats have been tried. In Sweden, for example, they use articulated lorries with trailers, giving two, or even three, points of articulation. In Alberta, Canada, they use two trailers to move loads over the Rockies. In Australia 'land trains' have four or five trailers to move through the outback. Perhaps the overall picture is that, within prevailing regulations, the type of vehicle is only limited by the designers' imagination.

Depending on conditions, road transport can normally carry loads up to, say, 20–30 tonnes. The European Union has a gross limit of 42 tonnes and different limits apply in other areas. In exceptional circumstances, very large loads can be carried, such as the loads of a thousand tonnes that are moved for oil companies in the Arctic. However, weight and size limits mean that road transport is more often used for smaller loads. These become relatively expensive, so road transport is generally used for shorter distances. Although it is a very simplistic view, you are more likely to see road transport used for delivering finished goods than bulky raw materials. Another problem is that lorries are particularly vulnerable to congestion and traffic delays.

Water

Both rail and road transport have the obvious limitation of only being used on land. Most supply chains use shipping to cross the oceans at some point, and over 90% of world trade is moved by sea. You can see the importance of shipping to a country like the UK, where 95% of freight arrives or leaves by ship, shipping is the fifth largest service sector exporter, the City of London insures 25% of the world's marine risk, the marine and repair business is one of the largest in Europe, there are 300 ports around the coast, and the surrounding waters are among the busiest in the world.[5]

There are basically three types of water transport – rivers and canals (usually called inland waterways), coastal shipping (moving materials from one port to another along the coast) and ocean transport (across the major seas). Many countries have well-developed river and canal transport, such as Canadian and US use of the St Lawrence Seaway, and European use of the Rhine. We normally associate river transport with smaller loads, perhaps narrow boats and barges. But river systems can carry ocean-going ships for surprisingly long distances. The Mississippi, for example, is navigable to Minneapolis, more than 2500 km from the Gulf of Mexico, and Chicago is a major port in the American prairies.

Realistically, though, most shipping is done by large vessels travelling through the world's shipping lanes. Some countries are fortunate enough to have a coastline that can be used for international transport, and cities such as Rotterdam, Hong Kong and New York have developed huge ports. The world's 20 biggest ports handle over half of all world trade.[6]

Some form of shipping is largely unavoidable for long journeys. There are many different types of vessel for various cargoes. Ships get considerable economies of scale, so many aim at moving big loads at low unit costs.

- *General cargo ships* are the standard design, with large holds that carry any type of cargo. Most of these are loaded by crane, although some have side doors that allow vehicles to drive on and off. Many ports around the world do not have facilities to handle the more specialised ships mentioned below, so these general-purpose vessels are very widely used.

- *Bulk carriers* carry large quantities of cheap bulk materials in large holds, such as grain or ores.

- *Tankers* carry any liquid, but by far the biggest movements are oil. Because of the economies of scale, these ships are built as big as possible.

- *Container ships* are specially designed to carry standard containers and their capacity is commonly rated in TEUs (20-foot equivalent units) or FEUs (40-foot equivalent units). A typical container ship carries around 5000 of these, with larger ones carrying 10,000.

- *Ferries* are usually RO-RO (roll-on roll-off) vessels that carry road vehicles over relatively short distances. There are, however, longer RO-RO routes between, say, Europe and America.

● *Barges*, which are towed behind ocean-going tugs. These are used for shorter routes where sea conditions are fairly reliable, such as between the USA and Puerto Rico. They have the advantage of being cheaper to run than normal ships.

● *Combination ships*. In addition to the specialised ships, many other designs are used, often to allow for dominant patterns of trade. Examples of such combination ships are the RO-RO/container ships that carry vehicles imported into the USA and return with bulk grain to Japan, and the oil-bulk vessels that carry oil from the Middle East and return carrying ores. One useful combination is passenger/container, as the passengers are ensured priority treatment in ports.

The main drawback with water transport is, of course, its inflexibility in being limited to appropriate ports. Journeys from suppliers and to customers inevitably need a change of mode, even if they are close to ports. In St Austell, UK, for example, china clay works are very close to specialised ports in Fowey, but the clay still has to be transported to the quayside. The other problem with shipping is that it is relatively slow, and needs time to consolidate loads and transfer them at ports. However, such transfers can be made efficient, and then coastal shipping can compete with road transport, even for relatively short distances.[7-9] The average water journey in the UK is 400 kilometres, so shipping can compete on, say, a Forth–Tees–Thames route.

One interesting aspect of shipping is the continued existence of conference services. This means that all carriers in a given area agree to charge a common price and regulate the frequency of their service. The justification of this cartel is that it guarantees a more regular service than would otherwise be available. However, many people question this idea of price fixing, and non-conference lines now offer deep discounts.

Air

Because of its low unit costs, water transport is the most common mode for international transport. Sometimes, though, its slow speed is unacceptable. If, for example, you run a factory in Argentina and a critical machine breaks down, you do not want the spare part to be put on the next scheduled ship from Japan, which will arrive in four weeks time. In such circumstances the alternative is air transport.

Passengers account for most airline business, with eight billion passenger kilometres flown a year in the UK.[3] This continues to grow despite some hiccoughs (in, say, 2001), with low-fare carriers (Ryanair, Virgin Express, Go, easyJet, buzz, and so on) accounting for around 25% of the market.[10] Airlines also carry a significant amount of freight, for products where speed of delivery is more important than the cost. In practice, this limits airfreight to fairly small amounts of expensive materials. Perhaps the most common movements are documents and parcel delivery, with carriers such as Federal Express and UPS.

There are three main types of operation. The first type is regular service, where major airlines use the cargo space in passenger aircraft that is not needed for baggage. The second type is cargo service, where operators run cargo planes on regular schedules. These are public carriers, moving goods for any customers. The third type is charter operations, where a whole aircraft is hired for a particular delivery.

In common with shipping, airlines have problems getting materials to and from their journeys. There are all sorts of facilities located around major airports for moving materials from sources onto the right planes, and then away from planes and out to customers. Unfortunately, these transfers again take time, and can reduce the benefits of air travel.

Another problem for airlines is their costs, over which they have very little control. They have a combination of high fixed costs (aeroplanes are expensive to buy) and high variable costs (due to fuel, landing fees, staff, and so on). It is expensive to keep planes flying, and there is no real way of reducing these costs. Competition can also be fierce, putting a limit on the amount they can charge, and this frequently sends new airlines into bankruptcy.

Pipeline

The main uses of pipelines are oil and gas together with the utilities of water and sewage. They can also be used for a few other types of product such as pulverised coal in oil.

Pipelines have the advantage of moving large quantities over long distances. Unfortunately, they have the disadvantages of being slow (typically moving at less than 10 km per hour), inflexible (only transporting between fixed points), and only carrying large volumes of certain types of fluid. In addition, there is the huge initial investment of building dedicated pipelines. Despite this initial investment, pipelines are the cheapest way of moving liquids – particularly oil and gas – over long distances. Local networks can add flexibility by delivering to a wide range of locations (such as supplies of water and gas to homes).

Choice of mode

Sometimes the choice of transport mode seems obvious: if you want to move heavy items between Singapore and Brisbane you will use shipping. For land journeys, many organisations seem happy to put materials on lorries without much thought for the alternatives. In practice, the choice of mode depends on a variety of factors. Perhaps the main ones are the nature of materials to move, the volume and distance. Other factors include:

- value of materials, as expensive items raise inventory costs and encourage faster modes
- importance, as even low-value items that would hold up operations need fast, reliable transport.
- transit times, as operations that have to respond quickly to changes cannot wait for critical supplies using slow transport
- reliability, with consistent delivery often being more important than transit time
- cost and flexibility to negotiate rates
- reputation and stability of carrier
- security, loss and damage
- schedules and frequency of delivery
- special facilities available.

Many other factors may be important for a final decision. Organisations that routinely use the cheapest mode may be performing badly by some of the other measures. Remember that transport costs are often a relatively small part of overall costs, and it can be worth paying more to get a rapid and reliable delivery. One of the early studies of logistics by Lewis et al.[11] showed that air freight can actually save money. It moves materials through the supply chain so quickly that organisations need fewer warehouses for distribution to customers – by paying more for transport they can reduce overall costs.

As a rule of thumb, the cheapest modes of transport are the least flexible. The following table shows a ranking for the cost, speed, flexibility and load limits of different modes of transport. The modes are ranked in order, with 1 being the best performance and 5 being the worst.

	Rail	Road	Water	Air	Pipeline
Cost	3	4	1	5	2
Speed	3	2	4	1	5
Flexibility	2	1	4	3	5
Volume/weight limits	3	4	1	5	2
Accessibility	2	1	4	3	5

Of course, organisations do not have to use the same mode of transport for an entire journey. They can break the journey into distinct stages and use the best mode for each stage. We will look at such intermodal journeys in the next section.

LOGISTICS IN PRACTICE

Alberta coalmines

Canada's largest coalmines are in the western province of Alberta. Unfortunately most of the demand for coal comes from power stations in the population centres of southern Ontario over 3000 km away.

The main competitors for coal in power stations are oil, gas, nuclear power and hydroelectricity. Coal is currently a popular choice as oil and gas are expensive, nuclear power has questions of long-term safety, and there is limited capacity for hydroelectricity. Alberta coal also has low sulphur content, which reduces the need for expensive flue-gas emission control equipment. There are, however, obvious problems with transport.

About three million tonnes of coal is shipped each year from Alberta to Ontario, with transport costs around $45 a tonne. The coal industry looks for ways of reducing this, and the alternatives considered are summarised below (see Figure 12.2).

■ *Rail and ship:* this is the current practice, with coal transported by rail from the mine to a terminal on the Great Lakes (usually Thunder Bay) and then by ship to a lakeside power station.

■ *Direct rail shipment:* moving coal by rail directly from the mine to a stockpile at a power station. This avoids the transfer to a ship, but replaces a sea journey with a considerably longer rail journey.

■ *High efficiency rail:* uses newly designed rail cars that increase maximum loads and reduce unit costs. With appropriate investment, high efficiency trains can be used to replace conventional trains in either of the first two options.

■ *West coast ports and Panama Canal:* this carries coal by train to a west coast port such as Vancouver, transfers it to ship for the journey through the Panama Canal and back through the St Lawrence Seaway to power stations in Ontario.

■ *Coal/oil agglomeration – eastbound:* Alberta is a major oil producer and the transport of oil and coal can be

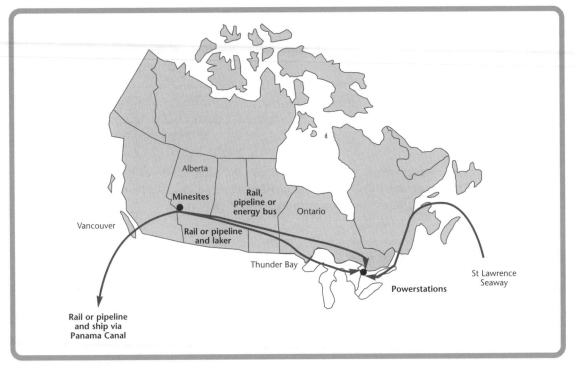

Figure 12.2 Transporting coal across Canada

LOGISTICS
IN PRACTICE
continued

combined. This crushes the coal at the mine and mixes it with crude oil to be pumped through a pipeline either directly to the power stations, or to a port on the Great Lakes. At the destination the slurry is separated, with coal being sent to the power stations and oil to markets in eastern Canada and the USA.

■ *Coal/oil agglomeration – westbound:* This is similar to the previous option, except that the slurry is piped to Vancouver for separation. The coal is put onto ships bound for the Panama Canal and St Lawrence Seaway, while the oil is sent to markets in western Canada and the USA.

■ *Energy bus,* which avoids the movement of coal by generating electricity near to the mines and using an inter-provincial electricity grid to send it for distribution in Ontario.

Analysing all the costs showed that a high efficiency rail service from the mine to Thunder Bay, followed by ship to the power station gives the lowest cost. This is marginally cheaper than the current arrangement, but needs more capital investment.

Source: Ash L. and Waters C.D.J. (1991) Simulating the transport of coal across Canada, *Journal of the Operational Research Society*, **42**(3), 195–204

INTERMODAL TRANSPORT

We have seen some factors that affect the choice of transport mode, but organisations do not have to use the same mode for an entire journey. Their best option is often to divide the journey into stages and use the best mode for each stage. This does, of course, depend on factors like the length of the journey, the relative costs and the penalty of moving between modes. But if you move materials from, say, Lanchow in central China to Warsaw in Poland, you might start by putting the goods on a truck, transferring them to rail for the journey across China to Shanghai, then onto a ship to Rotterdam, then back onto rail to cross Europe, and then truck for local delivery. Journeys that use several modes of transport are called **intermodal**.

INTERMODAL TRANSPORT refers to journeys that involve two or more different modes of transport.

The aim of intermodal transport is to combine the benefits of several separate modes, but avoid the disadvantages of each; perhaps combining the low cost of shipping with the flexibility of road, or getting the speed of air with the cost of road. The main problem is that each transfer between modes causes delays and adds costs for extra handling. You can experience this effect when you transfer between a bus and train, or between a car and ferry. Intermodal transport only works if this transfer can be done efficiently.

At the heart of intermodal transport are the systems for transferring materials between modes. The aim is to give a virtually seamless journey, and the best way of achieving this is to use modular or unitised loads. In effect, all materials are put into standard containers, and the equipment is arranged to move these containers.

The basic container is a metal box 20-feet long. This size has become somewhat restricting, and it is often replaced by a 40-foot box. Even this can be limiting, and the Hudson's Bay Company uses 53-foot containers on the trip from Vancouver to Montreal, reducing costs by 10–15%.[12]

Putting materials into these boxes eliminates the need to handle items individually, and the whole container goes from source to destination. Since these containers were introduced in 1956 on the trip between New York and Houston, they have transformed ideas about transport. In particular, transferring materials between modes has changed from a labour-intensive operation to a capital-intensive one. Huge **container ports** and **terminals** have been built around the world to move containers efficiently and with minimum delay from one type of transport to another, or from one carrier to another.

In the late 1960s ships spent about 60% of their time laid up in port for loading and unloading.[13] Largely due to containerisation, this has reduced dramatically, and ships can turn around in a few hours. A rule of thumb is that it takes one day to turn around a containership when it used to take three weeks to turn around a conventional ship. Over 70% of freight movements now use containers.[14]

Some of the benefits of containerisation include:[15]

- Simplified transport and flow of goods
- Easier and faster handling
- Genuine door-to-door service
- Faster deliveries
- Reduced loss due to damage, misplacement and pilferage

● Reduced packing costs
● Lower insurance costs
● Separation of incompatible goods
● Use of less congested routes
● Improved transport encourages trade.

Other types of intermodal transport

A very wide range of materials can be put into containers, but there are inevitably some that cannot, or are cheaper to transport by other means. Oil, for example, might be put into container-sized tanks (in the same way as bulk wine), but tankers or pipelines give cheaper alternatives. Non-standard containers might also be preferred for some journeys. Standard containers have to be strong enough to stack about eight tall, but if a company simply wants to transfer a box from rail to road, it can use 'swap bodies'. These are skeleton truck bodies that can be transferred to a rail car, but cannot stand the rough treatment of containers.

Another alternative to containers is **piggy-back transport**, where a lorry – or usually just the trailer – is driven onto a train for fast movement over a longer distance. You can see an example of this in the Channel Tunnel, where cars and lorries are driven onto a train for this part of their journey.

Another extension to this idea uses **land bridges**. These are used when materials cross land on what is essentially a sea journey. The most widely used examples are in the USA, where materials from the Far East cross the Pacific to the west coast of America, and then travel by rail on land bridges across to ports on the east coast, before continuing their sea journey to Europe. Two main links are the 'long bridge' in the north between Seattle and Baltimore, and the 'short bridge' in the south between Long Beach and New Orleans.

LOGISTICS
IN PRACTICE

Southampton Container Terminals Ltd

Southampton is one of the UK's busiest deepwater ports. It covers 176 acres, of which 135 acres is container stacking space.

On the ship side, the port is 4 km from the main international shipping lane around the south coast of England. The main access channel is dredged to 12.6 metres, with other berths dredged to 15 metres. This gives 1350 metres of continuous quay, which can handle 4 of the world's largest container ships at the same time.

Along the quays are 13 ship-to-shore gantry cranes for unloading container ships.

An important factor for unloading containers is the reach of the cranes. The cranes have to reach over containers stacked on the deck to lift the next one to unload, and the Southampton cranes have reaches up to 20 containers wide. They can lift up to 60 tonnes, and there is a floating crane for heavy lifts with a capacity of 200 tonnes.

On the land side straddle carriers move containers between the quay and the stack. There are 79 of these, each with a capacity of 40 tonnes. The stacking yard sorts containers and keeps them, usually in stacks 3

or 4 high, until they are sent inland or delivered to a ship at the quay. Throughput is fast, as it is in everyone's interest for the containers to spend a minimum time in these stacks.

The port is 2 km from the motorway network, and trucks can make this journey within 5 minutes. The major centres of Birmingham and Cardiff are around 200 km away. Multi-line sidings allow fast rail connections, and Freightliner run a main service of 13 trains a day. These connect to most major destinations in the UK.

Sources: company reports and website www.sct.uk.com

OWNERSHIP OF TRANSPORT

In Chapter 10 we saw how an important decision for warehousing is the ownership of facilities. The choice is essentially between privately owned, public or a combination of the two. With transport we again meet this decision. Is it better for an organisation to run its own transport fleet, to use public transport, or a combination of the two? With transport the more common terms are **in-house** or **own account transport** compared with **third-party transport**.

Own account transport

This has an organisation using its own transport fleet to move its materials. The most common form of private transport has large companies running their own fleets of trucks. This has the advantage of flexibility, greater control, closer integration of logistics and easier communications. Transport can also be tailored to the organisation's needs, with the best type of vehicles, fleet size, delivery schedule, customer service, and so on.

Own account transport can be expensive and an organisation should only run its own fleet when it is cheaper than using a specialist third-party carrier. Essentially, this means that own account transport must be run as efficiently as a specialised transport company. There are, however, potential cost savings as there is less pressure for transport to make a profit, possible tax advantages, and development grants. There are also intangible benefits, such as the marketing benefits of vehicles painted in identifiable livery and an impression of reliability and long-term dependability.

Only larger organisations can afford the capital investment and costs of running their own fleet. There are, however, ways of avoiding these costs. Most own account fleets are financed by some form of hiring or leasing, which gives a means of acquiring vehicles without having to find all the capital. Hire purchase, for example, spreads the payments over some period, while long-term hiring allows more flexible use. When you see a truck painted in J. Smith's livery, it does not necessarily mean that J. Smith actually owns the vehicle. He or she is more likely to be leasing it from a company that looks after maintenance, overheads, repairs, replacements and other running costs, in return for a fixed fee.

Third-party carriers

Specialised transport companies offer a range of services to other organisations. The advantage of this arrangement is that specialised companies run the transport, leaving the organisation to concentrate on its core operations. By using their skills and expertise the transport operators can give better services, or lower costs than own account transport. They might also be large enough to reduce costs through economies of scale, and they can get a number of operational benefits. They can, for example, consolidate smaller loads into larger ones and reduce the number of trips between destinations, or they can co-ordinate journeys to give backhauls, where delivery vehicles are loaded with other materials for the return journey.

Most third-party transport is provided by **common carriers**. These are companies like TNT and Excel Logistics which move materials on a one-off basis whenever asked by another organisation. If you want to send a parcel to Australia, you might use a parcel delivery service such as UPS, which acts as a common carrier.

Alternatively, an organisation can form a long-term relationship with a **contract carrier**. This contract carrier then takes over a part – often most of – the organisation's transport for some extended period. Schenker, for example, act as a contract carrier when they are responsible for all the movement of goods for Roche Diagnostics in the USA. Contract transport companies offer a wide range of services, ranging from an occasional parcel collection to running a large, dedicated fleet for an individual customer.

Choice of ownership

There are several factors to consider when choosing the best type of ownership.

- *Operating cost:* In different circumstances either own account or third-party transport might be cheaper, and there should be significant other benefits before an organisation moves away from their cheaper option.

- *Capital costs:* Capital is always scarce, and even if own account transport seems attractive, an organisation might find it difficult to justify the investment in vehicles. We have mentioned alternative arrangements for spreading the costs, so these analyses should be done carefully before reaching any conclusion.

- *Customer service:* Organisations must use transport that provides acceptable customer service in the best possible way. Sometimes, it is impossible to get a third-party carrier that can meets all requirements, and then own account transport is the only option – and, of course, vice versa.

- *Control:* An organisation clearly has greater control over transport – and therefore wider operations – if it runs its own transport. However, this control might be bought at a high price, and contract companies might offer equivalent services but without the overheads and inflexibility of a private fleet.

- *Flexibility:* The structure and operations of a private fleet are fairly rigid, as you cannot make quick adjustments to allow for changing circumstances. If there is a sudden peak in demand, you cannot increase the size of the fleet for a few days, and then reduce it again when the peak passes. In the same way, the fleet is structured to carry a certain mix of sizes and modes. Common carriers can make these adjustments much faster, as they rely on demand from some companies going through a trough while demand from other companies is peaking.

- *Management skills:* Managing transport needs specialised skills, which are not readily available in even the biggest organisation. This gives a strong argument for third-party carriers. Large transport companies can support the management teams with specialist skills, knowledge and experience of different conditions. A supporting argument says that an organisation with weak transport management suffers as it gives worse performance than competitors and becomes uncompetitive; one with strong transport management may be diverting valuable talent from the rest of the business.

- *Recruitment and training:* As well as being the most widely used, road transport is generally the most labour intensive. This gives high employment costs. There is also a shortage of skilled drivers, with many organisations finding it difficult to recruit and train suitable people. Both of these give an incentive to use third-party transport.

There are many factors to consider in the final decision, but overall – in common with warehousing – there is a clear trend towards third-party carriers. Many organisations – including the biggest – are reducing their own fleets, using more contract operators, and forming alliances. Again in common with warehousing, a common option is to use a mixture of own account and third-party carriers. Then an organisation can use its own transport for core activities, with full utilisation giving low costs. Any other transport needs are left to outside operators who deal with peaks and unusual demands.

Other services

An organisation can pass all its transport problems to a third-party carrier, but there are many other people who can offer their own specialised services. These can provide the special skills that are not usually available within a single organisation. Some organisations give fairly general advice, such as management consultants who work in logistics, and software companies that tailor packages for transport. Other experts give more specific services, such as freight forwarders and shipping agents. Many people might help with transport, and you can get the feel of their services from the following examples.

- *Common carriers:* As we have seen, these move materials between two points for any customer, usually in a one-off delivery using common facilities.

- *Contract carriers:* These offer transport services, but usually for a longer time. They take over some, or all, aspects of an organisation's transport for an agreed period. There are many possible arrangements, but they typically involve dedicated facilities set aside exclusively for one organisation.

- *Intermodal carriers:* Traditionally carriers have concentrated on one type of transport, such as shipping lines or road haulers. With the growth of intermodal transport, many companies offer a wider range of services and operate different types of transport. They typically look after all aspects of a journey between two specified points.

- *Terminal services:* Materials have to switch from one mode of transport to another, or move between different operators. These transfers may be done at ports, airports, terminals or container bases, which are run by separate organisations. The terminals do more than just transfer materials, and they might unload delivery vehicles, sort goods, break bulk for local delivery, concentrate goods for onward movement, load outgoing transport, keep track of all movements, and provide any other relevant services.

In this context you might hear of **demurrage**. Terminals earn money from their throughput, which they want to be as fast as possible. Any goods that are not collected as soon as they become available take up space and get in the way of other movements. To encourage companies to collect their materials promptly (perhaps within a day or two), terminal operators charge demurrage, which is a penalty for late collection and storage.

- *Freight forwarders:* One problem with third-party carriers is the expense of moving smaller loads. Unit transport costs fall with increasing quantity, and transport now focuses on standard loads, such as a full container load. If you only have enough material to fill part of a container, you have the obvious choice of leaving empty space – but then you are paying to move a whole container and only using part of it. An alternative is to use a freight forwarder. These are people who collect relatively small loads, and consolidate them into bigger loads travelling between the same points. A freight forwarder might, for example, combine six or seven smaller loads to get a full container, giving lower unit costs and faster delivery. Freight forwarders also provide all the administration needed to move materials through their journey, such as documentation, customs clearance, insurance, and so on.

- *Brokers:* A broker acts as an intermediary between customers and carriers. Effectively, they look at the goods to be moved, find the best routes and carriers and negotiate conditions. There are also specialised brokers who assist with particular parts of the journey, such as customs brokers who prepare the documents needed for customs clearance, get materials through customs and move them across international borders.

- *Agents:* These are usually local people who represent, say, shipping companies. They give a local presence and act as intermediaries between distant carriers and local customers, exchanging information, arrangements, and so on.

- *Parcel services:* These are similar to a Post Office, as they deliver small packages to any location. Companies such as Federal Express, United Parcel Service (UPS) offer very fast deliveries to almost any location in the world. Their strength is customer service, as they offer guaranteed next day delivery over long distances.

LOGISTICS IN PRACTICE

Christian Salvesen

In 1846 Christian and Theodore Salvesen founded a shipping and fishing company in Norway. Their company has been through a lot of growth, restructuring and change of focus. In 1997, it demerged its remaining non-core activities and after restructur-

ing in 1999 concentrated on its role as a major European logistics business. Their aim is, 'to manage clients' supply chains seamlessly across Europe under the single brand of Christian Salvesen'. They now work in partnership with manufacturers and retailers, controlling stock, and making sure that goods are delivered to customers precisely when they are needed. To support this, they have a fleet of 2500 vehicles, 5500 trailers and 14,000 staff working at 160 sites.

One of Christian Salvesen's major contracts is to distribute parts for Daimler-Chrysler in the UK. The problem is making sure that 300 franchised Mercedes-Benz and Chrysler dealers have adequate supplies of parts. The obvious option of having big stocks at each dealer is too expensive, so DaimlerChrysler meet demand from their European Logistics Centre at Milton Keynes, with rapid delivery guaranteed by Christian Salvesen.

At the centre of the operations is Christian Salvesen's SHARP (Shipments Handling And Reporting Programme). Every evening DaimlerChrysler enter the requirements of each dealer into this, and the parts are loaded onto large double-decked articulated trucks at Milton Keynes. These leave between 1900 and 2200 and travel to 11 feeder depots around the country. At the feeder depots they have an hour to transfer parts to local delivery vehicles. There are 35 of these, each of which delivers to up to 11 dealers, starting at midnight and finishing by 0800.

Sources: company reports and website at www.salvesen.com

ROUTING VEHICLES

Any organisation involved in transport has to consider many types of problem. We have discussed some of the most important, but there are always operational details to consider. The number of vehicles needed, type and size, special features required, routes used, assignment of loads and customers to vehicles, schedules, maintenance schedules, measures of service and quality, and so on. We cannot look at all these problems, but we can illustrate some principles by looking at the question of routing vehicles.

A basic routing problem looks for the best path for a delivery vehicle around a set of customers. There are many variations on this problem, all of which are notoriously difficult to solve. You can see this in the basic 'travelling salesman problem'. Imagine a salesman who has a number of customers to visit before returning home, and he or she wants to find the shortest journey (illustrated in Figure 12.3). This seems like a simple problem, until you think about the huge number of possible routes that have to be considered and compared. As we saw in Chapter 6, the number of possible routes is $n \times (n-1) \times (n-2) \times (n-3) \ldots 3 \times 2 \times 1$, where n is the number of customers to visits. For a problem of any size, it is impossible to imagine the huge number of possible routes, let alone compare them and find the best.

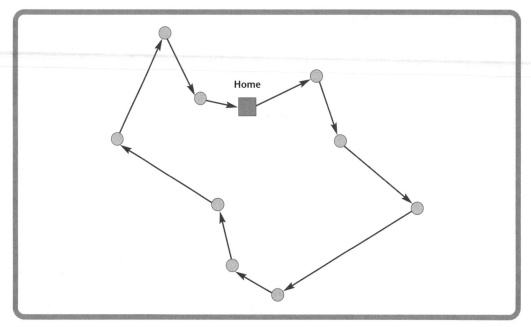

Figure 12.3 The travelling salesman problem

The travelling salesman problem is the basic routing problem, and real problems are much more complicated. They typically contain factors such as a fleet of different types of vehicles, multi-compartment vehicles, incompatible products, different logistics facilities, time windows for deliveries, varying speeds caused by traffic conditions, customers with different importance and conditions for deliveries, competing aims, variable delivery times, special equipment needed for some deliveries, uncertain costs, separate schedules for vehicles and drivers, and so on.

Many methods have been suggested for tackling routing problems but, like location, there are two general approaches. The first uses geographical arguments to look for the best routes, regardless of the actual roads. The second looks at the road network and finds shortest routes through it. Because of the increasing sophistication of electronic maps, the second of these is probably becoming more popular. The following list suggests some specific methods that have been proposed.

1. **Negotiations**: Finding acceptable routes is so complicated, with many subjective factors and people affected, that the best approach is often to negotiate a solution. This may not give the best technical answer, but it has the support of everyone concerned.

2. **Adjust previous plans**: Many routing problems are fairly stable, like postmen delivering letters. Then a useful approach has an experienced router reviewing present circumstances and updating previous routes to allow for any changes. This has the benefit of being relatively easy and causing little disruption. It also uses a well-understood procedure and experts can give results that are trusted by the organisation. Unfortunately, the results can also be of variable and uncertain quality, the routes may take a long time to design and they rely solely on the skills of a router.

3. **Other intuitive methods**: These include a range of methods that use the skills, knowledge and experience of routers, who typically use a series of heuristic rules that have been successful in the past.

4. **Maps**: Schedulers often find it easier to work with some form of diagrams, and the most popular are simple maps of key features. Then schedulers can draw routes and iteratively improve them. There are many guidelines to help with this, such as forming routes that are more or less circular, non-intersecting, no doubling back, and so on. Graphical approaches have the advantages that they are easy to use and understand, but they are really only one step better than an intuitive method.

5. **Spreadsheet calculations**: Using maps can show overall patterns, but they lose some of the details. An alternative is to concentrate on spreadsheet calculations and look at the patterns in the numbers. A common format for this lists the customers to be visited down the left-hand side and the time periods across the top.

6. **Simulation**: Simulation is one of the most flexible approaches to solving problems. It gives a dynamic view by imitating real operations over a typical period. Suppose that you want some information about proposed routes. You could sit in cabs and watch the process for some time, and see what was happening. This might give a good idea of the normal operations, but it would take a long time to get results and people may not work normally while there is someone watching. An alternative is to simulate the process. You use a computer to generate some typical features of the journey, and follow progress through the process. Rather than watching and timing a customer being served, for example, a computer generates typical service times – and any other features that you want.

7. **Expert systems**: These specialised programs try to make computers duplicate the thinking of a skilled scheduler. The basic skills, expertise, decisions and rules used by experts are collected in a knowledge base. A router then passes a specific problem to an inference engine, which is the control mechanism. This looks at the problem, relates this to the knowledge base and decides which rules to use for a solution. Expert systems have been developing for many years, and some organisations report useful results.

8. **Mathematical models**: Most of the previous approaches rely, at least to some extent, on the skills of a router. More formal mathematical approaches give optimal – or near optimal – solutions without any human intervention. In practice, routing has to include so many subjective and non-quantifiable factors, that optimal solutions in the mathematical sense may not give the best answers for the organisation. The most common mathematical approach uses linear programming. These methods are rather complicated, so they are generally limited to small problems. If, however, you have a problem where small changes in routes may give significant difference in costs, it is certainly worth looking at mathematical approaches.

There is a lot of standard software for tackling routing problems, such as Paragon, CAST and Optrack. Some of this uses standard procedures, but suppliers are often reluctant to publish details because of confidentiality. It can be a difficult job to compare all the software available and find the approach that best suits your needs.

WORKED EXAMPLE

A depot sited at (120,90) has to make deliveries to 12 customers at the following locations, and then return back to the depot. What is the best route?

Customer	X co-ordinate	Y co-ordinate
1	100	110
2	120	130
3	220	150
4	180	210
5	140	170
6	130	180
7	170	80
8	160	170
9	180	130
10	80	50
11	100	60
12	140	80

Solution

Real routing problems can have hundreds or thousands of locations to visit, and huge numbers of complicating factors. This very simple problem has 479,001,600 possible solutions from which we have to evaluate and pick the best. There are methods of doing this, usually included in routing software. One simple package gave the solution shown in Figure 12.4. You might check that this is the optimal result.

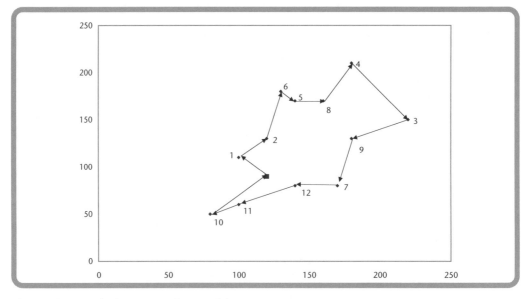

Figure 12.4 Solution to routing problem

CHAPTER REVIEW

❑ Transport is responsible for the movement of materials between facilities in the supply chain. It involves many related decisions about the best mode, ownership, organisation, routes, and so on.

❑ Transport is an essential part of logistics. e-Commerce can deliver intangible materials, but most products include goods which need transport for delivery to customers.

❑ There are five basic modes of transport – rail, road, air, water and pipeline. Each of these has different features and is best in different circumstances.

❑ The best transport between two points is usually intermodal, using the best mode for each leg of a journey. Transfers between modes can cause problems, so the aim is to create a seamless journey that combines the advantages of different modes.

❑ Organisations have a choice between owning their own transport, using third-party carriers, or some combination of the two. The best alternative depends on a number of factors, but there is a clear trend towards outsourced transport.

❑ Transport managers have to tackle many other problems. One concerns the routes to be used by vehicles. This is a surprisingly difficult problem, and many ways of tackling it have been suggested.

CASE STUDY — *Mount Isa Mines*

Mount Isa Mines is one of the world's great metal mines. Its main operations are at Mount Isa, in Queensland, Australia, where it mines adjacent deposits of copper and silver–lead–zinc ores. Production levels change with world demand and prices, but in a typical year 7 million tonnes of ore are mined to give 150,000 tonnes of copper and lead (containing silver) and 200,000 tonnes of zinc.

Mount Isa has serious transport problems. It produces huge quantities of ore in a remote area of Australia, while the main demand for finished metals is in the industrialised areas of the world, particularly Europe. The problem is to process the ores and move them to final markets as cheaply as possible.

You can see the scope of the problem from an outline of the journey for copper. This starts with underground explosions to break up the ore body. The broken ore is collected by front-end loaders and put onto ore trains that carry it to underground crushers. The crushed ore is then hoisted to the surface and stored in crude ore bins, with a capacity of 60,000 tonnes. A conveyor moves ore from these bins to another crusher, where it is reduced to about 10 mm, and passed to fine ore bins. The ore then goes to a rod-and-ball crusher for fine grinding, and is pumped to a floatation process, which produces a

C A S E   S T U D Y

continued

concentrate of about 25% copper. This concentrate is passed to smelters that roast it to remove some of the sulphur, smelt the roast product to remove iron and silica and leave a copper matte, and then oxidise the matte in a converter to remove more sulphur. The result at this stage is impure copper. This is sent to a casting furnace to remove most of the remaining impurities, and cast the copper into 300 kg ingots.

These operations are all carried out at the mine site, so there are two main logistics problems. The first moves huge quantities of materials from the mine to world markets, and the second moves materials needed by the mine, smelters and other operations into the remote site.

The copper ingots are taken by train to Townsville, 800 km away on the coast, for electrolytic refining, which removes any remaining impurities and gives almost completely pure copper. These facilities have a capacity of over 150,000 tonnes a year. At this point the copper is cast into its final form, of cake, bars, rods and wire. These are driven to the nearby port where they are shipped around the world.

Copper is only one of Mount Isa's products, and it has similar transport problems with lead and zinc. It also mines coal and gold, has organised its transport operations into a separate company, generates electricity and supplies water for the city of Mount Isa, and is involved in a wide range of mining and associated ventures.

C A S E   S T U D Y
Questions

- How important do you think transport is for the operations at Mount Isa?
- What alternatives are there for transport? What are the current arrangements and how might they be improved?
- Do other mining companies have similar transport problems?

P R O J E C T
Toorvik Transport Consultants

You have recently started work for Toorvik Transport Consultants, and are tackling your first study for a major customer. This customer buys electronic games from Japan, Singapore and Taiwan and imports them to Scandinavia. Now it is considering replacing some of the increasingly expensive games from Japan with cheaper models from China. How would you set about finding the different options for transporting these games? How would you start comparing these options?

DISCUSSION QUESTIONS

1. 'Transport is becoming increasingly less important, as e-commerce and other developments become widespread.' Do you think that this is true?
2. What types of technology are used in transport? How do you expect this to change in the future?
3. For most organisations road transport is the only realistic mode of transport. If this is true, why do so many people disapprove of heavy lorries? Are there any noticeable trends in the choice of transport mode?
4. One of the major trends in logistics is the move towards contract transport. Why?
5. An organisation with weak transport management suffers as it gives worse performance than more competent competitors and becomes uncompetitive; one with strong transport management may be diverting valuable talent from the rest of the business. What does this argument mean for transport management within an organisation?
6. There has been a huge amount of work done to develop optimal solutions to routing problems. In reality, most of this work remains theoretical and has not been implemented. Why is this?

REFERENCES

1. Office for National Statistics, (2001) *Annual Abstract of Statistics*, HMSO, London.
2. Ashford M. and Porter K. (1995) Exploiting the open frontiers of Europe, *Logistics Focus*, **3**(8), 2–6.
3. Department of the Environment, Transport and the Regions (2001) *Transport Statistics*, HMSO, London.
4. www.transtat.dtlr.gov.uk.
5. Cochran I. (1999) UK shipping, *Logistics and Transport Focus*, **1**(2), 22–5.
6. Karundawala G. (2000) World trade, Eighth Annual CIT Sri Lanka's conference, Colombo.
7. Anon. (2001) UK marine motorways study, *Logistics and Transport Focus*, **3**(4), 39.
8. Packer J.J. (1997) Roads-to-water revisited, IAME Conference, London.
9. www.logistics.som.hw.ac.uk.
10. Lewis C. (2000) Fortune favours the brash, *Logistics and Transport Focus*, **2**(4), 26–8.
11. Lewis H.T., Culliton J.W. and Steel J.D. (1956) *The Role of Air Freight in Physical Distribution*, Harvard Business School, Boston, MA.
12. Anon. (1965) The Bay unveils new container strategy, *Materials Management and Distribution*, December, p. 11.
13. Union Internationale Rail Route (2001) *Transport Statistics*, UIRR, Brussels.
14. Grainger A. (2000) Globalisation – implications for supply chains, *Logistics and Transport Focus*, **2**(2), 46–7.
15. Waters C.D.J. and Soman S.B. (1990) Containerised freight transport in developing countries, *Canadian Journal of Development Studies*, **9**(2), 297–310.

Further reading

Bamford C. (2001) *Transport Economics*, Heinemann, London.

Hensher D. (2001) *Transport – An Economic and Management Perspective*, Oxford University Press, Oxford.

CHAPTER 13

Global Logistics

CONTENTS

AIMS OF THE CHAPTER

After reading this chapter you should be able to:

- APPRECIATE the importance of international trade and its effect on logistics

- DESCRIBE the factors that encourage international trade

- DISCUSS the main difficulties met with international logistics

- OUTLINE some effects of border customs

- OUTLINE different ways of entering an international market

- DESCRIBE different structures for international organisation

INTERNATIONAL TRADE

Logistics and the economy

Despite short-term fluctuations in the economic climate, international trade continues to grow at a remarkable rate. Leontiades[1] notes that:

> One of the most important phenomena of the 20th century has been the international expansion of industry. Today, virtually all major firms have a significant and growing presence in business outside their country of origin.

This trade is based on the recognition that an organisation can buy things from a supplier in one country, use logistics to move them, and then sell them at a profit to a customer in another country. Improved communications, transport, financial arrangements, trading agreements, and so on, mean that organisations search the world to find the best location for their operations. Then international logistics move the related materials through long and complex supply chains.

INTERNATIONAL LOGISTICS occur when supply chains cross national frontiers.

In principle, international trade does not necessarily lead to international companies. In practice, however, the two are inseparable. If an organisation moves into a new country, it can keep a close check on new operations by controlling these from existing headquarters and giving local operations very little autonomy. This is, however, inflexible, and it does not allow local organisations to adapt to their own conditions or develop skills. An alternative is to devolve decisions. Then a company might become *international* (maintaining its headquarters in the home country and running worldwide activities from there), *multinational* (opening subsidiary headquarters around the world so that each area is largely independent) or *global* (treating the whole world as a single, integrated market). The distinction between these may not be so clear, and an organisation may choose other formats, perhaps working internationally in one area and multinationally in another.

Perhaps half of the trade between industrialised countries is accounted for by trade between subsidiaries of the same company.[2] In developed countries this is particularly noticeable, with a third of US exports being products sent by American companies to their overseas subsidiaries, and another third being products sent by foreign manufacturers back to their home market.

Some people prefer the term **global logistics**, to suggest integrated operations in an international setting. This can bring a whole range of new problems. Some of these are practical, such as physically moving materials across a frontier and organising transport over longer distances; some are cultural, such as speaking new languages and meeting different customer demands; some are economic, such as paying local taxes and tariffs.

It is patently obvious that the world is not a single homogenous area. There are differences in terrain, physical features, climate, infrastructure, population density, economic strength, political systems, cultures, and just about everything else. From a logistics point of view, any of these factors can give problems – it is, for example, more difficult to cross some national borders than it is to cross a mountain range, and a truck driver crossing Europe must adapt to repeatedly changing customs and languages.

One factor that is always important for logistics is the economic strength of a region. In general terms, stronger economies:

- move more materials, as they can afford to consume more products
- have more efficient logistics, due to better infrastructure, systems and support.

Greater prosperity allows efficient logistics, but there is a cycle and efficient logistics can actively contribute to prosperity. As well as giving employment to a large part of the population, logistics can encourage economic growth. The argument is that lower costs for logistics reduces the cost of delivered products – and thereby encourages sales, increases trade, opens new markets, breaks down local monopolies, increases competition and generally encourages business. This effect was noticed by Adam Smith who wrote in 1776: 'Roads, canals and navigable rivers ... (are) the greatest of all improvements.'[3]

Porter[4] looked at the reasons why nations are prosperous and said that 'a nation's ability to upgrade its existing advantages to the next level of technology and productivity is the key to its international success'. He listed four important factors for this:

- *factor condition* – which is a nation's ability to transform basic factors such as resources, education and infrastructure into competitive advantage
- *demand conditions* – such as market size, buyer sophistication and marketing
- *related and supporting industries* – which include logistics, partners and intermediaries
- *company strategy, structure and competition* – which give the market structure and features of domestic competition.

You can see that logistics appear – at least implicitly – several times on this list. To put it simply, trade increases prosperity, and trade depends on logistics.

Factors that encourage international trade

Governments have given almost universal support for increasing trade. Over the years they have signed many international agreements on trade, and have formed a range of organisations like the General Agreement on Tariffs and Trade (GATT), Organisation for Economic Co-operation and Development (OECD), and World Trade Organisation (WTO). There have also been significant developments in free-trade areas, such as the European Union, North American Free Trade Agreement, Association of South-East Asian Nations Free Trade Area and Southern Common Market of South America.

Largely as a result of these policies world trade continues to grow. The growth was about 10% in 2000 and 7% in 2001, compared with an average of 6.5% for the period 1990–99.[5] The value of merchandise exports in 2001 was about $6 trillion with commercial services adding another $1.5 trillion. The following list shows some factors that encourage this international trade:

- *Growing demand in new markets:* Many regions of the world are becoming more prosperous and are consuming more goods. Foreign companies recognise the opportunities in these growing markets and expand to sell their products in new markets.

- *Demand for foreign products:* Customers travel, watch television and use the Web to see products available in different areas. They demand new products that cannot be supplied by domestic companies.

⬤ *Convergence of market demands:* Centralised manufacturing only works if different markets accept the same products – or at least products with minor differences in the finishing. There is clear evidence for a convergence in tastes – which Ohmae calls 'Californianisation'[6] – which allows Coca-Cola, McDonald's, Toyota and Sony to sell the same products in virtually any country.

⬤ *Removal of trade barriers:* One of the major forces towards global free trade was the General Agreement on Tariffs and Trade (GATT) which stipulated that all its members should be treated equally. Countries in several regions have taken this idea further to create free trade areas. These have encouraged trade by easing trade restrictions and reducing tariffs, and are one reason why the amounts collected as tariffs fell from 20% of trade in the 1950s, to 7% at the beginning of the 1990s, and 3% by 2000.[7,8]

⬤ *Manufacturers aiming for economies of scale:* There have been significant changes in manufacturing operations, many of which depend on, or work best with, a stable, large-scale production. The best size for these facilities is often larger than demand from a single market. The result is centralised production, with economies of scale giving lower unit costs that more than cover any increased costs of logistics.

⬤ *Specialised support:* As we have already seen with warehousing and transport, many organisations are concentrating on their core competencies and are outsourcing other activities. A major industry has grown of specialised support companies that can help with, say, exporting, international transport, trade credit, foreign exchange, customs clearance, and so on.

⬤ *Integration of the supply chain:* Integration of the supply chain works towards a smooth movement of goods from initial suppliers through to final customers. This only becomes possible when national frontiers are transparent, and this means that the same organisation has to work on both sides of the border.

⬤ *Greater demands on suppliers:* Customers are putting more demands on suppliers – including just-in-time operations, total quality, strategic alliances, customisation, and so on. Local suppliers may not be able to meet these demands, and organisations may have to look further afield to find the best sources.

⬤ *Changing practices in logistics:* Developments in logistics can make trade easier. Containerisation, for example, made the movement of goods easier, cheaper and more reliable. This encouraged many companies to move profitably into new markets. Similarly, 'postponement', allows products to finish manufacture at a later point in the supply chain and be more flexible to customer demands.

⬤ *Improved communications among customers:* Satellite television, the Internet and other developing communication channels have made customers more aware of products from outside their local regions. This has stimulated demand in new markets, increased brand recognition and encouraged convergence in tastes and product demands.

⬤ *Improved communications in business:* Developments in information systems – ranging from EDI to on-board systems in vehicles – can fundamentally change the way organisations work. They allow more flexible operations, including efficient logistics in even remote areas.

LOGISTICS IN PRACTICE

Europeanisation of logistics

A single market was created within the European Union in 1993. This has had a considerable effect on logistics and wider operations. The amount of trade within the European Union has continued to grow, with more companies working internationally, and seeing the whole of the Union as their market.

Some specific changes are contributing to the 'Europeanisation' of business.

■ Companies are integrating their operations in different countries, using common processes and logistics practices
■ There is rationalisation of supply chains, with half of companies reducing the number of facilities they use
■ Rationalisation has lowered the costs of stock, warehousing and materials

■ There has been a significant increase in the number of warehouses serving more than one country – and a clear trend towards pan-European logistics centres
■ Service levels are continuing to rise to meet more demanding international customers
■ Opportunities for cost reduction and enhanced customer service have raised the profile of logistics as a core function
■ EDI has become an essential part of logistics.

Sources: Hefflinger T. (2002) *European Logistics*, THCo, Brussels; O'Sullivan D. (1995) Logistics in Europe, *Logistics Focus*, 4(6), 9–11

Effect at an organisational level

It is easy to talk about world trade and say that, 'world exports of office and telecom equipment rose by 10% to nearly $770 billion …'.[9] But these aggregate effects come from thousands of individual organisations deciding to expand their operations into new areas. More and more companies are doing this and working internationally but what makes them move in this direction? The single most important factor must be the organisation's product, and its suitability for international trade. The product that illustrates this best is the car.

Car manufacturers are among the biggest international operators. They buy materials and components from suppliers around the world, bring everything to central assembly plants, and then ship finished cars out to customers, who again might be anywhere around the world. This system works because of the huge economies of scale for car assembly, and the ability of logistics to move materials through international supply chains.

You can see the same effect in many manufacturers who aim for economies of scale by concentrating production in a single facility. A computer manufacturer, for example, might make keyboards in Brazil, monitors in the UK, speakers in France, motherboards in Singapore, disc drives in Japan, cases in China, and so on.

The reason why these companies can work internationally is that logistics is efficient enough to have a relatively small impact on the overall cost of the final product. This is measured by the **value density**.

The **VALUE DENSITY** is the ratio of a product's value to its weight or size.

Products with low-value density, like soft drinks, are expensive to move and logistics can form a significant proportion of their final cost. This encourages smaller suppliers who serve local needs. On the other hand, logistics adds a relatively small amount to the cost of high-value density products, such as computers. This encourages a few main suppliers to serve widespread, or global, needs.

There are, of course, many other product features that affect the feasibility of international operations. A well-known brand name can make international operations more attractive, and Nike, for example, can compensate for generally low-value density products by charging premium prices. Beer also has a low-value density, but some brands have well-established names, and significant economies of scale allow these to meet international demand from a few large breweries. The stage in a product life cycle is also important. Near the beginning of the life cycle profits are high and short lead times are more important than cost, thus encouraging local supplies. Later in the cycle, increased competition makes costs more important, and these might be reduced by the efficient, centralised stocks and consolidated transport that come with international operations.

Clearly some products are more suited to international trade than others. Some factors that encourage local, rather than international, suppliers are products that:

- have relatively low value, or value density
- deteriorate or have short shelf life
- are sensitive to cultural and other differences
- have little differentiation between competitors, or brand loyalty
- need high customer contact or personal service
- have less emphasis on cost
- give limited economies of scale in production
- generate social or political pressures to produce locally
- have uneven development of markets.

LOGISTICS IN PRACTICE

Trifast plc

TR Fastenings was formed in 1973, and was floated on the London Stock Exchange in 1994 as Trifast plc. By 1998 it employed 700 people, mainly in Uckfield, Sussex, where its main product was fasteners – like nuts and bolts. Although 90% of its customers are companies that originated in the US or Japan, 90% of its sales actually occur within the UK.

Trifast used to make nuts and bolts, but they had problems with fierce competition at a time when customers were shortening their supply chains and reducing the number of suppliers. To become more competitive, Trifast had to expand, and decided to move into Asia, Europe and the USA. Their strategy for expansion was to move from being a manufacturer of nuts and bolts to

LOGISTICS
IN PRACTICE
continued

being a service provider. Typically they visit a manufacturer, analyse their products, design exactly the type of fasteners needed, and then supply them. More than 60% of this trade comes from the electronics industry. Trifast cannot make all the fasteners themselves, so they source and manage the supply. This gives the opportunity to diversify. While they are managing the supply of fasteners, they can easily arrange the supply of associated parts, such as springs, plastic ties and pulleys. Then they can do some work on these, assembling parts into components – or kitting. This adds value for Trifast, and brings benefits to manufacturers, who have a guaranteed supply of materials, but only deal with one supplier.

Trifast's philosophy is now to form supply partnerships with manufacturers and their major sub-contractors. Through these partnerships they manage the supply of fasteners and just about any other high-volume, low-cost component. They have six systems for this. The basic system has a manufacturer faxing or e-mailing a list of materials it needs, and Trifast manages all

details of the delivery. The most sophisticated system has Trifast taking full responsibility for delivering components directly to bins on an assembly line.

As one example of their work, Trifast delivers 500 different parts directly to the assembly lines of seven Lear plants in Sweden. They store 150 tonnes of materials in a central warehouse and replace 64 separate suppliers.

Trifast started its international expansion by buying manufacturing plants in Singapore and Malaysia. It had considered opening distribution centres, but the stocks needed were too high. They then acquired companies in Ireland, Norway and Sweden, and established new companies in France and Hungary. They now have six manufacturing plants, 30 distribution divisions, an annual turnover of £122 million, 1000 employees, and carry 100,000 product lines.

Sources: company annual reports; Lawless J. (1998) Challenges of going global, *Sunday Times,* 26/4/98; website at www.trifast.com

PROBLEMS WITH INTERNATIONAL LOGISTICS

Differences in logistics

International logistics are different from national logistics, and it is not just a case of moving the same activities to another location. We can list some of the common differences as follows:

- international trade usually has much bigger order sizes, to compensate for the cost and difficulties of transport
- international markets are more erratic, with large variations in the demand and importance of any market
- most organisations have less experience with international logistics, so they are working in areas where they have less expertise

● there are more intermediaries, such as freight forwarders and customs agents
● the intermediaries and distances involved make relations with customers more difficult and remote
● communications become more difficult at a distance and across cultures
● terms of trade vary and may be unfamiliar
● financial arrangements can be less certain
● documentation is more complicated.

International trade is always difficult. If you imagine a simple transaction, where an organisation buys materials in one country, and arranges for them to be delivered to another country, you can begin to see the complications. It is not just a question of sending someone to another country to pick up the materials and bring them back. Also included are international banks to arrange the finances and exchange currencies, one government's regulations on exports and another government's regulations on imports, customs clearance with duties and taxes, transport operations in both countries, some mechanism for transferring materials between transport operators and across borders, translators for documents written in different languages, lawyers to check the contracts and conditions, and so on. As you can see, there is a surprising number of people involved in even a small transaction.

As with all logistics, a vital concern is the flow of information. This is obviously more difficult at a distance, and across borders. Unfortunately, it is also more important to have efficient information systems for long international supply chains, where there are more opportunities for things to go wrong. If a delivery is delayed at a border, both the supplier and customer want to know exactly what is happening, and how to solve any problems. But if the border is in a remote area, it can be difficult to get any information, let alone an accurate account of the situation. Intermediaries who help the flow of materials may actually cause problems with information flows. If several people are working on different aspects of movement, it may be difficult to co-ordinate their activities or assign responsibilities. Developments in mobile communications and EDI can certainly improve information flows, and some organisations are using this to get an advantage over their competitors. Other improvements come with the removal of trade barriers and harmonisation of business practices.

Problems with trade

Of course, the administrative difficulties are only one type of problem for international trade. As the European Union moved towards a single market, it identified three types of barrier:

● physical barriers, such as border controls and customer formalities
● technical barriers, such as differing health and safety standards
● fiscal barriers such as different rates of value-added tax and excise duties.

We can add some details to this list to show some of the issues for international logistics. These might appear at every border, and circumstances can change within a very short distance.

● *Political and legal systems:* The type of government and laws in different countries give significantly different conditions. Practices that are accepted in one country may be unacceptable in a neighbour. You can imagine one example from the past when Germany was divided. Simply stepping from West Germany to East Germany meant a change from a free market economy with systems aligned to western Europe (including private transport) to a centrally planned economy with systems aligned to the east (including nationalised transport).

● *Economic conditions:* Political systems directly affect the economy, and there are significant differences in prosperity, disposable income and spending habits. Sometimes there are very rapid changes, between, say, the borders of the USA and Mexico or Austria and the Czech Republic.

● *Competition:* This varies between very intense, market-driven competition in some countries, to state run monopolies in others. Logistics in, say, the Netherlands is particularly well developed and companies compete for business over a wide area.

● *Technology available:* Many logistics companies use sophisticated technologies for e-commerce, efficient customer response, satellite location, in-cab navigation, real-time routing, total communications, and a whole range of other developments. Although such technology is feasible, it does not mean that everybody uses it. Most of the world does not have access to, does not need, or cannot afford the latest technological development. In many areas the movement of loads depends on manual effort and bullock carts, and a lorry is the most advanced technology available.

● *Social systems and culture:* It is usually easier to trade with someone who has similar culture, habits, expectations, and so on. Even language differences give problems, so it would be easier for a company working in Belgium to open new facilities in France rather than, say, Sudan. You might assume that these differences are only important if dealing with widely separate locations, but there are many examples of people who live very close together, but seem to have little in common.

● *Finance:* There are many financial factors to consider. Some countries do not allow their currency to be taken out of the country, the value of some currencies fluctuates wildly or falls quickly, some banking systems are inefficient, sometimes exchanging money is difficult, and so on. A different type of problem comes with customs duties and tariffs for materials entering the country. We mention some of these in the next section.

● *Geography:* Transport is generally easier in straight lines over flat terrain. Crossing the American prairies is easy, but very few areas are laid out like this. Physical barriers that hinder transport include seas, mountain ranges, desserts, jungles, rivers, cities, national parks, and so on.

It is often the practical details that make the movement of materials across international frontiers time-consuming and irritating. You often hear of deliveries that are held up for days, simply because the driver cannot speak the same language as the customs people. Surveys typically suggest that the main problems found by exporters are as follows:

Main problem	Percentage of exporters
Export documentation	23
Transportation costs	20
High import duties	17
Cannot find foreign representatives with enough knowledge	16
Delay in transfer of funds	13
Currency fluctuations	12
Language barrier	10
Difficult to service products	10

LOGISTICS IN PRACTICE

Border crossings

Crossing international borders can be very time consuming. Trucks driving across the European Union might cross most borders without even slowing down, but when they hit the Polish border they might be delayed for days rather than hours. You can see some of the reasons for this when considering the border between Mexico and the USA.

The North American Free Trade Agreement (NAFTA) was signed in 1994 between the USA, Canada and Mexico. This allowed Mexico to protect local trucking companies by prohibiting USA and Canadian firms from operating within Mexico for ten years. Until this condition ran out, companies moving materials across the USA/Mexico border needed some procedures for actually crossing the frontier.

For a USA to Mexico crossing a US haulier delivers goods in a trailer close to the border. This company is likely to have lower rates than its Mexican counterpart, but it cannot move materials over the border. A cartage agent takes over the paperwork and organises the trailer's move through customs and across the border.

There a Mexican haulier picks up the trailer, and organises the journey onwards and to the customer. This haulier then returns the empty trailer near to the border, where a cartage agent again moves it through customs and across into the USA. Then the US haulier can pick it up and return.

This system is unusual, but it is not unusual to be held up at border customs. The most common cause of delay is queries over paperwork. Customs agents can usually sort this out fairly quickly, but EDI gives the opportunity for pre-clearance. An organisation sends a message ahead to a customs point that its vehicle is soon arriving at a border. The message gives details of materials carried, owners, destination, value, contact points, and any other relevant information. If all goes smoothly, customs clearance is agreed before the vehicle arrives, and it can continue its journey with little interruption.

Sources: Helfont G. (2002) *Customs Clearance in NAFTA*, Logistics Forum, Houston; Anon. (1994) Clearing customs, *Materials Management and Distributio*n, November, **24**

Customs barriers

Conventionally, customs duty is payable whenever materials enter a country. In practice, there is more than just customs duty, and it can be quite difficult to add all the taxes and duties to calculate the amount payable. Materials entering the European Union, for example, might have to pay customs duty, excise duty, import VAT, countervailing duties, anti-dumping duty, Common Agricultural Policy levies, and compensatory interest. These tariffs are not necessarily levied at the same rates, but there can be preferential rates. As an example, the duty on a television tube entering the European Union from Malaysia is 14%, from Thailand is 9.8%, from South Africa is 7.3% and from Poland is 0%.[10]

These are not the only costs of crossing a border, as companies have to pay the cost of compliance with export/import regulations, such as compulsory documentation and information requirements.

If materials cross a series of frontiers, they might have to pay these costs at every one. This would obviously raise prices and limit trade. As part of a policy to encourage trade, most countries do not charge duties on materials that are simply moving through, so that duty only becomes payable in the final destination. This is not always true, and sometimes charges are made on goods in transit. Normally, materials can also use customs' warehousing without paying duty. This allows normal port and warehousing operations, with duty paid when the materials are removed from the customs' warehouse and taken to their final market. This idea is extended in Free Trade Zones, which are duty- and tax-free areas within a country. These zones give larger areas for port and warehousing operations, and usually work like a container terminal. Even larger developments of this kind form customs unions. These are areas, like the European Union, that agree not to charge duties within their borders. Duty is paid when materials enter the union – which is seen as the final market – but they can then move freely without paying any more.

Of course, not everybody is in favour of removing barriers at international borders or encouraging trade. They argue that there should be strict controls over exports and, more particularly, imports. Thus considerations like excise duty and customs charges serve the main purposes of:

● preventing goods that are considered undesirable from entering a country
● protecting domestic producers from foreign competition
● generating revenue for the host country
● collecting statistics on trade.

ORGANISING INTERNATIONAL OPERATIONS

Ways of reaching foreign markets

If a company wants to send its products internationally, it does not have to work internationally itself. It can sell its products ex-works or free-on-board, which means that customers make all the arrangements for logistics. Obviously, though, for such transactions to succeed, someone has to work internationally – even if it is just the transport operator that physically moves materials across the border. If you imagine a manufacturer wanting to sell its products in a foreign country, it has five basic alternatives. The following list shows these in increasing order of investment and risk.

● *licensing or franchising*, where a local organisation makes the products to designs supplied by a foreign company; depending on circumstances, the foreign company might specify a range of procedures for operations, quality, tests, suppliers, and so on

● *exporting finished goods* and using local distributors to market them; the main risk here comes from increasing production to satisfy a demand that depends on the marketing company

● *setting up a local distribution network*; products are still exported to meet demand but the foreign company increases control of the supply chain by replacing the local marketing company by an owned subsidiary

- *exporting parts and using local assembly and finishing*; this needs facilities in the home market, but these can start very small, as seen in 'postponement'

- *full local production* with new manufacturing facilities either built specially or taken over from an existing company. This gives access to local knowledge and is often the only way of getting a presence in a controlled market.

A sixth alternative is to set up some form of joint venture with a local company. More substantial facilities can be opened through a partnership, allowing shared ownership, management skills, knowledge and risk. The level of commitment here can vary considerably, but local conditions often limit foreign ownership to no more than 49% of any joint venture.

Each of the six alternatives involves different levels of investment and risk – and clearly put different demands on the supply chain. The first two options use agents and do not involve the manufacturer directly in international operations; the last four involve some kind of local operations.

Opening full production can be very expensive and time consuming. When Nissan, Toyota and Mazda wanted a presence in the European Union, they spent billions of pounds and years of preparation opening new car plants in the UK. One faster way of getting a presence in a foreign market is to buy a company that is already working there. If an organisation is already working successfully in a market, then a larger company can buy it, inject cash and build on its assets. This is how Wal-Mart moved into the UK by buying Asda, which was the third biggest supermarket group.

Usually, organisations cannot afford this kind of investment or risk, and they adopt a more cautious approach. Typically, they expand their operations in a series of steps. In effect, they move down the list above, slowly increasing their investment and only moving on when each previous stage has proved successful.

LOGISTICS IN PRACTICE

Renfield Pharmaceuticals

Renfield Pharmaceuticals is a specialised branch of a major Swiss manufacturer, specialising in the treatment of hypertension and kidney damage. It works in many parts of the world, and uses a standard procedure for organising its expansion – or limiting its risks in less successful markets. This procedure can be summarised in the following steps:

1. Export to local trading companies and independent distributors. This gives limited sales, but it is a convenient way of testing the market. If the market looks attractive, Renfield move on to the next step.

2. Send a team of field representatives. These work with the local distributors, and also collect orders directly for Renfield. They can get experience in local conditions and make recommendations for the next step.

3. Set up a local distribution network. Occasionally Renfield buy local companies that have been distributing their products. Usually, they start up their own

L O G I S T I C S
I N   P R A C T I C E
continued

marketing and logistics organisation, which works in parallel with local companies. Over time, preferential trading terms allow the Renfield subsidiary to take a dominant position in the market. It always uses local employees and resources, but there is strong control from Renfield headquarters.

4. If the subsidiary distribution company develops a sizeable and profitable market, Renfield considers opening production facilities. In the first instance this is usually a packaging plant. Ingredients are sent in bulk from other Renfield plants, and the local plant arranges final production, packaging,

labelling, and passing to the distribution company.

5. After a reasonably long period of successful and profitable operations, with forecasts of continuing growth, Renfield consider larger production facilities. These typically make one or two of the company's main products, together with limited production of associated material. The mix of products and size of facilities depends on the country's population, economic conditions, trade and monetary restrictions, education levels, raw materials, and so on.

Source: company reports

Alternative types of organisation

Decisions about entering international markets depend on factors ranging from the organisation's strategy through to forecasts for economic growth. These are inevitably difficult, and need a clear appreciation of the costs and operations involved.

The incentive for international operations must come from the business strategy, which contains an aim of expansion. Then, perhaps the most important factor is that the new, foreign operations must fit into the general structure of the organisation. The logistics and other systems must be co-ordinated and work together. This includes a decision about whether to work nationally, internationally, multinationally or globally. These terms are overused to mean slightly different things, but essentially:

⬤ *National* organisations only work within their home market; if they want a presence in international markets, they export to marketing organisations in foreign countries.

⬤ *International* companies have facilities in different countries, but their work is really centred in one home country from which they control the activities of all subsidiaries.

⬤ *Multinational* companies lose the central control and have loosely linked, largely independent companies working in different geographical regions. The separate divisions have more flexibility to adjust operations and products to local needs. Two dominant company structures have divisions organised by geography or product. This is somewhat misleading, as no organisation can use either of these exclusively. An organisation with geographic divisions still needs some broader co-ordination of each product supply chain, and an organisation with product division still needs some regional structure.

● *Global* companies see the world as a single market; they usually make standard products for shipment anywhere in the world, using the locations where they can work most effectively and efficiently. Perhaps the main feature of global organisations is that they try to co-ordinate all their activities as if they supply a single market. Coca-Cola, for example, make the same products around the world, with all operations co-ordinated to meet demand as efficiently as possible.

Some people suggest that these descriptions can be misleading as they suggest that organisations adopt a single approach to all their operations – they use the single 'best' way of working. In reality, organisations have to be flexible and respond to local conditions, practices and demands. This needs a looser structure that can include many different types of operation, but gives a unified culture for the overall organisation. Such structures are sometimes called 'transnational'.

Achieving global operations

Levitt summarised the features of a global organisation by saying:[11]

> The multinational corporation operates in a number of countries and adjusts its products and prices in each – at high relative costs. The global corporation operates with resolute certainty – at low relative costs – as if the entire world (or major regions of it) were a single entity; it sells the same things in the same way everywhere.

There are clearly advantages in working globally, from both a logistics and operations point of view. Global organisations limit the range of products, concentrate research and development, ensure economies of scale, remove duplicated functions, simplify management structures, simplify the product design function, use standard processes, generate widespread expertise in products, give a unified marketing view, and so on. From a logistics point of view global operations can ensure that facilities are in the best locations, and that the same products move between any combination of facilities and customers. If there is a shortage of products in Sri Lanka the standard products can be shipped from stocks in Brazil rather than wait for the usual suppliers.

Ideally, then, organisations should aim for global operations, with their efficient operations and single, seamless market and organisation. Unfortunately, many organisations find it difficult to implement the strategies needed to achieve these. There are many barriers and problems including the following:[12]

● different regions demand different types of product
● products do not lend themselves to global operations
● global products are not viewed favourably and are rejected by customers
● organisations lack the human and technical resources needed to compete globally
● organisations cannot develop the right structures and strategies
● managers in different regions have different objectives for themselves and the organisation
● there are other cultural and economic differences that make co-ordination difficult
● each region, and country within the region, has a different infrastructure and facilities.

These factors, along with many others, make it impossible for most organisations to have global operations. Many organisations have started in this direction, but hit problems – often very simple ones like products that offend local tastes, lack of infrastructure or transport to get materials to their final destination. Such problems can even occur within relatively homogenous regions, such as western Europe.

Because of the practical difficulties, global operations are often viewed as a conceptual target rather than a realistic proposition. Nonetheless, there is clearly a trend for more companies to consider themselves as global.

Global supply chains

Managing the logistics of a global organisation is immensely complicated. It can involve the movement of huge quantities of materials around the world. Unfortunately, there is no single 'best' model for a global supply chain that can be used by every organisation. Each organisation has to find its own solution. Nonetheless, we can mention some common results, and the following list shows five common models for global logistics:

- *Sell globally but concentrate production and sourcing in one area.* Logistics then has a fairly simple job of moving materials from local suppliers into the organisation, but there are more problems with distribution from operations to international customers. To some extent this model gives fairly easy logistics, as the organisation is a pure exporter with global marketing rather than global operations. This can also be the most vulnerable to external pressures, as it is seen as concentrating economic benefits in one centre.

- *Concentrate production in one centre but buy materials and components from around the world.* Materials are now collected from distant suppliers, and products sold to distant customers. This gives, perhaps, the most difficult logistics with potential problems for both inward and outward logistics. It gives more widespread economic benefits, but the main value-adding activities are still concentrated in one location.

- *'Postponement' moves the finishing of production down the supply chain.* In a global context, postponement typically opens limited local facilities to complete production. This gives some opportunities for local value, but all components and parts are imported from main production centres. Because of the limited local input, low added value, and competition for local manufacturers, this kind of 'screwdriver' operation can be unpopular with host countries.

- *Operating as a local company, buying a significant proportion of materials from local suppliers.* The inward movement of materials is easier, as it becomes a local matter. Of course, this means that it may be vulnerable to changing local conditions. The products might be destined for local markets, or operations could be big enough to export to international customers. This is the most popular approach with host countries as it develops local skills and brings considerable economic benefit.

- *Some global operations have limited need of logistics.* A hamburger chain, for example, might work globally, but practicalities demand that it does not have an extended supply chain, but buys almost all materials locally and sells to local customers.

The features of the product and the company structure set the overall shape of a supply chain. A global company, for example, is unlikely to use the first model with centralised operations, as this is more like an 'international' company. There are, of course, many variations on these basic themes.

CHAPTER REVIEW

❏ International trade is continuing to grow very quickly. All of this trade depends on efficient logistics to move materials around the world.

❏ Many factors encourage international trade. Individual organisations are increasingly seeing the benefits of working in different countries. A key issue for such expansion is that the product must be attractive in international markets.

❏ There can be many problems for international logistics. Many of these are caused by the different conditions on either side of international borders. Some problems can be overcome by simple administrative arrangements; others are only solved by major initiatives, such as customs unions.

❏ An organisation does not have to work internationally itself to have a presence in overseas markets. It might, for example, export or use local distributors. There are several ways of entering international markets.

❏ Different companies can organise their international operations in different ways. Each has its own strengths and puts different emphasis on logistics. There is a general trend towards global operations, which see the world as a single integrated market.

❏ There are many possible structures for global supply chains.

C A S E   S T U D Y   *O'Daid Group*

Sean O'Daid runs part of a family business in Cork, Ireland, producing a range of natural conditioners for gardens. The main product is peat. This is dug from local bogs owned by the company, dried, shredded to give a uniform texture, treated to remove unwanted material and then compressed for packing into 25 kg and 50 kg bags. These are delivered throughout Ireland, but the highest sales are in the south around Cork, and east around Dublin.

Over the past 20 years, trade has varied, depending on the state of the economy and enthusiasm for gardening (which is often affected by television programmes). A more serious problem is the environmental damage done by peat extraction, and

C A S E   S T U D Y   *continued*

which is encouraging gardeners to look for environmentally friendly alternatives. O'Daid Garden Products is a small company, but they extract more than 10,000 tonnes of peat a year. Continuing at this rate of extraction, their accessible reserves will last about a century. Sean summarises this situation by saying, 'we have lots of peat in the ground, but demand is certainly falling, and is likely to go even lower. We are actively developing new materials as alternatives to peat, but these are more expensive and will probably be more attractive in the longer term. In the medium term we want to exploit our existing reserves, and get a smooth transition to the new products. In particular, we want to increase current peat production, and start exporting to the UK and the rest of Europe.'

Sandra O'Daid runs another part of the family business. She imports materials to make a range of high-value Celtic jewellery, which she exports to 42 countries around the world. Her materials are largely gemstones and precious metals from South Africa and Australia. Her main exports are to the countries around the Pacific Rim, particularly Singapore and Australia. Last year sales from her traditional customers fell slightly, and she started looking for sales in the Middle East and South America.

C A S E   S T U D Y
Questions

- How would you compare the logistics requirements of these two parts of the family business? What problems are they each likely to face? How can these be overcome?
- Do you think that expanding internationally is a reasonable strategy for Sean? Can he learn anything from Sandra's experience?

P R O J E C T
Parcel Transport

Imagine that you want to send a parcel of books weighing 100 kg from the UK to Peru. Find the alternatives available for transport, and identify the best. Describe in detail the journey of your package, and list the people involved in each stage. What specific problems would you meet? If you were a publisher wanting to sell 100 kg of books a week in Peru, how would this affect your approach to logistics?

DISCUSSION QUESTIONS

1. What are the main differences between logistics within a single country and logistics that span a number of different countries? What are the specific problems of working internationally?
2. By their nature, all supply chains must be international. Do you think this is true?
3. Some regions of the world present particularly difficult problems for logistics. What regions do you think might prove difficult to work in, and why?
4. There is a growing number of free trade areas. Why? Do they really allow free trade between members? If free trade is such a good idea, why do countries not simply remove all their duties and tariffs on trade?
5. Why are companies moving towards global operations? What are the implications for logistics?

REFERENCES

1. Leontiades J.E. (1985) *Multinational Business Strategy*, D.C. Heath & Co., Lexington, MA.
2. Julius D.A. (1990) *Global Companies and Public Policy*, Royal Institute of International Affairs, London.
3. Smith A. (1776) *The Wealth of Nations*, London.
4. Porter M. (1990) Why nations triumph, *Fortune*, 12/03/90, pp. 54–60.
5. www.wto.org.
6. Ohmae K. (1985) *Triad Power – The Coming Shape of Global Competition*, Free Press, New York.
7. Grainger A. (2000) Globalisation – implications for supply chains, *Logistics and Transport Focus*, **2**(2), 46–7.
8. Anon. (1998) World trade systems at 50, *Financial Times*, 18/5/98.
9. World Trade Organization (2001) *International Trade Statistics*, WTO, Geneva.
10. Grainger A. (2000) Customs and international supply chain issues, *Logistics and Transport Focus*, **2**(9), 40–3.
11. Levitt T. (1983) The globalization of markets, *Harvard Business Review*, May/June.
12. Jain S. (1989) Standardisation of international marketing strategies, *Journal of Marketing*, **53**, January.

Further reading

Ernst R. et al. (1998) *Global Operations Management and Logistics*, John Wiley, Chichester.
Wood D.F. (1994) *International Logistics*, Chapman & Hall, London.

Index

WITHDRAWN